CORPORATE ENTREPRENEURSHIP

Entrepreneurial Development within Organizations

CORPORATE ENTREPRENEURSHIP

Entrepreneurial Development within Organizations

MICHAEL H. MORRIS
University of Hawaii

DONALD F. KURATKO
Ball State University

THOMSON
™
SOUTH-WESTERN

Australia · Canada · Mexico · Singapore · Spain · United Kingdom · United States

SOUTH-WESTERN

™

THOMSON LEARNING

Corporate Entrepreneurship

Michael H. Morris, Donald F. Kuratko

For permission to use material from this
text or product, contact us by
Tel (800) 730-2214
Fax (800) 730-2215
http://www.thomsonrights.com

ISBN: 0-03-033726-7

To the leading ladies in our lives:
Jennifer, Jessica, Julia, and Katie
—Michael H. Morris

Debbie, Christina, and Kellie
—Donald F. Kuratko

———————————■———————————

THE ENTREPRENEURIAL CHALLENGE
CONFRONTING ORGANIZATIONS

The global economy is creating profound and substantial changes for organizations and industries throughout the world. These changes make it necessary for business firms to carefully examine their purpose and to devote a great deal of attention to selecting strategies in their pursuit of the levels of success that have a high probability of satisfying multiple stakeholders. In response to rapid, discontinuous, and significant changes in their external and internal environments, many established companies have restructured their operations in fundamental and meaningful ways. In fact, after years of restructuring, some of these companies bear little resemblance to their ancestors in their business scope, culture, or competitive approach. The challenge for organizations in today's marketplace is to build a competitive advantage. This can only be accomplished through continuous innovation and the creation of new ideas. While major corporations acknowledged this need during the last decade, they floundered through reductions in force, downsizing, rightsizing, budget cuts, and depressed morale in their workforce. How could an organization develop innovations when its personnel were being pressured to do more with less?

The answer was found in another sector of the economy—the entrepreneurial sector. During the last ten years, new incorporations averaged 600,000 a year. Entrepreneurs and their new ventures generated millions of jobs to offset the huge reductions by Fortune 500 firms. Celebrity entrepreneurs like Steven Jobs of Apple Computer, Fred Smith of Federal Express, Debbi Fields of Mrs. Fields Cookies, and Bill Gates of Microsoft captured the economic spotlight by demonstrating that it is people—not institutions—that create new ideas. More importantly, these new ideas grew into major corporations, and in some cases, major competitors within the Fortune 500. Harsh lessons were learned and corporations realized that the same entrepreneurial spirit in people who developed these new ventures may be present within the corporate boundaries. The new century is seeing corporate strategies focused heavily on innovation. This new emphasis on entrepreneurial thinking developed during the *entrepreneurial economy* of the 1980s and 1990s.

Tom Peters and Robert Waterman began a revolution in popular literature with their best seller, *In Search of Excellence.* They exposed some of the excellent companies utilizing the innovative capabilities of their people to accomplish corporate renewal. Rosabeth Moss Kanter followed with her book, *The Change Masters*, and later, *When Giants Learn to Dance*. The idea of entrepreneurship inside an organization was uncovered and documented. Peter Drucker's (1985) book *Innovation and Entrepreneurship* provided guidelines for innovative activity whether inside an organization or outside. In one of his most profound statements, he pointed out that:

> "Entrepreneurship is based upon the same principles, whether the entrepreneur is an existing large institution or an individual starting his or her new venture single-handed. It makes little or no difference whether the entrepreneur is a business or a nonbusiness public-service organization, not even whether the entrepreneur is a governmental or non-governmental institution. The rules are pretty much the same, the things work and those that don't are pretty much the same, and so are the kinds of innovation and where to look for them. In every case, there is a discipline we might call Entrepreneurial Management."

The concept of "Corporate Entrepreneurship" became viable when Gifford Pinchott (1985) released his book *Intrapreneuring*, in which he coined the term "intra" (within) "preneurship" (derived from entrepreneurship). The gimmick word became a popular representation of corporate entrepreneurship. Pinchott's book outlined the guidelines and recommendations for people inside organizations to bring forth and develop new ideas into actual business ventures.

Some experts claimed that the two terms were mutually exclusive. You could not have entrepreneurship within a corporation. However, most executives began to pursue the possibility of eliciting new ideas and new innovations from their employees. The success stories have been remarkable but they don't offer a simple strategy for duplication. Corporate entrepreneurship is a complex process because it challenges so many of the preexisting structures and processes of each organization.

Over the last decade, there has been a growing interest in the use of corporate entrepreneurship as a process for corporations to enhance the innovative abilities of their employees and, at the same time, increase corporate success through the potential creation of new corporate ventures. However, the creation of corporate entrepreneurial activity can be difficult since it involves radically changing traditional forms of internal organizational behavior and structural patterns.

The pursuit of corporate entrepreneurship has arisen from a variety of pressing problems including: (1) increased global competition; (2) continual downsizing of organizations seeking greater efficiency; (3) dramatic changes, innovations, and improvements in the marketplace; (4) perceived weaknesses in the traditional methods of corporate management; and (5) the exodus of innovative-minded employees who are disenchanted with bureaucratic organizations. This loss of talented employees is intensified by the new appeal of entrepreneurship as a legitimate career and the increased developments in the venture capital industry (as well as informal capitalists) that enable the financing of more new ventures.

This book provides a framework for understanding the critical elements involved with the corporate entrepreneurial revolution. Through a close examination of the nature of entrepreneurship in established companies, its vision and direction, the environment that must be developed, and the entrepreneurial orientation for the future, we believe you will gain a stronger perspective on the entrepreneurial mindset. Such a mindset will help organizational leaders transform their companies through corporate entrepreneurship. It will help you to not merely face the revolution but actually create it. As Gary Hamel states in his book *Leading the Revolution*, "I am no longer a captive to history. Whatever I can imagine, I can accomplish. I am no longer a vassal in a faceless bureaucracy. I am an activist, not a drone. I am no longer a foot soldier in the march of progress. I am a *Revolutionary*."

ORGANIZATION OF THE BOOK

The chapters of *Corporate Entrepreneurship: Entrepreneurial Development Inside Organizations* are systematically organized around the nature of entrepreneurship in established organizations. More than simply discussing the concept in general, this book develops the details in understanding the pertinent elements needed to implement an entrepreneurial strategy inside existing organizations.

Section I (Chapters 1–4) introduces the nature of entrepreneurship inside established companies. Examining the evolution of corporations and the entrepreneurial imperative that is needed today, the application of entrepreneurship inside established companies is presented. A careful look at the concept of entrepreneurial intensity makes clear the different levels of entrepreneurship in organizations. Finally, the differences between start-up and corporate entrepreneurship are clearly delineated.

Section II (Chapters 5–9) focuses on the vision and direction of entrepreneurial activity inside corporations. From an individual perspective, the corporate entrepreneur and creativity are examined. From an organizational perspective, product innovation and technology are discussed along with a development of corporate entrepreneurial strategy. A final chapter addresses the obstacles to corporate entrepreneurship that exist in many organizations.

Section III (Chapters 10–13) develops the important elements for a supportive environment needed in corporate entrepreneurship. Structure, control numbers, human resource practices, and company culture are all critical factors in the corporate environment. Each of these factors is thoroughly examined within the context of entrepreneurial activity.

Section IV (Chapters 14–16) concentrates on the entrepreneurial orientation of organizations as they progress in the future. The measurement of an organization's entrepreneurial activity is discussed for the purpose of assessing the degree of success realized by these efforts. The concept of entrepreneurship in government organizations is presented since privatization and entrepreneurial behavior are becoming more recognized in public policy. Finally, the book concludes with a focus on how to sustain the entrepreneurial process and develop into the innovative organization of tomorrow. After all, tomorrow is where the entrepreneurial mind already resides.

ACKNOWLEDGMENTS

Many individuals played important roles in helping us develop and refine our book, and they deserve special recognition. We would like to express our appreciation to the following people, who believed in this book and who worked closely with us on this project, in particular Tracy Morse, Acquisitions Editor; Jana Pitts, Development Editor; Heather Hogan, Assistant Editor; Beverly Dunn, Market Strategist; and Barrett Lackey, Project Manager.

We would like to extend a special acknowledgment to Maggie A. Ailes, Executive Assistant for the Midwest Entrepreneurial Education Center, and Donna Hensley of the Page Center for Entrepreneurship for their administrative support and word processing efforts on the manuscript. Their constant dedication and support were invaluable. Also, many thanks to Minet Schindehutte for her standard of excellence and assistance in helping to develop some of the ideas in these chapters. We would also like to acknowledge Barb J. Terlap of the Midwest Entrepreneurial Education Center for her development of the Intrapreneurial Insights for each chapter.

Finally, we would also like to express a special appreciation to Neil A. Palomba, retiring dean of the College of Business at Ball State University, for all his years of leadership and enthusiastic support of entrepreneurship.

Michael H. Morris
Miami University

Donald F. Kuratko
Ball State University

SERIES IN ENTREPRENEURSHIP

Advisory Editor for Entrepreneurship—**Donald F. Kuratko**
The Stoops Distinguished Professor of Entrepreneurship and Founding Director
of the Entrepreneurship Program at Ball State University

Foegen
Business Plan Guidebook with Financial Spreadsheets
Revised Edition

Hodgetts and Kuratko
Effective Small Business Management
Seventh Edition

Hornsby and Kuratko
The Human Resource Function in Emerging Enterprises

Kuratko and Hodgetts
Entrepreneurship: A Contemporary Approach
Fifth Edition

Kuratko and Welsch
Strategic Entrepreneurial Growth

Morris and Kuratko
Corporate Entrepreneurship

Ryan and Hiduke
Small Business: An Entrepreneur's Plan
Fifth Edition

AUTHOR PROFILES

DR. DONALD F. KURATKO is the Stoops Distinguished Professor of Entrepreneurship and Founding Director of the Entrepreneurship Program, College of Business, Ball State University. In addition, he is Executive Director of The Midwest Entrepreneurial Education Center. Dr. Kuratko is the first professor ever to be named a Distinguished Professor for the College of Business at Ball State University. He has published over 150 articles on aspects of entrepreneurship, new venture development, and corporate entrepreneurship. His work has been published in such journals as the *Strategic Management Journal, Academy of Management Executive,* the *Journal of Business Venturing, Entrepreneurship Theory & Practice,* the *Journal of Small Business Management,* the *Journal of Small Business Strategy, Family Business Review,* and the *Advanced Management Journal.*

Dr. Kuratko has authored eight books, including the leading entrepreneurship book in American universities today, *Entrepreneurship: A Contemporary Approach,* 5th ed. (2001), as well as *Strategic Entrepreneurial Growth* (2001), *Entrepreneurial Strategy* (1994), *Effective Small Business Management,* 7th ed. (2001), *Management,* 3rd ed. (1991), and *Corporate Entrepreneurship* (2002). In addition, Dr. Kuratko has been consultant on corporate intrapreneurship and entrepreneurial strategies to a number of major corporations, among them Anthem Blue Cross/Blue Shield, AT&T, United Technologies, Ameritech, The Associated Group (Acordia), Union Carbide Corporation, ServiceMaster, and TruServ.

The academic program in entrepreneurship that Dr. Kuratko developed at Ball State University has received national acclaim, including such honors as The George Washington Medal of Honor (1987); The Leavey Foundation Award for Excellence in Private Enterprise (1988); National Model Entrepreneurship Undergraduate Program Award (1990); The NFIB Entrepreneurship Excellence Award (1993); the National Model Entrepreneurship Graduate Program Award (1998) and the National Model Innovative Pedagogy Award for Entrepreneurship (2001). The Midwest Entrepreneurial Education Center (which Dr. Kuratko developed at Ball State University) received the Quality Improvement Award from the state of Indiana (1998, 1999, & 2000) and the NASDAQ Center for Entrepreneurial Excellence Award (2000). In addition, Ball State University's Entrepreneurship Program has continually earned high national rankings, including: Top 20 in *Business Week*; Top 15 in *Success* magazine; Top 10 business schools for entrepreneurship research over the last ten years (MIT study); and Top 5 in *U.S. News & World Report*'s elite ranking (including the #1 state university for entrepreneurship).

Dr. Kuratko's honors include: Professor of the Year for five consecutive years at the College of Business, Ball State University, as well as the Ball State University College of Business Teaching Award 14 consecutive years. Dr. Kuratko holds the distinction of being the only professor in the history of Ball State University to achieve all four of the university's major lifetime awards which include: Ball State University's Outstanding Young Faculty (1987); Outstanding Teaching Award (1990); Outstanding Faculty Award (1996); and Outstanding Researcher Award (1999). Dr. Kuratko was also honored as The Entrepreneur of the Year for the state of Indiana (sponsored by Ernst & Young, Inc. Magazine, and Merrill Lynch) and was inducted into the Institute of American Entrepreneurs Hall of Fame (1990). In addition, Dr. Kuratko was named the National Outstanding Entrepreneurship Educator for 1993 by the U.S. Association for Small Business and Entrepreneurship and in 1994, he was selected one of the Top Three Entrepreneurship Professors in the United States by the Kauffman Foundation, Ernst & Young, *Inc.* Magazine, and Merrill Lynch. In 2000, he was honored with the Thomas W. Binford Memorial Award for Outstanding Contribution to Entrepreneurial Development by the Indiana Health Industry Forum. In 2001 Dr. Kuratko was named a 21st Century Entrepreneurship Research Fellow by the National Consortium of Entrepreneurship Centers.

DR. MICHAEL H. MORRIS holds the Harold and Sandy Noborikawa Chair in Entrepreneurship and Marketing at the University of Hawaii. Before that, he held the Cintas Endowed Chair in Entrepreneurship at Miami University in Oxford, Ohio, and is the Director of the Thomas C. Page Center for Entrepreneurship. During his tenure there, Miami was selected as the National Model Undergraduate Entrepreneurship Program. He also serves as Visiting Professor of Entrepreneurship and Marketing at the Graduate School of Business, University of Cape Town, where he coordinates the Supporting Emerging Enterprises (SEE) Program. In addition, he is the Managing Director of PenteVision, an executive education and consulting firm, and has been a principal in three entrepreneurial start-ups. Professor Morris received his Ph.D. in marketing from Virginia Tech in 1983. His dissertation, on organizational buying behavior, won top honors that year from the Academy of Marketing Science. He also holds a Master of Science degree in economics, an MBA, and a Bachelor of Arts degree, also in economics.

In addition to *Corporate Entrepreneurship*, Dr. Morris has published *Business to Business Marketing* (3nd edition, Sage, 2001) *Market-Oriented Pricing* (Quorum Books, 1991) and *Entrepreneurial Intensity* (Quorum Books, 1998). He has also authored or co-authored over one hundred articles in such academic publications as the *Journal of Business Research*, the *Journal of Management*, *Entrepreneurship Theory and Practice*, *Industrial Marketing Management*, *Long Range Planning*, the *Journal of the Academy of Marketing Science*, the *Journal of International Business Studies*, the *European Journal of Marketing*, *Futures*, the *Journal of Business Ethics*, the *Journal of Business Venturing*, and the *Marketing Education Review*. His recent research interests have included small venture strategy, corporate entrepreneurship, the marketing and entrepreneurship interface, public sector innovation, and price management.

Professor Morris has also been active in executive education and consulting with a variety of institutions and companies around the world. He has taught in the executive programs sponsored by the Graduate School of Business, University of Cape Town (South Africa), the University of Porto (Portugal), the University of Malta, Henley Management School (U.K.), the University of the Pacific, and others. His corporate clients have included AT&T, Dupont, British Petroleum, De Beers, 3-M Pharmaceutical, Ogilvy and Mather, Premier Foods, the State of California, United Telephone, and a wide array of others. He has also initiated two entrepreneurial start-ups.

Dr. Morris is also a former Fulbright Scholar (South Africa, 1993). He has served as Chair of the American Marketing Association's Task Force on the Marketing and Entrepreneurship Interface and is currently the editor of the *Journal of Developmental Entrepreneurship*. He has received recognition both for his teaching and research, and was twice honored by Pi Sigma Epsilon as their national Faculty Advisor of the Year. In 2001 Dr. Morris was named a 21st Century Entrepreneurship Research Fellow by the National Consortium of Entrepreneurship Centers.

CONTENTS

CHAPTER 9
UNDERSTANDING THE OBSTACLES TO CORPORATE ENTREPRENEURSHIP 171

SECTION III DEVELOPING AN ENVIRONMENT TO SUPPORT ENTREPRENEURSHIP 189

CHAPTER 10
STRUCTURING THE COMPANY FOR ENTREPRENEURSHIP 191

THE NATURE OF ENTREPRENEURSHIP IN ESTABLISHED COMPANIES

───────■───────

"Wealth in the new regime flows directly from innovation, not optimization; that is, wealth is not gained by perfecting the known, but by imperfectly seizing the unknown."

— KEVIN KELLY,
"NEW RULES FOR THE NEW ECONOMY," WIRED

───────■───────

CORPORATE EVOLUTION AND THE ENTREPRENEURIAL IMPERATIVE

INTRODUCTION

Companies are not static—they are continually changing. Lately, it seems that the rate of change has accelerated. In fact, many of those who have been part of the evolution (and revolution) of corporations in recent years have an amazing story to tell. The past quarter century has produced an immense transformation in the functions, patterns, and cycles of organizations. Many of the conventional rules of business no longer apply. Fundamental assumptions about employees, products, control of resources, technologies, and markets have been challenged and in some cases discarded altogether. For many firms, turbulence in their external environments has become a way of life.

In the midst of all of this, the relevance of the traditional theories and principles that guide managerial practice is being questioned. On the one hand, conditions and relationships among variables within companies have changed to the point that different models and theories are required to address the practical needs of the contemporary executive. As a result, managers have been surfeited with a whole range of new concepts and tools from total quality management and business process reengineering to right-sizing, outsourcing, and self-directed work teams. We can call this the "new management thinking." On the other hand, many of the basic lessons and principles of good business practice still apply. It is important to remember the adage, "Those who do not learn from the past are sure to repeat it."

In this chapter, we will examine some of the basic tenets of management and organizational growth. Many of these tenets will set the stage for the chapters to come. Our purposes are to explore the changing shape of the managerial challenge in companies, to build on the relevant lessons of conventional management theory, and to identify a new paradigm for achieving sustainable competitive advantage. As we shall see, entrepreneurship represents a unifying framework for successful management practice in the 21st century.

TRADITIONAL MANAGEMENT: SETTING THE STAGE

Most contemporary organizations have managers schooled in the basic principles of management theory. The traditional functions of planning, organizing, leading, and controlling, which have been stressed in business schools for decades, are still prevalent today. The newer methods of innovative management do not replace these basic fundamentals. Rather, the newer methods are different and sometimes unique applications of, or adjustments to, many of the basic functions.

Management is a universal consideration. Almost every problem faced by groups of people, formal organizations, and even nations can be at least partially solved through effective and efficient management practices. Firms in the private sector continually strive to increase their managerial efficiency and effectiveness, as do organizations in the public sector. Management is the process of setting objectives and coordinating the efforts of personnel in order to attain them. Note that by its very definition, management involves getting things done through other people. The manager must be a planner, communicator, coordinator, leader, motivator, and controller; and most of all, the manager must be a facilitator. He or she must smooth the way not only for the performance of subordinates, but also for the accomplishment of change through people.

ART OR SCIENCE?

Is management an art or a science? This question is often asked by both practitioners and students of management. The answer is that management is *both* an art *and* a science. As an art, management requires the use of behavioral and judgmental skills that cannot be quantified or categorized the way scientific information can be in the fields of chemistry, biology, and physics. For example, management involves communicating, motivating people, leading, and using qualitative judgment, intuition, gut feeling, and other nonquantifiable abilities.

Management is a science as well, in that it requires the use of logic and analysis. The manager arrives at a solution by systematically observing, classifying, and studying facts in relation to the problem at hand. The scientific aspects of management have been greatly advanced by the development of computers and applicable mathematical formulas. Today there are quantitative techniques that can be used for dealing with a variety of management-related problems, ranging from the control of inventory to the reduction of customer waiting time.

When dealing with people, managers approach management as an art; when dealing with material things (including systems, processes, and so on), they approach it as a science. The approach used most often varies at different levels of the organizational hierarchy. At the lower levels of an organization, managers most often face problems that can be resolved using scientific techniques — for example, problems in work flow, machine replacement, and overall efficiency. At the upper levels, managers most often solve problems using judgment, reflection, thought, and intuition. Successful managers at all levels of the hierarchy, however, need to employ both the art and science of management.

■ FIGURE 1.1

Relative Amounts of Conceptual, Human, and Technical Skills Needed for Effectiveness at Various Levels of the Management Hierarchy

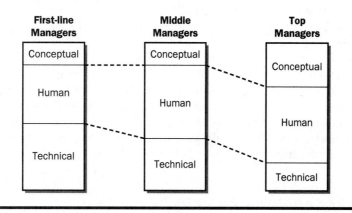

SOURCE: Hodgetts, R. M., and D. F. Kuratko. 1991. *Management,* 3rd ed. Fort Worth: Harcourt Brace Jovanovich..

MANAGERIAL SKILLS

There are three different kinds of managerial skills: technical, human, and conceptual (Katz 1974). As seen in Figure 1.1, the requisite degree of each kind of skill varies, depending on the manager's level in the management hierarchy.

Technical skill is the ability to use the techniques, procedures, and tools of a specific field. This skill is particularly important at the first line of the organization where the manager needs to know how the work is done.

Human skill is the ability to communicate, motivate, and lead individuals and groups. An understanding of human relations and organizational behavior is most important to managers in the middle ranks of the management hierarchy. Because these managers are concerned with directing lower-level supervisors and other middle managers, their jobs are more human than technical in nature. The ability to persuade, negotiate with, and coordinate the activities of others is the key to their success.

Conceptual skill is the ability to plan, coordinate, and integrate all of the organization's interests and activities. It is most important at the upper levels of the organization where long-range forecasting and planning are the principal activities. To chart the organization's course, the top manager must be able to balance the demands of the organization's various departments and units with the demands of the external environment

Notice in Figure 1.1 that as a manager progresses up the hierarchy, the importance of technical skill decreases while the importance first of human skill and then of conceptual skill increases.

EFFICIENCY VS. EFFECTIVENESS

Although often used interchangeably in today's organizations, the terms *efficiency* and *effectiveness* have different meanings. The distinction is important because successful managers tend to be *both* efficient and effective (Sayles 1993).

Efficiency is measured by dividing output by input. It is an economic concept. A manager who initiates a cost-cutting program that reduces overall departmental expenses by 10 percent is improving efficiency. The amount of work being done (output) remains the same while the cost of producing this output (input) declines.

Effectiveness pertains to the manager's ability to choose appropriate objectives and the means for achieving them. While efficiency means doing things right, effectiveness means doing the right things. Of the two, effectiveness is more important. The reason is perhaps best explained by Peter Drucker (1964), the well-known management writer and consultant, who has noted that, "The pertinent question is not how to do things right but how to find the right things to do, and to concentrate resources and efforts on them."

MANAGERIAL FUNCTIONS

Let us further consider the four basic functions of traditional management: planning, organizing, leading, and controlling. Each can be briefly elaborated upon:

Planning is the process of setting objectives and then determining the steps needed to attain them. In carrying out this process, organizations often rely on many different aspects of planning, including the formulation of purposes or missions, objectives, strategies, policies, procedures, rules, programs, and budgets. These elements of planning vary in nature and scope; some are developed at one level of the hierarchy exclusively while others are developed at every level. The planning process itself consists of five steps: (1) awareness of the opportunity, (2) establishment of objectives, (3) determination and choice of alternative courses of action, (4) formulation of derivative plans, and (5) budgeting of the plan.

Organizing is the process of assigning duties to personnel and coordinating employee efforts in order to ensure maximum efficiency. Organizing is a natural outgrowth of planning and decision making. Once the organization knows what goals it wants to achieve, it can organize them. To organize, the manager must consider both structure and people. In dealing with structure, the manager's primary concerns are departmentalization, job descriptions, organizational charts and manuals, and organizational design. In organizing people, the manager works on delegation and decentralization of authority, job design, coordination, and overall people–structure fit. The purpose is to meld the structure and the people.

Leadership is the process of influencing people to direct their efforts toward the achievement of some particular goal. To be good leaders, managers must be knowledgeable about human behavior, the concept of leadership, and communication.

■ FIGURE 1.2

MANAGEMENT AS A TRANSFORMATION PROCESS

Feedback into the System

Organizational Boundary

INPUT	MANAGERIAL TRANSFORMATION PROCESS				OUTPUT
	Planning the Enterprise's Direction	Organizing the Enterprise's Structure	Leading and Motivating the Enterprise	Controlling the Enterprise's Operations	
Workers	• Nature of planning	• Departmentalization	• Nature of human behavior	• Control process	Products
Managers	• Types of plans	• Span of control		• Control techniques	Services
Government	• Basic mission	• Delegation and decentralization	• Individual's needs and motivation		Profits
Customers	• Strategic planning			• Information technology	Employee satisfaction
Economy	• Portfolio management	• Human resources forecasting	• Group characteristics	• Operations management	
Technology		• Selection process	• Leadership behavior		
Suppliers	• Decision-making process			• Human conflict	
Other environmental variables		• Training and development	• Contingency leadership theory	• Change process	
				• Organizational development in action	
			• Communication process		

Organizational Boundary

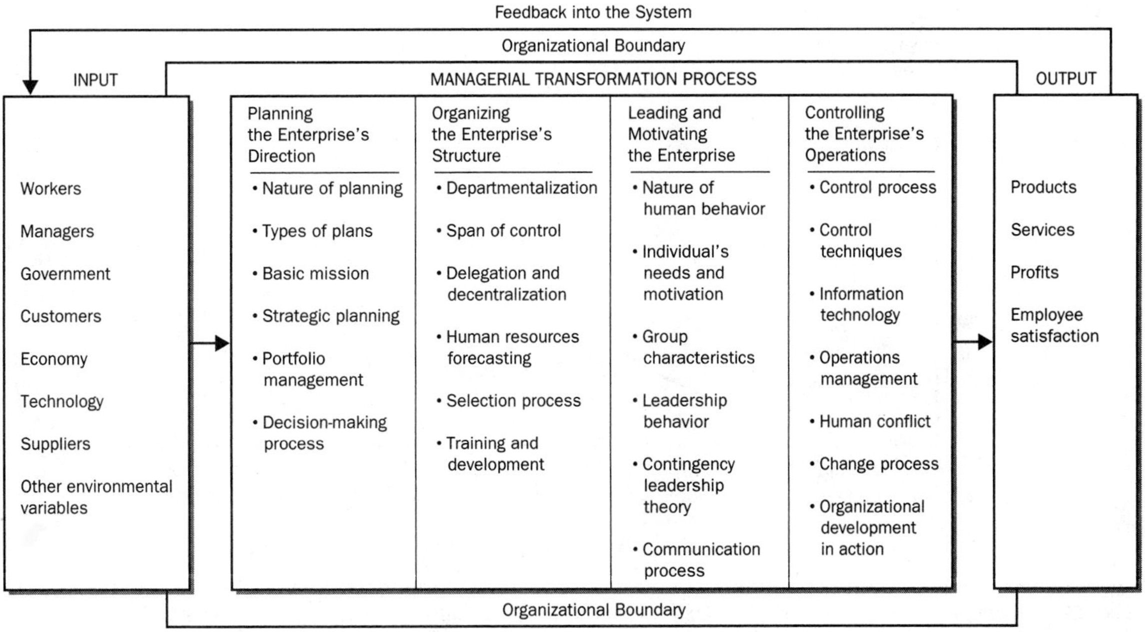

SOURCE: Hodgetts, R. H., and D. F. Kuratko. 1991. *Management*, 3rd ed. Fort Worth: Harcourt Brace Jovanovich.

The *controlling* process consists of three steps: (1) establishment of standards, (2) comparison of results against standards, and (3) correction of deviations. Every organization needs to control both operations and people. Techniques for controlling operations vary, depending on what needs to be controlled. Managers must also know how to meet the challenge of managing conflict and change, inevitable events in every organization.

The manager's job by its very nature is system oriented (Ghoshal and Bartlett 1995). Managers oversee the transformation process through which inputs are transformed into outputs (Figure 1.2). For example, they supervise new employees (inputs) who produce a certain number of units per hour (outputs). Managers are responsible for planning, organizing, staffing, influencing, leading, and controlling. To carry out these responsibilities efficiently and effectively, they must understand how the organization interacts with the external environments and how the different parts of the organization work together (Bartlett and Ghoshal 1997).

■ **FIGURE 1.3**

A VENTURE'S TYPICAL LIFE CYCLE

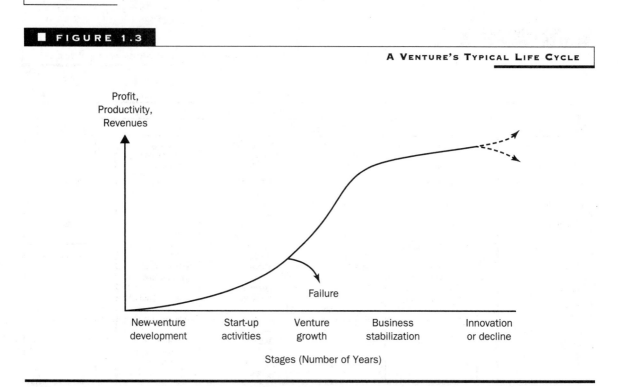

SOURCE: Kuratko, D. F., and R. M. Hodgetts. 2001. *Entrepreneurship: A Contemporary Approach,* 5th ed. Fort Worth: Harcourt College.

HOW COMPANIES EVOLVE: INTERNAL TRANSFORMATIONS

Organizations experience the natural patterns of life cycle stages, from initial venture development through start-up activities, venture growth, stabilization, diversification, innovation, and/or decline. Figure 1.3 illustrates this traditional model of corporate evolution. Other observers have described these stages in different terms. For example, Adizes (1998) developed the analogy of life cycle passages from nature and used the terms *courtship, infancy, go-go, adolescence, prime, maturity,* and *death.* Greiner's (1972) classic article on evolution and revolution within organizations depicted the stages as creativity, direction, delegation, coordination, and collaboration. In short, authors may differ in terminology, but they generally agree that organizations evolve through life cycles. Using the basic terms from Figure 1.3, let's examine the stages of evolution and the management practices involved.

STAGES OF DEVELOPMENT

The first stage, *new-venture development,* consists of those activities associated with the initial formulation of the venture. This initial phase is the foundation of the entrepreneurial process and requires creativity and assessment. In addition to the accumulation and expansion of resources, this is a creative, assessment, and networking stage for initial entrepreneurial strategy formulation. The general philosophy, mission, scope, and direction of the enterprise are determined during this stage.

The second stage, *start-up activities,* encompasses the foundation work needed for creating a formal business plan, searching for capital, carrying out marketing activities, and developing an effective entrepreneurial team. These activities typically demand an aggressive entrepreneurial strategy with maximum efforts devoted to launching the venture. Start-up activities are typified by strategic and operational planning steps designed to identify the firm's competitive advantage and to uncover feasible sources of funding. Marketing and financial considerations tend to be paramount during this stage (Crandall 1987).

The *growth stage* often requires major changes in entrepreneurial strategy. Competition and other market forces call for reformulation of strategies. Kuratko (1988) asserts that some firms find themselves "growing out" of business because they are unable to cope with the growth of their ventures. Highly creative entrepreneurs sometimes are unable, or unwilling, to meet the administrative challenges that accompany this stage of growth. As a result, they leave the enterprise and move on to other ventures.

The *stabilization stage* is a result of both market conditions and the efforts of the organization. During this stage, a number of developments commonly occur, including increased competition, consumer indifference to the organization's good(s) or service(s), and/or saturation of the market with a host of "me-too" look-alikes. Sales often begin to stabilize, and the organization must begin thinking about where the enterprise will be going over the coming five to ten years. This stage is often a "swing" stage in that it precedes the period when the firm either swings into higher gear and greater profitability or swings toward decline or failure. During this stage, innovation is often critical to future success.

The final stage is a choice of innovation (strategic renewal) or decline. Firms that fail to innovate will die. Those enterprises that are financially successful will often try to acquire other innovative firms, thereby ensuring their own growth. Also, many firms will work on new product/service development in order to complement current offerings.

All of the stages of a venture's life cycle are important strategic points, and each requires a different set of strategies. However, the key focus of this book is on what happens after the period of rapid growth and development of a company — once it has stabilized, become relatively large, and implemented somewhat sophisticated management systems. Our concern is with how firms lose the edge, the sense of urgency — the entrepreneurial spirit.

KEY FACTORS AS ORGANIZATIONS MATURE

A number of critical factors affect the extent to which companies remain dynamic or become lethargic. These factors are control, responsibility, tolerance for failure, and change and flexibility.

Control.   Growth and size bring about problems in command and control. In dealing with them, three vital questions need to be answered: Does the control system imply trust? Does the resource allocation system imply trust? Is it easier to ask permission than to ask forgiveness? These questions reveal a great deal about the control of a firm. If the questions are answered "yes," the organization is moving toward an effective blend of control and participation. If the questions are answered "no," the reasons for the negative response should be closely examined.

Responsibility.   As the business evolves, the distinction between authority and responsibility becomes more apparent. This is because authority always can be delegated, but it is also important to create a sense of worker responsibility. It is through responsibility that flexibility, innovation, and a supportive environment are established. People tend to look beyond the ordinary limits of their job if a sense of responsibility is developed. Sustainable entrepreneurship requires innovative activity and shared responsibility of everyone in the organization.

Tolerance for Failure.   No matter how large or successful a company becomes, it is still important to maintain a tolerance for failure. The level of failure that the entrepreneur experienced and learned from at the start of the venture should be the same level expected, tolerated, and learned from in later stages. Although no business should seek failure, to continually innovate and grow will require a degree of tolerance, as opposed to punishment, for failure.
Three distinct forms of failure should be distinguished:

1. *Moral Failure:* This form of failure is a violation of internal trust. Since the firm is based on mutual expectations and trust, this violation can result in serious negative consequences, and should not be tolerated.
2. *Personal Failure:* This form of failure is brought about by a lack of skill or application. Usually, responsibility for this form of failure is shared by the firm and the individual. Normally, there is an attempt to remedy the situation in a mutually beneficial way.
3. *Uncontrollable Failure:* This form of failure is caused by external factors and is the most difficult to prepare for or deal with. Resource limitations, strategic directions, and market changes are examples of forces outside the control of employees. Top management must carefully analyze the context of this form of failure, while viewing it as a valuable learning experience.

Change and Flexibility.   Plans, strategies, leadership approaches, and operating methods all are subject to continual changes as the organization matures. Retaining an innovative and opportunistic posture requires a sense of variation from the norm. It should be realized, however, that change holds many implications for the enterprise in terms of resources, people, and structure. It is therefore important that flexibility regarding change be preserved as companies evolve into large diversified entities. Such flexibility allows for faster managerial response to threatening environmental conditions.

■ TABLE 1.1

CHANGING ORGANIZATIONAL PRACTICES
THROUGH CORPORATE GROWTH

Organization Practice	Stage 1	Stage 2	Stage 3	Stage 4	Stage 5
Management focus	Make and sell	Efficiency of operations	Expansion of market	Consolidation of organization	Problem solving and innovation
Organization structure	Informal	Centralized and functional	Decentralized and geographical	Line-staff and product groups	Matrix of teams
Top management style	Individualistic and entrepreneurial	Directive	Delegative	Watchdog	Participative
Control system	Market results	Standards and cost centers	Reports and profit centers	Plans and investment centers	Mutual goal setting
Management reward system	Ownership	Salary and merit increases	Individual bonus	Profit sharing & stock options	Team bonus

SOURCE: Adapted from Greiner, L. E. 1972. "Evolution and Revolution as Organizations Grow," *Harvard Business Review* (July–August): 45.

CHANGING ORGANIZATIONAL PRACTICES: DEALING WITH CRISIS POINTS

As this discussion has illustrated, organizations evolve through a life cycle of stages. Every organization and its component parts are at different stages of development at any given point in time. The task of management is to be aware of these stages; otherwise, it may not recognize when the time for change has come, or it may act to impose the wrong solution.

Table 1.1 provides a vivid picture of how organizational practices change through five stages of development. Management focus, organizational structure, management style, control systems, and reward systems are all illustrated as changing through the different stages of development.

Understanding the stages of development and the changing organization practices that are needed for each stage allows today's managers to be in a position to *predict* future problems and thereby to prepare solutions and strategies before new crises arise. Managers often fail to realize that organizational solutions that are not flexible and changing could create problems for the future. Organizational evolution is not an automatic affair; it is a contest for survival. To move ahead, companies must consciously introduce planned structures that not only are solutions to a current crisis, but also are fitted to the *next* phase of development. This requires considerable self-awareness on the part of top management as well as great interpersonal skill in persuading other managers that change is needed.

Each stage of the organization's life cycle demands specific managerial actions because of the "crisis points" that are encountered. If the organization is able to develop strategies to move beyond the crisis point, then growth will continue. Each of these points presents challenges to an organization's growth (Greiner 1972).

In the first stage, creativity is the driving force in developing the business. The crisis point is one of leadership. As the company grows, larger production runs require knowledge about the efficiencies of manufacturing. Increased numbers of employees cannot be managed exclusively through informal communication; new employees are not motivated by an intense dedication to the product or organization. Additional capital must be secured, and new accounting procedures are needed for financial control. So here is the first critical developmental choice — to locate and install a strong business manager who is acceptable to the founders and who can pull the organization together.

In the second stage, a crisis develops from demands for greater autonomy on the part of lower-level managers. The solution adopted by most companies is to move toward greater delegation. Yet it is difficult for top managers who were previously successful at being directive to give up responsibility.

The third stage brings about a sense of losing control over a highly diversified field operation. Autonomous managers prefer to run their own shows without coordinating plans, money, technology, and manpower with the rest of the organization. Freedom breeds a parochial attitude.

In order to regain some control, organizational leaders will develop a myriad of procedures and centralized systems during the fourth stage. However, the proliferation of systems and programs begins to exceed its utility. Procedures take precedence over problem solving, and innovation is dampened. In short, the organization has become too large and complex to be managed through bureaucratic programs and rigid systems.

The final stage presents the most serious crisis — confronting the "sustainable growth wall." In attempting to develop a managerial ability to deal with sustainable entrepreneurial growth, many managers confront constraints that seem too onerous to overcome. Thus, many organizations begin a process of steady decline. A sense of infallibility combined with internal turmoil keep the company from recognizing the signs of change in the external environment. The wrong opportunities are emphasized, key talent leaves the firm, and the organization becomes vulnerable to takeover. The company has become a dinosaur.

MANAGING ONGOING GROWTH AND CHANGE

Managing continuous growth and encouraging entrepreneurial development often depend on the degree to which appropriate values and attitudes are inculcated in the organization's members. Developing a corporate culture that fosters the achievement of organizational goals is a central task. According to Timmons (1999), some of these values and attitudes include the following: expecting the unexpected, anticipating the end of rapid growth, assessing the meaning of growth for the firm and maintaining focus, developing sources of objectivity, thinking like an entrepreneurial company, developing appropriate leadership, and fostering company culture.

- *Expecting the unexpected:* Anything can happen in an entrepreneurial organization and it probably will. Maintaining a flexible attitude is paramount for individuals as well as organizations.

- *Anticipating the end of rapid growth:* It is easy to be seduced into thinking that growth will never end. But explosive growth inevitably slows down at some point. This may occur for a variety of external reasons: market maturation or saturation, product or technology obsolescence, and/or the emergence of strong competition. It may also come from internal sources. The organization may be unable to marshall its resources and sustain further growth.

- *Assessing growth and maintaining focus:* Traditional standards say growth is good and more growth is better. Maintaining earning trends and steady growth are important from a capital markets perspective. However, the rapidly growing company must avoid overextending itself and should maintain a strategic view consistent with its resource base. It must continuously anticipate future needs in such areas as supplies, manufacturing capacity, money, space, and people.

- *Developing sources of objectivity:* Rapid growth can be intoxicating. Maintenance of outside perspectives discourages "star syndrome" attitudes and promotes a more objective point of view. It is more important to know the difference between reality and hype than to believe one's own press releases. Monitoring the competitive environment either formally or informally is critical, and infinitely preferable to flying blind. Procedures for environmental scanning can be beneficial. Finally, attention to strategic planning that is neither overly rigorous nor unstructured will help preserve a sense of objectivity and reality-testing in a dynamic environment.

- *Thinking like an entrepreneurial company:* In an entrepreneurial firm, the resource base is typically much thinner, which means that backup systems and resources are not available in the same quantity and quality as in large bureaucratic entities. The key is that everyone in the larger company needs to think and act in terms of risk versus rewards and develop a mentality of using resources wisely while continuing to pursue entrepreneurial projects.

- *Developing appropriate leadership:* The leadership of an entrepreneurial corporation must act as champions for new projects, establish an "express lane" for their development, and provide creative direction and support for new initiatives.

■ *Fostering company culture:* Culture commonly refers to a sense of social reality created collectively by a particular group over time. Thus, the notion of culture as manageable is paradoxical. Yet, for the entrepreneurial corporation, culture is something that must be managed actively. There is no time to wait for culture to emerge. Managing corporate culture allows the entrepreneurial firm to grow continuously and innovate more effectively.

TURBULENT ENVIRONMENTS AND THE NEED FOR A NEW PARADIGM

The business environment today is all about *change*. This is not a radical or new revelation. Heraclitus stated in 500 BC that "nothing endures but change." However, the pace and magnitude of change is dramatically greater than ever before. It is continuous change and thus a never ending stream of new challenges is derived from each segment or component of the external environments of companies. Let's examine a few of these components.

Never in history has the pace of technology been so fast, with technology life cycles getting shorter, and technological advances leapfrogging one another. The economic environment is less predictable, can change directions more quickly, and is influenced by variables that were insignificant thirty years ago. Competitors appear more quickly, come from unexpected directions, and redefine and take over entire industries overnight. And, while external resources are always scarce and unknown, the marketplace demands ever-increasing choice, quality, and efficiency. Markets are more specialized, segmented, and "niched," and the mass market is dead. Customers themselves are harder to classify because of the changing societal environment, and, of course, government is continually raising the regulatory and legal standards. (Table 1.2 illustrates the increasing complexities in these environments.) As a result of these extreme changes in the external environment, corporations are confronted with intensified pressures to produce within the growing framework of shortened decision windows, diminishing opportunity streams, changing decision constituencies, increased resource specialization, lack of predictable resource needs, fragmented markets, greater risk of resource and product obsolescence, and a general lack of long-term control. Never before have incumbency and past experience in business been worth so little while innovation and risk taking are worth so much.

How are today's firms reacting to this new extreme challenge? A veritable cornucopia of new strategic initiatives seems to be preoccupying the time of most executives. These include downsizing, unbundling, focusing on core businesses divesting others, reengineering, decentralizing, outsourcing, restructuring, relying on self-directed work teams, and more. It seems like a continuous search for the quick solution. In spite of all the efforts to respond traditionally, the Fortune 500 continued to reduce their work forces over the last ten years by eliminating

■ **TABLE 1.2**

INCREASING COMPLEXITIES IN TODAY'S ENVIRONMENTS

Environment	Description
Technological environment	Acceleration/obsolescence
Economic environment	Unpredictable
Competitive environment	Increasing/threatening
Market environment	Demanding/fragmented
Resource environment	Scarce/unknown
Customer environment	Diverse/challenging
Regulatory environment	Increasing/aggressive
Global environment	Rising/sophisticated

millions of jobs. Thus, the reality is that external turbulence is forcing a fundamental internal transformation. It is all about experimentation, as management looks for the right structure, the right approach to control, the right leadership style, and the right way to reward employees.

But what is the "end game"? What is the real quest as managers sort through the theories, concepts, and new approaches? The answer is and always will be sustainable competitive advantage. But the rules have changed here as well. The quest for competitive advantage can no longer be found simply in lower costs, or higher quality, or better service. Instead, it lies in the following:

- ■ Adaptability
- ■ Flexibility
- ■ Speed
- ■ Aggressiveness
- ■ Innovativeness

. . . and these five words come down to one — *entrepreneurship*.

Advantage lies in finding ways to tap the spirit of Richard Branson, Michael Dell, Anita Roddick, and other great entrepreneurs within the mainstream of big companies — on the production floor, in the sales force, among the purchasing agents.

Continuous innovation (in terms of products, processes, and administrative routines and structures) and an ability to continually redefine the competitive playing field are among the skills that will define corporate performance in the global economy of the 21st century. As Steven Brandt (1986) of Stanford University stated, "The challenge is relatively straightforward. The United States must upgrade its innovative prowess. To do so, U.S. companies must tap into the creative power of their members. Ideas come from people. Innovation is a capability of the many. That capability is utilized when people give commitment to the mission and life of the enterprise and have the power to do something with their capabilities."

THE ENTREPRENEURIAL IMPERATIVE:
A PERSISTENT SENSE OF URGENCY

The ability to manage an entrepreneurial mindset is the most vital requirement for business success. Growth means embracing change, and the management of change is one of the most underdeveloped skills among managers. This is a great challenge, because it often encompasses the art of balancing fairly stable and dynamic factors (Duck 1993). Thus, the survival and growth of any organization requires that the management possess strategic and tactical skills as well as entrepreneurial abilities. The specific skills and abilities that are needed will depend in part on the organization's current stage of development.

Adizes (1978) emphasized the four major roles that any effective organization must exhibit. Using the acronym PAEI, Adizes outlined each critical role:

> A well-managed organization must *Produce* the results for which it exists. It must also achieve its results efficiently. It must be *Administered*, that is, its decisions must be made in the right sequence and with the right timing and right intensity. In the long run, a well-managed organization must adapt to its external environment. The *Entrepreneurial* role focuses on adaptive changes, which requires creativity and risk taking. And to ensure that an organization can have a life span longer than that of any of its key managers, the fourth role—*Integration*—is necessary to build a team effort. Effective and efficient management over the short and long term requires the use of all four roles. (p. 169)

While it can be argued that all four roles are needed, it becomes apparent that today's organizations have become efficient in producing, administering, and integrating. However, the entrepreneurial role may be *the* most critical role for the exponential changes facing organizations in this new millennium.

The entrepreneurial manager (1) perceives an opportunity, (2) pursues this opportunity, and (3) believes that success in exploiting the opportunity is possible (Stevenson and Jarillo-Moss 1986). This belief is often due to the uniqueness of the idea, the strength of the product, or some special knowledge or skill possessed by the manager. These same factors must be translated throughout the organization itself as the business grows.

Corporate entrepreneurship represents a framework for the facilitation of ongoing change and innovation in established organizations. It provides a blueprint for coping effectively with the new competitive realities that companies encounter in the global marketplace. As we shall see in the coming chapters, corporate entrepreneurship transcends the strategy, structure, culture, control systems, rewards, and human resource management practices of a company. It redefines the purpose of the enterprise, so that the philosophy becomes one of "healthy dissatisfaction," of continually putting the company's own products and services out of business with better ones, with leading customers instead of following them, and with turning traditional assumptions about price and performance on their heads.

In order to establish a strategy of corporate entrepreneuring, organizations need to allow the freedom and provide the capital that corporate entrepreneurs require to develop their ideas. Unfortunately, it is no simple process to move a traditional hierarchical firm to the point that developing entrepreneurship becomes a meaningful and important component of its strategy.

Traditional management practices that have focused upon completing tasks more efficiently are not sufficient solutions to new challenges. Firms need to become more flexible and creative as well as more tolerant of failure. In fact, failure needs to be seen as a learning process. Corporate entrepreneurs must be stimulated, supported, and protected.

Whether we call it the "new economy," the "digital economy," the "Internet economy," or simply the "new world order," the entrepreneurial imperative is obvious. Innovate or dissipate may become the mantra for this millennium.

The growing interest in corporate entrepreneurship is not surprising given the complex, discontinuous, hypercompetitive, nanospeed world that organizations must face. The pressing problems mentioned above have stripped away the security of traditional management practices and thrust organizational leaders into a revolution. Gary Hamel, one of the leading strategists today, believes that leaders must find, ignite, and sustain the revolution rather than be destroyed by it. Hamel (2000) points to the inevitable "diminishing returns" experienced by most organizations using traditional strategies. Following are a few key questions managers must ask themselves:

- How much more cost savings can the company wring out of its current business? Are managers working harder and harder for smaller and smaller efficiency gains?

- How much more revenue growth can the company squeeze out of its current business? Is the company paying more and more for customer acquisition and market share gains?

- How much longer can the company keep propping up its share price through share buybacks, spin-offs, and other forms of financial engineering? Is top management reaching the limits of its ability to push up the share price without actually creating new wealth?

- How many more scale economies can the company gain from mergers and acquisitions? Are the costs of integration beginning to overwhelm the savings obtained from slashing shared overhead costs?

- How different are the strategies of the four or five largest competitors in the industry from the company's strategy? Is it getting harder and harder to differentiate the company from its competitors?

If managers answer "not much" and "yes" more than a couple of times, the company may be reaching the point of diminishing returns. Once this is acknowledged, organizational leaders can begin the tasks of learning the entrepreneurial perspective and developing the entrepreneurial intensity required to navigate through the challenging years ahead.

INTRAPRENEURIAL INSIGHT

FROM THOSE WHO HAVE BEEN THERE

L.D. DeSimone, Chairman and CEO of 3M

Among B-schools and industry pundits, 3M is widely known for its creative inventions. While it is not company policy, it is understood that its 8,000 researchers are expected to spend up to 15 percent of their time working on unapproved projects. It is this kind of an entrepreneurial environment that many corporations seek to emulate. However, whether it's the lack of financial ability to support such activity or the lack of an appropriate management team, many still struggle to accomplish such a mission.

Management at 3M is so flexible and trusting that it doesn't get concerned if it doesn't hear from an employee for a long period of time. If someone's creative energy is noticeably waning, the person is simply relocated to a department where his or her original, hire-able energy can be revitalized and put to good use. The hiring process is a key part of 3M's creative, entrepreneurial environment. According to DeSimone, 3M rededicated itself in the early '90s to hiring people who intuitively understand the discipline of the marketplace. Furthermore, a personality profile with innovative characteristics was derived and used to formulate questions used in interviews for technical positions. Using inquiries such as "What kind of projects did you initiate as a child?" and "Were you ever so creative that your parents got upset with you?" has kept 3M in the limelight and in the forefront of intrapreneurship and innovation.

George N. Hatsopoulos, Chairman and CEO of Thermo Electron Corporation

For many years, Thermo Electron used the usual cash bonuses and stock options to maintain and motivate employees. This works well in many corporations, but it didn't take long for Thermo Electron to realize that well-performing stocks were indicative of the success of the whole company, not just one particular unit—thus no real intrinsic motivation. The result: spin-outs. The publicly traded spin-outs, unlike many spin-offs, remain as part of the business family (Thermo Electron does keep a majority interest) and have the desired effect on employee attitude and work ethic. Over twelve years, the corporation supported twelve spin-outs by providing financial and legal services, employee benefits administrations, risk management, and investor relations for a simple 1 percent of revenues. In 1995, 80 percent of its 12,000 employees worked for spin-outs, many of which had stock options in spin-outs other than their own and had options valued at $1 million or more.

William F. O'Brien, President and CEO of Starlight Telecommunications

While working at GTE, William O'Brien and his colleague, Pete Nielsen, experienced how tough it can be to "dance with an elephant." At the time, O'Brien was in

SUMMARY AND CONCLUSIONS

The past twenty-five years have produced immense changes in the functions, patterns, and cycles of organizations. These changes, however, are typically adaptations (sometimes extreme) of more traditional theories, methods, and practices that were developed over the last century. We examined in this chapter some of the basics of traditional management and organizational growth in order to respect the past and fully appreciate the more innovative approaches suggested by corporate entrepreneurship.

charge of African sales and Nielsen was in charge of satellite-based networks. Their idea was to develop telecommunications services in Africa. GTE has a new ventures group that supports creativity and idea-generation within the corporate walls. However, for O'Brien and Nielsen, after two years of working with senior management and refining their business plan on their own time, the project was denied. Unfortunately, protocol was that new ventures couldn't be funded unless the supervisors for whom you worked signed off on the initiative. Their main sponsor had retired, and the successor didn't want to lose their talent to another division. Both O'Brien and Nielsen ultimately resigned and started Starlight Telecommunications, which is now making waves in the African telecom industry.

While reflecting on his experience with GTE, O'Brien developed three guidelines for true entrepreneurship: (1) Corporate goals relating to new ventures should be identified and dis-seminated, and managers should be encouraged to support spin-offs that advance these goals; (2) Employees who identify new business ideas should be protected and rewarded; and (3) Proposals should move quickly through the approval process.

BILL HARRIS, EXECUTIVE VICE PRESIDENT OF INTUIT; FORMER PRESIDENT AND CEO OF CHIPSOFT, WHICH INTUIT ACQUIRED IN 1993

For Intuit, acquiring the entrepreneurial edge wasn't the problem. It was maintaining it. The company grew fast, and it grew well—management easily recognized the fact that they were not going to be able to "maintain their entrepreneurial agility" as they went from a $50 million to a $500 million entity. Like Thermo Electron, Intuit's CEO decided to break up the organization into eight core-product units, each under the direction of a different general manager and customer mission. Suddenly, the only centralized issues were management information systems (MIS) and compensation. Harris knew that to sustain cutting-edge innovation and be truly entrepreneurial, "we must encourage and allow our people—at all levels—to respond completely and immediately to our customers." He believed that continued entrepreneurial thinking in this unpredictable business will occur by encouraging employees to look to the customer for inspiration and instruction rather than the boss. While this action might not always have the best results, Intuit would rather reward intelligent failure than succumb to a diminishing quality of effort. Intuit fosters such creativity by investing one-third to one-half of its operating income in unproved and unprofitable new products. It took six years and multiple attempts before QuickBooks ever made a profit for the company.

SOURCE: Adapted from DeSimone, L. D., G. N. Hatsopolous, and W. F. O'Brien. 1995. "How Can Big Companies Keep the Entrepreneurial Spirit Alive?" *Harvard Business Review* (November–December): 3–9.

The chapter examined the evolutionary stages (internal changes) that corporations experience and the crisis points that they encounter. We then discussed the turbulent and "extreme" environments that today's corporations face from the external side. It is the entrepreneurial imperative that may be the most important breakthrough in surviving and growing companies in this fast and furious environment. The chapters ahead present the road map for understanding this imperative.

REFERENCES

Adizes, I. 1978. "Organizational Passages: Diagnosing and Treating Life Cycle Problems of Organizations," *Organizational Dynamics* (Summer): 169–187.

Bartlett C., and S. Ghoshal. 1997. "The Myth of the Generic Manager," *California Management Review* 40 (Fall): 92–116.

Brandt, S. C. 1986. *Entrepreneuring in Established Companies.* Homewood: Dow-Jones-Irwin.

Crandall, R. E. 1987. "Company Life Cycles: The Effects of Growth on Structure and Personnel," *Personnel* (September): 28–36.

Drucker, P. F. 1964. *Managing for Results.* New York: Harper & Row.

Duck, J. D. 1993. "Managing Change: The Art of Balancing," *Harvard Business Review* (November–December): 109–118.

Ghoshal, S., and C. Bartlett. 1995. "Changing the Role of Top Management: Beyond Structure to Process," *Harvard Business Review* (January–February): 86–96.

Greiner, L. E.. 1972. "Evolution and Revolution as Organizations Grow," *Harvard Business Review* (July–August): 37–46.

Hambrick, D. C., and L. M. Crozier. 1985. "Stumblers and Stars in the Management of Rapid Growth," *Journal of Business Venturing* (January): 31–45.

Hamel, G. 2000. *Leading the Revolution.* Boston: Harvard Business School Press.

Jarillo, J. C. 1989. "Entrepreneurship and Growth: The Strategic Use of External Resources," *Journal of Business Venturing* 4: 133–147.

Katz, R. L. 1974. "Skills of an Effective Administrator," *Harvard Business Review* (September–October): 90–102.

Kuratko, D. F. 1988. "Managing Entrepreneurial Growth." *Entrepreneurship Development Review* (Winter): 1–5.

O'Neill, H. M. 1983. "How Entrepreneurs Manage Growth." *Long Range Planning* (February): 117.

Osborne, R. L. 1994. "Second Phase Entrepreneurship: Breaking Through the Growth Wall," *Business Horizons* (January–February): 80–86.

Sayles, L. R. 1993. "Doing Things Right: A New Imperative for Middle Managers," *Organizational Dynamics* (Spring): 5–14.

Stevenson, H. H., and J. C. Jarillo-Mossi. 1986. "Preserving Entrepreneurship as Companies Grow." *Journal of Business Strategy* (Summer): 10.

Timmons, J. 1999. *New Venture Creation.* Boston: Irwin/McGraw Hill.

APPLYING ENTREPRENEURSHIP
TO ESTABLISHED COMPANIES

INTRODUCTION

Entrepreneurship is more than the starting of a business. Although venture creation can certainly be an important facet of entrepreneurship, it's not the complete picture. In fact, it's not even a requisite condition. Seeking and capitalizing on opportunity, taking risks beyond security, and having the tenacity to push an innovative idea through to reality represent the essence of what entrepreneurs do. An entrepreneurial perspective can be developed in any individual. It is a perspective that can be exhibited inside or outside an organization, in profit or not-for-profit enterprises, and in business or nonbusiness activities. The purpose is to turn innovative ideas into organizational realities. Entrepreneurs create the new, while replacing or destroying the old. They challenge assumptions and bend or break rules.

We are in the midst of a global entrepreneurial revolution. Look at the indicators. It is not just that venture start-ups are at an all-time high. The rate of new product and service introduction is at record levels in most industries. The same can be said for patents issued and the licensing of new products and processes. The development, application, and enhancement of new technologies are occurring at a breathtaking pace. New forms of business organization and business relationship are appearing almost daily. Entrepreneurial thinking and acting are changing the way business is conducted at every level and in every country. It does not matter if you are a company in Los Angeles, Johannesburg, or Peking—entrepreneurship is redefining what you make, how you make it, where you sell it, and how you distribute it.

The entrepreneurial revolution is a silent but profound one. It is not about glamour and fanfare. While there is a tendency to think of entrepreneurs as heroes or celebrities, they are quite ordinary people. They do extraordinary things as a function of vision, hard work, and passion. They are not necessarily trying to change the world, even if in fact that is the outcome. Dissatisfaction with the status quo, along with a sense that things can be improved, that there is a better way, drive the actions of the entrepreneur. For the entrepreneur, entrepreneurship is not a discrete event that happens at a point in time. Rather, it is a philosophy of business and a philosophy of life.

Having established some of the basic precepts of management in Chapter 1, we will introduce in this chapter the fundamental building blocks of entrepreneurship. These include an examination of what entrepreneurship is and is not. Many of the popular myths regarding entrepreneurship will be explored. Dispelling these misconceptions is important for the successful application of entrepreneurship in a corporate context. The process nature of entrepreneurship will be analyzed. Finally, integrative models that are useful for conceptualizing entrepreneurship in an established organization are presented.

DEFINING ENTREPRENEURSHIP

Although the term *entrepreneurship* has been in use for well over 200 years, there remains considerable disagreement over its meaning. People seem to hold widely disparate views regarding who is an entrepreneur, what an entrepreneurial venture looks like, and the nature of the activities that constitute entrepreneurial behavior. Although literally hundreds of perspectives have been presented, seven of the most prevalent themes are summarized in Table 2.1. One study performed a content analysis of key words and phrases in definitions of entrepreneurship appearing in journal articles from the leading academic journals as well as in popular textbooks from major publishing houses (Morris and Lewis 1993). The results are summarized in Table 2.2. As can be seen, fifteen key terms appear at least five times in the sample. The most common terms include starting or creating a new venture; innovating or creating new combinations of resources; pursuing opportunity; marshalling necessary resources; risk-taking; profit-seeking; and creating value.

Gartner (1990) concludes that a universal definition has yet to emerge but suggests we are talking about a single phenomenon, albeit one with multiple components. The relative importance of these different components can vary according to the environmental context within which an entrepreneurial event occurs. However, one definition seems to incorporate all aspects of the entrepreneurial phenomenon. Entrepreneurship is "the process of creating value by bringing together a unique package of resources to exploit an opportunity" (Stevenson et al. 1999).

The definition has four key components. First, entrepreneurship involves a process. It is manageable, can be broken down into steps or stages, and is ongoing. Moreover, as a process, entrepreneurship can be applied in *any* organizational context. Second, entrepreneurs create value where there was none before. They create value within organizations, and they create value in the marketplace. Third, entrepreneurs put resources together in a unique way. Unique combinations of money, people, procedures, technologies, materials, facilities, packaging, distribution

■ TABLE 2.1

Creation of Wealth	Entrepreneurship involves assuming the risks associated with the facilitation of production in exchange for profit.
Creation of Enterprise	Entrepreneurship entails the founding of a new business venture where none existed before.
Creation of Innovation	Entrepreneurship is concerned with unique combinations of resources that make existing methods or products obsolete.
Creation of Change	Entrepreneurship involves creating change by adjusting, adapting, and modifying one's personal repertoire, approaches, and skills to meet different opportunities available in the environment.
Creation of Employment	Entrepreneurship is concerned with employing, managing, and developing the factors of production, including the labor force.
Creation of Value	Entrepreneurship is a process of creating value for customers by exploiting untapped opportunities.
Creation of Growth	Entrepreneurship is defined as a strong and positive orientation towards growth in sales, income, assets, and employment.

SOURCE: Morris, M. H. 1998. *Entrepreneurial Intensity*. Westport: Quorum Books.

■ TABLE 2.2

Term	Number of Appearances
1. Starting/founding/creating	41
2. New business/new venture	40
3. Innovation/new products/new market	39
4. Pursuit of opportunity	31
5. Risk-taking/risk management/uncertainty	25
6. Profit-seeking/personal benefit	25
7. New combinations of resources, means of production	22
8. Management	22
9. Marshalling resources	18
10. Value creation	13
11. Pursuit of growth	12
12. A process activity	12
13. Existing enterprise	12
14. Initiative-taking/getting things done/proactiveness	12
15. Create change	9
16. Ownership	9
17. Responsibility/source of authority	8
18. Strategy formulation	6

*Terms receiving five or more mentions.

SOURCE: Morris, M., P. Lewis, and D. Sexton. 1994. "Reconceptionalizing Entrepreneurship: An Input-Output Perspective," *SAM Advanced Management Journal* 59, No. 1 (Winter): 21–31.

channels, and other resources represent the means by which entrepreneurs create value and differentiate their efforts. Fourth, entrepreneurship is opportunity-driven behavior. It is the pursuit of opportunity without regard to resources currently controlled (Stevenson et al. 1999). The unique combination of resources fits well with some unrecognized or unmet opportunity.

Timmons (1999) takes us further in elaborating on what entrepreneurs do. He views entrepreneurship as the ability to create and build a vision from practically nothing. Fundamentally, it is a human, creative act. It is the application of energy to initiate a novel concept or build an enterprise or venture, rather than just watching or analyzing. This vision requires a willingness to take calculated risks—and then to do everything possible to reduce the chances of failure. Entrepreneurship also includes the ability to build a team with complementary skills and talents. It is the knack for sensing an opportunity where others see chaos, contradiction, and confusion. It is possessing the know-how to find, marshal, and control resources (often owned by others).

Entrepreneurship is also a highly misunderstood phenomenon. Many stereotypes and oversimplifications exist, which helps explain why differences exist over such basic questions as the definition of entrepreneurship. It is these misunderstandings that lead some to be skeptical of the application of entrepreneurship to larger, established organizations. Let us explore and attempt to dispel some of the myths and misconceptions.

DISPELLING THE MYTHS AND SIDESTEPPING THE FOLKLORE

It is not unusual for executives to question the relevance of entrepreneurship for their organizations. Some are concerned with the difficulties and implications of applying entrepreneurship; others simply do not believe that it applies or has meaning in a big company. Such skepticism can often be traced to certain long-standing beliefs about entrepreneurship, myths that have developed over years and that reflect limited knowledge and research in the field. As many observers have noted, the study of entrepreneurship is still emerging, and "folklore" will prevail until it is dispelled with contemporary research findings. Listed below are ten of the most notable myths, together with an explanation regarding why each is inaccurate or incomplete (Kuratko and Hodgetts 2001 and Morris 1998).

1. "ENTREPRENEURS ARE BORN, NOT MADE"

The prevailing idea that the characteristics of entrepreneurs cannot be taught or learned, that they are innate traits with which one must be born, has a long history. These traits include achievement motivation, aggressiveness, initiative, drive, willingness to take risks, tolerance of ambiguity, analytical ability, and self-confidence. Today, however, it is recognized that traits and characteristics associated with entrepreneurial behavior are heavily influenced by environmental conditions (family, work, peer group, social) and that each of us has significant entrepreneurial potential. The challenge is to help people recognize and develop these characteristics within themselves.

2. "ENTREPRENEURSHIP IS ABOUT INVENTION"

The idea that entrepreneurs are inventors is a result of misunderstanding and tunnel vision. While many inventors are also entrepreneurs, there are numerous entrepreneurs who do not invent anything. They do tend to engage in various kinds of innovative activity and/or capitalize on the creative ideas of others. For example, Ray Kroc did not invent the fast-food franchise, but his innovative ideas made McDonald's the largest fast-food enterprise in the world. Moreover, the innovativeness of many entrepreneurial concepts can be found in the operating process, the pricing approach, the packaging, the distribution method, or some other means of value creation that does not entail inventing a new product. There is some level of innovativeness in entrepreneurship, but innovative behavior takes many forms.

3. "ENTREPRENEUR PROFILE"

Many books and articles have presented checklists of characteristics of the successful entrepreneur. These lists were neither validated nor complete; they were based on case studies and on research findings among achievement-orientated people. Today we realize that a standard entrepreneurial profile is hard to compile. The environment, the venture itself, and the entrepreneur all interact, resulting in many different types of profiles. Put another way, there are different kinds of entrepreneurs. Successful entrepreneurs are more likely to benefit from an "entrepreneurial perspective" within themselves than to fit a particular profile.

4. "ALL YOU NEED IS LUCK TO BE AN ENTREPRENEUR"

Being at the right place at the right time is always an advantage. But "luck happens when preparation meets opportunity" is an equally appropriate adage. Prepared entrepreneurs who seize opportunity when it arises often appear to be "lucky." They are, in fact, simply better prepared to deal with situations and turn them into successes. What appears to be luck really is preparation, determination, desire, knowledge, and innovation.

5. "ENTREPRENEURS ARE EXTREME RISK-TAKERS (GAMBLERS)"

Risk is a major element in the entrepreneurial process. However, the public's perception of the risk assumed by most entrepreneurs is distorted. While it may appear that an entrepreneur is gambling on a wild chance, the fact is that the entrepreneur is usually assuming a moderate or calculated level of risk. Most successful entrepreneurs work hard through planning and preparation to mitigate or minimize the risk involved. Few of them like risk. They seek to manage risk in order to better control the destiny of their vision.

6. "Entrepreneurs Are Academic and Social Misfits"

The belief that entrepreneurs are academically and socially ineffective may be a reaction to the fact that some business owners started successful enterprises after dropping out of school or quitting a job. In many cases, the importance of such an event has been blown out of proportion in an attempt to "profile" the typical entrepreneur. Historically, in fact, educational and social organizations did not recognize the entrepreneur. They abandoned him or her as a misfit in a world of corporate giants. Business education, for example, was aimed primarily at the study of corporate activity. Today, the successful entrepreneur wears two hats, one of visionary change agent and one of effective manager. He or she is typically adept socially, economically, and academically. No longer a misfit, the entrepreneur is now viewed as a professional.

7. "All Entrepreneurs Need Is Money"

It is true that a venture needs capital to survive; it is also true that a large number of business failures occur because of a lack of adequate financing. However, many other resources, such as a skilled and balanced team, technical and selling capabilities, distribution channels, licenses, and more, are vital for entrepreneurial success. Money is not always a guarantee that the right resources are put together in the right way at the right time. Also, entrepreneurs do not own all the resources that they use — they are adept at borrowing, sharing, leasing, renting, and networking resources. Further, having money is not a bulwark against failure. Failure because of a lack of proper financing often is an indicator of other problems: managerial incompetence, lack of financial understanding, poor investments, poor planning, and the like. To entrepreneurs, money is a resource but never an end in itself.

8. "Ignorance Is Bliss for Entrepreneurs"

The myth that too much planning and evaluation lead to constant problems — that analysis leads to paralysis — does not hold up in today's competitive markets, which demand detailed planning and preparation. Identifying the strengths and weaknesses of a concept or venture, setting up clear timetables with contingencies for handling problems, and minimizing these problems through careful strategy formulation are all key factors for successful entrepreneurship. Thus careful planning — not ignorance of it — is the mark of an accomplished entrepreneur.

9. "THE HIGH FAILURE RATE MYTH"

It is true that many entrepreneurs suffer a number of failures before they are successful. They follow the adage "if at first you don't succeed, try, try, again." In fact, failure can teach many lessons to those willing to learn and often leads to future successes. This is clearly shown by the corridor principle, which states that with every venture launched, new and unintended opportunities often arise. The 3M Company invented Post-it notes using a glue that had not been strong enough for its intended use. Rather than throw away the glue, the company focused on finding another use for it and, in the process, developed a multimillion-dollar product. Yet, the statistics of entrepreneurial failure rates have been misleading over the years. In fact, one researcher, Bruce A. Kirchoff, has reported that the "high failure rate" most commonly accepted may be misleading. Tracing 814,000 businesses started in 1977, Kirchoff found that more than 50 percent were still surviving under their original owners or new owners. Furthermore, 28 percent voluntarily closed down, and only 18 percent actually "failed" in the sense of leaving behind outstanding liabilities. In a corporate context, success rates of projects and products also exceed 50 percent.

10. "ENTREPRENEURSHIP IS UNSTRUCTURED AND CHAOTIC"

There is also a tendency to think of entrepreneurs as gunslingers—as people who shoot from the hip and ask questions later. They are assumed by some to be disorganized and unstructured, leaving it to others to keep things on track. The reality is that entrepreneurs are heavily involved in all facets of their ventures, and they usually have a number of balls in the air at the same time. As a result, they are typically well-organized individuals. They tend to have a system, perhaps elaborate, perhaps not, but personally designed to keep things straight and maintain priorities. In fact, their systems may seem strange to the casual observer, but they work.

When doing something entrepreneurial, one is dealing with the unknown, and there is a need to be tolerant of ambiguity. Unanticipated developments arise all the time. Success is often a function of how prepared one is for the unknown and how well one is positioned to capitalize on the unanticipated. The entrepreneur's ability to meet daily and weekly obligations, to simultaneously grow the venture, and to move quickly when novel events occur is strongly affected by his or her organizing capabilities. Plans, outlines, forecasts, checklists, timetables, budgets, databases, and pert charts are examples of tools that the contemporary entrepreneur always keeps close at hand.

The conclusion is that entrepreneurship is a planned activity that can be managed as a process, involves risk, requires innovation, and can be applied in virtually any organizational context. In addition, it is an activity requiring significant dedication, perseverance, and adaptability. Virtually anyone is capable of being entrepreneurial, and many people manage to be entrepreneurial on a continuous basis.

THE ENTREPRENEURIAL PROCESS

One of the most valuable contributions to our understanding of entrepreneurship is the general recognition that a process is involved. It is a process that occurs in an organizational setting, including larger, established companies. Considerable attention is devoted to describing the steps or stages involved and identifying factors that both constrain and facilitate the process. Although the process has been described in various ways, it generally consists of the following stages:

- identifying an opportunity
- defining a business concept
- assessing resource requirements
- acquiring those resources
- implementing and managing the concept
- harvesting the concept or venture

Of the numerous methods and models that attempt to structure the entrepreneurial process and its various components, we shall examine two of the more interesting approaches here. (See also the special issue on models of the process in *Entrepreneurship: Theory and Practice*, 1993, Volume 17, No. 2.) First, we will discuss the "assessment process" based on the work of Robert Ronstadt (1984). Then we will assess the "input-output model" developed by Michael Morris (1998). Both of these perspectives attempt to describe the entrepreneurial process as a consolidation of diverse factors.

An "Entrepreneurial Assessment" Approach

Our first model focuses on the individual, arguing that entrepreneurship should be approached from the vantage point of a person's career, rather than from the perspective of the particular concept he or she is developing or the organizational context within which he or she is operating (Ronstadt 1984). At the heart of the model is the need to make ongoing assessments of the entrepreneur, the concept or venture, and the environment. These assessments should be made using qualitative, quantitative, strategic, and ethical criteria. Figure 2.1 provides an illustration.

Successful entrepreneurship occurs as the result of (a) the preparation, characteristics, and values of the individual entrepreneur or champion and the fit of the individual with the concept or venture; (b) a unique, well-defined, internally consistent and viable business concept; and (c) a favorable set of environmental conditions. Importantly, the results of the assessments in each of these areas must be compared to the stage of the person's entrepreneurial career: early, middle, or late. Thus, the types of entrepreneurial concepts the entrepreneur pursues and the contexts in which he or she pursues them are likely to vary over the stages of his or her career. The perspective is consistent with the notion of entrepreneurship as a

ENTREPRENEURIAL ASSESSMENT APPROACH

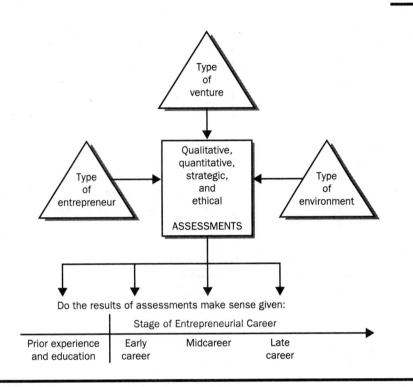

SOURCE: Ronstadt, R. C. 1984. *Entrepreneurship.* Dover: Lord Publishing.

lifetime philosophy, manifesting itself in different ways over time and providing a theme or direction to an individual's professional and personal development.

AN "INTEGRATIVE" APPROACH

A more integrative picture of the entrepreneurial process is provided by Morris et al. (1994). Presented in Figure 2.2, this model is built around the concepts of inputs to the entrepreneurial process and outcomes from the entrepreneurial process. The input component of Figure 2.2 focuses on the entrepreneurial process itself and identifies five key elements that contribute to the process. The first is environmental opportunities, such as a demographic change, the development of a new technology, or a modification to current regulations. Next is the individual entrepreneur, the person who assumes personal responsibility for conceptualizing and implementing a new venture. The entrepreneur develops some type of business concept to capitalize on the opportunity (e.g., a creative approach to solving a

■ **FIGURE 2.2**

AN INTEGRATIVE MODEL OF ENTREPRENEURIAL INPUTS AND OUTCOMES

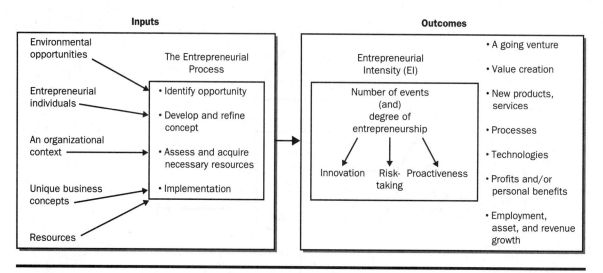

SOURCE: Morris, M., P. Lewis, and D. Sexton. 1994. "Reconceptualizing Entrepreneurship: An Input-Output Perspective," *SAM Advanced Management Journal* 59, No. 1 (Winter): 21–31.

particular customer need). Implementing this business concept typically requires some type of organizational context, which could range from a sole proprietorship run out of the entrepreneur's home or a franchise of some national chain to an autonomous business unit within a large corporation. Finally, a wide variety of financial and nonfinancial resources are required on an ongoing basis. These key elements are then combined throughout the stages of the entrepreneurial process. Stated differently, the process provides a logical framework for organizing entrepreneurial inputs.

The output component of Figure 2.2 first includes the level of entrepreneurship being achieved. As we shall discuss in more detail in the next chapter, entrepreneurship is a variable. Thus, the process can result in any number of entrepreneurial events and can produce events that vary considerably in terms of how entrepreneurial they are. Based on this level of "entrepreneurial intensity," final outcomes can include one or more going ventures, value creation, new products and processes, new technologies, profit, jobs, and economic growth. Moreover, the outcome can certainly be failure and thereby bring about the economic, psychic, and social costs associated with failure.

This model not only provides a fairly comprehensive picture regarding the nature of entrepreneurship, but can also be applied at different levels. For example, the model describes the phenomenon of entrepreneurship in both the independent start-up company and within a department, division, or strategic business unit of a large corporation. This brings us to an examination of the entrepreneurial process at the level of the established company or organization.

THE NATURE OF CORPORATE ENTREPRENEURSHIP

DEFINING THE CONCEPT

Corporate entrepreneurship is a term used to describe entrepreneurial behavior inside established midsized and large organizations. Related terms include *organizational entrepreneurship, intrapreneurship,* and *corporate venturing.* Operational definitions of corporate entrepreneurship have evolved over the past thirty years. For example, Damanpour (1991) noted that corporate innovation is a very broad concept that includes the generation, development, and implementation of new ideas or behaviors. An innovation can be a new product or service, an administrative system, or a new plan or program pertaining to organizational members. In this context, corporate entrepreneurship centers on reenergizing and enhancing the firm's ability to acquire innovative skills and capabilities.

Zahra (1991) has observed that "corporate entrepreneurship may be formal or informal activities aimed at creating new businesses in established companies through product and process innovations and market developments. These activities may take place at the corporate, division, business unit, functional, or project levels, with the unifying objective of improving a company's competitive position and financial performance." Guth and Ginsberg (1990) stress that corporate entrepreneurship encompasses two major phenomena: new venture creation within existing organizations and the transformation of organizations through strategic renewal.

A related point of view defines corporate entrepreneurship as the process whereby an individual or a group of individuals, in association with an established company, creates a new organization or instigates renewal or innovation within the current organization (Sharma and Chrisman 1999). Under this definition, strategic renewal (which is concerned with organizational revitalization involving major strategic and/or structural changes), innovation (which is concerned with introducing something new to the marketplace), and corporate venturing (corporate entrepreneurial efforts that lead to the creation of new business organizations within the corporate organization) are all important and legitimate parts of the concept of corporate entrepreneurship.

FRAMEWORKS FOR UNDERSTANDING CORPORATE ENTREPRENEURSHIP

The concept of corporate entrepreneurship combines the critical elements of entrepreneurship we have discussed up to this point with the strategic requirements and development of corporations. Research concerning corporate entrepreneurship has been rapidly increasing over the past few years. A variety of frameworks

■ FIGURE 2.3

FITTING CORPORATE ENTREPRENEURSHIP INTO STRATEGIC MANAGEMENT

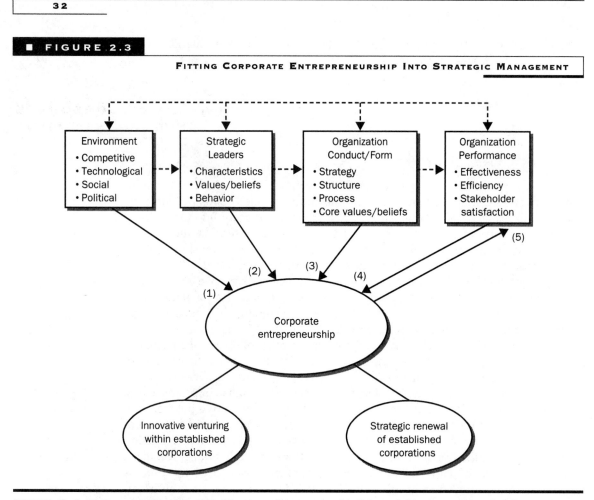

SOURCE: Guth, W. D., and A. Ginsberg. 1990. "Corporate Entrepreneurship," *Strategic Management Journal* 11 (Summer): 5–15.

have been developed that contribute to our understanding of and the accomplishment of entrepreneurial activities inside companies.

A DOMAIN FRAMEWORK

Guth and Ginsberg (1990) have provided a framework for developing knowledge about corporate entrepreneurship. They argue that the domain of corporate entrepreneurship encompasses two types of processes: internal innovation (venturing through the creation of new businesses within existing organizations) and strategic renewal initiatives that transform operations within organizations. Figure 2.3 illustrates this model. Key components in this model include the environment, strategic leaders, organization form, and performance. Each component represents an important element affecting the nature and outcomes of corporate entrepreneurship.

■ FIGURE 2.4

AN INTERACTIVE MODEL OF CORPORATE ENTREPRENEURING

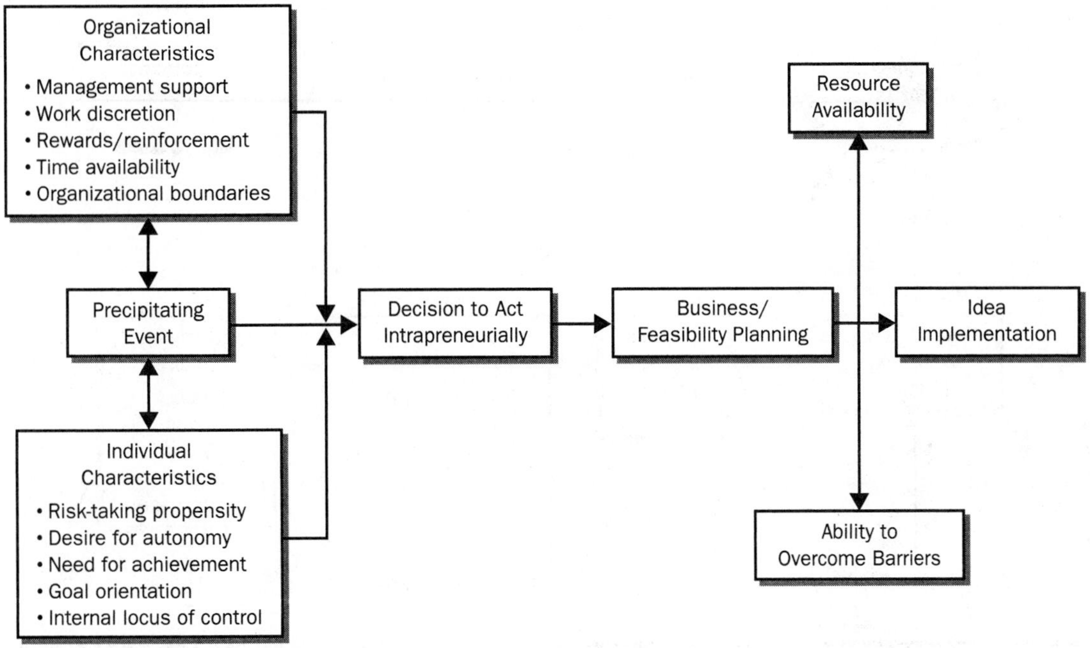

SOURCE: Hornsby, J. S., D. W. Naffziger, D. F. Kuratko, and R. V. Montagno (1993). "An Interactive Model of the Corporate Entrepreneurship Process," *Entrepreneurship Theory and Practice* 17, No. 2 (Spring):31.

AN INTERACTIVE FRAMEWORK

An alternative framework can be found in the work of Hornsby et al. (1993). They focus on the interaction of organizational factors and individual characteristics that is ignited by a precipitating event that leads to successful corporate entrepreneurship. Figure 2.4 illustrates this interactive model. The precipitating event could be a change in company management, a merger or acquisition, development of new technology, or some other event that acts as the impetus for the interaction between individual characteristics and organizational factors.

A STRATEGIC INTEGRATION FRAMEWORK

Yet another perspective approaches entrepreneurship as an overall orientation within a company. The focus here is on the integration of entrepreneurship throughout the entire organization, rather than merely viewing entrepreneurship as a discrete activity or event or behavior. That is, entrepreneurship is not just something that a person or team does. Rather, it captures the essence of what an

■ FIGURE 2.5

STRATEGIC INTEGRATION OF ENTREPRENEURSHIP THROUGHOUT THE ORGANIZATION

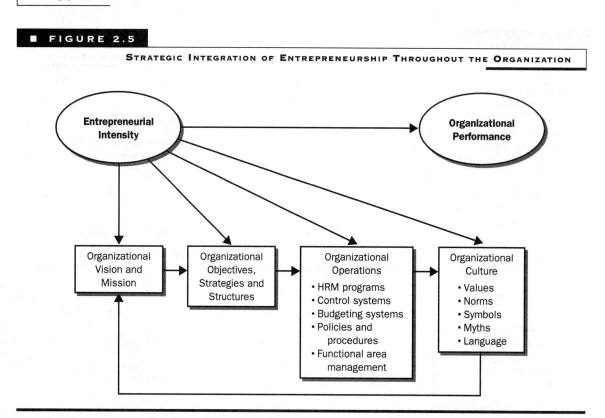

SOURCE: Adapted from Covin, J. G., and D. P. Slevin. 1991. "A Conceptual Model of Entrepreneurship as Firm Behavior," *Entrepreneurship Theory and Practice* 16, No. 1 (Fall): 7–26.

organization is about and how it operates. Originally developed by Covin and Slevin (1991), Figure 2.5 indicates that entrepreneurial orientation or intensity has a direct and positive influence on company performance. It does so because it is interwoven with the vision and mission of the firm; the strategies, objectives, and structures of the organization; the company's operations; and the overall organizational culture. The major purpose of this integrative model is to allow for considerable managerial intervention and thus reduce the view of corporate entrepreneurship as serendipitous or mysterious.

The overall theme behind all of these frameworks is a revitalization of personal creativity, product and process innovation, and ongoing managerial development in companies. The strategies and insights presented in the models here can serve as a foundation for understanding the current increase in entrepreneurial action inside organizations. Further, they can guide the efforts of managers striving to create work environments that are supportive of the entrepreneurial spirit. In the chapters ahead, we will further investigate how to create such environments, while identifying specific ways in which corporate entrepreneurship can serve as the source of competitive advantage in companies.

INTRAPRENEURIAL INSIGHT

RULES FOR FOSTERING AN INNOVATIVE ORGANIZATION

RULE #1 - UNREASONABLE EXPECTATIONS

■ Only when people subscribe to the unreasonable goals will they start searching for breakthrough ideas.

■ There are no mature industries, only mature managers who unthinkingly accept someone else's definition of what is possible.

RULE #2 - ELASTIC BUSINESS DEFINITION

■ Too many companies define themselves by what they do rather than by what they know (core competencies) and what they own (strategic assets).

RULE #3 - A CAUSE, NOT A BUSINESS

■ Revolutionaries draw much of their strength from their allegiance to a cause that goes beyond growth, profits, or even personal wealth accumulation.

■ The courage to leave some of oneself behind and strike out for parts unknown comes not from some assurance that "change is good" but from a devotion to a wholly worthwhile cause.

RULE #4 - NEW VOICES

■ Let the youth be heard.

■ Listen to the periphery.

■ Let newcomers have their say.

RULE #5 - AN OPEN MARKET FOR IDEAS

■ Create a market for entre-preneurial ideas inside your company.

■ New ideas are the currency of the realm.

RULE #6 - CREATE AN OPEN MARKET FOR CAPITAL

■ Within a corporation, why set the hurdle for accessing a small investment for the purpose of funding an

unconventional idea, building a prototype, or designing a market trial at the same difficulty as involved when obtaining a large, irreversible investment?

RULE #7 - OPEN A MARKET FOR TALENT

■ "A" people work on "A" opportunities.

■ Provide incentives for employees who are willing to take a "risk" on something out of the ordinary.

RULE #8 - LOW-RISK EXPERIMENTATION

■ Being revolutionary does not mean being a high-risk taker.

■ False dichotomy: Cautious follower vs. high-risk taker. Neither is likely to pay off in the age of revolution.

SOURCE: Adapted from Hamel, G. 2000. *Leading the Revolution.* Boston: Harvard Business School Press.

SUMMARY AND CONCLUSIONS

In this chapter we have attempted to lay a foundation for understanding entre-preneurship. We noted the many perspectives regarding who (is an entrepre-neur?), what (do they do?), why (do they do it?), where (or in what kind organizational setting?), and how (following what kind of process?). An attempt was made to identify some common elements among the diverse viewpoints. These included creating a new concept or venture, innovating or creating new combinations of resources, pursuing opportunity, marshaling necessary resources, risk-taking, profit-seeking, and creating value. Using these common elements, a definition of entrepreneurship was presented. The key to this definition is the notion that entrepreneurship is a manageable process consisting of specific stages and that it can be applied in virtually any organizational setting.

The ability to apply entrepreneurship to midsized and large organizations requires that we dispense with many of the myths and misconceptions regarding entrepreneurship. A number of these misconceptions were discussed. The underlying need is to remove the mystique from both the entrepreneur as a person and the phenomenon of entrepreneurship as it occurs in practice. Entrepreneurship is about vision and insight, but also about hard work, perseverance, and adaptability. Entrepreneurs themselves are ordinary people who, working through teams, create the new. Importantly, entrepreneurial potential is something that resides in each and every employee in a company.

Entrepreneurship occurs as a function of the interactions among a number of key variables. Two general perspectives were presented on these variables. The first of these approached things from the perspective of the career stages of the individual who pursues an entrepreneurial initiative. The second looked at the pursuit of entrepreneurship from the vantage point of critical inputs and outcomes. Both of these perspectives are equally applicable to start-up entrepreneurship and corporate entrepreneurship.

Finally, the concept of corporate entrepreneurship was formally introduced. Three frameworks were provided for understanding the unique nature of entrepreneurship when it happens inside an established organization. The reality is that entrepreneurship in corporations takes many forms and manifests itself in many ways. Moreover, companies can differ significantly in terms of how entrepreneurial they are. This last point, which is concerned with the variable nature of entrepreneurship, will be the subject of our attention in the next chapter.

REFERENCES

Covin, J. G., and D. P. Slevin. 1991. "A Conceptual Model of Entrepreneurship as Firm Behavior," *Entrepreneurship Theory and Practice* 16, No. 1: 7–26.

Damanpour, F. 1991. "Organizational Innovation: A Meta-analysis of Determinant and Moderators," *Academy of Management Journal* 34: 355–390.

Gartner, W. B. 1990. "What Are We Talking About When We Talk About Entrepreneurship?" *Journal of Business Venturing* 5: 15–28.

Guth, W. D., and A. Ginsberg. 1990. "Corporate Entrepreneurship," *Strategic Management Journal* (Special Issue) 11: 5–15.

Hornsby, J. S., D. W. Naffziger, D. F. Kuratko, and R. V. Montagno. 1993. "An Interactive Model of the Corporate Entrepreneurship Process," *Entrepreneurship Theory and Practice* 17, No. 6 (Spring): 29–37.

Kuratko, D .F., and R. M. Hodgetts. 2001. *Entrepreneurship: A Contemporary Approach,* 5th ed. Ft. Worth: Harcourt College.

Morris, M. H. 1998. *Entrepreneurial Intensity.* Westport: Quorum Books.

Morris, M. H., and P. S. Lewis. 1991. "Entrepreneurship as a Significant Factor in Societal Quality of Life," *Journal of Business Research* 13, No. 1 (August): 21–36.

Ronstadt, R. C. 1984. *Entrepreneurship.* Dover: Lord Publishing.

Sharma, P., and J. J. Chrisman. 1999. "Toward a Reconciliation of the Definitional Issues in the Field of Corporate Entrepreneurship," *Entrepreneurship Theory and Practice* 23, No. 3 (Spring): 11–28.

Stevenson, H. H., H. I. Grousbeck, M. J. Roberts, and A. Bhide. 1999. *New Business Ventures and the Entrepreneur.* Homewood: Irwin.

Timmons, J. A. 1999. *New Venture Creation*, 5th ed. Homewood: Irwin.

Zahra, S. A. 1991. "Predictors and Financial Outcomes of Corporate Entrepreneurship: An Exploratory Study," *Journal of Business Venturing* 6, No. 4 (July): 259–286.

LEVELS OF ENTREPRENEURSHIP IN ORGANIZATIONS: ENTREPRENEURIAL INTENSITY

What does it mean to characterize an organization as "entrepreneurial"? We make the mistake of thinking in either–or terms, as in "that's an entrepreneurial firm, while that one is not." However, entrepreneurship is not something an organization either has or does not have; it is a variable. There is some level of entrepreneurship in every organization. Even in the largest, most staid and conservative companies, elements of entrepreneurial behavior can be found somewhere in the firm. Within the most bureaucratic government organizations, one can find highly entrepreneurial people. The question becomes one of determining how entrepreneurial a given organization is. The answer to this question lies in the three underlying dimensions of entrepreneurship: innovativeness, risk-taking, and proactiveness. Let us explore each of these dimensions in greater detail.

EXPLORING THE DIMENSIONS OF ENTREPRENEURSHIP

INNOVATIVENESS

The first dimension that characterizes an entrepreneurial organization is innovativeness. Here, the concern is with the relative emphasis on concepts or activities that represent a departure from what is currently available. Simply stated, to what extent is the company doing things that are novel, unique, or different?

A range, or continuum, of possibilities exists (Figure 3.1). Does the concept address a need that has not previously been addressed, as the first laser surgical tool did? Does it change the way one goes about addressing a need, as the original fax machine or the microwave oven did? Is it a dramatic improvement over

■ FIGURE 3.1

A RANGE OF OPTIONS: INNOVATIVENESS AS IT
APPLIES TO PRODUCTS AND SERVICES

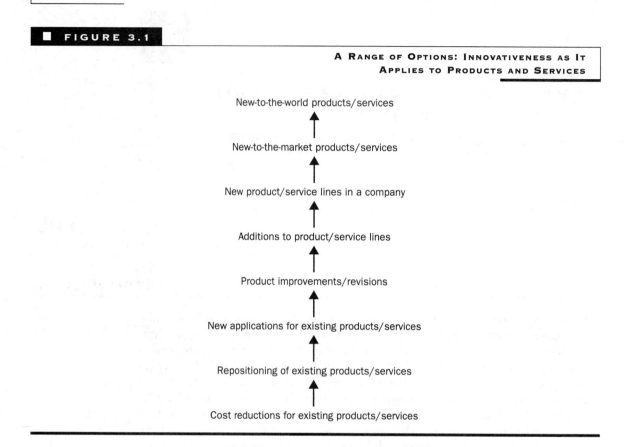

New-to-the-world products/services

↑

New-to-the-market products/services

↑

New product/service lines in a company

↑

Additions to product/service lines

↑

Product improvements/revisions

↑

New applications for existing products/services

↑

Repositioning of existing products/services

↑

Cost reductions for existing products/services

conventional solutions, as the cellular telephone or the electric automobile are? Does it represent a minor modification or improvement to an existing product, as a longer-lasting lightbulb or less fattening dessert products do? Is it just the geographic transfer of a proven product, such as the sale of frozen yogurt in a country where the product is unknown?

In addition to these product examples, innovation can take the form of new or improved services. The tremendous growth of the service sector is a testimonial to the entrepreneurial spirit at work. America Online (AOL), MSNBC, The Discovery Zone, E*Trade, and La Petite Daycare Centers represent just a few of the thousands of successful entrepreneurial service concepts. In fact, given their intangible nature and the ease with which they can be replicated, services lend themselves to continuous innovation and improvement. American Express is an excellent example of a company that is continually looking for service line extensions, modifications, and enhancements.

The third innovation frontier is in processes, or finding new and better ways to accomplish a task or function (Table 3.1). Many entrepreneurial ventures offer products that are fairly standard and certainly not unique. However, they have come up with highly innovative process innovations that are a major source of

■ **TABLE 3.1**

A RANGE OF OPTIONS: INNOVATIVENESS AS IT APPLIES TO PROCESSES

Degree of Innovation	Type of Process
Major new process	Administrative systems
Minor new process	Service delivery systems
Significant revision of existing process	Production methods
Modest improvement of existing process	Financing methods
	Marketing or sales approaches
	Procurement techniques
	Compensation methods
	Supply chain management techniques
	Distribution methods
	Employee training programs
	Pricing approaches
	Information management systems
	Customer support programs
	Logistical approaches
	Hiring methods

competitive advantage (i.e., they result in lower costs, faster operations, more rapid delivery, improved quality, or better customer service). Examples include innovative production techniques, distribution approaches, selling methods, purchasing programs, or administrative systems. Consider the novel hub-and-spoke transport system used by Federal Express to provide quick and dependable overnight parcel delivery service or the highly inventive production techniques mastered by Nucor that result in high-quality and affordable specialty-grade steel produced in a mini-mill.

RISK-TAKING

Anything new involves risk, or some likelihood that actual results will differ from expectations. Risk-taking involves a willingness to pursue opportunities that have a reasonable likelihood of producing losses or significant performance discrepancies. Our emphasis is not on extreme, uncontrollable risks, but instead on the risks that are moderate and calculated. Entrepreneurship does not entail reckless decision making. It involves a realistic awareness of the risks involved—including financial, technical, market, and personal—and an attempt to manage these risks. These risks are reflected in the various resource allocation decisions made by an individual or organization as well as in the choice of products, services, and markets to be emphasized. Risk-taking can thus be viewed as both an individual-level trait as well as an organization-level concept.

An interesting perspective on calculated risk-taking is provided by Hamel and Prahalad (1993). They use the analogy of the baseball player who comes to bat,

RELATING INNOVATIVENESS TO RISK

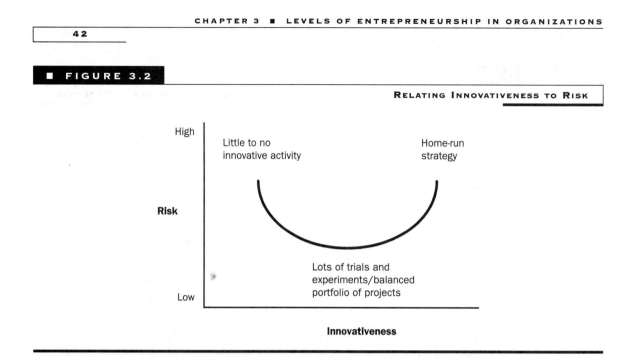

concentrates intently on perfecting his/her swing, and strives to hit a home run. Further, the batter is preoccupied with his/her batting average. Obviously, if he or she comes to bat only twice and gets a hit on one of those occasions, the result is a .500 batting average. Unfortunately, companies often approach the development of new products, services, and technologies as does our baseball player. They pursue few projects, rely on cautious, "go-slow" strategies that aim to perfect the concept, and hold off on introduction until they are certain they have a major winner. Meanwhile, scrappier competitors move more quickly and beat them to the punch.

Successful hits are a function of both one's batting average and the number of times one comes to bat. The message is that entrepreneurs and entrepreneurial companies need to come to bat more often. Risks are better managed by focusing on frequent, lower-risk market incursions with a variety of new product and service options targeted to different segments and niches. By engaging in lots of experiments, test markets, and trial runs, the entrepreneur is better able to determine what works and what does not. Such quickened learning may come at the expense of minor failures, but it is also likely to ensure more sustainable long-term successes.

One might be tempted to assume that innovativeness and risk-taking are directly correlated: that doing more innovative things means taking higher risks and vice versa. In reality, the relationship may be more complex, as pictured in Figure 3.2. Here, the relationship is pictured as a curvilinear function. As can be seen, risk is high when the company ignores new product and service opportunities and engages in little to no innovation. Companies that do not innovate are faced with a higher risk of not perceiving market and technology shifts that are capitalized on by competitors. But risk is also high when companies take the

■ **FIGURE 3.3**

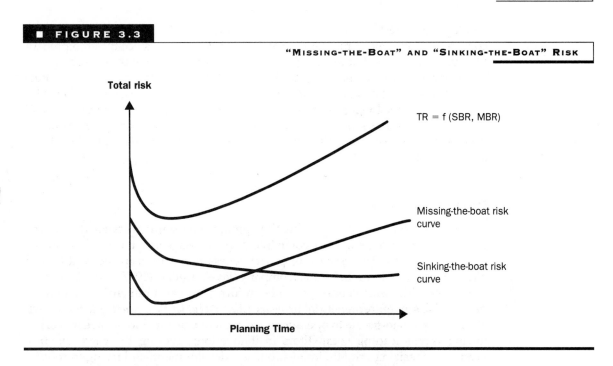

Total risk

$TR = f(SBR, MBR)$

Missing-the-boat risk curve

Sinking-the-boat risk curve

Planning Time

opposite track and attempt to come up with breakthrough innovations that create new markets and redefine industries. In Figure 3.2 this is referred to as a "home-run" strategy. In between these two end-points is the Hamel and Prahalad strategy discussed above. Risk is lower and more manageable when lots of trials and experiments are pursued all the time; in effect, a balanced portfolio of innovation projects is being managed. We shall further investigate the concept of an "innovation portfolio" in Chapter 7.

It is also critical to note that, from an entrepreneurial standpoint, there are actually two sides to the risk equation. Discussions of risk generally focus on what happens if the entrepreneur pursues a concept and it does not work out. This side of the equation has been labeled "sinking the boat" risk by Dickson and Giglierano (1986). It is reflected in such factors as a poorly thought-out concept, bad timing, an already well-satisfied market, inadequate marketing and distribution approaches, and inappropriate price levels. The other side of the equation is called "missing the boat" risk, or the risk in not pursuing a course of action that would have proven profitable. It occurs when the entrepreneur delays acting on a concept for too long and is preempted by competitors or changing market requirements. Here, the entrepreneur is being too cautious or conservative and often seeks more security in the form of additional market research, financial data, or input from consultants.

Figure 3.3 illustrates the relationship between these two types of risk. With more planning time, "sinking the boat" risk steadily declines, since the entrepreneur is able to refine his/her concept; put together a better resource package; and identify more effective approaches to production, marketing, and other operational concerns. Meanwhile, "missing the boat" risk initially falls, since the entrepreneur identifies fatal flaws that represent reasons to rethink or shelve the concept.

He or she may let competitors be the first to the market, let them make the mistakes from which he or she can learn, then enter with a much better market solution. However, the longer the delay in action, the more likely that competitors will move quickly and lock up the market opportunity or that the market opportunity itself will disappear. Total risk, then, becomes a function of the outcomes if one acts and if one does not.

PROACTIVENESS

The third dimension of entrepreneurship, proactiveness, is less easy to define. The opposite of reactiveness, it has come into popular usage as a term to describe an action orientation. The essence of proactiveness is captured in the well-known Nike slogan "Just do it." At a company level, Miller (1987) associates proactiveness with assertiveness, which he in turn views as a dimension of strategy making. He sees entrepreneurial firms as *acting on rather than reacting to* their environments. His short scale to operationalize proactiveness includes three items: following versus leading competitors in innovation; favoring the tried and true versus emphasizing growth, innovation, and development; and trying to cooperate with competitors versus trying to undo them.

Proactiveness is concerned with implementation, with taking responsibility and doing whatever is necessary to bring an entrepreneurial concept to fruition. It usually involves considerable perseverance, adaptability, and a willingness to assume responsibility for failure. In his study of the strategic orientation of business enterprises, Venkatraman (1989) uses the term to refer to a continuous search for market opportunities and experimentation with potential responses to changing environmental trends. He suggests it is manifested in three key ways:

1. Seeking new opportunities that may or may not be related to the present line of operations;

2. Introducing new products and brands ahead of competition; and

3. Strategically eliminating operations that are in the mature or declining stages of the life cycle.

Proactive behavior has also been approached as a person's disposition to take action to influence his/her environments (Bateman and Crant 1993). This perspective holds that the behavior of people is both internally and externally controlled and that situations are as much a function of individuals as individuals are themselves functions of their environments. As Buss (1987) has put it, people are not "passive recipients of environmental pressures": they influence their own environments. This approach to proactiveness is one that fits with corporate entrepreneurship very well — namely, that people can intentionally and directly change their current circumstances, including aspects of their work environment.

To illustrate the proactiveness dimension, consider the engineer from a large telecommunications company whose job involves delivering engineering services to customer sites, many of which are in remote locations. Routinely, crews must drive company trucks loaded with sensitive technical equipment to these customer sites. Traveling along bumpy, rural, and sometimes dirt roads, the equipment is often damaged or knocked out of calibration. The field crews often have to wait at a site while more equipment is sent out from the head office, or they must return another day. Our engineer takes it upon himself to fix the problem in his free time. He obtains resources by "begging, borrowing, and stealing" from the organization. Lo and behold, he comes up with a design for the truck bed that would allow the truck to be driven through a veritable hurricane without the equipment losing calibration or otherwise being damaged.

Is this proactive? Yes and no. Our engineer certainly has done much more than analyze a problem; he has produced a solution. But proactiveness is more than this. The engineer must sell the solution to his boss, who likely will not have the time or money to support the engineer. He then has to persist in selling it to the organization, which will entail building a coalition of supporters, overcoming large numbers of obstacles, and demonstrating adroit political skills. This is where the real proactiveness comes into the picture. If, in the end, the company's truck fleet is converted to his design, successful entrepreneurship has occurred. Even better than this would be the subsequent licensing of the design to other companies.

This distinction drawn here is similar to the distinction between the inventor and the (corporate) entrepreneur. Inventors are more than dreamers, in that they translate an idea into a product. But entrepreneurs go further, and this is the essence of proactiveness. Entrepreneurs may invent a product or process or rely on someone else's invention. Their real contribution lies in recognizing, properly defining, and effectively communicating the potential of the invention and then in achieving acceptance for the invention within the company, getting it implemented (if it is a process), launching it (if it is a product), and achieving commercial success or failure.

COMBINATIONS OF THE DIMENSIONS: THE CONCEPT OF DEGREE

Different combinations of these three dimensions are possible. A given entrepreneurial event (new product, service, or process) might be highly or only nominally innovative, entail significant or limited risk, and require considerable or relatively little proactiveness. Accordingly, the "degree of entrepreneurship," refers to the extent to which events are innovative, risky, and proactive. This does not mean that more of each of the three dimensions of entrepreneurship is necessarily better.

ENTREPRENEURSHIP AS A VECTOR

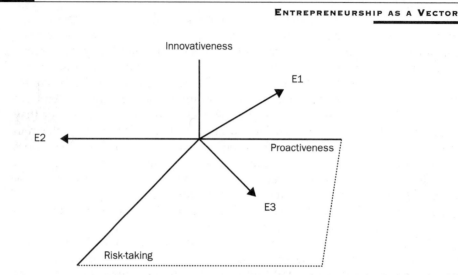

Rather, entrepreneurship is ideally a balanced process, and the appropriate degree depends on the situation.

To visualize this, entrepreneurship might be conceived of as a vector in three-dimensional space, as shown in Figure 3.4. Three situations (E1, E2, and E3) are portrayed in Figure 3.4. The first situation (E1) represents a firm or group of managers/entrepreneurs that is highly innovative or proactive but highly risk averse. The second situation (E2) finds another firm or group of managers/ entrepreneurs that is highly innovative and risk-taking to the point of gambling but lacking in proactiveness—the persistence and ability to implement entrepreneurial concepts. The third firm or group of managers/entrepreneurs (E3) has a more or less balanced entrepreneurial orientation.

Two observations can be made. First, while the discussion in Figure 3.4 applies to firms or groups of managers/entrepreneurs, it could just as well apply to departments or functions within firms, such as sales management or selling, and obviously the vector could be applied to an individual. Thus, there could be individuals who are indeed too innovative and not proactive enough or who attempt to overcome personal limitations in innovativeness by taking disproportionate risks — perhaps to the extent of gambling on products, customers, or sources of supply. Second, the entrepreneurial mix, or the magnitude and direction of the vector, is obviously not standard or easy to calculate and specify.

■ FIGURE 3.5

DICHOTOMIZING THE ENTREPRENEURIAL
DIMENSIONS OF RISK-TAKING AND INNOVATIVENESS

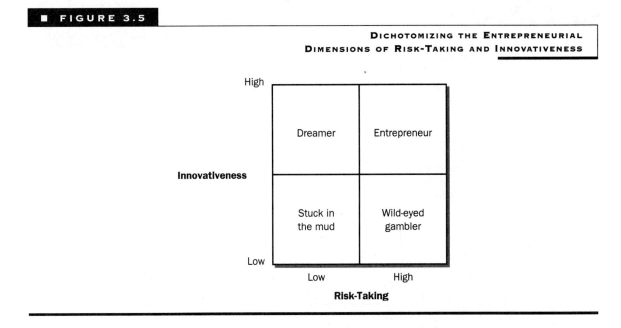

Rather, it depends on situations within industries or sales environments. Thus, for example, high-tech markets might require greater levels of innovative input for success than would fast-moving consumer goods markets, and real estate sales situations might reward greater risk-seeking than would situations in telemarketing.

Another worthwhile approach would be to examine the position of an organization, a department within an organization, or an individual on a matrix formed by any two of the three dimensions, and to consider the implications of this. For example, consider the application of the risk-taking and innovativeness dimensions to a sales department within a company. The sales department might find itself in one of four positions, as illustrated in Figure 3.5. The "stuck-in-the-mud" sales manager would seldom innovate or be willing to assume the risks that such innovation would require. The "dreamer" would be highly innovative in thinking but unwilling to take the risks to give the innovations the chance of success. Taking risks would be all the "wild-eyed gambler" did—the concepts on which risks were taken would not be innovative or creative but would merely be risky "bets." The entrepreneurial sales manager would balance risk-taking and innovativeness, realizing that innovative ideas also necessitate some risk-taking. Similarly, two-by-two grids can also be used to examine the dichotomies of innovativeness and proactiveness and risk-taking and proactiveness.

■ FIGURE 3.6

THE ENTREPRENEURIAL GRID

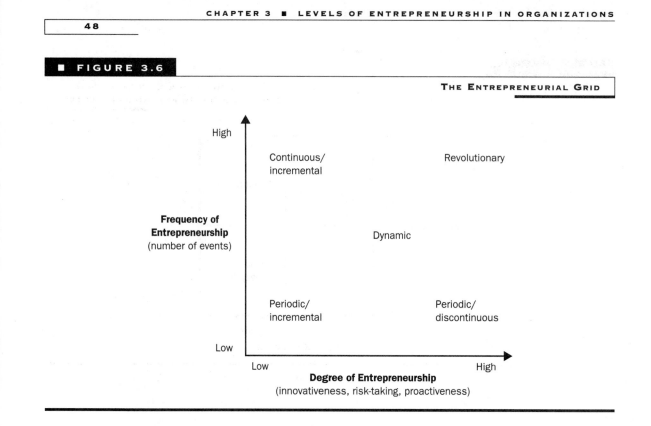

ENTREPRENEURIAL INTENSITY: COMBINING DEGREE AND FREQUENCY OF ENTREPRENEURSHIP

We began the chapter by noting that entrepreneurship is a variable. An entrepreneurial event varies in the degree of entrepreneurship, or how much innovativeness, risk-taking, and proactiveness is involved. Just as important is the question of how many entrepreneurial events take place within a company over a given period of time. We will refer to this as the "frequency of entrepreneurship." Some companies produce a steady stream of new products, services, and processes over time, while others may very rarely introduce something new or different.

This brings us to the concept of "entrepreneurial intensity." To assess the overall level of entrepreneurship in a company, the concepts of degree and frequency must be considered together. Any number of combinations can result. Thus, a firm may be engaging in lots of entrepreneurial initiatives (high on frequency), but none of them are all that innovative, risky, or proactive (low on degree). Another company may pursue a path that emphasizes breakthrough developments (high degree) that are done every four or five years (low frequency).

To better understand the entrepreneurial intensity (EI) concept, consider Figure 3.6. Here, a two-dimensional matrix has been created with the number, or frequency, of entrepreneurial events on the vertical axis, and the extent or degree to which these events are innovative, risky, and proactive on the horizontal axis. We refer to this matrix as the "entrepreneurial grid." For purposes of illustration, five sample scenarios have been identified in Figure 3.6, and these have been labeled Periodic/Incremental, Continuous/Incremental, Periodic/Discontinuous, Dynamic, and Revolutionary.

Each of these reflects the variable nature of entrepreneurial intensity. For example, where few entrepreneurial events are produced, and these events are only nominally innovative, risky, and proactive, the organization can be described as Periodic/Incremental in terms of its (modest) level of EI. Similarly, an organization that is responsible for numerous entrepreneurial events that are highly innovative, risky, or proactive will fit into the Revolutionary segment of the entrepreneurial matrix and will exhibit the highest levels of EI.

While Figure 3.6 depicts five discrete segments, it is important to note that these segments have been arbitrarily defined to provide an example of how EI may vary. Amounts and degrees of entrepreneurship are relative; absolute standards do not exist. Further, any given organization could be highly entrepreneurial at some times and not very entrepreneurial at others. Consequently, they could occupy different segments of the matrix at different points in time.

APPLYING THE ENTREPRENEURIAL GRID TO ORGANIZATIONS

The entrepreneurial grid is a very useful tool for managers attempting to define the role of entrepreneurship within their organizations. By identifying where the company falls in the grid, management is effectively defining the firm's entrepreneurial strategy. Consider an application of the grid to five successful companies (Figure 3.7). These are firms that exhibit varying degrees of EI, and as a consequence, are representative of different spaces or scenarios.

They include the following:

■ *Wendy's*. Started in 1969, this highly successful fast-food chain rapidly captured third place in the industry by developing an innovative product/service delivery system and by targeting a relatively untapped market consisting of young adults with a desire for higher-quality food. Throughout the years, it has maintained a competitive advantage by responding to environmental trends. For example, an increasing demand for convenience led Wendy's to pioneer drive-up window service, and shifting consumer preferences for lighter, lower-calorie meals were met through the introduction of salads and baked potatoes. Responding to saturated demand and heightened competitive intensity, a "value menu" was added. While none of these activities can be considered highly innovative, Wendy's can be credited with introducing a few creative changes to the fast-food industry. As such, Wendy's is representative of the Periodic/Incremental segment of the entrepreneurial grid.

■ FIGURE 3.7

APPLYING THE ENTREPRENEURIAL GRID AT THE ORGANIZATIONAL LEVEL

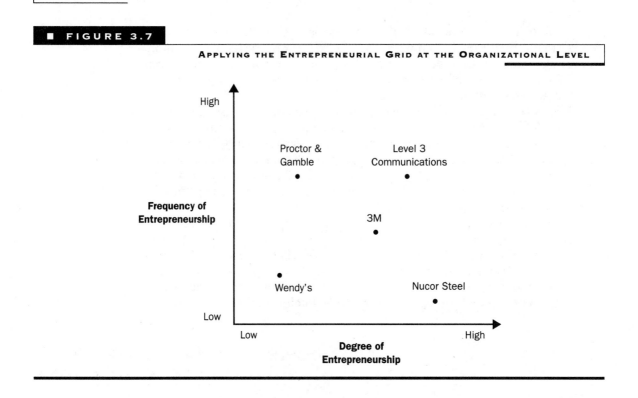

■ *Procter & Gamble* (P&G). With the leading brand in twenty-two of forty product categories in which it competes, P&G has remained on top in the highly competitive consumer packaged goods industry by placing priority on research and development. The result has been a continuous stream of product improvements, with an occasional new product entry. P&G excels at evolutionary adaptations to, and improvements in, existing product concepts. Therefore, this company is representative of the Continuous/ Incremental segment of the grid.

■ *Nucor.* Founded in 1968 as a mini-mill that produced steel construction joints, Nucor introduced a radically new technical process for producing sheet metal in small electric arc furnaces. It mastered the ability to produce a ton of sheet steel in three-quarters of a man-hour versus the conventional three man hours. In addition to transforming the competitive and economic structure of the steel industry, this innovation has affected the cost structure of firms in many other industries (e.g., automobile, construction). Therefore, while Nucor has been responsible for a few entrepreneurial initiatives, its efforts have had a relatively dramatic effect on several industries. As such, Nucor represents Periodic/Discontinuous entrepreneurship.

- *Minnesota Mining and Manufacturing Company (3M).* The 3M Company's unique talent is finding commercial uses for new product technology, developing that technology into dozens of marketable forms, and finding novel applications for these products. An example is Scotch cellophane tape, from which many successful products were derived. 3M sets a goal of achieving 25 percent of annual sales from products that have been developed in the last five years. The system of innovative products that come from this firm suggest that it is representative of the Dynamic segment of the entrepreneurial grid.

- *Level 3 Communications.* Capitalizing on fundamental changes in communication technology, Level 3 is the first company to build an end-to-end Internet Protocol (IP) international communications network from the ground up. Characterized as the very model of a modern major bandwidth merchant, the company is currently building more than 20,000 miles of fiber-optic networks in the US and Europe. Level 3's IP-based network also includes undersea capacity across the Atlantic and Pacific. Packing its network with fiber and spare conduits for future upgrades, Level 3 serves such data-intensive customers as internet service providers (ISPs) and telecom carriers. Services include dedicated circuits, Internet access, server and network equipment collocation, and dark fiber leasing. The speed and aggressiveness of Level 3, its high-risk profile, and its visionary approach to the future suggest the company is closer to the Revolutionary sector of the grid.

These companies represent a study in contrasts. Consider a comparison of Nucor's major technological advancement in the production of steel to the constant flow of new products and processes that come from cross-functional ranks of 3M or the development of the drive-up window concept to the development of laser technology. Yet, each firm has an effective strategy for EI that has proven to fit with its internal and external environments and to be profitable.

Where a company falls in the entrepreneurial grid will vary depending on a number of internal and external factors. Internally, entrepreneurship is more in evidence where company structures are flat, control systems contain a measure of slack, appraisal systems include innovation and risk-taking criteria, jobs are broad in scope, and reward systems encourage a balance of individualism and group orientation. Externally, industries that are highly concentrated and have little direct competition, demand that is captive, technologies that rarely change, and margins that are comfortable will likely contain companies with low EI scores. Frequency of entrepreneurship may be directly related to the intensity of competition and amount of market heterogeneity, while degree of entrepreneurship is likely to be related to the rate of technological change in an industry and amount of product heterogeneity.

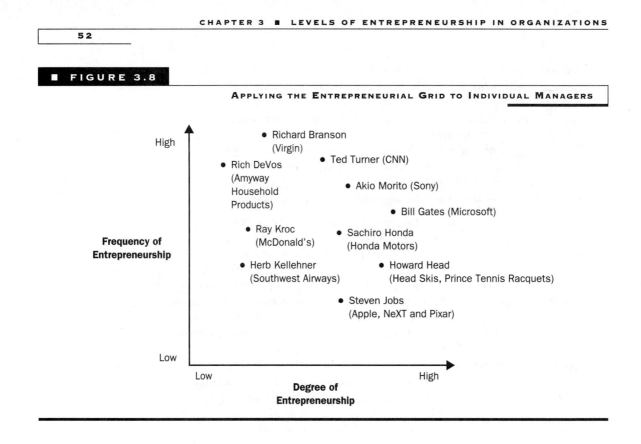

■ FIGURE 3.8

APPLYING THE ENTREPRENEURIAL GRID TO INDIVIDUAL MANAGERS

APPLYING THE GRID AT THE LEVEL OF THE INDIVIDUAL MANAGER

There are many types of corporate entrepreneurs. Some are technically oriented, some are aggressive promoters of a concept, and others are good managers. In the next chapter, we will explore some of their characteristics in more depth. However, it is also important to focus on the ways in which a manager is entrepreneurial. Managers differ significantly in terms of their own entrepreneurial profiles, and the entrepreneurial grid can also serve as a useful means for diagnosing these profiles.

In essence, the concepts of degree and frequency discussed above apply as well at the individual level as they do at the organizational level. Thus, someone such as Ted Turner not only does things that are fairly innovative, risky, and proactive (e.g., the initial launch of Cable News Network), but he also demonstrates a high frequency of entrepreneurship. In a relatively short period of time, Mr. Turner rolled out Headline News, CNN International, CNN Airport, CNN en Espanol, CNNfn.com, TNT, TBS Superstation, Turner Classic Movies, Cartoon Network, and more.

Entrepreneurs can fall into different areas on the entrepreneurial grid. Figure 3.8 provides some hypothetical examples. If we consider someone like

Richard DeVos, founder of Amway Products, his profile probably falls into the Continuous/Incremental segment, since his orientation has been a steady stream of complementary lines and product improvements. Bill Gates of Microsoft might be characterized as a Dynamic entrepreneur, since he has championed a substantial number of significant software innovations. Howard Head, who personally drove the development of the metal ski in the 1950s and the oversize Prince tennis racket in the 1970s, most likely falls into the Periodic/Discontinuous area of the grid. Finally, someone like Herb Kelleher, of Southwest Airlines fame, has built his very service-oriented company around a clearly defined strategy and a people-oriented management style. He probably would fall more in the Periodic/Incremental section of the grid.

Another way in which the grid might be applied to individuals would involve characterizing how the entrepreneur approaches external change. Many individuals achieve success by quickly adapting to environmental change. Others base their efforts on actually creating major change in the environment. Ray Kroc was a great adapter, while Steven Jobs is more of a change agent. If we drew a vertical line at the mid-point of the horizontal, or "degree," axis, the former group would fall on the left-hand side of the grid, while the latter group would fall on the right-hand side.

Environmental circumstances are apt to influence the personal strategy an individual pursues in terms of where he or she falls on the grid. Not only might the industry and market conditions influence an individual's personal strategy, but so too might such factors as the perceived cost of failure at different times, developments in his or her personal life, his or her past record of entrepreneurial success or failure, and the extent to which he or she is working alone or as part of a sanctioned company team. In addition, positioning in the grid is probably influenced by other psychological traits, such as the person's need for achievement, locus of control, risk-taking profile, and tolerance of ambiguity.

THINGS WE KNOW AND DON'T KNOW ABOUT ENTREPRENEURIAL INTENSITY

Our understanding of entrepreneurial intensity in organizations is in its infancy. Of the studies that have been done to date, perhaps the most significant finding concerns a very basic question: does it matter? Do companies with stronger entrepreneurial orientations perform better? The answer is an unequivocal "yes." Researchers have demonstrated statistically significant relationships between EI and a number of indicators of company performance. Examples of such indicators include profits, the income-to-sales ratio, the rate of growth in revenue, the rate of growth in assets, the rate of growth in employment, and a composite measure of twelve financial and nonfinancial criteria (e.g., Covin and Slevin 1989, 1990; Davis, Morris, and Allen 1991; Miller and Friesen 1983; Morris and Sexton 1996; Peters and Waterman 1982; Zahra 1986). This linkage between EI and performance appears to be especially strong for companies that operate in increasingly turbulent environments. Rapid rates of change and threatening developments in the external environment force firms to find ways to be more entrepreneurial.

This does not mean that more entrepreneurship is always better. The likelihood is that there are norms for entrepreneurial intensity in every industry. Such norms suggest there is no best place to be in the entrepreneurial grid—the ideal point is industry and market specific. Further, as noted below, it is also time specific. The better-performing firms are those that demonstrate a stronger entrepreneurial orientation than their counterparts in the same industry. But norms for industries vary widely. One might expect a grocery retail chain to be higher on frequency, lower on degree, with a heavier emphasis on process innovation than on product innovation. Alternatively, leading pharmaceutical companies will likely approach the dynamic sector of the grid, with high frequency of new products and a portfolio of innovations that includes both incremental advances and breakthrough products.

Within companies, entrepreneurial orientations can be expected to differ significantly among various divisions, units, departments, and areas. In addition, there is no pattern such that marketing departments in companies are relatively more entrepreneurial or procurement departments are always less entrepreneurial. Not only will entrepreneurial orientation differ by company, but an entrepreneurial manager can guide a staid, conservative unit of any kind towards a more entrepreneurial profile. At the same time, the more a given unit or department must operate under conditions of turbulence, financial uncertainty, and other threats, the more one would expect a higher entrepreneurial profile in that unit or department.

There is also much we do not know. For example, to what extent does the relative importance of degree versus frequency vary depending on such strategic factors as the pace of technological change in an industry, the levels of competitive intensity, or the heterogeneity of market demand? Under what conditions is degree versus frequency the strongest contributor to company performance? It is also necessary to determine if frequency and degree contribute equally to short-term as opposed to long-term performance. It may be that frequency has more of a short-term impact, whereas degree is better able to impact long-term outcomes. Although hypothetical, such a possibility is implicit in the work of Hamel and Prahalad (1991). Using a baseball analogy of hitting many singles versus attempting to hit a home run, they emphasize the value of companies pursuing multiple smaller projects at one time as opposed to pursuing one potentially breakthrough project. A risk-reward trade-off is involved in which the former are thought to generate short- and immediate-term profits, whereas the latter significantly impacts long-term profitability.

Another critical question concerns the types and amounts of costs associated with EI. Resource requirements are likely to vary considerably at different levels of EI within a given industry, and the shape of the cost curve should be estimated. A related question concerns the failures that result from EI. Product and service failure rates are likely to be positively associated with both the frequency and

INTRAPRENEURIAL INSIGHT

INnovation: Out with the Old and IN with the New

"The problem is never how to get new, innovative thoughts into your mind, but how to get old ones out."

— DEE HOCK, BUSINESS VISIONARY AND CREATOR OF VISA

In his eclectic book, *The Circle of Innovation,* Tom Peters presents to the reader fifteen stopping points, or ideas, along a circle that he believes lead to innovation — a topic he professes to be obsessed with. One of those ideas is that "You can't live without an eraser." Peters feverishly puts forward the idea that forgetting what's *been* done and focusing on what *can or needs* to be done is the key to success. Take the following examples. Bill Gates initially viewed the Internet as a passing fad. Soon after, without looking back at his previous mindset, he set out to make Microsoft a building block for it. For years, retailer Banana Republic attempted to ape Gap. Finally the company realized its attempts were futile and started anew with a high-end image and gained an immediate 18 percent rise in same-store sales. GM forgot the traditional way of selling and servicing cars and created Saturn.

■ *Forget hesitation.* Wayne Gretzky said it best: "You miss 100 percent of the shots you don't take."

■ *Forget failure.* Failure doesn't just come before success in the dictionary.

■ *Forget rules.* They were meant to be broken.

■ *Forget balance.* Make yourself and others uncomfortable — stir things up.

■ *Forget propriety.* Some of the greatest inventions were once deemed ridiculous.

■ *Forget consensus.* While you're waiting for it, someone else is stealing your idea.

IF YOU ALWAYS DO WHAT YOU'VE ALWAYS DONE, YOU'LL ALWAYS GET WHAT YOU'VE ALWAYS GOTTEN.

Silicon Valley is a hotbed of forgetters and innovators. Success secrets include a tolerance of failure and treachery, the pursuit of risk, enthusiasm for change, openness to collaboration, variety, and an "anybody can play" attitude. Peters includes the Silicon Valley Test in his book as a way for an organization to gauge its likelihood of success Silicon Valley style. Address the following statements with *Yes!, Sometimes,* or *Never!* to determine your organization's need for a Strategic Forgetting Plan.

■ Failure is tolerated around here, even considered a good thing.

■ Ideas flow readily, without hoarding by this person (department) or that.

■ We're willing to swing for the fences and accept a relatively low batting average.

■ We spend (time and money) heavily on investing in unit and individual renewal.

■ We thrive on change.

■ We are diversity freaks, and politics is rarely the basis for rewards or promotion.

■ We groove on our service/product and are determined that it should be as cool as they come.

■ We don't try to reinvent the wheel; we take a new idea and test it . . . fast.

■ We're always working with others/outsiders on new projects, big and small.

■ We think anyone can be a big winner.

SOURCE: Adapted from Peters, T. 1997. *The Circle of Innovation.* New York: Alfred A. Knopf, 75–121.

degree components of EI, and research is needed to determine which is greater and why.

Entrepreneurial intensity also is likely to play a role in determining relationships among the nature of the external environment facing a company, the strategy of the company, and the internal structure of the company. It would seem that EI serves a potentially critical role in integrating these three variables. As a case in point, firms experiencing higher levels of environmental turbulence may require higher levels of EI to survive and grow, which in turn generates corporate strategies that are more aggressive (e.g., focusing on new product and market development) as well as structures that are more flexible, decentralized, and open.

Finally, it is not clear that high levels of entrepreneurial intensity are sustainable. It may be that there are patterns to a company's entrepreneurial performance over time. One theory is that companies alternate, or "cycle," between fairly dynamic periods of higher entrepreneurial intensity and periods where innovations are more incremental and intensity is lower (e.g., Slevin and Covin 1990). During these less intense periods, the focus is more on consolidation and administrative control. Yet, there are companies, such as 3M, that sustain a given level of entrepreneurship for extended periods.

SUMMARY AND CONCLUSIONS

With today's competitive conditions, many senior executives recognize the need for more entrepreneurship in their companies. However, they often struggle when attempting to define what it really means to be entrepreneurial and how entrepreneurship should manifest itself within their individual businesses. In this chapter, we have provided a beginning point. Management must first determine where the firm falls in the entrepreneurial grid; the relative importance of frequency and degree; and the specific types of innovation, risk-taking, and proactive behaviors that are consistent with the firm's strategic direction.

We have also introduced the concept of entrepreneurial intensity. There is nothing special about this particular term, but there is much support for it as a managerial concept. Researchers and consultants have used such terms as entrepreneurial posture, organic emphasis, entrepreneurship level, and entrepreneurial aggressiveness to talk about what, in essence, is the same thing (Cheah 1990; Covin and Slevin 1991; Jennings and Seaman 1990; Keats and Bracker 1988; Schaefer 1990; Stuart and Abetti 1987). The key for managers is to specify the "dominant logic" of the firm and the extent to which entrepreneurial intensity is part of that dominant logic. In subsequent chapters, we will further examine the interplay between dominant logic, entrepreneurial intensity, and corporate strategy.

Entrepreneurial intensity must become a key activity ratio that is monitored on an ongoing basis within organizations. Assessment at the level of the organization can be used to benchmark and track levels of entrepreneurship, establish norms and draw industry comparisons, establish entrepreneurship goals, develop strategies, and assess relationships between EI and company performance variables over time. At the individual manager level, assessments can be useful in helping managers and others to examine and refine their own leadership styles as well as in characterizing employee behavior over time.

REFERENCES

Bateman, T. S., and J. M. Grant. 1993. "The Proactive Component of Organizational Behavior: A Measure and Correlates," *Journal of Organizational Behavior* 14 (March): 103–118.

Buss, D. M. 1987. "Selection, Evocation and Manipulation," *Journal of Personality and Social Psychology* 53, No. 4: 1214–1221.

Cheah, H. B. 1990. "Schumpeterian and Austrian Entrepreneurship: Unity within Duality," *Journal of Business Venturing* 5 (December): 341–347.

Covin, J. G., and D. P. Slevin. 1989. "Strategic Management of Small Firms in Hostile Behavior," *Entrepreneurship Theory and Practice* 16 (Fall): 7–25.

Davis, D., M. Morris, and J. Allen. 1991. "Perceived Environmental Turbulence and Its Effect on Selected Entrepreneurship, Marketing and Organizational Characteristics in Industrial Firms," *Journal of the Academy of Marketing Science* 19 (Spring): 43–51.

Dickson, P. R., and J. J. Giglierano. 1986. "Missing the Boat and Sinking the Boat: A Conceptual Model of Entrepreneurial Risk." *Journal of Marketing* 50: 43–51.

Hamel, G., and C. E. Prahalad. 1991. "Corporate Imagination and Expeditionary Marketing," *Harvard Business Review* 69, No. 4 (July–August): 31–93.

Jennings, D. F., and S. L. Seaman. 1990. "Aggressiveness of Response to New Business Opportunities Following Deregulation: An Empirical Study of Established Financial Firms," *Journal of Business Venturing* 5 (October): 177–189.

Keats, B. W., and J. S. Bracker. 1988. "Toward a Theory of Small Business Performance: A Conceptual Model," *American Journal of Small Business* 13 (Spring): 14–58.

Miller, D., and P. H. Friesen. 1983. "Innovation in Conservative and Entrepreneurial Firms: Two Models of Strategic Momentum," *Strategic Management Journal* 3, No. 1: 1–25.

Miller, D. 1987. "Strategy Making and Structure: Analysis and Implications for Performance," *Academy of Management Journal* 30, No. 1: 7–32.

Morris, M. H., and D. L. Sexton. 1996. "The Concept of Entrepreneurial Intensity," *Journal of Business Research* 36, No. 1: 5–14.

Morris, M. H., D. L. Sexton, and P. Lewis. 1994. "Reconceptualizing Entrepreneurship: An Input-Output Perspective," *SAM Advanced Management Journal* 59, No. 1 (Winter): 21–31.

Peters, T., and R. Waterman. 1982. *In Search of Excellence*. New York: Harper & Row.

Schaefer, D. S. 1990. "Level of Entrepreneurship and Scanning Source Usage in Very Small Businesses," *Entrepreneurship Theory and Practice* 15, No. 1: 19–31.

Slevin, D. P., and J. G. Covin. 1990. "Juggling Entrepreneurial Style and Organization Structure—How to Get Your Act Together," *Sloan Management Review* 31 (Winter): 43–53.

Stuart, R., and P. A. Abetti. 1989. "Start-up Ventures: Towards the Prediction of Initial Success," *Journal of Business Venturing* 2, No. 3: 215–230.

Venkatraman, N. 1989. "Strategic Orientation of Business Enterprises: The Construct, Dimensionality, and Measurement," *Management Science* 35 (August): 942–962.

Zahra, S. A. 1986. "A Canonical Analysis of Corporate Entrepreneurship Antecedents and Impact on Performance," In *Best Paper Proceedings*. Pearce and Robinson, eds. 46th Annual Meeting, Academy of Management, 71–75.

4

Differences Between Start-Up and Corporate Entrepreneurship

Entrepreneurship has long been associated with bold individuals who persevere against the odds in creating a new venture. The entrepreneur is often thought of as a type of hero, with celebrity status given to such luminaries as Mary Kay Ash (Mary Kay Cosmetics), Jeff Bezos (Amazon.com), Richard Branson (Virgin), Anita Roddick (The Body Shop), and Michael Dell (Dell Computer). Obviously, in the vast majority of instances, entrepreneurship is not so glamorous. Most start-up efforts are fairly opportunistic and highly individualistic endeavors that become all-consuming in terms of the demands on the entrepreneur. They also tend to produce a fair number of failures. When successful, they result in the creation of a new company. The majority of these new companies remain relatively small throughout their existence.

All of these characteristics raise problems when we start speaking of entrepreneurship within a larger, established company. For instance, do companies really want bold, aggressive, risk-taking individuals all over the place? Is opportunistic behavior consistent with the planned, controlled, strategic direction of a firm? Are corporate entrepreneurs really "starting up" anything when the company exists and has an established market presence? Are stockholders willing to let management "bet the farm" on some entrepreneurial initiative? Two consequences of questions such as these are a) considerable confusion about the nature of corporate entrepreneurship, and b) a certain skepticism about whether entrepreneurship is even possible within larger companies.

Given such confusion and skepticism, it is important to understand both the similarities and the differences between start-up entrepreneurship and entrepreneurship in an established organization. In this chapter, we will compare and contrast the two types of entrepreneurship, examine the implications of the major differences, and explore the principal forms entrepreneurship takes when applied in an established enterprise.

ENTREPRENEURSHIP IS ENTREPRENEURSHIP: UNDERSTANDING THE SIMILARITIES

Consider two commonly accepted definitions of entrepreneurship: "the pursuit of opportunity without regard to resources currently controlled" and "the process of creating value by putting together a unique combination of resources to exploit an opportunity" (Stevenson et al. 1999). Both perspectives get to the essence of what entrepreneurship is about, and neither says anything about starting a small business. In fact, the context within which entrepreneurship occurs is not part of the definitions. Rather, the focus is capitalizing on opportunity by coming up with a unique concept that creates value for a customer. This phenomenon can occur in start-up ventures, small firms, midsized companies, large conglomerates, nonprofit organizations, and even public sector agencies (see Chapter 15).

Another fundamental precept in entrepreneurship is that a process is involved. The fact that entrepreneurship entails a process suggests that it has steps or stages, is manageable, and is ongoing. Moreover, it is a process that can be applied in any organizational context. The stages of this process presented in Chapter 2 are the same ones involved with corporate entrepreneurship. Opportunities must be identified, resources mustered, concepts implemented, and ventures or initiatives harvested. Similarly, the major objectives to be accomplished in each stage remain the same.

We have also approached entrepreneurship as a variable consisting of the underlying dimensions of innovativeness, risk-taking, and proactiveness. These dimensions characterize entrepreneurial efforts no matter where these efforts occur. There are start-up ventures that are only nominally innovative or risky and ones that are highly entrepreneurial. Now consider the corporate context. When Frito Lay introduced Baked Lays Potato Chips, the initiative was relatively low on innovativeness, risk-taking, and proactiveness, while Ford Motor Company's original introduction of the Taurus automobile or General Motors launch of the Saturn Company were both high in terms of the three entrepreneurial dimensions. Further, degree and frequency of entrepreneurship combine to form entrepreneurial intensity, and we saw in Chapter 3 how this concept is applicable both to larger companies and to corporate managers.

The message is that the basics are the same: entrepreneurship is entrepreneurship. Table 4.1 summarizes many of the basic similarities between start-up and corporate entrepreneurship. Understanding these similarities is important for at least three reasons. First, this understanding helps dispense with the notion that corporate entrepreneurship is just a popular management fad and that interest in

■ **TABLE 4.1**

SIMILARITIES BETWEEN START-UP
AND CORPORATE ENTREPRENEURSHIP

- Both involve opportunity recognition and definition.
- Both require a uniqe business concept that takes the form of a product, service, or process.
- Both are driven by an individual champion who works with a team to bring the concept to fruition.
- Both require that the entrepreneur be able to balance vision with managerial skill, passion with pragmatism, and proactiveness with patience.
- Both involve concepts that are most vulnerable in the formative stage, and that require adaptation over time.
- Both entail a window of opportunity within which the concept can be successfully capitalized upon.
- Both are predicated on value creation and accountability to a customer.
- Both find the entrepreneur encountering resistance and obstacles, necessitating both perseverance and an ability to formulate innovative solutions.
- Both entail risk and require risk-management strategies.
- Both require the entrepreneur to develop creative strategies for leveraging resources.
- Both involve significant ambiguity.
- Both require harvesting strategies.

it will fade once the consultants and popular business writers move on to the next new tool, concept, or perspective. By recognizing that entrepreneurship is a universal concept, we begin to understand that it lies at the heart of the corporation. Sustainable competitive advantage is impossible without it. Entrepreneurship is not a quick fix or an operational experiment in companies. In fact, the company that is not interested in developing and tapping into the entrepreneurial potential of its employees has effectively signed its own death warrant — the question is only one of whether it will be a quick demise or a slow, lingering decline.

Second, it is vital that both the senior executives who commit the company to an entrepreneurial path and the champions within organizations who are expected to carry out the entrepreneurial mission understand the phenomenon with which they are dealing. Entrepreneurship is real; it entails risks; failure is likely; and the psychological, emotional, and financial costs can be significant. Employees in companies should think of themselves as entrepreneurs. They should not think of themselves as *somewhat like* entrepreneurs. The corollary, of course, is that senior executives must let them be entrepreneurs — with all that this encompasses.

Third, virtually all of the research on entrepreneurship has emphasized the start-up context. The commonalities between start-up and corporate entrepreneurship suggest that company executives can learn much from examining what we know about the start-up context, rather than discarding those insights as irrelevant.

It is for the reasons cited above that words such as *intrapreneurship,* coined by Gifford Pinchot to describe entrepreneurship in established companies, can be misleading. They make corporate entrepreneurship sound like either something completely unique or as if it were the stepchild of entrepreneurship, borrowing some of the name but not really constituting the real thing. Therefore, instead of using the term *intrapreneurship,* throughout this book we use the term *corporate entrepreneurship* to indicate that the fundamentals do not change, only the context.

THE CORPORATE CONTEXT: IDENTIFYING THE KEY DIFFERENCES

At the same time, there are important differences to keep in mind for those pursuing entrepreneurial initiatives in established companies (Table 4.2). Entrepreneurship is often conceptualized in terms of risks and rewards, and both have distinct nuances in a corporate setting. While the types of risk (e.g., financial, market, supplier, competitive, etc.) are similar, at issue is the party who actually takes the risks. In a start-up context, all of the risk falls on the entrepreneur. Although successful entrepreneurs are typically adroit at sharing or spreading risk, they are ultimately accountable for the risks being incurred. They have a considerable amount on the line financially, professionally, and personally. The other side of the equation finds the start-up entrepreneur in a position to earn unlimited rewards. Most of them do not become millionaires, but the possibility exists. The reward picture is affected by another key aspect of the start-up context. The entrepreneur owns all or a considerable portion of the company. He or she can realize returns not simply though a salary, but through dividend payments, through licensing fees paid to himself/herself, through a range of perquisites, and through capital gains from selling shares of stock as the value of the company increases.

With corporate entrepreneurs, most of the risks are being assumed by the company. In fact, the major risk taken by the entrepreneur is career related. By pursuing new concepts rather than simply concentrating on normal job responsibilities, especially where concepts are highly innovative or encounter severe resistance within the company, the entrepreneur may jeopardize future pay increases, career advancement, and even his/her job. Correspondingly, the entrepreneur generally finds real limitations to the possible rewards he or she can realize if the concept is successfully implemented, and most of the returns go to the company. Further, as the entrepreneur generally owns little to none of the company, returns are limited to salary and perhaps a bonus, with some companies going so far as to offer a small share of the profits or cost savings that result from the entrepreneur's efforts. All too often, there are concerns that the entrepreneur should not earn amounts that exceed the salaries of his/her superiors.

Start-up entrepreneurs own more than the company. They own their ideas, concepts, and intellectual contributions. A product that is invented or a new customer

■ **TABLE 4.2**

CORPORATE AND START-UP ENTREPRENEURSHIP:
MAJOR DIFFERENCES

Start-Up Entrepreneurship	Corporate Entrepreneurship
Entrepreneur takes the risk	Company assumes the risks, other than career-related risk
Entrepreneur "owns" the concept and business	Company owns the concept, and typically the intellectual rights surrounding the concept
Entrepreneur owns all or much of the business	Entrepreneur may have no equity in the company, or a very small percentage
Potential rewards for the entrepreneur are theoretically unlimited	Clear limits are placed on the rewards entrepreneurs can receive
One misstep can mean failure	More room for errors, company can absorb failure
Vulnerable to outside influence	More insulated from outside influence
Independence of the entrepreneur (although the successful entrepreneur is usually backed by a strong team)	Interdependence of champion with many others; may also have to share credit with several people
Flexibility in changing course, experimenting, or trying new directions	Rules, procedures, and bureaucracy hinder the entrepreneur's ability to maneuver
High speed of decision making	Longer approval cycles
Little security	Job security
No safety net	Dependable benefit package
Few people with whom to talk	Extensive network for bouncing around ideas
Limited scale and scope, at least initially	Potential for sizeable scale and scope fairly quickly
Severe resource limitations	Access to finances, R&D, production facilities for trial runs, an established sales force, an existing brand, existing distribution channels, existing databases and market research resources, and an established customer base

service approach that is implemented belongs to the entrepreneur. He or she personally identifies with the concept and enjoys a sense of pride when it succeeds. In a corporation, ideas and concepts belong to the organization. There can still be a sense of pride, but the employee must be prepared for the ways in which the company will modify the concept, the extent to which it will support the concept, and the people who will take credit for the success of the concept. In this sense, the employee not only does not have legal ownership, but his/her sense of psychological ownership is also undermined.

Until the venture is well established, which can take many years, the start-up entrepreneur enjoys little security. He or she may take a deficient salary at the outset, and earnings may be tied to company performance. Failure of the company means loss of his/her job and livelihood. The company may not be able to afford extensive benefits packages. Conversely, the corporate entrepreneur generally knows he or she has a job tomorrow; receives a dependable and often attractive salary; and is provided with excellent health and disability insurance, a pension fund, and associated benefits. In a sense, the corporate entrepreneur has much more of a safety net should things go wrong. As we shall see in subsequent chapters, the desire for security is a factor that distinguishes the corporate entrepreneur and an incentive for him or her not to leave the company and strike out on his or her own.

Related to the distribution of risks and rewards is the vulnerability of the start-up entrepreneur. The venture can be dramatically affected by external developments such as a supplier that fails to deliver, a regulatory change, or an economic downturn. Further, regardless of how successful the start-up entrepreneur is from the start or the levels of sales achieved, one major misstep (e.g., running out of cash, the addition of a new product that does not fit, hiring the wrong employee, expanding too quickly) can quickly put the entrepreneur out of business. The corporate entrepreneur is certainly affected by external developments but is also more insulated from their impacts. For instance, the corporation's bargaining power with suppliers is typically greater, as is the ability to find and switch to a new supplier. The financial stability of the company, the well-developed infrastructure (operations, sales, R&D, logistics, etc.), and the established lines of products and services all combine to make the corporate entrepreneur less vulnerable. He or she has more time and resources to endure negative developments.

While external forces can be especially problematic for the start-up entrepreneur, the corporate entrepreneur deals with a number of unique internal challenges. In an established corporation, the entrepreneur does not enjoy the relative independence enjoyed by the start-up entrepreneur. Rather, the corporate entrepreneur's success is directly tied to his/her ability to win approval from various managers (or to get managers to "look the other way"), obtain resources and cooperation from key departments or units, and build coalitions or alliances. The entrepreneur's project can be terminated at any time, sometimes for arbitrary reasons. Alternatively, other corporate priorities can lead to the sidelining of what appear to be very promising projects. Not only does the entrepreneur have less personal control over the destiny of his/her concept, but he or she is also far more interdependent with others than independent. This characteristic also affects outcomes, since even if the concept or idea is successful, the corporate entrepreneur may or may not receive the credit, but almost certainly a number of other people will share the credit.

The internal corporate environment has two other distinguishing aspects. The size and scope of the established company are such that the firm cannot operate without sophisticated administrative and control systems. These systems typically imply a level of bureaucracy and red tape. Approval cycles can be relatively slow, while the entrepreneur must move the idea or concept through numerous approval levels. Alternatively, the start-up entrepreneur has much more flexibility, can change course relatively easily, and is able to move with greater speed.

Finally, and perhaps most significantly, comes the question of resources. The start-up entrepreneur operates under severe resource constraints, and these constraints often result in significant modifications of the core concept and the directions the business takes. The rate at which the venture is able to grow is often hindered by these constraints, while failure to grow can mean missed opportunities and greater vulnerability to competitor entreaties. The corporate entrepreneur is in a very different situation. While he or she usually does not control the needed resources, the resources are available in ample supply within the organization. Consider just a few of the preexisting resources available in many established companies. In addition to money, the company might be expected to have a known brand name, an established customer base, market research capabilities, market intelligence databases, distribution channels in place, relationships with suppliers, technical or research and development staff, production facilities, and more. The skilled entrepreneur finds creative ways to tap into these resources.

Let's assume that the corporate entrepreneur is successful. Because of the resources of the company, a new product or service can achieve global distribution fairly quickly. A new process can be implemented throughout the organization and affect the way thousands of employees do their jobs. It could take the start-up entrepreneur many years to get a venture to the same point in terms of its impact. Stated differently, the corporate entrepreneur can operate on a bigger scale and scope much more quickly.

A resource that corporate entrepreneurs often take for granted, but one that makes a considerable difference is "people to talk with." In the early stages, the start-up entrepreneur is often extremely worried about someone stealing the idea, moving faster, and taking the opportunity for himself or herself. Start-up entrepreneurs can develop a certain paranoia, where they are hesitant to say too much to anyone about their concept. The corporate entrepreneur is in a very different situation. There are experienced, knowledgeable people throughout the company with whom he or she can explore the idea, test it, and make modifications and refinements. This internal network of expertise can also be a source of insights regarding how to effectively position the concept within the company.

THE POLITICAL FACTOR

Of special note when considering factors that distinguish corporate entrepreneurship is organizational politics. Organizations are nothing more than the people within them, and these people differ in terms of their needs, objectives, values, and capabilities. As a result, organizations are filled with politics, and political factors will be instrumental in the success or failure of any entrepreneurial initiative within an established company.

The need for political skills is tied to three major challenges faced by the corporate entrepreneur: achieving credibility or legitimacy for the concept and the entrepreneurial team, obtaining resources, and overcoming inertia and resistance (Block and MacMillan 1993). The entrepreneur is usually limited in terms of formal power within the organization. Further, the more innovative or different the concept, the more skeptical people are likely to be of its viability or value. The entrepreneur must achieve credibility by giving others within the organization a "reason to believe." Some of the ways legitimacy might be established include building and using an influence network, securing endorsements from senior executives or other significant players, making small advances and sharing the credit with others, sharing valuable information with those who hold positions of key influence, and demonstrating competence by helping others with their problems while also asking for help.

When it comes to obtaining resources, corporate entrepreneurs are good "bootstrappers." They identify underutilized resources within the firm and use some of the tactics above to convince resource owners to share them. They are adroit at borrowing, begging, and scavenging for resources.

The greatest challenge lies in overcoming inertia (e.g., the new idea represents change, and people are usually comfortable with the status quo, see no need for change, or feel the new idea will create work for them) and overt resistance (e.g., the new idea threatens the positions of others or will take resources away from them). In reality, an unlimited number of political tactics are available to the corporate entrepreneur. These will be examined in more depth in Chapter 9. Examples of tactics the entrepreneur might employ include creative use of existing rules, creative ways to evade existing rules, use of alliances and coalitions, use of negotiation ploys, reliance on the exchange of personal favors, and efforts to educate or provide information to others, among many others.

IMPLICATIONS OF THE DIFFERENCES

Sustainable entrepreneurship is more likely where managers recognize the implications of these differences between the start-up and corporate contexts. Implications can be drawn for the motivation and attitudes, time horizons, accountability, risk orientation, skills, and operating styles of the corporate entrepreneur.

The corporate entrepreneur does not want to do all the things necessary to start a business of his/her own. He or she is not looking to get rich. Rather, the corporate entrepreneur's motivation has more to do with the desire to create something successful, to bring to fruition an idea that he or she really believes in, to put his or her own mark on something that will make a substantive contribution to the company. Corporate entrepreneurs enjoy the security of the company and, while frustrated with the bureaucracy, they identify with the organization. They have a healthy cynicism about many of the systems within the company, but also appreciate the need to be politically savvy. Just as important is the motivation of the entrepreneur's sponsor. One observer has argued that the sponsor "is motivated not by personal ambition but by a desire to serve the corporation and an admiration for the maverick's way of operating" (Pinchot 1985).

The corporate context finds the entrepreneur with a number of conflicting pressures that he or she must balance. One of the key conflicts concerns time. Corporate entrepreneurs are self-driven, with self-imposed timelines and performance benchmarks. Yet, the timeline for moving a project through to completion is almost always at odds with the normal monthly, quarterly, and annual performance review cycles of the corporation. The development cycle of an entrepreneurial project can be anywhere from two to ten or more years. The challenge becomes one of a) performing satisfactorily on the normal performance measures, while b) meeting self-imposed goals for project development and completion, and c) ensuring that self-imposed goals exceed anything that senior management would ever have expected.

In a related vein, measures of the entrepreneur's performance may not be as clearcut in a corporation. In a start-up context, there are numerous readily identifiable and visible performance measures. A business is established, jobs are created, sales levels and profits are achieved, and investors receive a rate of return. With the corporation, if the innovation is a product or service, again the entrepreneur has sales and profit measures to assess, but many factors beyond his or her control affect these financial performance measures. For instance, sales revenue may be influenced by the performance of other products in the company's line, by levels of sales effort, and by marketing support. Profits are affected by the costs that are allocated to the product or service. When the innovation is a process, then performance measures might relate to cost savings, shortened operating cycles, improved customer-service levels, or some other indicator. The key for the corporate entrepreneur is to identify performance measures that he or she can influence, build them into his or her plan, and track performance along the way.

Start-up entrepreneurs like to think of themselves as their own boss. Technically, they are. However, they frequently have other stockholders or partners to whom they are accountable, and may also be beholden to financiers, suppliers, and distributors. The corporate context finds the entrepreneur with a different set of masters. He or she reports to a boss but is also accountable to the sponsor and to any of the senior managers whose departments have lent support along the way. If he or she is part of a team in a matrix-type structure, the entrepreneur has to be concerned about the senior executives in all the areas represented on the team.

Because they stay in a company instead of going it alone, we might expect corporate entrepreneurs to be fairly risk averse. This is not the case. Since the company is effectively assuming much of the risk that surrounds the concept, the entrepreneur might actually tend to take greater risks. It is the company's money to lose, although the entrepreneur's job is at stake. However, few companies fire people because they try something entrepreneurial and fail. It is far more likely that people try something entrepreneurial, get frustrated because of the resistance and obstacles within the company, and leave on their own. The reality is that corporate entrepreneurs are moderate risk takers. They tend to first look at a situation carefully and identify all the associated risk factors (customer, competitor, financial, political, job-related, etc). They then develop strategies for managing or mitigating the risks. They also craft approaches for communicating the risks and risk-management strategy to key managers within the company. This is a critical element for success. The risks must be positioned in a way that fits the general risk profile of the company and is politically acceptable.

One of the most daunting tasks confronting senior executives, based on the differences discussed above, involves creating a sense of autonomy and ownership in an environment where the employee may actually have relatively little of each. This is a theme to which we will return in the chapters to come. No one action or program will accomplish this task. It requires a well-crafted mix of decision variables, including company structure, planning approaches, control systems, reward and appraisal systems, internal communication styles, employee training programs, and aspects of the company culture.

In the end, the challenge of getting employees to act on their entrepreneurial potential may not be as difficult as retaining employees who have been entrepreneurial. In our work with successful corporate entrepreneurs, we frequently ask them why they do not quit and start their own ventures. Their responses are directly related to the differences we have noted above. Following are the three most common answers:

1. The resource base that I can tap into;
2. The potential to operate on a fairly significant scope and scale fairly quickly;
3. The security I enjoy when operating in an existing company.

We also ask successful corporate entrepreneurs why they would leave. This question produces a variety of responses, but organizational politics always ranks high on the list.

Thus, it becomes critical that senior management create environments where employees have a sense that resources can be accessed if an idea is sound and they are willing to fight for it. Further, management must find ways to reinforce the ability of anyone in the firm to champion an idea and get it implemented throughout the corporation in a reasonable time span. In addition, they must invest in the development of people. There is little sense of security if companies are less than loyal to their employees and employees are less than loyal to their companies. Entrepreneurial firms like Southwest Airlines find that it makes sense to invest in employees first, that value creation for customers follows, and that this is followed by wealth creation for stockholders.

■ **TABLE 4.3**

CHARACTERIZING THE SEVEN MAJOR FORMS
OF CORPORATE ENTREPRENEURSHIP

Traditional R&D: "Leave it to the technical guys."

Ad hoc venture teams: "Here's the concept, the budget, and the deadline—go to it."

New venture groups: "We want a factory for breakthrough concepts."

Champions and the mainstream: "It's up to everyone, including you."

Acquisitions: "We can buy growth and obtain the products, markets, and technologies of others."

Outsourcing: "Let's have someone else develop it for us, and then we'll make the money."

Hybrid forms: "We can mix and match the other approaches to fit our context."

THE FORMS ENTREPRENEURSHIP TAKES IN COMPANIES

Up to this point, we have spoken about corporate entrepreneurship as a phenomenon that produces innovation in companies. But it is not a single phenomenon; it can take a variety of different forms. Each of these forms further distinguishes the corporate setting from the start-up venture.

For instance, entrepreneurship can come from above, below, or from separate units (Vesper 1984; Guth and Ginsberg 1990). That is, senior management could chart a bold new strategic direction for the firm such as the decision by Ball Corporation, a major maker of food and beverage containers, to move into aerospace technologies or the decision by Walt Disney Company to establish retail stores in malls. Alternatively, entrepreneurship can be the result of initiatives from below. An employee has an idea for a radically improved approach to getting products to distribution points on time, a way to make money selling add-on services to customers, or a product-line extension. Or the source of the entrepreneurship could be a separate department or unit that has been set up for the explicit purpose of innovation. The creation of the New Ventures Division at Procter and Gamble would be a case in point.

Going a step further and building on the early work of Schollhammer (1982), we believe there are seven major forms taken by corporate entrepreneurship (Table 4.3). The first of these can be termed "traditional R&D [research and development]." Many companies have a department staffed by people who are technically qualified, and they work on improving existing products and developing new ones. It is not always called Research and Development, but the focus is generally on technical advancements and overcoming technical obstacles. The work is research-based, and there are any number of projects underway at a given time. These projects are usually closely tied to the current strategic direction of the firm. Some of them may represent bold new concepts, while others are replications of achievements by other firms. In essence, it becomes the job of this department to produce the new products, making it easy for everyone else in the company to escape responsibility for innovation.

The second form is the "ad hoc venture team." The senior management group commits to an opportunity or finds itself needing to respond to an impending competitive threat. It puts together a team of employees, charges them with coming up with a specific innovation, and sets them up autonomously, out of the corporate mainstream. Team members often come from diverse parts of the company, and some may come from outside. The venture team usually has more freedom and flexibility and does not have to operate within many of the standard systems and procedures that govern the rest of the company. They may be given ample financial resources but a demanding timeline for project completion. A case in point is the venture team that developed IBM's original personal computer. Trying to quickly switch directions and make up lost ground, IBM located the team in Boca Raton, Florida, and gave them a very clear mission and a very tight deadline. Such teams tend to be good at accomplishing the specific mission, but not at producing sustained entrepreneurship.

A number of firms have taken the venture team concept a big step further and have created "new venture divisions." Here, a permanent unit is established with the objectives of breakthrough innovation and the creation of entirely new markets. In a sense, the division or group is a kind of incubator where bold new ventures can be formulated and brought to life. By separating this division from the rest of the company, the theory is that traditional assumptions relied on within the firm's normal operations will be abandoned, including assumptions about customers, products, distribution, costs, technology, and competitors. While the types of innovations produced will typically reflect the core capabilities of the company, the focus is on finding innovations that move the company in major new strategic directions. The new market opportunities must have huge market potential to be considered. One of the great challenges of these divisions lies in producing new products and services that, once they are launched, will be supported by mainstream operating units. That is, it can be quite difficult to get an operating division to adopt or take ownership of an initiative that they played no role in creating.

A principal focus of this book is entrepreneurship that derives from "champions and the mainstream." This form of entrepreneurship originates from any level or department in the organization. Employees recognize opportunity and develop innovative concepts and then attempt to sell them to senior management. They become "champions" and seek out higher level "sponsors." They beg and borrow resources, often relying on informal networks, exchanging favors, and doing considerable development work in secret, or at least prior to formal approval and support for the concept. In fact, many of these concepts are rejected multiple times by management, but the champion perseveres in keeping the idea alive and adapting it into a form management will accept.

Some companies prefer to achieve entrepreneurial growth through "acquisitions," or purchasing other companies. A classic example is Cintas Corporation, a highly innovative supplier of uniforms in the workplace. It has become the dominant player in the industry through an aggressive acquisitions strategy. The key here is strategic fit, making acquisitions that are related to the core competencies of the company or acquiring skills, technologies, and customers that complement the strategic direction of the company. The challenge for Cintas, an inherently entrepreneurial company, is to instill its values and culture in each new acquisition.

Rather than acquiring another firm, a growing number of companies are buying some of the intellectual capital of other companies and individuals. In effect, they are "outsourcing innovation." For some, this is a realistic path simply because of the significant infrastructure and personnel costs associated with having the necessary in-house capabilities. For others, it is more about timing and speed. The rapid pace of technological change, the many parallel and complementary technological advances that are happening in many fields, and the difficulty in making substantive progress on a whole array of projects at the same time find the firm relying on others. They either acquire the rights to an invention or effectively pay someone else to develop it while retaining ownership.

Lastly, any number of "hybrid forms" are possible. The reality is that organizations are experimenting today in attempts to spur entrepreneurial performance. Even within the six forms described above, there is considerable variance across firms. An example of a hybrid form would be the company that tries the new venture division approach, but instead of having one corporate-level new venture division, it attaches new venture divisions to each of the major units within the company. Alternatively, champions might be found within the mainstream who are empowered to outsource some of the new product development work as they move a project through to completion.

These various forms of corporate entrepreneurship are likely to produce different kinds of outcomes. While there is no clear empirical evidence, we can make some general propositions. For example, the traditional R&D approach will often have a strong technology-push orientation (see Chapter 7 for further discussion of this concept), suggesting projects are undertaken that result in technically superior products, but for which the market may not have sufficient need, at least at the present time. Many R&D departments are better at invention than at entrepreneuring, suggesting they too often produce inventions that are "commercially challenged." The degree of innovativeness is also likely to vary across these forms. Bolder breakthroughs would seem more likely from new venture groups and traditional R&D, while the mainstream might produce more incremental innovation, with ad hoc teams and outsourcing somewhere in between. Speed of innovation is an especially interesting issue. The performance record of many R&D departments and new venture groups suggests they are not

ENTREPRENEURIAL THINKING AT HEWLETT-PACKARD

Even back in the mid-1990s, before talented employees rushed to dot.coms to make millions on stock options and IPOs, employee performance and morale was directly tied to a feeling of ownership within a company. When managers eliminated standard procedures and allowed for employees to truly utilize their knowledge, skills, and abilities, enjoyment at work and true productivity were the end result. At Hewlett-Packard, this practice worked wonders when two managers gave up control of a thirty-five-member team and created a new companywide distribution process in less than nine months. As one team leader put it, "When people are free to define their own goals and roles at work, their commitment intensifies, and the job becomes more personally meaningful."

Mei-Lin Cheng and Julie Anderson were given the task of reengineering HP's twenty-six-day, multibillion-dollar distribution process into one that was shorter, technologically sound, and, ultimately, made customers happier. Only after they had shortened the cycle from twenty-six to eight days and gotten funding for the project's second year did Anderson start to realize how the team managed to be so effective. "We took things away: no hierarchy, no titles, no job descriptions, no plans, no step-by-step milestones of progress." As it has been said before, to level out the playing field, they checked their titles, and weapons, at the door. "Everyone felt the time pressure. They asked us (managers) how to organize the work, and we just said, 'Start.'" Fortunately, the team came to the conclusion that if they took the traditional route, with members working on separate facets of the project, they'd run into the same problem of system integration later.

Frustration ensued among the team members without any guidance or supporting words. Cheng and Anderson held out, however, stressing that if they provided an answer to a question, it might not be the right one—that no one person can see the whole system perfectly. They knew that multiple minds working on a solution without functional barriers would provide for the best outcome. This nontraditional project-management technique left Cheng and Anderson giving obtuse answers to the higher-ups, but there was still no interference when their progress finally came to a halt.

The team was arguing about whether they were ready to execute some orders on the new system when one member associated their situation with that of Bill Murray's in the movie *Groundhog Day*. The plot has Murray reliving the same day, trying to figure out how to get to the next day, by altering small actions each time the day began anew with "I Got You Babe" playing on his alarm clock. With this in mind and with the '60s tune as their theme song, the HP team set out to fix their problem one step at a time, learning as they went along. Anderson coined it as "practicing," stating that people in business too rarely get a chance to practice. When the team accepted that they didn't have to have it perfect the first time they tried, they made effective decisions, overcame struggles, and were able to define the priorities. "Our approach is to jump in, bite off what we can chew, and learn as we go. You've got to start without knowing where the journey is going to take you," said Cheng.

The entrepreneurial, out-of-the-box thinking at Hewlett-Packard didn't come as a result of ownership *of* the company. It came from ownership of an idea, a project, and of a job *at* the company. By taking away structured decision making, traditional roles and responsibilities, and allowing the team to utilize Legos, beans, and Mr. Potato Heads, Anderson built "the capacity to learn, first in individuals and ultimately in the organization." Team members believed that they were smart enough and could do what they were hired to do without anticipating orders, permission, and denials. Their stress lightened, and they enjoyed their jobs more. "That's because there's not a tradeoff between personal life and work life," said one member.

SOURCE: Sherman, S. 1996. "Secrets of HP's 'Muddled' Team," *Fortune* (March): 116–120.

all that timely in terms of getting projects completed and ready for launch. Alternatively, ad hoc venture teams, outsourcing, and champions in the mainstream are likely to produce much faster results. While this is just conjecture, it suggests that the senior management group needs a realistic set of goals and performance expectations as it decides to implement a given form. There is also no reason that all of the forms above could not be operating in a given company, with differing roles and performance standards established for each.

SUMMARY AND CONCLUSIONS

Entrepreneurship is not limited to starting a business. It is about putting resources together in a unique way to exploit an opportunity. As such, entrepreneurship is a universal concept that can be applied in any organizational context. In fact, the business world is filled with start-up firms that are not especially entrepreneurial and any number of large firms that are highly entrepreneurial.

In this chapter we have explored the commonalities and differences between the start-up context and the corporate context. Large companies can learn a great deal from the experiences of start-up entrepreneurs. Sadly, too many corporate executives see their situation as far more sophisticated and complex than that of the start-up, so they close their minds to potential lessons regarding the ways in which small companies acquire and leverage resources, conduct guerrilla approaches to marketing and finance, structure themselves, style decision making, approach budgeting, and so forth.

At the same time, corporate entrepreneurs must operate in an environment filled with nuances and obstacles to which a start-up entrepreneur could not relate. Risks, rewards, ownership, security, vulnerability, bureaucracy, politics, and resources are all very different in a corporate context. Moreover, entrepreneurship takes a variety of unique forms in the corporation, and each of these forms poses its own distinct set of problems and opportunities for both the entrepreneur and the senior management of the firm. In the final analysis, we can conclude that entrepreneurship in a company is like entrepreneurship in a start-up, only different.

REFERENCES

Block, Z., and I. C. MacMillan. 1993. *Corporate Venturing: Creating New Businesses within the Firm*. Boston: Harvard Business School Press.

Guth, W. D., and A. Ginsberg. 1990. "Corporate Entrepreneurship," *Strategic Management Journal* (Special Issue) 11: 5–15.

Pinchot, III, G. 1985. *Intrapreneuring*. New York: Harper and Row.

Pinchot, III, G., and R. Pellman. 1999. *Intrapreneuring in Action*. San Francisco: Berrett-Koehler.

Schollhammer, H. 1982. "Internal Corporate Entrepreneurship," In *Encyclopedia of Entrepreneurship*. Englewood Cliffs: Prentice Hall.

Stevenson, H. H., M. J. Roberts, D. E. Grousbeck, and A. Bhide. 1999. *New Business Ventures and the Entrepreneur*. Homewood: Richard D. Irwin.

Vesper, K. H. 1984. "Three Faces of Corporate Entrepreneurship: A Pilot Study," In *Frontiers of Entrepreneurship Research*. Wellesley: Babson College.

ENTREPRENEURIAL VISION AND DIRECTION

———————————■———————————

The greatest difficulty in the world is not for people to accept new ideas,
but to make them forget about old ideas.

—JOHN MAYNARD KEYNES, ECONOMIST

———————————■———————————

5

WHO IS THE CORPORATE ENTREPRENEUR?

Of all the elements necessary for successful corporate entrepreneurship, the individual "champion" or "intrapreneur" is the most critical. Without the visionary leadership and persistence demonstrated by this individual, little would be accomplished. Someone must come up with a concept, a vision, a dream. He or she must translate this dream into products and processes within some sort of organizational context. He or she must champion the concept to a wide range of publics and partners. He or she must adapt the concept to reflect the realities encountered within the environment. And he or she must persevere in overcoming the normal and the arbitrary obstacles that are thrown into his or her path.

In this chapter, we will examine what is known about entrepreneurial individuals. Their personality characteristics will be explored from both a positive and negative perspective. Types of entrepreneurs will be identified. A model will be presented that captures the set of variables that lead an individual to pursue an opportunity. While most of the research on individual characteristics and behaviors has been done on start-up or independent entrepreneurs, many parallels can be drawn for corporate entrepreneurship. The unique differences of individuals who do entrepreneurial things in larger companies will also be explored.

THE ENTREPRENEURIAL PERSONALITY

The single most researched question within the field of entrepreneurship is, "Who is the entrepreneur?" A variety of somewhat conflicting findings have been

■ **TABLE 5.1**

COMMON TRAITS AND CHARACTERISTICS ASSOCIATED
WITH THE ENTREPRENEURIAL INDIVIDUAL

Drive to achieve
Internal locus of control
Calculated risk-taking
Tolerance of ambiguity
Commitment/perseverance/determination
Independence
Self-confidence & optimism
Tolerance for failure
Persistent problem solving
Opportunity orientation
Integrity and reliability
High energy level
Resourcefulness
Creativity and innovativeness
Vision
Team building

SOURCE: Kuratko, D. F., and R. M. Hodgetts. 2001. *Entrepreneurship: A Contemporary Approach,* 5th ed. Fort Worth, TX: Harcourt College.

produced regarding the psychological and sociological makeup of entrepreneurs. Many of these studies suffer from significant methodological problems. Nonetheless, there do appear to be a few characteristics around which a consensus has emerged. On the psychological side, there is some agreement on at least six characteristics. (See Table 5.1 for a more comprehensive list of psychological traits associated with the entrepreneurial personality.) The available evidence identifies entrepreneurs as being more motivated by achievement than power, money, status, acceptance, or any other considerations. They are driven by the task, the challenge, the opportunity to accomplish what others said could not, would not, or should not be done. Money certainly counts, but it is a by-product. Financial rewards serve as a scorecard, telling the entrepreneur that he or she is making progress.

Entrepreneurial individuals also demonstrate a strong internal locus of control. Unlike those who believe that external events control their lives and dictate what happens around them, entrepreneurs are change agents. They fundamentally believe that, with enough time and effort and their own involvement, they can change their workplace, their markets, their industries—in short, their environments.

Entrepreneurial individuals are calculated risk takers. The entrepreneur tends to be about a 5.5 on a 10-point scale, where 1 = risk avoidant and 10 = bold gambler. Calculated risk taking can be defined as pursuit of a course of action that has a reasonable chance of costly failure, where failure is a significant negative difference between anticipated and actual results. It is calculated in the sense that (a) the individual has considered and attempted to estimate (at least conceptually) the likelihood and magnitude of the key risk factors; and (b) he or she has attempted to manage or mitigate the key risk factors through good planning and managerial decision-making.

The very nature of the entrepreneurial process demands that the entrepreneur demonstrate a high "tolerance of ambiguity." Things do not have to fit a precast mold or follow an exact pattern. In fact, they are often messy, imprecise, and there is tremendous uncertainty regarding whether he or she is on the right path and what unanticipated obstacles lie around the next bend. The entrepreneurial process will inherently move in new and unanticipated directions. Most successful entrepreneurs find that, if their concept is implemented and achieves success, it will look quite different than the concept they first started with. This is not because of poor conceptualizing or planning; it is the fundamental nature of the game.

Entrepreneurs are self-motivated, self-reliant, and prefer a degree of autonomy when accomplishing a task. The perception that they have room to maneuver in affecting their own destiny is highly valued. Finally, it is generally agreed that entrepreneurs are tenacious and demonstrate significant perseverance. Other common findings, about which there is less consensus, suggest that entrepreneurs are versatile, persuasive, creative, well-organized, extremely hard-working, and competitive (Morris 1998).

Perhaps the two most significant conclusions that can be drawn from attempts to understand the traits and characteristics of the entrepreneur are that entrepreneurs are not born and that no single prototype of the entrepreneur exists. Although filled with controversy, the research makes it clear that traits associated with entrepreneurial behavior are strongly influenced by the environment and are developed over time. The list of traits and characteristics in Table 5.1 does not contain items that are clearly genetic, such as intelligence, physical prowess, or artistic talent. The tendency to be self-confident, to have an internal locus of control, or to be achievement motivated is the result of family, educational, social, and work experiences. Further, there is entrepreneurial potential in everyone. Our second conclusion concerns the tendency to look for a single profile of the entrepreneur. In reality, entrepreneurs differ significantly in terms of their risk profiles, need for independence, locus of control, and other characteristics. It would seem, instead, that there are different types of entrepreneurs. We shall discuss some of the major types that have been identified later in the chapter.

Characteristics such as the ones discussed above have important implications for corporate entrepreneurship. While entrepreneurs will differ markedly on a given characteristic, recognizing the key characteristics helps managers and employees know where to focus in developing a given individual's entrepreneurial potential. Although it may not be possible to teach someone to be an entrepreneur, it is certainly possible to help them develop their achievement motivation, tolerance of ambiguity, or appreciation for calculated risk-taking. In addition, implications can be drawn for the design of the work environment. As managers make decisions about company structure, controls, rewards, policies, and other areas that define the work environment, these decisions must be made in a manner that is compatible with the types of characteristics associated with entrepreneurship. A work environment that does not allow a degree of autonomy, penalizes risk-taking, and discourages individual action is not one in which employees are likely to discover and act on their entrepreneurial potential.

THE DARK SIDE OF ENTREPRENEURSHIP

The rewards, successes, and achievements of entrepreneurs have been extolled by many observers. However, a "dark side" of entrepreneurship also exists. That is, a potentially destructive element resides within the energetic drive of successful entrepreneurs. In exploring this dual-edge perspective, Manfred Kets de Vries (1985) notes specific negative factors that can permeate the personality of entrepreneurs and dominate their behavior. Although each of these factors possesses a positive aspect, it is important for entrepreneurs to understand the potentially destructive aspects. While this "dark side" is descriptive of start-up entrepreneurs, it can also be manifested in corporate entrepreneurship.

Entrepreneurial activity entails risk. While they are rarely *directly* proportional, higher reward usually means higher risk. So concepts that are more innovative or involve bolder breaks with current practice typically represent higher risk and also higher reward. However, there are some risks that do not result in any reward. Also, beyond some level, risk may continue to rise while reward does not. This is why entrepreneurs tend to evaluate risk very carefully. The manner in which they confront risk is a potential dark side for entrepreneurs. Entrepreneurs face a number of different types of risk, and these can be grouped into four basic areas.

Financial Risk.   In most new ventures the individual or corporation puts a significant amount of financial resources at stake. This money or these resources will, in all likelihood, be lost if the venture fails. That is, financial risk is greater when the more non-retrievable assets are invested in an innovative concept. In a start-up context, this can mean financial ruin, while in a corporate context, a highly visible failure can affect stock value and bond ratings.

Career Risk.   A question frequently raised by would-be entrepreneurs is the effect of pursuing an entrepreneurial concept on their career, job advancement, vertical and lateral mobility, job rewards, and general marketability. This is a major concern to managers who have a secure organizational job with a high salary and a good benefit package.

Family and Social Risk.   Doing something entrepreneurial requires a tremendous amount of the individual's energy and time, especially when he or she has a regular job to perform. Consequently, his or her other commitments may suffer. Entrepreneurs who are married, and especially those with children, expose their families to the risks of an incomplete family experience and the possibility of permanent emotional scars. In addition, old friends may vanish slowly because of missed interaction.

Psychic Risk.   The greatest risk may be to the well-being of the entrepreneur. A lost job can be replaced; lost time can be attributed to learning or to laying the groundwork for a future entrepreneurial pursuit; financial losses can be recovered; spouse, children, and friends can usually adapt. But some entrepreneurs who have suffered catastrophes have been unable to bounce back, at least not immediately. The psychological impact has proven to be too severe for them.

Entrepreneurs can also fail to appreciate the fact that risks such as these are shared with other people, and/or that other people are affected by the downside when things do not work out. In addition, risk is related to stress. The hazardous potential of entrepreneurial stress has been the focus of a number of research studies (Akande 1992; Buttner 1992). In general, stress can be viewed as a function of discrepancies between a person's expectations and ability to meet demands, as well as discrepancies between the individual's expectations and personality. If a person is unable to fulfill role demands, then stress occurs.

Given the struggle for resources and support, entrepreneurs must bear the responsibility for their mistakes while playing a multitude of roles, such as salesperson, recruiter, spokesperson, and negotiator. These simultaneous demands can lead to role overload. Being entrepreneurial requires a large commitment of time and energy, often at the expense of family and social activities. Finally, entrepreneurs are often working alone or with a small number of employees, even when they are operating in a large company.

Some of the most common entrepreneurial goals are independence, wealth, and work satisfaction. Research studies indicate that those who achieve these goals often pay a high price. A majority of entrepreneurs surveyed had back problems, indigestion, insomnia, or headaches. To achieve their goals, however, these entrepreneurs were willing to tolerate stress and its side-effects. The perceived rewards justified the costs.

In addition to the challenges of risk and stress, the entrepreneur also may experience the negative effects of an inflated ego. In other words, some of the characteristics that usually propel entrepreneurs into success, such as the need for control, sense of distrust, desire for success, and ceaseless optimism, also reflect themselves in the following negative ways.

AN OVERBEARING NEED FOR CONTROL

Entrepreneurs are driven by a strong sense that they can change their environments. They desire to control both their venture and their destiny. Their internal locus of control can spill over into a preoccupation with controlling everything. An obsession for autonomy and control may cause entrepreneurs to work in structured situations only when they have created the structure on their terms. This has serious implications for networking in an entrepreneurial team, since entrepreneurs can visualize the external control by others as a threat of subjection or infringement on their will. It also has potentially detrimental implications for working in a corporate context, where collaboration is critical and control is exerted by other people, procedures, and systems over which the entrepreneur has little influence.

A Sense of Distrust

To remain alert to competition, customers, and government regulations, entrepreneurs are continually scanning the environment. Not only are they on the watch for developments that could undermine their ventures, but also they try to anticipate and act on developments before others have had the chance. They tend to distrust the motives of others, thinking others are trying to either kill the entrepreneur's idea or steal it. This distrustful state can result in their focusing on trivial things, causing them to lose sight of reality, to distort reasoning and logic, and to take destructive actions.

An Overriding Desire for Success

The overwhelming desire to succeed is often tied to a person's ego. The individual is driven to succeed and takes pride in demonstrating his or her success. Although entrepreneurs frequently find (or perceive) that the odds are stacked against them and that problems without clear solutions never seem to stop coming, they also have faith that they will ultimately prevail. Thus, they can develop a certain sense of defiance, while denying any feelings of insignificance. Their belief in themselves evolves into a conviction that they are indispensable, that without them the project either will fail or it will be much less than it could be. The person and his or her ego become more important than the needs of the project. The likelihood of this happening is even greater in a corporate context, where the entrepreneur is required to play politics, share credit, swallow pride, and invest precious time in activities that have little to do with moving a project forward. The loss of perspective can alienate others and ensure the demise of a project.

Unrealistic Optimism

The ceaseless optimism that emanates from entrepreneurs (even in the bleakest times of a project or venture) is a key factor in the drive toward success. Entrepreneurs maintain a high enthusiasm level that gives others a sense of faith and conviction when a concept seems unworkable or the obstacles seem overwhelming. However, when taken to an extreme, this optimistic attitude can lead to a fantasy approach that undermines the credibility of the venture and the entrepreneur. A self-deceptive state may arise in which entrepreneurs ignore trends, facts, and reports and delude themselves into thinking everything will turn out fine. This type of behavior can lead to an inability to handle the reality of project setbacks and needs.

These examples do not imply that all entrepreneurs fall prey to the negative side or that each of the characteristics presented always gives way to dysfunctional behaviors. Yet, companies that wish to encourage entrepreneurial behavior on the part of their employees should recognize both the upside and downside. The corporate environment represents a counter-balance to some of these negative behaviors, such as unrealistic optimism—but the environment must also be somewhat tolerant of the idiosyncrasies of the entrepreneurial personality.

MOTIVATING ENTREPRENEURIAL BEHAVIOR

Although research on the psychological characteristics of entrepreneurs has not provided an agreed-on "profile," it is still important to recognize the contribution of psychological factors to the entrepreneurial process. In fact, the willingness to pursue entrepreneurial concepts and the willingness to devote himself or herself to a concept over time are directly related to an entrepreneur's personal make-up. In an interesting attempt to explain the motivational process that drives entrepreneurial behavior, Naffziger et al. (1994) propose the dynamic model that appears in Figure 5.1. Let's apply this model in a corporate context.

The decision to behave entrepreneurially results from the interaction of several factors. An individual has an idea or recognizes an opportunity. The tendency to act on it (as well as the manner in which he or she acts) is the result of the interplay between his or her personal characteristics, the individual's personal goal set, his or her personal environment, the current business environment, and the nature of the innovative idea (Reuber and Fischer 1999).

However, before he or she actually acts on the idea, the individual takes into account two additional considerations. The first of these involves a comparison of his or her perceptions of the probable outcomes were the idea to be successfully implemented with the personal outcomes he or she has in mind. In a corporate setting, this comparison is influenced by the past experiences of the individual within the company and the experiences of others with which the individual is familiar. Next, an individual looks at the relationship between the implementation approach that would be required and likely outcomes from that approach. Here, the potential entrepreneur is concerned with what it will take to garner resources and support, overcome obstacles, and ensure the final concept meets market requirements. Again, the comparison is influenced by past experiences. Further, the more times the individual has attempted to pursue new ideas in the company, the more likely he or she has developed implementation approaches that work.

Assuming the concept is pursued, the strategy and managerial approaches of the corporate entrepreneur result in some sort of outcome within the firm. This could range from a hugely successful new product or market to a glorious failure. It could also result in concepts that are perpetually in limbo within the company or that never get out of the development process, regardless of how much has been spent. According to the model, the entrepreneur's expectations are finally

■ FIGURE 5.1

A MODEL OF ENTREPRENEURIAL MOTIVATION

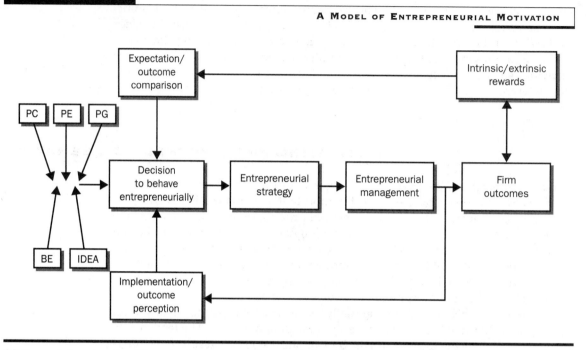

PC, Personal characteristics; PE, personal environment; PG, personal goals; BE, business environment.

SOURCE: Naffziger, D. W., J. S. Hornsby, and D. F. Kuratko. 1994. "A Proposed Research Model of Entrepreneurial Motivation," *Entrepreneurship Theory and Practice* 33 (Spring 1994), p. 33.

compared with these actual firm outcomes. Future entrepreneurial behavior is based on the results of all of these comparisons. When outcomes meet or exceed expectations, the entrepreneurial behavior is positively reinforced, and the individual is motivated to continue to behave entrepreneurially, either within the current venture or possibly through the initiation of additional ventures, depending on the existing entrepreneurial goal. When outcomes fail to meet expectations, the entrepreneur's motivation will be lower and will have a corresponding impact on the decision to continue to act entrepreneurially. These perceptions also affect subsequent implementation methods relied upon by the corporate entrepreneur.

ARE CORPORATE ENTREPRENEURS DIFFERENT?

The discussion up to this point has concentrated on what is known about entrepreneurs in general and how this knowledge might apply in a corporate context. However, just as the corporate setting is very different from the start-up setting, the corporate entrepreneur (or intrapreneur) is also a different kind of person.

Intrapreneurs are not necessarily the inventors of new products, services, or processes (although they often are), but they turn ideas or prototypes into profitable realities. They are the drivers behind the implementation of innovative concepts. They are team builders with a commitment and the necessary drive to see ideas become realities. Importantly, they are very ordinary people who tend to do extraordinary things.

Entrepreneurial action can be thought of in terms of stages of conceptualization and implementation. From the employee's perspective, we can think of these as the stages of dreaming and doing. There are many people in an organization that dream, or come up with new ideas. The issue from an entrepreneurial perspective concerns how much responsibility they take not only for refining their ideas into a workable or viable form, but also for selling ideas, overcoming resistance, and following through on implementation. The shortage in most companies is not of dreamers, but of doers. Figure 5.2 characterizes different types of people in organizations based on the extent to which they focus on the conceptualization part of things, or on making it happen. Thus, inventors and planners identify possibilities, while conventional managers focus on an action agenda. Corporate entrepreneurs represent a strong mix of vision and depth of action. They are the dreamers who do.

The corporate entrepreneur begins with an idea. This idea typically starts as a vision, which might be fairly loosely defined. In a sense, he or she goes through a "daydreaming phase." Here, the intrapreneur mentally examines the process he or she will have to follow to take the idea from concept to successful implementation. Different pathways are thought through, and potential obstacles and barriers are mentally examined. The intrapreneur of the Pontiac Fiero, Hulki Aldikacti, provides an example. When Aldikacti first came up with the idea for the Fiero, he was unsure of what the car should look like. So he built a wooden mock-up of the passenger compartment. He then sat in the model and imagined what it would feel like to drive the finished car. This helped him develop and perfect the final project.

Corporate entrepreneurs can move quickly to get things done. They are goal-oriented, willing to do whatever it takes to achieve their objectives. They are also a combination of thinker, doer, planner, and worker. Dedication to the new idea is paramount, since their action-orientation must be balanced against perseverance and tenacity. They must struggle to keep an idea alive, often after higher-level managers, committees, and others have "killed" it two or three times. Intrapreneurs often expect the impossible from themselves and consider no setback too great to make their venture successful. They are self-determined pursuers of a vision who go beyond the call of duty in achieving their goals.

When faced with failure or setback, intrapreneurs employ an optimistic approach. First, they do not admit they are beaten; they view failure as a temporary setback to be learned from and dealt with. It is not seen as a reason to quit. Second, they view themselves as responsible for their own destiny. They do not blame their failure on others but instead focus on learning how they might have done better. By objectively dealing with their own mistakes and failures, intrapreneurs learn to avoid making the same mistakes again, and this, in turn, is part of what helps make them successful.

■ **FIGURE 5.2**

THE INTRAPRENEURIAL FRAMEWORK

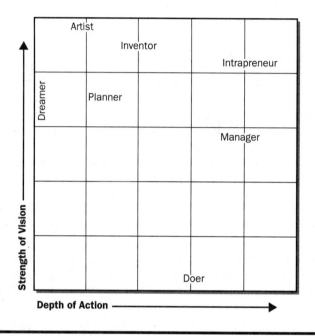

SOURCE: Adapted from Pinchott, G. III. 1985. *Intrapreneuring*. New York: Harper & Row.

It could be argued that the discussion above could be applied equally to those who start new independent ventures and those who champion innovation in larger companies. And yet, there are critical differences between these two individuals. Table 5.2 draws a fairly detailed comparison between the characteristics and skills of the intrapreneur, those of the start-up or independent entrepreneur, and those of traditional managers.

An examination of the items in Table 5.2 reveals some important insights into the nature of the corporate entrepreneur. These individuals are closer to the traditional start-up entrepreneur than to the traditional corporate manager, but they have certain things in common with both. They desire a degree of autonomy, but also want access to corporate resources. Security matters to them, and they respond to corporate rewards and recognition. At the same time, they are cynical about many of the processes and systems within the company, but also optimistic that they can find ways around the rules and bureaucracy. They are more politically adept than the typical start-up entrepreneur, but more willing than the typical manager to get their hands dirty and do whatever task needs to be done.

■ TABLE 5.2

Characteristic	Traditional Manager	Entrepreneur	Intrapreneur
Primary motives	Wants promotion and other traditional corporate rewards; power motivated	Wants freedom; goal oriented, self-reliant, and self-motivated	Wants freedom of access to corporate resources; goal oriented and self-motivated, but also responds to corporate rewards and recognition
Time orientation	Responds to quotes and budgets; to weekly, monthly quarterly, and annual planning horizons; and to the next promotion or transfer	Uses end goals of five- to ten-year growth of the business as guides; takes action now to move to next step along the way	End goal of three to fifteen years, depending on the type of venture; urgency to meet self-imposed and corporate timetables
Tendency to action	Delegates action; supervising and reporting take most energy	Gets hands dirty; may upset employees by suddenly doing their work	Gets hands dirty; may know how to delegate but, when necessary, does what needs to be done
Skills	Professional management; often business-school trained; uses abstract analytical tools, people-management and political skills	Knows business intimately; more business acumen than managerial or political skill; often technically trained if in technical business; may have had formal profit-and loss responsibility in the company	Very much like the entrepreneur, but the situation demands greater ability to prosper within the organization; needs help with this
Attitude toward courage and destiny	Sees others being in charge of his or her destiny; can be forceful and ambitious, but may be fearful of others' ability to do him or her in	Self-confident, optimistic, and courageous	Self-confident and courageous; many are cynical about the system but optimistic about their ability to outwit it
Focus of attention	Primarily on events inside corporation	Primarily on technology and marketplace	Both inside and outside; sells insiders on needs of venture and marketplace but also focuses on customers
Attitude toward risk	Cautious	Likes moderate risk; invests heavily but expects to succeed	Likes moderate risk; generally not afraid of being fired, so sees little personal risk
Use of market research	Has market studies done to discover needs and guide product conceptualization	Creates needs; creates products that often cannot be tested with market research; potential customers do not yet understand them; talks to customers and forms own opinion	Does own market research, an intuitive market evaluation, like the entrepreneur

continued

■ **TABLE 5.2**

CONTINUED

Characteristic	Traditional Manager	Entrepreneur	Intrapreneur
Attitude toward status	Cares about status symbols (corner office, etc.)	Happy sitting on an orange crate if job is getting done	Considers traditional status symbols a joke; treasures symbols of freedom
Attitude toward failure and mistakes	Strives to avoid mistakes and surprises; postpones recognizing failure	Deals with mistakes and failures as learning experiences	Sensitive to need to appear orderly; attempts to hide risky projects from view so as to learn from mistakes without political cost of public failure
Decision-making style	Agrees with those in power; delays making decisions until a feel of what bosses want is obtained	Follows private vision; decisive, action oriented	Adept at getting others to agree with private vision; somewhat more patient and willing to compromise than the entrepreneur but still a doer
Who serves	Pleases others	Pleases self and customers	Pleases self, customers, and sponsors
Attitude toward the system	Sees system as nurturing and protective; seeks position within it	May rapidly advance in a system; then, when frustrated, may reject the system and form his or her own company	Dislikes the system but learns to manipulate it
Problem-solving style	Works out problems within the system	Escapes problems in large and formal structures by leaving and starting over alone	Works out problems within the system or bypasses them without leaving
Family history	Family members worked for large organizations	Entrepreneurial small-business, professional, or farm background	Entrepreneurial small-business, professional, or farm background
Relationship with parents	Independent of mother; good relations with father but slightly dependent	Absent father or poor relations with father	Better relations with father but still stormy
Socioeconomic background	Middle class	Lower class in some early studies; middle class in more recent ones	Middle class
Educational level	Highly educated	Less well educated in earlier studies; some graduate work but not Ph.D. in later ones	Often highly educated, particularly in technical fields, but sometimes not
Relationship with others	Perceives hierarchy as basic relationship	Perceives transactions and deal making as basic relationship	Perceives transactions within hierarchy as basic relationship

SOURCE: Adapted from Pinchot III, G. 1985. *Intrapreneuring.* Harper & Row, pp. 54–56. Copyright 1985 by Gifford Pinchott III. Adapted by permission of Harper Collins Publishers.

CATEGORIES OF ENTREPRENEURS

Earlier, we noted that there is no single prototype of the entrepreneur. The same is true of the corporate entrepreneur. There may actually be a number of different types. As an example, Kao (1991), differentiated between creative or charismatic and conventional entrepreneurs. The former tend to do something that is more innovative, has a higher risk profile, and is more growth oriented than the latter.

Alternatively, Miner (1996) concludes that four different types of entrepreneurs exist, each of which achieves success by approaching entrepreneurship from a different route.

These include the following:

THE PERSONAL ACHIEVER (THE CLASSIC ENTREPRENEUR)

- High need for achievement
- Need for performance feedback
- Desire to plan and set goals
- Strong individual initiative
- Strong personal commitment and identification with their organization
- Internal locus of control
- Belief that work should be guided by personal goals, not those of others

THE SUPER-SALESPERSON (ACHIEVES SUCCESS THROUGH NETWORKING, SELLING, AND PEOPLE SKILLS)

- Capacity to understand and feel with another, to empathize
- Desire to help others
- Belief that social processes, interactions, and relationships are important
- Need to have strong positive relationships with others
- Belief that the sales force is crucial to carrying out company strategy
- Experience in selling

THE REAL MANAGER (STRONG MANAGERIAL SKILLS COMBINED WITH AGGRESSIVE GROWTH ORIENTATION)

- Desire to be a corporate leader
- Desire to compete
- Decisiveness
- Desire for power
- Positive attitudes to authority
- Desire to stand out from the crowd

THE EXPERT IDEA GENERATOR (EXPERTISE PLUS CREATIVITY)

- Desire to innovate
- Love of ideas, curious, open minded
- Belief that new product development is crucial component of company strategy
- Good intelligence; thinking is at center of his or her entrepreneurial approach
- Intelligence as a source of competitive advantage
- Desire to avoid taking risks

If we apply this scheme to the corporate context, personal achievers would be the type of bold, visionary, risk takers that are typically associated with the classic entrepreneur. Super-salespeople would be entrepreneurial employees who successfully push concepts as a function of their networking and people skills. Real managers are more power oriented and tend to systematically and aggressively grow an internal venture. Expert idea generators, or technopreneurs, are inventors or creators, typically with a strong technical background. While they will champion a new idea within the organization and through implementation, they most enjoy the opportunity to go back and invent more new things. They are somewhat more risk-averse.

There may be other kinds of entrepreneurs in companies. However, this framework provides a beginning point for recognizing some of them. The critical point here is that corporate entrepreneurs take on various forms and exhibit different styles. They can differ in terms of their relative risk profiles, sources of motivation, managerial capabilities, and other characteristics.

MYTHS ABOUT CORPORATE ENTREPRENEURS

Given the similarities between independent and corporate entrepreneurs, some of the myths regarding the former are also applied to the latter. That is, supervisors and peers in an organization have a tendency to stereotype employees who demonstrate strong entrepreneurial proclivities. Consider the following five myths, together with the countervailing reality:

Myth: The primary motivation of intrapreneurs is a desire for wealth; hence, money is the prime objective.

Fact: The primary motivation of intrapreneurs is the process of innovation: freedom and ability to innovate. Money is only a tool and a symbol of success.

Myth: Intrapreneurs are high risk takers—they are gamblers who play for high stakes.

Fact: Moderate risk taking is a more realistic description of the intrapreneur's actions. Because of his or her insatiable desire to achieve, small, calculated, and analyzed risks are the preferred stepping-stones of these individuals.

Myth: Because intrapreneurs lack analytical skills, they "shoot from the hip." This has led to a philosophy of "luck is all you need."

Fact: Intrapreneurs are fairly analytical. Although it may appear they are lucky and shoot from the hip, in truth, they are well prepared, understand innovation, and perceive market needs very well.

Myth: Intrapreneurs lack morals or ethics because of their strong desire to succeed. They do not care how they succeed, just as long as they succeed.

Fact: In today's demanding, educated, and critical society, where companies and their actions tend to be visible to the public, intrapreneurs tend to be highly ethical and have moral convictions consistent with society's expectations. If they do not have these convictions, they do not survive.

Myth: Intrapreneurs have a power-hungry attitude and are most interested in building an empire. They want the venture to grow as big and as fast as it can.

Fact: Most intrapreneurial enterprises are small and relatively conservative. The individual is more interested in the profit and growth of the concept or venture than in empire building. The focus is on doing things right rather than doing them big.

Many inside the organization view entrepreneurial individuals as threatening. They disturb comfort zones and create change. As a result, there is a tendency to cling to such stereotypes or otherwise negatively portray the motives and actions of the entrepreneurial employee. For this reason, executives should clearly define the nature and role of the internal champion, communicate to everyone in the company the importance of this role, and publicly reinforce the image of those who fill this role with recognition and rewards.

CRITICAL ROLES IN CORPORATE ENTREPRENEURSHIP

Entrepreneurship can happen anytime and anywhere in a company. The managerial challenge concerns how to make it sustainable—how to maintain the desired frequency and degree of entrepreneurship on an ongoing basis. Achieving continuous entrepreneurship requires that the firm recognize the specific roles that must be filled for an entrepreneurial event to successfully occur. Further, an environment must be created where people are expected to take on one or more of these roles on a regular basis. The key roles are defined as follows:

Initiator: Triggers a new entrepreneurial event, either by recognizing some external threat or opportunity, identifying some internal need, or pursuing ongoing innovation initiatives. This role could be filled by the champion or by someone else.

Sponsor/Facilitator: The patron or senior management advocate of the initiative, pushing for its acceptance and completion, playing a major advising or mentoring role as it unfolds, and perhaps housing it. This high-level person acts as buffer, protector, and modifier of rules and policies and helps the venture obtain the needed resources.

Champion/Manager: Takes the lead in directing the project, overseeing and coordinating the project, adapting key aspects along the way, sustaining the project as obstacles and opposition arise, and bringing it through the implementation phase.

Team Supporter: Augments the team, playing a secondary or more minor role and providing expertise, intelligence, analysis, and marketing plans/programs on behalf of the initiative.

Reactor: Plays more of a devil's advocate role, providing market intelligence and insights that serve to either pinpoint weaknesses in the entrepreneurial idea, possible ways in which it should be revised or refined, or reasons it should or should not be pursued.

While all of these roles need to be filled, the two most critical ones are the champion and the sponsor. The focal point of any entrepreneurial initiative is the champion. The unique demands of the corporate environment require that the individual filling the champion role must be able to wear many hats at the same time. However, he or she cannot be expected to wear all the necessary hats, and this is why a well-constructed team and strong network are important. Fifteen more specific jobs that must be accomplished in order to bring an entrepreneurial concept to fruition include the following:

Researcher/Analyzer: Gathers intelligence, assesses potential, evaluates key factors in the market;

Interpreter/Strategist: Identifies patterns, trends, future development and draws implications for project development;

Visionary/Inventory: Provides creativity, intuition, and judgment in recognizing opportunities and ways to capitalize upon them;

Catalyst or leader: Provides motivation and impetus for getting project off the ground;

Endorser: Endorses the entrepreneurial concept and lends credibility to the pursuit of the concept by the project champion;

Team player: Plays a collaborative role with people from other specialty areas;

Resource provider: Assists with information—human, financial, and other inputs—to exploit opportunity;

Problem solver: Responds to a particular question or challenge that the innovation team encounters along the way;

Coordinator: Helps to bring together and integrate key inputs and resources over time;

Negotiator: Helps bridge differences among various involved parties regarding what the project or concept should consist of, its scope, its resource commitment levels, and its timetable;

Politician: Helps overcome internal resistance and gains top management support;

Change manager: Oversees any strategic redirection, modification of infrastructure, and employee training or reorientation necessary to implement a new initiative;

Missionary: Motivates and inspires management and all relevant interest groups regarding ongoing need for innovation;

Opportunist: Reacts quickly to emerging developments; provides new direction if necessary;

Critic/Judge: Identifies key flaws, downside risks, likely impact on other parts of the business.

In terms of their skill set, corporate entrepreneurs often start their first internal initiative as specialists. That is, the individual may specialize in one area, such as marketing or research and development, but once the entrepreneurial initiative gets underway, he or she is forced to learn all the facets of the venture. The intrapreneur soon becomes a generalist with many skills.

The success of the champion is also closely linked to the ability to find the right sponsor. Let us take a closer look at this key individual.

THE IMPORTANCE OF SPONSORS

In the corporate environment, the announcement of new ideas triggers the "impatience clock." Intrapreneurs need to be shielded from impatient executives who are driven by results. A results orientation can sometimes destroy the innovation before it ever gets off the ground. Therefore, sponsors are corporate managers at higher levels in the organization willing to protect intrapreneurs by building environments of safety around them. Sponsors aid the intrapreneur in gaining access to resources and information and have a sincere belief in the intrapreneur's vision. They also assist in keeping the entrepreneurial project "under the radar screen," where it has less visibility and is not as likely to become a target for elimination.

Most important, sponsors protect the intrapreneur from being fired if certain corporate rules are violated.

Outlined below are some of the questions to ask when attempting to identify a sponsor for an innovative project (Pinchot 2000).

- Has this person been challenged and yet proceeded anyway? Is the person willing to handle controversy?
- Does the person have a deep personal commitment to innovation and innovative people?
- Can you gain the respect of this person?
- How important is another step up the corporate ladder to this person?
- Does this person know when to fight, when to give up gracefully, and when it really does not matter?
- Does the person understand clearly the corporate decision-making structure?
- Does this person have the respect of other key corporate decision makers and have access to them?

Establishing mutual trust with a sponsor may be the most important aspect of working within a corporate environment. The selection of a sponsor should not only reflect the personality and position of the champion, but also the nature of the innovative project. It is worthwhile for the champion to consider three specific aspects of the project itself before deciding the level, functional background, and particular identity of the sponsor to be approached:

Nonfinancial resources: Time, facilities, equipment, advice, and personnel needed by the champion to successfully complete the innovative project;

Investment: Venture money to keep the project moving along and avoid needless delays;

Critics: The extent of political opposition likely to be encountered by the champion; the sponsor must be willing and able to defend the intrapreneur and deter the critics.

It is also important to recognize the potential for retirements, promotions, and transfers to alter the sponsor-intrapreneur relationship. Loss of the sponsor or organizational changes that make the sponsor less able to influence the progress of a particular project can lead to the demise of a project. It is therefore important to establish a formal network as soon as possible.

HOW SUBORDINATES VIEW THE ENTREPRENEURIAL MANAGER

From the vantage point of the subordinate, what attributes are associated with having an entrepreneurial boss? Do employees really want to work for an entrepreneurial manager? In a major study, Pearce, Kramer, and Robbins (1997) attempted to answer these questions. The research involved 102 managers and over 1,500 subordinates. The findings identified the following eleven key behaviors that define an entrepreneurial manager:

- Efficiently gets proposed actions through red tape and into practice;
- Displays enthusiasm for acquiring skills;
- Quickly changes course of action when results are not being achieved;
- Encourages others to take the initiative for their own ideas;
- Inspires others to think about their work in new and stimulating ways;
- Devotes time to helping others find ways to improve products and services;
- Goes to bat for good ideas of others;
- Boldly moves ahead with a promising new approach when others might be more cautious;
- Vividly describes how things could be in the future and what is needed to get there;
- Gets people to rally together to meet a challenge;
- Creates an environment where people get excited about making improvements.

Six months after having subordinates evaluate managers on these eleven behaviors, the researchers assessed the satisfaction levels of employees with the managers. Results of the data analysis clearly indicated support for the idea that managers who are entrepreneurial in their behavior have a positive impact on their subordinates' satisfaction. The findings demonstrated that, as entrepreneurial behaviors increased, subordinates' satisfaction with supervision increased. Whereas 62 percent of the subordinates of entrepreneurial managers reported high levels of satisfaction, 69 percent of subordinates of more bureaucratic managers reported low levels of satisfaction with their supervisors. Further, for eight of the eleven behaviors cited above, there were significant differences between high and low subordinate satisfaction.

It appears, then, that there are payoffs from having a company that is more entrepreneurial in the form of higher financial performance and also payoffs from having managers who are more entrepreneurial in the form of more highly satisfied employees.

THE ENTREPRENEURIAL MINDSET

Even the most entrepreneurial of managers can lose the entrepreneurial edge. The day-to-day pressures, the administrative demands of organizational policies and

■ FIGURE 5.3

THE INTRAPRENEURIAL MINDSET

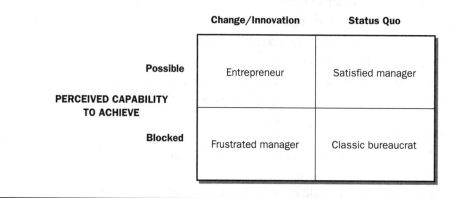

FUTURE GOALS

SOURCE: Kuratko, D. F. and R. M. Hodgetts. 2001. *Entrepreneurship: A Contemporary Approach*, ed 5. Fort Worth, TX: Harcourt College.

procedures, and the need for more systematic approaches as an innovative concept grows into a large internal enterprise force the intrapreneur to become more administratively oriented. Figure 5.3 illustrates the danger of entrepreneurs evolving into bureaucrats who in turn stifle innovation. The classic bureaucrat believes in the status quo while blocking all initiatives for change. The entrepreneur believes in change as the future goal and perceives that people in the company have the capabilities to achieve change. Thus the entrepreneurial mindset is one of belief in change and innovation while recognizing and developing the capabilities to achieve such changes. Table 5.3 provides an outline of the key characteristics of this mindset.

In order to maintain this "entrepreneurial mindset," the manager must assume certain ongoing responsibilities (McGrath and MacMillan 2000). The first responsibility involves "framing the challenge." In other words, there needs to be a clear definition of the specified challenges that everyone involved with innovative projects should accomplish. It is important to think in terms of and regularly reiterate the challenge. Second, leaders have the responsibility to "absorb the uncertainty" that is perceived by team members. Entrepreneurial leaders make uncertainty less daunting. The idea is to create the self-confidence that lets others act on opportunities without seeking managerial permission. Employees must not be overwhelmed by the complexity inherent in many innovative situations. A third responsibility is to "define gravity"—that is, what must be accepted and what

■ TABLE 5.3

CHARACTERISTICS OF THE ENTREPRENEURIAL MINDSET

1. *They passionately seek new opportunities.* Habitual entrepreneurs stay alert, always looking for the chance to profit from change and disruption in the way business is done. Their greatest impact occurs when they create entirely new business models. New business models revolutionize how revenues are made, costs are incurred, or operations are conducted, sometimes throughout an entire industry. One reason that the emergence of the Internet as a new medium of business has been accompanied by dizzyingly high company valuations is that investors perceive its potential to profitably transform virtually every aspect of economic life.

2. *They pursue opportunities with enormous discipline.* Habitual entrepreneurs not only are alert enough to spot opportunities, but make sure that they act on them. Most maintain some form of inventory, or register, of unexploited opportunities. They make sure that they revisit their inventory of ideas often but they take action only when it is required. They make investments only if the competitive arena is attractive and the opportunity is ripe.

3. *They pursue only the very best opportunities and avoid exhausting themselves and their organizations by chasing after every option.* Even though many habitual entrepreneurs are wealthy, the most successful remain ruthlessly disciplined about limiting the number of projects they pursue. They go after a tightly controlled portfolio of opportunities in different stages of development. They tightly link their strategy with their choice of projects, rather than diluting their efforts too broadly.

4. *They focus on execution—specifically, adaptive execution.* Both words are important. People with an entrepreneurial mindset execute—that is, they get on with it instead of analyzing new ideas to death. Yet they are also adaptive—able to change directions as the real opportunity, and the best way to exploit it, evolves.

5. *They engage the energies of everyone in their domain.* Habitual entrepreneurs involve many people—both inside and outside the organization—in their pursuit of an opportunity. They create and sustain networks of relationships rather than going it alone, making the most of the intellectual and other resources people have to offer and helping those people to achieve their goals as well.

SOURCE: McGrath, R., and I. MacMillan. 2000. *The Entrepreneurial Mindset.* Boston: Harvard Business School Press.

cannot be accepted. The term *gravity* is used to capture limiting conditions. For example, there is gravity on the earth, but that does not mean it must limit our lives. If freed from the psychological cage of believing that gravity makes flying impossible, creativity can permit us to invent an airplane or spaceship. This is what the entrepreneurial mindset is all about—seeing opportunities where others see barriers and limits. A fourth responsibility of entrepreneurial leadership involves "clearing obstacles" that arise as a result of internal competition for resources. This can be a problem especially when the entrepreneurial innovation is beginning to undergo significant growth. A growing venture will often find itself pitted squarely against other (often established) aspects of the firm in a fierce internal competition for funds and staff. (See Chapter 9 on corporate obstacles.) Creative tactics, political skills, and an ability to regroup, reorganize, and attack from another angle become invaluable. A final responsibility for entrepreneurial leaders is to keep their finger on the pulse of the project. This involves constructive monitoring and control of the developing opportunity.

In the contemporary organization, all managers must be entrepreneurs. As such, responsibilities such as those described here must become a core part of how every manager's job is defined. Doing so will help limit the extent to which individual champions begin that inexorable transition from corporate entrepreneur to corporate bureaucrat.

A FINAL THOUGHT: ARE YOU A CORPORATE ENTREPRENEUR?

Before we leave this discussion regarding the nature of entrepreneurial individuals, it may be helpful for the reader to assess his or her own entrepreneurial profile. Gifford Pinchot (1985) proposes the following short set of items as a quick test. (Answer yes or no to each question.)

1. Does your desire to make things work better occupy as much of your time as fulfilling your duty to maintain them the way they are?
2. Do you get excited about what you are doing at work?
3. Do you think about new business ideas while driving to work or taking a shower?
4. Can you visualize concrete steps for action when you consider ways to make a new idea happen?
5. Do you get in trouble from time to time for doing things that exceed your authority?
6. Are you able to keep your ideas under cover, suppressing your urge to tell everyone about them until you have tested them and developed a plan for implementation?
7. Have you successfully pushed through bleak times when something you were working on looked as if it might fail?
8. Do you have a network of friends at work whom you can count on for help?
9. Do you get easily annoyed by others' incompetent attempts to execute parts of your ideas?
10. Can you consider trying to overcome a natural perfectionist tendency to do all the work yourself and share the responsibility for your ideas with a team?
11. Would you be willing to give up some salary in exchange for the chance to try out your business idea if the rewards for success were adequate?

Ten Rules of the Entrepreneurial Insurgent

Change Agents quickly became a thing of the past, making way for the more versatile title of Entrepreneurial Insurgent. Change Agents were hot commodities, brought into corporations to shake things up. Insurgents, brought out of the context of government resistance, bring rebellion into the corporate environment and do much more than just act as a catalyst for change. Becoming a change insurgent is as simple as adding a comma and the two words to the end of your current title — who says titles are overrated? The question is, do you have what it takes?

Manage the blood supply. The only way to keep an organization innovative and alert for new opportunities is to maintain a fresh perspective. You may have a $5 million company, but why not hire someone who knows how to run a $100 million company?

Find, hire, and promote people who make you and the organization uncomfortable. Everyone knows that when things get comfortable, it's time to get uncomfortable. The problem is, most people don't recognize a comfortable situation. Yes-men and brownnosers won't keep an organization ready for action in this era riddled with change. Hire an eclectic staff with different views, backgrounds, and talents — hopefully you'll be surprised with what you get.

Undermine or subvert "relations" people. In the old economy, relations people were paid well to maintain the status quo. No upheavals allowed; no press releases warranted. Companies are now thriving on the demands of customers, suppliers, and technology. Complaints and turmoil should be routed around the public relations department (e-mail works perfectly) to land in the laps of those who really can do something about the problem.

Conduct heat. If you always do what you've always done, you'll always get what you've always gotten. Friction and tension in an organization can be a good thing. If everyone knows what everyone is up to and responsible for, then the heat will be on for everyone to perform. Passing the buck and avoiding responsibility will never get a problem solved correctly.

Turn the company geeks and salespeople into change allies. Change happens. It happens because technology improves and consumers want everything bigger, better, and faster. Having the employees closest to the catalysts work closer together just makes sense.

Hold change resisters' hands. You know who they are. The ones that use phrases like, "If it ain't broke, don't fix it" and "That seems risky." Change, for them, is a red flag. Their very definition of success lies within last year's annual report. Initially, they will need support, but once they realize how and why change is good, the team will be stronger than ever.

Use tough love. Change resisters do so with the company's best interests in mind. Or at least that's what they'll tell you. As a change insurgent you must value their concern while also letting them know that when the time comes, change is going to happen with or without them.

New times demand new measures. Dramatic company change can easily be lost in the details and put on the back burner. To compete in the new, ever-changing economy, new strategies need new benchmarks, and old processes need to be redefined.

Just do it. It's easier to ask for forgiveness than it is to ask for permission. Need more be said? Hint: It is, however, best to act on informed decisions.

When you've got to go, you've got to go. A successful change insurgent can only do so much — within any organization, the title is temporary. The knowledge, skills, and abilities of any given change insurgent are learned within a specific context and environment but can be expanded and developed outside the proverbial four-walled cell. When the work is done and the environment for change is in place, a change insurgent can continue to work or take the new skill and do magic in other organizations.

ADAPTED FROM: Reich, R. B. 2000. "Your Job Is Change," *Fast Company* 5, No. 39 (October): 140–150.

Pinchot suggests that if you have answered *yes* more times than *no,* it is likely that you are already behaving like an entrepreneur.

SUMMARY AND CONCLUSIONS

The entrepreneurial personality takes on many forms. While there are some characteristics common to most entrepreneurial individuals such as achievement motivation, internal locus of control, calculated risk taking, and tolerance for ambiguity, there is no single profile or prototype. Further, entrepreneurs are not born. The entrepreneurial potential is rich in every employee in a company, no matter what his or her background or position.

In this chapter, the concept of entrepreneurial motivation was explored. We also examined the dark side of entrepreneurship so as to note some of the dysfunctional aspects of entrepreneurial behavior. Characteristics that distinguish corporate entrepreneurs from independent or start-up entrepreneurs and from conventional managers were identified. While there are also similarities among these three types, the corporate entrepreneur is closer in nature to the start-up entrepreneur than to the conventional manager. Just as important is the need to recognize the different kinds of entrepreneurs that can be found in a corporate setting, and an attempt was made to describe at least four different types.

Sustainable entrepreneurship is dependent on the ongoing ability of companies to fill a set of key roles, the two most important of which were the champion and the sponsor. Champions must wear many hats, and a number of their responsibilities were identified. The nature and scope of these responsibilities make it clear that corporate entrepreneurship does not happen without teams where other individuals can wear some of the required hats. When seeking someone to serve as sponsor, there is a need to achieve a fit not only between the champion and the targeted person but also between the entrepreneurial concept and the type of sponsor selected. Criteria for a good sponsor were suggested.

The chapter concluded with a look at how employees define an entrepreneurial manager. It is noteworthy that employees demonstrate higher levels of job satisfaction when they perceive their boss is entrepreneurial. Finally, the need for all managers to adopt and regularly refresh an entrepreneurial mindset was examined. There is a proclivity for the most entrepreneurial of employees to lose that edge over time. To avoid this tendency, a set of responsibilities was prescribed — responsibilities that should be a mainstay in the job description of every manager.

REFERENCES

Akande, A. 1992. "Coping with Entrepreneurial Stress," *Leadership & Organization Development Journal* 13, No. 2: 27–32.

Block, Z., and I. MacMillan. 1993. *Corporate Venturing.* Boston: Harvard Business School Press.

Busenitz, L., and J. B. Barney. 1997. "Differences Between Entrepreneurs and Managers in Large Organizations: Biases and Heuristics in Strategic Decision-Making," *Journal of Business Venturing* 12: 9–30.

Buttner, E. H. 1992. "Entrepreneurial Stress: Is It Hazardous to Your Health?" *Journal of Managerial Issues* 13, No. 2 (Summer): 223–240.

Chen, C. C., P. G. Greene, and A. Crick. 1998. "Does Entrepreneurial Self-Efficacy Distinguish Entrepreneurs from Managers," *Journal of Business Venturing* 13: 296–316.

Cooper, A. C., and K. W. Aerz. 1995. "Determinants of Satisfaction for Entrepreneurs," *Journal of Business Venturing* 10 (November): 439–458.

Gartner, W. B. 1989. "Some Suggestions for Research on Entrepreneurial Traits and Characteristics," *Entrepreneurship Theory and Practice* 14 (Fall): 27-38.

Herron, L., and H. J. Sapienza. 1992. "The Entrepreneur and the Initiation of New Venture: Launch Activities," *Entrepreneurship Theory and Practice* 17 (Fall): 49–55.

Johnson, B. R. 1990. "Toward a Multidimensional Model of Entrepreneurship: The Case of Achievement Motivation and the Entrepreneur," *Entrepreneurship Theory and Practice* 15 (Spring): 39–58.

Kao, J. J. 1991. *The Entrepreneur.* Englewood Cliffs: Prentice Hall.

Kets de Vries, M. F. R. 1985. "The Dark Side of Entrepreneurship," *Harvard Business Review* 63 (November/December): 160–167.

Kuratko, D. F., and R. M. Hodgetts. 2001. *Entrepreneurship: A Contemporary Approach,* 5th ed. Fort Worth: Harcourt College.

Kuratko, D. F., J. S. Hornsby, and D. W. Naffziger. 1997. "An Examination of Owner's Goals in Sustaining Entrepreneurship," *Journal of Small Business Management* 35 (January): 24–33.

McGrath, R. G., and I. MacMillan. 2000. *The Entrepreneurial Mindset.* Boston: Harvard Business School Press.

Miner, J. B. (1996). *The Four Routes to Entrepreneurial Success.* San Fancisco: Berrett-Koehler.

Morris, M. H. 1998. *Entrepreneurial Intensity.* Westport: Quorum Books.

Morris, M. H., M. Schindehutte, and D. F. Kuratko. 2000. "Trigger Events, Corporate Entrepreneurship, and the Marketing Function," *Journal of Marketing Theory and Practice* 8, No. 2 (Spring): 18–30.

Naffziger, D. W., J. S. Hornsby, and D. F. Kuratko. 1994. "A Proposed Research Model of Entrepreneurial Motivation." *Entrepreneurship Theory and Practice* 19 (Spring): 29–42.

Pearce III, J. A., T. R. Kramer, and K. D. Robbins. 1997. "Effects of Managers' Entrepreneurial Behavior on Subordinates," *Journal of Business Venturing* 12: 147–160.

Pinchot III, G. 1985. *Intrapreneuring.* New York: Harper & Row.

Pinchot III, G., and R. Pellman. 1999. *Intrapreneuring in Action.* San Francisco: Berrett-Koehler.

Rabin, M. A. 1996. "Stress, Strain, and Their Moderators: An Empirical Comparison of Entrepreneurs and Managers," *Journal of Small Business Management* 34 (January): 46–58.

Reuber, A. R., and E. Fischer. 1999. "Understanding the Consequences of Founder's Experience," *Journal of Small Business Management* 39 (February): 30–45.

Shaver, K. G., and L. R. Scott. 1991. "Person, Process, Choice: The Psychology of New Venture Creation," *Entrepreneurship Theory and Practice* 16 (Winter): 23–45.

Stewart, W. H., W. E. Watson, J. C. Carland, and J. W. Carland. 1999. "A Proclivity for Entrepreneurship: A Comparison of Entrepreneurs, Small Business Owners, and Corporate Managers," *Journal of Business Venturing* 14: 189–214.

6

CREATIVITY AND THE CORPORATE ENTREPRENEUR

Two Theories and the Need to Take a Leap

What does is take to get people to act in an entrepreneurial manner? Consider two possibilities. Theory 1 is that certain people are born to be entrepreneurial, that they are destined to become entrepreneurs, and that they will do so when they are ready. Theory 2 holds that everyone, or at least most people, have innate entrepreneurial potential. People simply need to discover and channel that potential, and there are things that can be done to help them along the way. These two theories result in very different implications for how a company can foster entrepreneurship. With Theory 1, the company that wants to encourage entrepreneurship must go out and hire entrepreneurial people. Internally, senior management must, in effect, pick the winners, meaning they must try to identify the innately entrepreneurial employees and then invest in or provide resources to those individuals. Alternatively, Theory 2 suggests that the job of senior management is to create a work environment that is highly conducive to entrepreneurship and that employees will naturally "step to the plate."

It is our position that entrepreneurs are not necessarily "born," and that many of the key traits associated with entrepreneurial behavior are a function of a person's family, social, educational, and work experiences (see Chapters 2 and 5). Thus, we adhere to Theory 2. To the extent that we are correct, the task of management is to design work environments with the proper set of incentives, role models, resource pools, control systems, and structures. How to create such an environment is the focus of Section III of this book.

With both of the theories above, and especially with Theory 2, there remains a fundamental challenge. It is said that "you can lead a horse to water, but you cannot make him drink." The same is true for entrepreneurial behavior in companies. An inappropriately designed work environment will surely destroy the entrepreneurial spirit in companies, but a well-conceptualized environment does not guarantee that employees will act in an entrepreneurial fashion. In the end, the employee must make the personal commitment and take the entrepreneurial leap. The beginning point for employees is to recognize their own creative potential and then to systematically manage that potential within the organization.

This chapter will examine ways in which people can develop breakthrough ideas on the job. Specifically, we will explore the nature of individual and group creativity in organizations. Our interest is both in identifying ways for employees to think about their own creativity and in ways for managers to facilitate employee creativity.

DEFINING CREATIVITY IN A COMPANY

Creativity is the soul of entrepreneurship. It is required in spotting the patterns and trends that define an opportunity. It is needed to develop innovative business concepts. Most importantly, the corporate entrepreneur has to be highly creative in getting a sponsor, building and using a network, obtaining management buy-in for the concept, forming a team, coming up with resources, and overcoming the many obstacles that will be thrown into his/her path.

While many perspectives exist, creativity can be defined as the application of a person's mental ability and curiosity to discover something new. It is the act of relating previously unrelated things. In fact, much of the work on creativity tends to focus on the ability to relate and connect, to put things together in a novel way. Thus, while entrepreneurship is about making things happen and deals with the practical challenges of implementation, creativity is the capacity to develop new ideas, concepts, and processes.

People are inherently creative. Some act on that creativity all the time, others stifle it, and most of us are somewhere in between. The reality is that employees often do not realize when or how they are being creative. Further, they fail to recognize the many opportunities for creativity that arise within their jobs on a daily basis. Miller (1999) notes that we are all creative in many different ways. Table 6.1 summarizes seven general ways in which people are creative.

In a business context, creativity is more than originality. There is a pragmatic dimension in that creative approaches or solutions must also be useful and actionable in the context of the company and its competition situation. Amabile (1998) suggests that there are three components of successful creativity in organizations: expertise, motivation, and creative thinking skills. Expertise encompasses what a person knows and can do. It defines the intellectual space that he/she uses to explore and solve problems. Motivation can be extrinsic (desire to achieve company rewards and awards) or intrinsic, with the latter being the most critical. Intrinsic motivation refers primarily to passion and interest, or the person's internal desire to do something. The person is driven by the challenge and joy of accomplishment.

■ TABLE 6.1

THE ARENAS IN WHICH PEOPLE ARE CREATIVE AT WORK

William Miller argues that people often do not recognize when they are being creative, and they frequently overlook opportunities to be creative. He suggests that the path to creativity begins by first recognizing all of the ways in which we are or can be creative. People in organizations can channel their creativity into seven different arenas:

- **Idea Creativity:** thinking up a new idea or concept, such as an idea for a new product or service or a way to solve a problem.
- **Material Creativity:** inventing and building a tangible object such as a product, an advertisement, a report, or a photograph.
- **Organization Creativity:** organizing people or projects, and coming up with a new organizational form or approach to structuring things. Examples could include organizing a project, starting a new type of venture, putting together or reorganizing a work group, and changing the policies and rules of a group.
- **Relationship Creativity:** innovating approach to achieving colloboration, cooperation, and win-win relationships with others. The person who handles a difficult situation well or deals with a particular person in an especially effective manner is being creative in a relationship or one-on-one context.
- **Event Creativity:** producing an event or occasion, such as an awards ceremony, team outing, or annual meeting. Finding a way to bring two opponents together. The creativity here also encompasses décor, ways in which people are involved, sequence of happenings, background, and so forth.
- **Inner Creativity:** changing one's inner self. Being open to new approaches to how we do things and thinking about ourselves in different ways. Achieving a change of heart, or finding a new perspective or way to look at things that is a significant departure from how one has traditionally looked at them.
- **Spontaneous Creativity:** acting in a spontaneous or spur-of-the-moment manner such as coming up with a witty response in a meeting, an off-the-cuff speech, a quick and simple way to settle a dispute, or an innovative appeal when trying to close a sale.

SOURCE: Adapted from Miller W. C. 1999. *Flash of Brilliance.* Reading: Perseus Books.

Creative thinking skills refer to the particular ways individuals approach problems and solutions and the techniques they use for looking at a problem differently, seeking insights from other fields of endeavor, challenging assumptions, and so forth. One of the most important conclusions from Amabile's impressive work in the area is that managers can influence all three of these components of creativity. The organization must emphasize managerial practices that result in employees being challenged, that provide them with freedom, and that give them access to resources. Similarly, practices that result in well-designed, mutually supportive, and diverse work teams are likely to spur creativity. Also valuable is encouragement from supervisors for creative outputs and reinforcement in terms of the values, systems, and structures of the organization.

THE CREATIVE PROCESS

Creativity is too often associated with brainstorming. Here the general idea is that people must simply open up their minds, let everything go, apply no constraints, be positive, and generate as many ideas as possible. Out of this activity will come a creative solution. However, it is important to recognize that creativity is much more than brainstorming. In fact, brainstorming is but one of many tools or techniques that can be useful in creative problem solving.

On one level, creativity is messy, random, and unscientific. On another level, structure plays a role in creativity, and those who approach creativity from a more systematic perspective tend to come up with a lot more great ideas. The key to this distinction is to recognize that creativity involves heuristics, not algorithms. Algorithms are complete mechanical rules or formulas for solving a problem or dealing with a situation. Heuristics are incomplete guidelines or rules of thumb that can lead to learning or discovery. Thus, if there is no clear path the employee must create one. Finding the appropriate path to a creative solution is much easier if the employee first approaches creativity as a logical process and then utilizes some of the available creative problem-solving techniques as he/she moves through the process. While it is generally accepted among researchers and consultants that a process is involved in creativity, there are different opinions regarding the nature of that process. Figure 6.1 summarizes seven views regarding the steps or stages involved in successful creativity. On further examination, these perspectives have much in common. Accordingly, we believe the following five-stage approach captures the essence of all of them.

The process begins with a problem or question or challenge. What is labeled "preparation" is a stage where the individual attempts to define the problem, gather information, and look for the right answer. Too often, people jump in looking for the solution without really understanding the real problem or question. In many instances, the different individuals in a work group think they are all solving the same problem, but because of their differing interpretations and assumptions, they are effectively solving different problems. This is why Hirchberg (1998) suggests that an individual must first ask creative questions before coming up with creative answers. He encourages questions that are surprising, provocative, destabilizing, that emanate from skewed vantage points, and that open new routes to a subject. The most simple questions can serve to get around constraining assumptions and help the employee get to the root of the true problem.

As a rule, the creative solution does not simply come. In fact, the route an individual pursues in trying to come up with the solution can become circuitous, confusing, and far removed from the beaten path. It leads to a series of dead ends that seem further and further removed from a viable solution, and the "frustration" stage sets in. This frustration is caused by and magnified by a set of creative blocks, a subject to which we will return shortly. Most people, arriving at the frustration stage, give up or settle for a solution that is rather uncreative and closer to the status quo.

If a person consciously steps away from the problem and puts it on the back burner, he/she is in the "incubation" stage. The individual is, in effect, nonintentionally working on the problem. Further, he/she is either consciously or unconsciously removing some of the key blocks. There may also be more data gathering in this stage, although it also may not be intentional. Insights can be found in

■ **FIGURE 6.1**

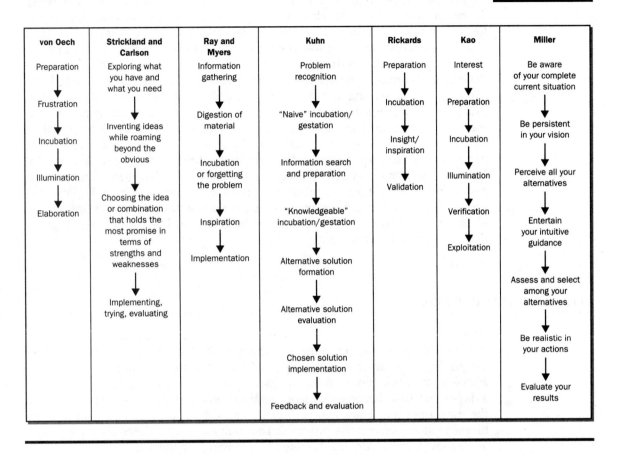

von Oech	Strickland and Carlson	Ray and Myers	Kuhn	Rickards	Kao	Miller
Preparation	Exploring what you have and what you need	Information gathering	Problem recognition	Preparation	Interest	Be aware of your complete current situation
Frustration		Digestion of material	"Naive" incubation/ gestation	Incubation	Preparation	Be persistent in your vision
Incubation	Inventing ideas while roaming beyond the obvious	Incubation or forgetting the problem	Information search and preparation	Insight/ inspiration	Incubation	Perceive all your alternatives
Illumination	Choosing the idea or combination that holds the most promise in terms of strengths and weaknesses	Inspiration	"Knowledgeable" incubation/gestation	Validation	Illumination	Entertain your intuitive guidance
Elaboration		Implementation	Alternative solution formation		Verification	Assess and select among your alternatives
	Implementing, trying, evaluating		Alternative solution evaluation		Exploitation	Be realistic in your actions
			Chosen solution implementation			Evaluate your results
			Feedback and evaluation			

areas, pursuits, or activities that are far afield of the actual problem and may be quite removed from the person's own background or field of expertise.

The employee next sees a ray of light, a thread, or a piece of a possible solution. There may be an "aha" moment. This stage, called "illumination," involves the employee's coming up with the outline or core of an answer. The answer often needs to be refined, adapted, expanded, tested, and further revised. Not only are there likely to be pragmatic problems in actually applying the solution, but the employee also has to make changes as he/she tries to sell the idea to management. This is the stage of "elaboration."

Of course, the process is usually not as linear as it might sound. There could be points of incubation throughout, with some of them lasting quite long and some being very short. There may be feedback loops, where an insight at one point leads the employee to discard a principle or assumption made at an earlier point, suggesting a need to go back and move in a direction that was earlier rejected. There may also be little "eurekas" along the way, and these may come together to form an overall solution, rather than a single big eureka in the illumination stage.

As an employee moves through the creative process, it is also helpful to think of the stages in terms of divergence and convergence (Leonard and Swap 1999). Divergence is breaking from familiar, established ways of seeing and doing. It is a concern with generating lots of options and truly novel ideas, regardless of their practicality. Convergence is the achievement of some agreement regarding the merits of a given idea and the value in pursuing that idea. It is a reality check in terms of the implementation issues. Individuals or groups go back and forth from divergence to convergence when they are successfully managing their creativity. Effective creativity requires balance, or equal time, for divergence and convergence. In fact, the failure to produce highly creative answers may be linked to groups that either spend too much time generating and discussing options, or, alternatively, devote most of their effort to taking an idea to task and arguing detailed implementation issues.

THE CREATIVE BLOCKS

People do not need to be creative for most of what they do in a given day. In fact, they develop patterns and routines without which their lives would be in chaos. They then adopt attitudes that are consistent with maintaining the status quo. However, the same type of thinking that allows a person to function efficiently on a day-to-day basis becomes a major constraint when trying to be creative. That is, the guidelines and rules people find so valuable in everyday life become the blocks to their own creative potential. The ability to master the creative process on an ongoing basis is very much linked to removing the blocks.

Roger von Oech (1998) argues that there are ten critical blocks to creativity. These are summarized in Table 6.2. In essence, he is arguing that employees are more likely to come up with breakthrough ideas if they look for multiple solutions, are illogical and impractical, break existing rules, are playful and not worried about looking foolish, embrace ambiguity, and recognize that failure is a sign of progress. Two additional blocks are especially relevant for corporate entrepreneurship. People miss creative opportunities because they are too narrow and focused in their jobs. By stating, "That's not my area," possibilities are ignored because they do not fit a person's job description or are outside of a person's education, experiences, and professional field. As von Oech (1998) notes, "It's hard to see the dynamite idea behind you by looking twice as hard in front of you." The key lies in the employee's willingness to look beyond his or her field or job responsibilities; to explore how other disciplines approach similar problems; and to adopt different frames of reference, languages, and assumptions. Creative

THE CREATIVE BLOCKS

■ TABLE 6.2

"The Right Answer"	The fallacy that there is only one correct solution solution to a problem
"That's not logical"	The belief that logic is fine for the development and application of ideas, but stifles creativity
"Be practical"	The tendency to allow practical considerations to kill concepts, halt the search for ideas, and deter us from considering alternative solutions
"Follow the rules"	Ignoring the fact that most revolutionary ideas are disruptive violations of existing systems and beliefs
"Avoid ambiguity"	Strict adherence to one fixed perspective on a situation
"To err is wrong"	Failure to see the connection between error and innovation: when you fail, you learn what doesn't work and can adjust
"Play is frivolous"	Unwillingness to acknowledge the creative power of play
"That's not my area"	Restriction of creativity through thinking that is overly narrow and focussed
"Don't be foolish"	Unwillingness to think unconventionally out of fear of appearing foolish
"I'm not creative"	The worst of the blocks: self-condemnation that trumps talent, opportunity, and intelligence

SOURCE: Adapted from von Oech, R. 1998. *A Whack on the Side of the Head.* New York: Warner Books.

individuals are explorers, looking in other areas for ideas. They find history in a hardware store or fashion in a steel factory. They indulge hobbies and read publications in diverse fields and then bring all of this to bear on job-related challenges. Lastly, the worst of the blocks is the "I'm not creative" one. A difference between people who are consistently creative and those who are not is that the former think of themselves as creative, while the latter assume they are not. The latter come to depend on the former any time a creative solution is needed. The objective evidence suggests that we are all rich in creative potential, regardless of what we believe about ourselves.

Where do these blocks to creativity originate? Consider three sources. As the discussion above makes clear, employees impose the blocks on themselves based on their own perceptions. Second, fellow employees impose them on their coworkers. Refrains such as "That's not your job," "Don't be foolish," and "That's not logical" are commonly heard in team meetings, planning sessions, and hallway conversations. Even where the employee does not actually hear such phrases, he/she perceives a need not to look foolish or step beyond his/her job responsibilities in front of coworkers. Finally, the workplace itself is a source of blocks. Certain companies may not tolerate failure, may penalize rule bending or breaking, or may assign people to jobs with extremely narrow job descriptions. A host of variables that characterize the internal environment come into play, variables that we will examine in greater depth in Part III of this book.

THE CREATIVE EMPLOYEE:
PROBLEM-SOLVING STYLES

Although there is latent creativity in every employee of a company, people are not all creative in the same way. They have different thinking or cognitive styles. A very popular way to label these styles involves distinguishing individuals based on whether they are "left-brained" or "right-brained." The left-brained thinker arrives at solutions through a more analytical, logical, sequential approach to problem solving. The right-brained thinker relies more on an intuitive, values-based, nonlinear approach to framing and solving a problem. The cognitive styles of people can also be reflected in work styles and decision-making activities, including a person's preference for working with others versus alone, learning about something versus experiencing that something, and making quick decisions versus generating lots of options no matter how urgent the matter at hand.

A more comprehensive view of thinking styles, or what some have called "brain operating systems" (Hall 1995) grows out of the work of Ned Hermann over the past twenty-five years. He posits a model that groups thinking styles into the following four categories:

1. *Thinking Style A:* Intuitive, rule breaking, imaginative

2. *Thinking Style B:* Logical, fact-based, bottom-line oriented

3. *Thinking Style C:* Organized, planned, detailed

4. *Thinking Style D:* Interpersonal, emotional, people-focused

These styles are summarized in the four quadrants pictured in Figure 6.2. Within each quadrant is a synopsis of the thinking and problem-solving preferences of people who fall into that category. It is possible that individuals use each of the quadrants to varying degrees when doing certain tasks. However, over time, people develop a preference for a particular thinking mode. They develop skills for the types of tasks or methods associated with that thinking mode. None of these four thinking styles is necessarily better than the others. Each is capable of producing significant creativity. The key becomes the nature of the problem and the decision-making context.

A given person's cognitive preferences shape his or her leadership styles and communication patterns. But the people who work for that person or the team members with whom that person must interact can differ significantly in terms of their own cognitive preferences. They process information and solve problems in different ways. The failure to appreciate these differences is often a cause not only of the failure to produce a truly creative solution but also of frustration and conflict. Because one person's style is to gather as much information as possible, absorb it, and then generate a solution does not mean a fellow group member is effective at doing things in the same way.

As a result, thinking styles have important implications for creativity in work environments. People in companies have great ideas all the time, but they often go unheard, get ignored, or are discounted. The problem often lies not with the

■ FIGURE 6.2

EMPLOYEE PROBLEM-SOLVING STYLES
AND THE HERMANN BRAIN DOMINANCE PROFILE

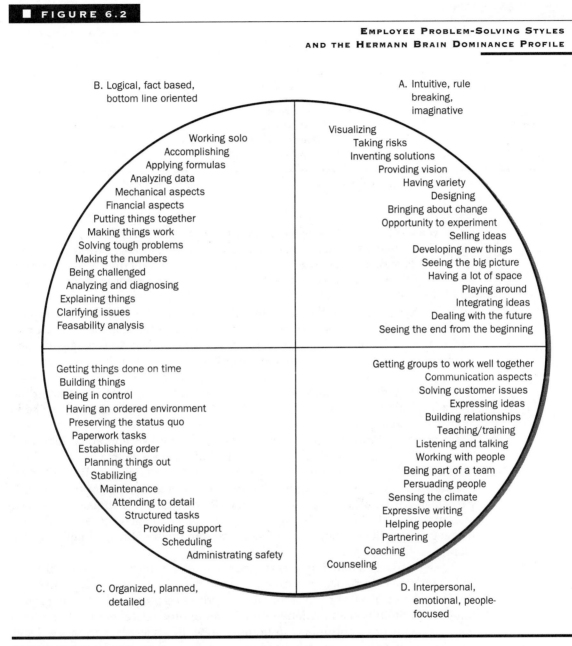

B. Logical, fact based, bottom line oriented

Working solo
Accomplishing
Applying formulas
Analyzing data
Mechanical aspects
Financial aspects
Putting things together
Making things work
Solving tough problems
Making the numbers
Being challenged
Analyzing and diagnosing
Explaining things
Clarifying issues
Feasability analysis

A. Intuitive, rule breaking, imaginative

Visualizing
Taking risks
Inventing solutions
Providing vision
Having variety
Designing
Bringing about change
Opportunity to experiment
Selling ideas
Developing new things
Seeing the big picture
Having a lot of space
Playing around
Integrating ideas
Dealing with the future
Seeing the end from the beginning

Getting things done on time
Building things
Being in control
Having an ordered environment
Preserving the status quo
Paperwork tasks
Establishing order
Planning things out
Stabilizing
Maintenance
Attending to detail
Structured tasks
Providing support
Scheduling
Administrating safety

Getting groups to work well together
Communication aspects
Solving customer issues
Expressing ideas
Building relationships
Teaching/training
Listening and talking
Working with people
Being part of a team
Persuading people
Sensing the climate
Expressive writing
Helping people
Partnering
Coaching
Counseling

C. Organized, planned, detailed

D. Interpersonal, emotional, people-focused

SOURCE: Ned Herrman Group.

■ **TABLE 6.3**

LINKING STAGES IN THE PROCESS TO PROBLEM-SOLVING APPROACHES

Creativity Stage	Activity	Psychological Style
Interest	Environmental scanning	Intuition/emotion
Preparation	Preparing the expedition	Details/planning
Incubation	"Mulling things over"	Intuition
Illumination	The "eureka" experience	Intuition
Verification	Market research	Details/rationality
Exploitation	Captain of industry	Details/rationality

SOURCE: Kao, J. J. 1989. *Entrepreneurship, Creativity and Organization.* Englewood Cliffs: Prentice-Hall.

employee's idea or creative vision; rather, it may be that his/her thinking or cognitive style differs from that of his/her boss or coworkers. People are judging both the methods someone uses to get to an idea and the idea itself from the unique perspective of their own thinking style. Similarly, when an employee is trying to sell an idea to someone within the organization, presenting it in a manner consistent with the thinking style of the recipient can be instrumental in obtaining support.

The implications for management are also considerable. A manager must recognize that different people have different thinking styles. Accordingly, he/she purposely designs a full range of approaches and perspectives into the organization, unit, or department. While insisting that cognitively diverse employees must respect one another's thinking styles, the manager is purposely trying to foster the collision of ideas, frames of reference, assumptions, and approaches. He/she is actively managing those collisions.

Consider the formation of two work teams. One consists entirely of individuals who utilize Thinking Style A. Another includes people with all four thinking styles. Will one group be more creative? Research from the Eureka Ranch (1998), a leading creativity center, suggests that the "whole brain" group, or the one with participants from all thinking styles, can out-create groups populated with just one thinking style. What is also apparent is that the homogeneous and heterogeneous groups will be creative in different ways and will not respond in a similar manner to the same stimuli.

We can also relate thinking styles to the stages of the creative process. Different skills are more important at particular stages in the process, as suggested in Table 6.3. Here, Kao's (1989) version of the creative process is presented. Thinking styles built around intuition and emotion may be more productive in identifying relevant problems or opportunities to undertake, while styles that prioritize detail and rationality will be especially good in the verification and exploitation of a creative concept. To the extent that these inferences hold true in a corporate context, they reinforce the value of work groups with diverse thinking styles.

Table 6.3 also indicates that critical activities occur in each stage of the creative process, such as information search and environmental scanning in the first stages

■ FIGURE 6.3

THE CREATIVE PROCESS: RELEVANT ROLES

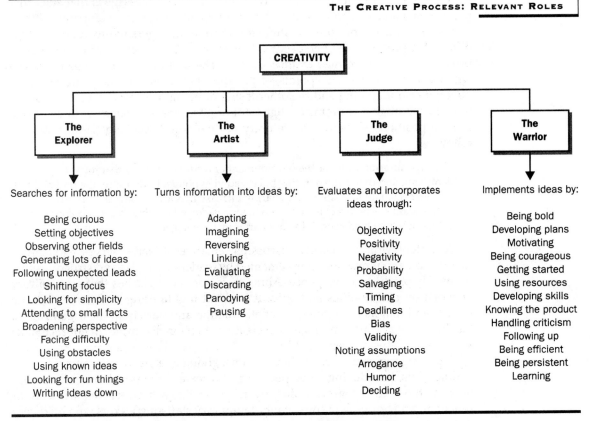

SOURCE: von Oech, R. 1986. *A Kick in the Seat of the Pants.* New York: Harper and Row.

and doing market research in the verification stage. Consistent with the changing activities that require attention is the notion that the role of the individual changes as the creative process unfolds. Different roles require unique skill sets (Figure 6.3). For instance, von Oech (1986) stresses the need to be an explorer when searching for new insights and perspectives, an artist when turning resources into new ideas, a judge when assessing the merits of a concept, and a warrior when attempting to achieve organizational acceptance and implement the idea.

THE NEED FOR FRICTION

Creativity involves a paradox. In an era where considerable attention is devoted to the need in organizations for teamwork, cooperation, consensus, and conflict avoidance, it may be that companies also need to highlight differences. On the one hand, creative organizations demonstrate great teamwork and collaboration. On the other hand, they feature diversity and friction. The message is that such friction can be good. Collisions are a vibrant source of energy in a company.

The fostering of entrepreneurship requires that managers figure out how to get different approaches and perspectives to grate against one another in a productive process that can be termed *creative abrasion*. The point is not to create a scenario where colliding ideas, viewpoints, or priorities battle one another, with one winning out or dominating and the other losing or being discarded. Nor is the objective to encourage compromise, alignment of positions, or watering down of one or both positions so as to achieve unity of direction. Hischberg (1998) notes the following:

> "Creative abrasion calls for the development of leadership styles that focus on first identifying and then incorporating polarized viewpoints. In doing so, the probabilities for unexpected juxtapositions are sharply increased, as are the levels of mutual understanding. The irony is that out of a process keyed on abrasiveness, a corporate culture of heightened sensitivity and harmony is achieved."

Consistent with the earlier discussion, creative abrasion serves to facilitate divergence, and it must be complemented by leadership styles and structures that ultimately produce convergence. Abrasion is not about clashes that are arbitrary or based on personalities and egos. It is about highlighting differences that are natural and that increase the level of stimulation and variety in the organization. Further, there are different degrees of creative abrasion. Examples of efforts to take advantage of this concept could include hiring people who are not like current staff; putting together interfunctional teams; giving a team two seemingly incompatible goals; introducing a perspective that threatens the positions and assumptions of those in the group; blurring responsibilities between departments or functions; and bringing in consultants, temporary staff, or speakers who hold very different points of view. Management of abrasion is an art. It requires patience and a sense of when to let the friction run its course and when to interfere so as to avoid permanent dead ends.

CREATIVITY TECHNIQUES AND CREATIVE QUALITY

A treasure trove of techniques and methods are available for use at different stages in the creative process. Techniques exist for generating creative concepts and ideas (e.g., brainstorming, role playing, mind mapping), techniques for overcoming negativity (the "yes and" rather than "yes but" rule, which states that concerns about new ideas must be phrased in ways that find the positive in them), and techniques for reaching convergence (e.g., backcasting, or imagining future scenarios and backing up to the present). The list is virtually endless as can be seen in such books as Michalko's *Thinkertoys* (1991), Hall's *Jump Start Your Brain* (1995), or Rickard's *Creativity at Work* (1988). Table 6.4 provides a few examples.

■ **TABLE 6.4**

EXAMPLES OF CREATIVE PROBLEM-SOLVING TECHNIQUES

- Brainstorming
- Reverse Brainstorming
- Mind Mapping
- Lateral Thinking Techniques
- Synetics
- Gordon Method
- Force Fit Technique
- Checklist Method
- Free Association
- Forced Relationships
- Collective Notebook Method
- Knight's Move Thinking
- Heuristics
- Scientific Method
- Kepner-Tregoe Method
- Value Analysis
- Attribute Listing Method
- Morphological Analysis
- Perceptual Mapping
- Matrix Charting
- Sequence-Attribute/Modification Matrix
- Inspired (Big Dream) Approach
- Parameter Analysis

SOURCE: Adapted from Hisrich, R. D., and M. Peters. 1998. *Entrepreneurship*. Burr Ridge: Irwin McGraw-Hill.

The value of these techniques and exercises is likely to vary based on an employee's thinking or problem-solving style. People with a particular thinking style (see the quadrants in Figure 6.1) may respond more to certain techniques or stimuli than will those who have a different thinking style.

The purpose of these types of exercises and techniques and the reason for approaching creativity in a more systematic manner is to improve the quality of the creative output. In fact, producing a higher *quantity* of creative ideas is not of much value unless the end result is higher *quality* in terms of the ultimate concept or solution. This is an important point. While creativity itself is not something an employee can see or feel or touch, the quality of an individual's or group's creativity can be judged. Although many criteria are available for judging creativity, a good beginning point is to consider the following three standards:

1. *Overt benefit*—to what extent does the idea or concept convey a clear benefit or advantage to a user or customer? In what ways does it create value, and how much value is being created?

2. *Reason to believe*—what supporting evidence is the employee able to provide, and is a user or customer likely to accept that the concept or idea will deliver the same level of benefits that the employee claims?

3. *Dramatic difference*—how unique or different is the employee's concept or idea from current or conventional solutions? Is it an incremental or breakthrough advance? Can it be meaningfully differentiated from existing solutions on a sustainable basis?

Although creativity will always be an art, organizations need not view it as unmanageable. There is a role for structure, standards, expectations, and measures of performance. Clearly, creativity often happens inadvertently, and employees are frequently not conscious of the fact that they are being creative. Even so, their creative productivity is apt to be enhanced when they recognize the many ways in which they are currently creative, understand their own immense creative potential, and adopt systematic approaches for tapping that potential.

SUMMARY AND CONCLUSIONS

Creativity is the foundation upon which entrepreneurship is built. The corporate entrepreneur requires creative solutions to an array of challenges and obstacles as a concept goes from conceptualization to implementation. In the end, entrepreneurship in larger organizations cannot happen without technical creativity, political creativity, resource creativity, marketing creativity, and more.

Creativity in organizations is about destruction and construction. It requires the abandonment of certain assumptions, the rejection of accepted precepts, and the elimination of established methods. It also results in concepts or solutions that can disrupt the work lives of people in companies, making them break out of patterns and comfort zones. But creativity also brings with it a fresh start, a new way, a freedom from the constraints of what was, and a path to what can be. It is a manifestation of the human spirit, such that the act of successful creativity is by itself a tremendous source of employee motivation and pride. To create is to matter, to count, to make a difference, to have an impact, and to be a source of value.

Employees are creative without knowing it, and many creative things they do happen on the spur of the moment. Yet, the employee's ability to be a continued source of creative contribution is tied to an understanding of a) a person's own immense creative potential; b) a recognition of the many ways in which he or she is and can be creative; c) an appreciation for his or her own thinking or problem-solving style; d) a recognition of the different thinking styles of those with whom he or she works and to whom he or she reports; and e) an understanding of the nature of the creative process and some of the techniques for facilitating the mastery of that process time and time again.

Corporate entrepreneurs operate in differing capacities within an organization. The challenges of successful creativity are likely to vary depending upon the particular role the corporate entrepreneur is playing. Figure 6.4 provides a synopsis of the different challenges confronting the creative entrepreneur when he or she is in the position of subordinate, team member, manager, and founder/CEO. What becomes evident from each of the boxes in Figure 6.4 is that while creativity should be the oil that lubricates an organization and allows it to move in new directions, in many companies it is treated as a foreign substance that will disrupt the workings of the firm's motor.

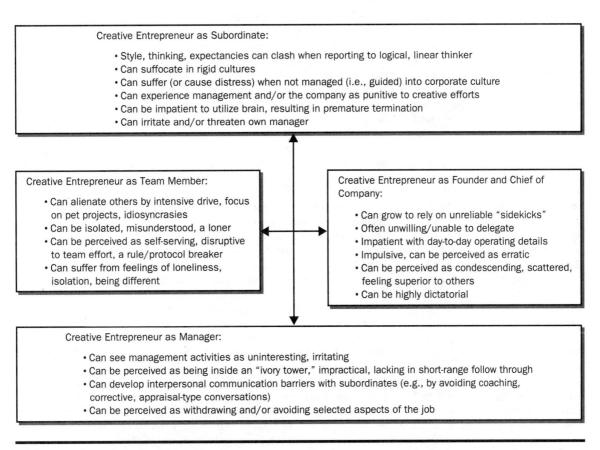

■ **FIGURE 6.4**

COMMON CHALLENGES FACING THE CREATIVE CORPORATE ENTREPRENEUR

Creative Entrepreneur as Subordinate:

• Style, thinking, expectancies can clash when reporting to logical, linear thinker
• Can suffocate in rigid cultures
• Can suffer (or cause distress) when not managed (i.e., guided) into corporate culture
• Can experience management and/or the company as punitive to creative efforts
• Can be impatient to utilize brain, resulting in premature termination
• Can irritate and/or threaten own manager

Creative Entrepreneur as Team Member:

• Can alienate others by intensive drive, focus on pet projects, idiosyncrasies
• Can be isolated, misunderstood, a loner
• Can be perceived as self-serving, disruptive to team effort, a rule/protocol breaker
• Can suffer from feelings of loneliness, isolation, being different

Creative Entrepreneur as Founder and Chief of Company:

• Can grow to rely on unreliable "sidekicks"
• Often unwilling/unable to delegate
• Impatient with day-to-day operating details
• Impulsive, can be perceived as erratic
• Can be perceived as condescending, scattered, feeling superior to others
• Can be highly dictatorial

Creative Entrepreneur as Manager:

• Can see management activities as uninteresting, irritating
• Can be perceived as being inside an "ivory tower," impractical, lacking in short-range follow through
• Can develop interpersonal communication barriers with subordinates (e.g., by avoiding coaching, corrective, appraisal-type conversations)
• Can be perceived as withdrawing and/or avoiding selected aspects of the job

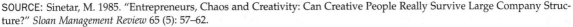

SOURCE: Sinetar, M. 1985. "Entrepreneurs, Chaos and Creativity: Can Creative People Really Survive Large Company Structure?" *Sloan Management Review* 65 (5): 57–62.

Organizations tend to be insensitive to the nuances and idiosyncrasies of the individual who is attempting to be creative. While there are many things a company can do to encourage and support this individual, the ultimate issue is one of freedom (Sinetar 1985). The creative employee seeks freedom in the general area of his or her work and the way in which the work gets done. He or she seeks freedom to ask novel or disturbing questions. Most fundamentally, he or she seeks freedom to develop unusual solutions to the problems and opportunities confronted by the organization.

How Does Disney Do It?

Just as some companies fear losing their employees if the creative spark hits them, others are secure enough to encourage creative thinking, free association, and the complete reconfiguration of a project. Such is the case at the Disney Corporation, arguably the most creative organization in the world. Michael Eisner and his team of executives, artists, and "imagineers" continually amaze the public with new parks; cruise ship vacations; media productions; and an extensive, interactive, visually pleasing Web site. Four new parks, in California, Tokyo, Paris, and Hong Kong, will open by 2005.

Three times per year at Disney, any employee can pitch an animated film idea to Eisner and three other vice presidents during the *Gong Show*. To ensure that even the most meek and mild get a chance at expressing their creativity, coworkers are utilized to help fine-tune presentations and give live action support if necessary. The executive team listens to an average of forty ideas each session and makes it a point to give immediate feedback, whether good or bad. Peter Schneider, president of feature animation in

the '90s and current chairman of Walt Disney Studios, emphasized the importance of telling the presenters why their ideas will or will not work. "We don't pull our punches. If you do that enough and people don't get fired or demoted, they begin to understand that no matter how good, bad, or indifferent the idea, it can be expressed, accepted, and thought about." The box-office hit, *Hercules,* was a result of the *Gong Show*. The employee's original story line didn't make it into production, but he still received what Schneider referred to as a "first treatment" — a very generous cash reward with payments spread out between idea inception and the release of the movie.

Once a movie is in production, the environment of employee-driven decisions still reigns. According to Schneider, the only management intervention is in setting the deadlines and budget. With those parameters in place, the directors and imagineers are free to do whatever it takes to get it done. Seventy-five percent of the time, this method works wonders. The directors are allowed to pick their crew — enough of an

incentive for employees to give any project their best effort.

Disney employees' creative energy is also fueled by the fact they not only can be themselves but also can feel appreciated and valued. For a company that is so closely involved with its customers on all levels and in all divisions, it only makes sense that the top brass associate with the individuals that make everything happen. On one occasion, a ping-pong tournament found Michael Eisner and hourly artists playing together during lunch hours. The structure at Disney is so employee-friendly that the low person on the totem pole didn't let Eisner win.

Revenues for the Disney Corporation totaled $25.4 billion for the fiscal year 2000, with $4 billion being retained as operating income. Disney has 2 billion shares of common stock outstanding, with no single person or group as the beneficial owner of more than 5 percent of either class of the common stock.

SOURCE: McGowan, Joe. 1996. "How Disney Keeps Ideas Coming." *Fortune* 133 (April): 131–134.

REFERENCES

Amabile, T. 1998. "How to Kill Creativity," *Harvard Business Review.* 76 (September–October): 77–87.

Eureka Ranch. 1998. *The Value of Thinking Styles.* Workshop Manual. Cincinnati: Richard Saunders International.

Hall, D. 1995. *Jump Start Your Brain.* New York: Warner Books.

Hirshberg, J. 1998. *The Creative Priority.* New York: Harper Books.

Kao, J. J. 1989. *Entrepreneurship, Creativity and Organization*. Englewood Cliffs: Prentice- Hall.

Leonard, D., and S. Straus. 1997. "Putting the Company's Whole Brain to Work," *Harvard Business Review* 75 (July–August): 111–121.

Leonard, D., and W. Swap. 1999. *When Sparks Fly*. Boston: Harvard Business School.

Michalko, M. 1991. *Thinkertoys*. (Berkeley, CA: Ten Speed Press)

Miller, W. C. 1999. *Flash of Brilliance*. Reading: Perseus Books.

Rickards, T. 1988. *Creativity at Work*. Brookfield: Gower Publishing.

Sinetar, M. 1985. "Entrepreneurs, Chaos and Creativity: Can Creative People Really Survive Large Company Structure?" *Sloan Management Review* 65 (5): 57–62.

von Oech, R. 1986. *A Kick in the Seat of the Pants*. New York: Harper and Row.

von Oech, R. 1998. *A Whack on the Side of the Head*. New York: Warner Books.

PRODUCT INNOVATION, TECHNOLOGY, AND THE CORPORATION

THE PRESSURE TO INNOVATE

Creativity leads to innovation, and entrepreneurship drives the process — from the first ray of creative light through to commercialization and harvesting. To innovate is to introduce within a company or marketplace new methods, processes, technologies, products, or services. Simply put, an innovation is a new way of doing something. And as we saw in Chapter 3, innovativeness is one of the three underlying dimensions of entrepreneurship. It occurs in varying degrees, ranging from new-to-the-world products or services to minor improvements or new applications of an existing product or process.

Companies today find that they must innovate more than in times past. Much of the pressure to innovate is due to external forces, including the emergence of new and improved technologies, the globalization of markets (resulting in intensified competitive pressures), the fragmentation of markets (resulting in intensified customer pressures), government deregulation, and dramatic social change. Financial markets are also penalizing companies that fail to demonstrate an effective innovation strategy. However, internal pressures exist as well. One of the great challenges facing companies in the 21st century concerns the ability to attract and retain high-quality employees. Employees are attracted to companies that are experimenting, trying new things, and continually learning.

The push for more innovation manifests itself in a variety ways. The most obvious manifestation is an increase in the number of innovation projects underway within a company at a given point in time. We will expand on this pattern later when the concept of the innovation portfolio is introduced. Coupled with this is an increase in the number of new products and services launched each year. Companies are also finding they must become faster, facing pressures to significantly reduce the time from idea generation to product launch. The ability to do so, and to produce products and services the market will accept, increasingly requires that more departments and functional areas within the firm get heavily involved in the innovation process. All of this suggests greater resource commitment, including people, money, time, facilities, and equipment. In fact, the innovation dynamic taking place within firms is such that the winners in any industry over the next five years will be those firms whose product portfolios are 30 percent bigger and whose spending on innovation is 50 percent greater than it is today. Further, as much as 40 percent of their revenues will be coming from products and services that they do not currently sell.

Less clear is the impact of heightened innovation activity on success rates. On the one hand, companies might expect that the more they innovate, the better they get at it. Correspondingly, the ratio of new concepts generated to actual products launched should go down, while the financial performance of the products that are launched should improve. On the other hand, more activity means the company is increasingly moving into territory (i.e., technologies, markets, distribution approaches) with which it is unfamiliar, making failures more probable. In addition, companies are likely to find innovation activity increasing in most firms. This means more products get introduced than markets can sustain, again pushing up the failure rate.

It is our opinion that the second scenario is more likely. Firms must prepare to experience more failure, not less. But failures on individual projects in an environment of continued innovation, adaptation, and learning will spell greater overall success for the firm. And as we shall see in this chapter, the issue is not simply a question of how much innovation activity takes place within the firm. Far more important is the way a firm manages the complexities and ambiguities that surround innovation.

INNOVATION CREATES DILEMMAS

If innovation were simple or cheap, companies would do a lot more of it. The irony is that companies actually resist something that is so vital to their futures. For too many firms, the tendency is to innovate only when they are in trouble or in response to a competitor's move. Some of this tendency can be traced to the adage "If it ain't broke, don't fix it," so managers focus their efforts on maximizing the success of proven products and services in the face of immediate competitive threats. Innovation is about tomorrow, and managers are concerned with the here and now. But at a deeper level, innovation is an activity that challenges many of the basic principles of management.

Consider the expression *management of innovation*. It might be construed as an oxymoron, or contradiction in terms. *Management* implies control, while *innovation* is about the unknown and is often unpredictable. How does a manager control the

■ **TABLE 7.1**

SIXTEEN DILEMMAS OF INNOVATION

1. Not all entrepreneurs are innovators, and not all innovators are entrepreneurs, but successful entrepreneurship tends to involve continued innovation (in products, services, and processes/methods).

2. Innovation is about the unknown. Management is about control. How do you control the unknown?

3. Innovation is about breaking the rules. People who break rules don't last long in organizations.

4. Successful innovation tends to occur when there are constraints, routines, and deadlines. There is a need for both freedom and discipline, and the issue is one of balance.

5. Failure is likely if the firm does not innovate. But the more the firm innovates, the more it fails.

6. An innovation succeeds because it addresses customer needs. Yet, when you ask customers about their needs, many do not know or cannot describe them to you except in very general terms.

7. Innovating is risky. Not innovating can be more risky. Innovating more actually reduces risks.

8. Innovation can be revolutionary or evolutionary. The costs, risks, and returns of both types differ, and both require different structures and management styles.

9. A company that innovates is frequently making its own products obsolete when there was still profit potential in those products.

10. Innovation requires supporting infrastructure to be successful, and the existing infrastructure is often inadequate. However, these infrastructure needs may not become apparent until after the innovation is developed.

11. While innovation is more technically complex and costly today, most breakthrough innovation does not come from large companies or corporate R&D labs with sizeable budgets, but from individual inventors and entrepreneurs.

12. People who design innovations typically seek to perfect their new product or service, making it the best possible. But the marketplace wants it to be "good enough," not perfect. The additional time and money necessary to make the innovation "best possible" drive up prices beyond what the customer will pay and result in missed opportunity.

13. Technology-driven innovation leads to dramatic new products that prove to be "better mousetraps" nobody wants. Customer-driven innovation leads to minor modifications to existing products or "me-too" products meeting a competitive brick wall.

14. While typically associated with genius or brilliance, innovation is more often a function of persistence.

15. While innovation is associated with breaking the rules of the game (e.g., 3-M), it frequently entails playing an entirely different game (e.g., Starbucks, Deli).

16. Being first to market is not consistently associated with success, while being second or third is not consistently associated with failure.

unknown? Quite simply, he or she does not. While this does not mean innovation cannot be managed, it does suggest that traditional approaches to management may not apply. In fact, innovations represent departures from the past, meaning they often break with established rules and challenge traditional ways of thinking and doing. Further, the corporate entrepreneur must break rules to accomplish innovation in most firms. This creates a dilemma, in that employees who regularly break rules typically do not last long in most companies.

The reality is that innovation poses a large number of dilemmas for corporate managers, as illustrated in Table 7.1. While creating the new, innovations make existing products obsolete, including possibly some of the company's own successful products. Because of this and the tendency for new products to receive a larger share of production, marketing, and distribution resources, many inside the firm have an incentive to resist innovation. Another dilemma considers the extent to which the firm is first to market. There is a first mover advantage in most markets, but the first mover also frequently makes the most critical mistakes. The firm that is reasonably quick, but a second or third mover has a chance of ultimately being the winner. The evidence is quite mixed with regard to which firms will ultimately succeed or fail in a new product category.

There is also the dilemma of control. Innovation works because employees are given a level of freedom, autonomy, and discretion. That is, there is a degree of flexibility in terms of rules, controls, and processes. At the same time, successful innovation often occurs where there is pressure, deadlines, routines, and operating constraints. In fact, breakthroughs often do not come from large research laboratories with sizeable budgets, but from individuals and smaller entrepreneurial units operating under much tougher limitations.

TYPES OF INNOVATION AND THE RISK FACTOR

An additional dilemma concerns the relationship between innovation and risk. To appreciate this relationship, it is important to first establish the different types of innovation. A distinction can be drawn among four innovation types, as follows:

Discontinuous innovation—a breakthrough innovation. It usually results in products or services that address a need that has not been addressed before or that change the way customers go about addressing a need. The integrated circuit, cellular telephone, and microwave oven were discontinuous innovations when they were first introduced.

Dynamically continuous innovation—a dramatic improvement over the existing state-of-the art solution. It is not as disruptive to buyer behavior as discontinuous innovation. The first electric toothbrush and laptop computer represent examples.

Continuous innovation—incremental or step-at-a-time innovation. With this type of innovation, performance of an existing product is enhanced, new features or options are added, and/or new applications are developed. Making a lightbulb burn for an extra 100 hours, adding a new flavor to a line of soft drinks, or adding a safety feature to a machine tool would represent continuous innovation.

Imitation—copying, adapting, or mimicking the innovations of other firms. If Kodak successfully introduces a new type of film for use in general photography, it is likely that Fuji will be forced to introduce its version of the same thing.

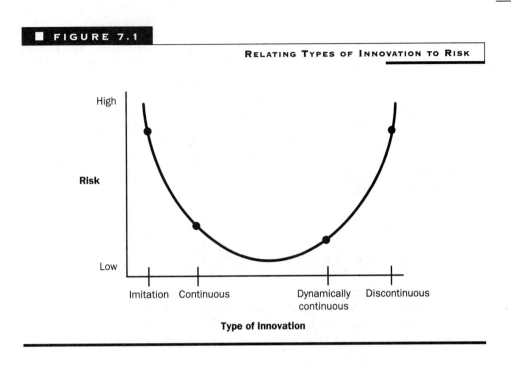

■ FIGURE 7.1

RELATING TYPES OF INNOVATION TO RISK

Type of Innovation

Companies tend to devote most of their resources toward continuous innovation and imitation. On the surface, this would seem to be a prudent risk-management strategy. That is, it might be postulated that risk is highest with discontinuous innovation and steadily declines as a company moves down the list toward imitation. However, this is not the case. As Figure 7.1 suggests, the risk equation is U-shaped, with high levels of risk both at the imitation and discontinuous innovation ends of the continuum.

The company that innovates only in response to the moves of other firms and pursues an imitation strategy is incurring high risk principally because of the nature of the contemporary business environment. With the pace of technological and marketplace change, the imitative company is apt to miss out on entire market opportunities by the time it is able to respond to an innovative new product or service. When the firm does move, it finds its role to be that of niche player in the marketplace. It also becomes harder and harder to catch up as innovative competitors move from incremental advances in a current technology to a major advance using a new technology. Meanwhile, new competitors emerge from other industries to attack the firm's most profitable lines of business with innovative marketing, distribution, and customer service approaches.

At the same time, firms that engage in breakthrough innovation are often moving into uncharted waters where no one has been before. Consequently, there is high risk of market failure through improper market analysis, mismatch of technology to market needs, or inadequate design of marketing programs. In many instances, the window of opportunity has yet to open, and the firm is too early.

Sometimes the requisite infrastructure to support the innovation, including logistical systems and service networks, is inadequate. In still other cases, the firm is unable to penetrate the market beyond the so-called innovators and early adopters because the value package represented by a new product or service fails to have general market appeal.

In the middle of the continuum, risks are more moderate. The firm is continually improving existing products and discovering new market applications, while also adding new products to its product mix that represent significant advances in the current state-of-the-art product. Further, and as we saw in Chapter 3, risk is managed not by pursuing less innovation, but by innovating more and by innovating more intelligently.

WINNERS: COMPANIES THAT INNOVATE WELL

A number of researchers have attempted to characterize the best practices of companies that seem to be especially good at innovation. That is, what are the things that these firms do that seem to make a difference? Let us consider three perspectives.

Synectics, a leading international firm specializing in innovation consulting, studied the innovation practices and performance of 150 major U.S. companies (Synectics 1993). The analysis produced the following three categories of firms: Stars, Seekers, and Spectators. The Stars were high-performing companies that had successfully integrated innovation and creativity into their daily business practices. Seekers were companies that displayed a number of appropriate innovation practices but came up short in terms of innovation performance and companywide commitment to innovation. Spectators tended to acknowledge the importance of innovation but provided little support for it. They shunned formal programs for innovation and were reluctant to seek outside ideas and perspectives.

The Stars had a number of characteristics that distinguished them from the other two groups, and Synectics concluded that a number of them were critical for sustained innovation. These characteristics included the following:

- Having CEO's that were heavily involved in fostering innovation;
- Defining innovation as critical to long-term company success;
- Attaching great importance to the concept of managing change;
- Having the words *innovation* and *creativity* in their mission statements;
- Demonstrating an openness to outside ideas;
- Having formal programs for idea generation and problem solving;
- Placing strong emphasis on cross-function communications;
- Implementing programs to encourage employees to talk to customers;
- Increasing levels of investment in R&D and a strong focus on product development;

■ **TABLE 7.2**

FINDINGS OF THE **PDMA** BEST INNOVATION PRACTICES STUDY

In one of the major benchmarking studies of corporate innovation in American companies, the Product Development Management Association (PDMA) surveyed 189 large companies that are active innovators. Below are some of their more notable findings:

1. Over 76 percent of the responding companies now use multidisciplinary teams to develop new products.
2. Only 56.4 percent of the companies have a specific new product strategy; only 54.5 percent have a well-defined new product development process; 32.8 percent still had neither one!
3. It takes the average company in the study 2.95 years to develop innovative types of new products.
4. Formal financial criteria to measure the performance of new products are developed by 76 percent of the companies.
5. Having insufficient resources is the most frequently mentioned obstacle to successful product development.
6. Companies are developing one successful new product for every eleven new product ideas or concepts they consider.
7. Over a recent five-year period, the companies introduced an average of 37.5 new products, whereas the median was 12. These figures are expected to increase to 45 and 20, respectively, during the next five-year period.
8. The companies achieved a success rate of 58 percent of the products they introduced during the recent five-year period.
9. The companies spent 52 percent of their new product expenditures on new products that were financially successful.
10. In 1990, 32 percent of company sales came from new products introduced during the previous five years. In 1995, the respondents expect that 38 percent will come from new products introduced during the 1990–1995 period.

SOURCE: Page, A. L. 1993. "Assessing New Product Development Practices and Performance: Establishing Crucial Norms," *Journal of Product Innovation Management* 10: 273–290.

■ Creating budgets allocated exclusively to innovation;
■ Providing rewards for individual creativity and innovation;
■ Spending time in meetings that were highly productive.

The companies that were Stars also tended to outperform the other firms not only in terms of sales and profit growth but also in such areas as employee satisfaction, employee retention, and product/service quality.

A separate study was conducted under the auspices of the Product Development and Management Association (Page 1993). Their "Best Practices Survey" attempted to establish norms across companies in the new product development area. Table 7.2 highlights some of the key findings. Among other insights, their results indicated a tendency to have a formal innovation strategy, rely heavily on cross-functional teams, and use formal criteria to measure new product performance. Additional noteworthy findings included the fact that firms anticipated on average that they would introduce twenty new products over the next five years, while the new product success rate approximated 58 percent (see also Table 7.3).

■ TABLE 7.3

SUCCESS RATES FOR CORPORATE INNOVATION

	Success Rate[1]	% Profit Success[2]	NP Sales %[3]	NP Profit %[4]
Full sample	59.0%	54.6%	32.4%	30.6%
The best	79.8%*	78.0%*	49.2%*	49.2%*
The rest	52.5%*	47.1%*	25.2%*	22.0%*
Product type				
Manufactured goods	59.6%	55.3%	34.0%†	32.4%†
Services	58.2%	52.7%	24.1%†	21.7%†
Technology base				
High tech	60.5%	56.5%	42.3%*	38.8%*
Mixed	60.0%	55.3%	28.7%*	26.9%*
Low tech	55.2%	50.3%	23.7%*	24.5%*
Market served				
Consumer products	58.1%	53.2%	36.2%	32.9%
Mix of both	60.8%	55.2%	24.9%	23.1%
Business to business	58.6%	54.5%	33.4%	32.0%
Annual sales				
≤$24 million	62.3%	56.8%	40.7%*	37.2%*
$25 to $99 million	60.7%	57.4%	33.2%*	35.2%*
$100 to $499 million	60.9%	56.0%	28.6%*	27.6%*
≥$500 million	53.0%	48.9%	23.7%*	18.8%*

[1]*Success Rate:* Percentage of products commercialized in the last five years that were categorized as successes.

[2]*Percentage of profit success:* Percentage of products commercialized in the last five years that were categorized as financial successes.

[3]*NP sales percentage:* Dollar sales of products commercialized in the last five years as a percentage of total sales.

[4]*NP profit percentage:* Dollar profits from products commercialized in the last five years as a percentage of total profits.

*Anova test: $p < 0.01$; †Anova test: $P < 0.05$

SOURCE: Page, A. L. 1993. "Assessing New Product Development Practices and Performance: Establishing Crucial Norms," *Journal of Product Innovation Management* 10: 273–290.

For every eleven ideas that entered the new product development process, one product was successfully launched. Just over half the budget spent on new product development was spent on products that proved to be successful.

A third perspective comes from the anecdotal observations of such respected observers as Gary Hamel (2000), Tom Peters (1997), and Thomas Kuczmarski and colleagues (2001). Based on their consulting interactions with large cross-sections of companies, these authors reinforce many of the findings cited above. They provide other insights as well, such as the tendency for highly innovative companies to manage a portfolio of innovations and to have a systematic and well-defined new product development process. These are customer-centered companies but also employee-centered companies. They take the entire business

■ FIGURE 7.2

INNOVATION AS A LINEAR PROCESS

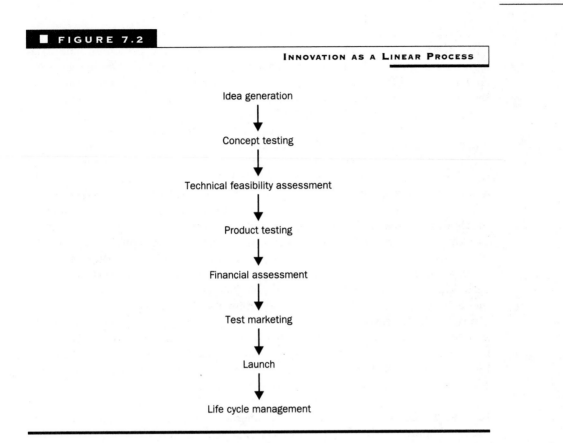

Idea generation

↓

Concept testing

↓

Technical feasibility assessment

↓

Product testing

↓

Financial assessment

↓

Test marketing

↓

Launch

↓

Life cycle management

concept (or value-creating package) as the starting point for innovation, rather than just a product or service. Employees in these firms demonstrate a passion for innovation and a clear focus in terms of the key things they are trying to accomplish with their innovative efforts.

APPROACHES TO INNOVATION: THE PROCESS

Effective management of innovation requires that the firm make two overarching decisions. The first decision concerns the process to be employed by the firm, while the second decision involves the organization or structuring of employees around the process.

The new product or service development process usually does not evolve in a neat, orderly fashion. In fact, there is a certain level of chaos to be found in the most successful of projects. Nonetheless, there are some key steps that generally must be accomplished to produce a commercially viable new product. These are outlined in Figure 7.2.

Ideas for innovations come from a variety of sources, both inside and outside the company. Effective innovators have a system for regularly generating and cataloging ideas, and this includes both active (e.g., patent searches, attending research conferences and trade shows, conducting market research, internal brainstorming sessions) and passive (informal conversations at work, ideas that come to an employee while doing some other task) search efforts. The largest number of ideas are discarded during the screening stage. The company applies a set of evaluative criteria to the ideas and rates them. Of key concern are fit with the company (e.g., skills, capabilities, strategic direction) and fit with the market (e.g., clearly identified need, competitive opening, growth potential). The remaining ideas are next subjected to a concept-testing phase, where a hypothetical product is explained to relevant audiences, including customers, to get their reactions. Potential benefit segments are identified. Focus groups, interviews, and surveys are often used. Business cases are then prepared for the most promising surviving concepts. These concepts, now fairly well defined around some core benefit, must then be transformed into a physical product (or service delivery model) and undergo performance testing. Technical feasibility analysis involves establishing more exact technical requirements for designing and producing the product and ensuring these requirements can be met on a reasonable time and cost schedule. A physical product or service model is engineered, and unit production costs are estimated. Design engineers may conceive different versions of the product (or service delivery system) based on the many trade-off decisions that must be made among product attributes. Next comes technical product or service testing, which subjects the innovation to a rigorous examination of tolerances and performance capabilities under differing circumstances. Products are often placed in customer locations (or beta test sites), and their use is monitored. Profitability analysis is then performed to determine break-even points in terms of the initial investment and rates of return that will be realized based on projected cash flows. To confirm initial sales projections and finalize decisions regarding price, packaging, promotion, and distribution, test marketing is then performed using a representative subset of the intended market. Lastly, market launch efforts have become fairly complex and sophisticated undertakings that are often initiated a year or more before a product or service hits the market. The firm is attempting to successfully penetrate the innovators and early adopters, while laying the ground for penetration of the more general market.

Although a logical evolution of necessary activities, the innovation process is rarely so linear or smooth. It normally involves considerable feedback and requires multiple iterations in accomplishing a given activity. These iterations might involve progress in one area or by one team that then necessitates adjustments in another area, and subsequent progress in the second area then requires new work in the first area. Extensive information must be shared back and forth across the various individuals and units involved in the process. Given these characteristics, many firms have found the "stage-gate" system to be an effective approach to the innovation process.

With the stage-gate system, creative activities that move the project forward are separated from evaluation activities (Figure 7.3). The stages consist of a number of

■ FIGURE 7.3

THE INNOVATION PROCESS AS STAGES AND GATES

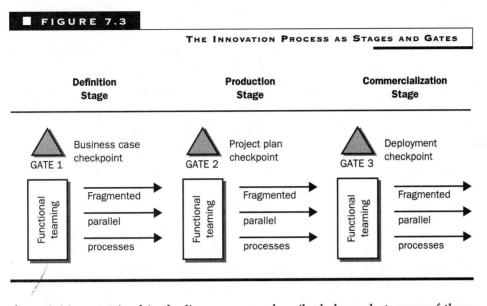

the activities contained in the linear process described above, but many of these activities are done in parallel or extensively overlap one another. Parallel processing demands concurrent problem solving instead of sequential steps, which will result in less recycling and reworking. Thus, in the first stage, idea generation and concept testing may occur in tandem. This stage would then be followed by a gate in which some concepts are eliminated and a decision is made to further invest in certain other concepts, allowing them to move into the next stage. Now, technical work and initial financial analysis may be done and a prototype produced. Then comes an evaluative gate and so forth. Thus, rather than a single major go/no-go decision early in the process, such decisions are made at each gate, meaning a project can be killed right up to the point of launch. The stage-gate system is closer to what firms do in practice, with a typical reliance on from four to six stages, multiple activities in a stage, and a go/no-go decision after each stage.

APPROACHES TO INNOVATION: STRUCTURES TO SUPPORT PROJECTS

Having conceptualized a process to guide innovation efforts, the company must organize people around that process. This can be the more difficult task, for it requires a structure that not only gets the right inputs into the process at the right time, but also one that facilitates both creative abrasion and cross-functional collaboration. The goal is also to get employees to take ownership of a project, getting as many people as possible believing that they invented the product or service.

A host of structural challenges surrounds new product development. Who should be involved in which projects, at what stages or points in the projects, in

Type of Organizational Structure	Description	Advantage(s)	Disadvantage(s)
New product division	Large and self-sufficient division	Centralized coordination and control Top management attention assured Resources adequate Long-term commitment	Coordination with other divisions Inflexibility due to size Opportunity for vested interests
New product department	Department within division	Specialization Integration of efforts	Few resources Less authority
New product manager	One manager who is responsible for a new product	Simplicity	Can overwhelm one manager Cooperation from others difficult
Product or brand manager	New product responsibility added to normal duties	Best for line extensions or modifications	Not suited to truly innovative products Manager torn between regular and new product duties
New product committee	Standing committee with diverse representation	Several functional areas involved	Dilutes responsibility across members
Cross-functional project team	New product group set up for the duration of a project	Flexible, fluid, involves diverse perspectives	Often hard to get functional department support
Task force or ad hoc committee	Temporary matrix approach	Taps specialized managers on full-time or part-time basis	Multiple demands placed on group members
Venture team	Internal as well as external personnel used	Brings in outsiders' expertise	May garner resources greater than the worth of the project
Outside suppliers	Contract with another company to develop product	Utilizes specialists for independent work	Can be costly Coordination and control problems
Multiple organization forms	Use of hybrid forms depending on nature of project	Form designed to fit needs to the project	Difficulties in managing, coordinating, and evaluating the efforts of several unique structural forms

what capacity, accountable for what deliverables, and evaluated on what criteria? Who will play the role of champion for a given project, and how can different champions be identified, motivated, and compensated? How does the firm achieve trust, openness, communication, cooperation, and team spirit among departments and among key managers insofar as innovation activities are concerned?

Many structural options are available for addressing these challenges. Table 7.4 provides a synopsis of ten different structural approaches used by firms to produce new products. When deciding which of these to use, management is effectively deciding the extent to which the structure is more:

Simple versus Complex

Centralized versus Decentralized

Formal versus Informal

Autonomous versus Integrated

Highly Specialized versus More Generalist

Full-time versus Part-time

Thus, as one moves from the traditional R&D department to a new product committee to a cross-functional team, the structure gets more complex, authority becomes more decentralized, and rules and processes become more informal. At the same time, unit autonomy becomes greater, and the group of people working on the project is more specialized. It is also likely as one moves across these three structural alternatives that decision making and conflict resolution become less hierarchical and more participative. Information will flow more horizontally than vertically, and information sharing is likely to increase.

Companies are experimenting with new structures essentially on a trial-and-error basis. Much remains to be learned about what works and why. It does appear that the effectiveness of a given approach depends upon the type of innovation activity undertaken. For instance, venture teams are more likely to produce disruptive innovations and to do so on a fairly timely basis. Product managers can be expected to come up with line extensions or minor modifications of existing products. The greatest trend appears to be toward the use of multiple structural forms. Page (1993) reported that, while multidisciplinary teams are by far the most widely used organizing structure, better than half of the companies he surveyed were using multiple forms such as a cross-functional team and a new products department or new products manager. Other evidence suggests that the degree of fit between the innovative team or venture and the mainstream organization affects the success of innovations. That is, regardless of the particular structural form, success is more likely where there are high levels of awareness, commitment, and connection between the venture unit and the corporate parent (Thornhill and Amit 2001).

THE NEED FOR A CHAMPIONS PROGRAM

A formal champions program is another valuable structural ingredient. Such a program encourages ambitious and talented entrepreneurs from throughout the organization to suggest, develop, champion, and implement new products. Champions believe deeply in an idea and badly want senior management's blessing to go after it. The champion's role is to encourage the project during its critical stages, keep key decision makers and sponsors aware of the project's status, mentor team members, help the team get its needs met, and enthusiastically promote the project at the highest levels of the company. Product champions also have to be true believers in the development team.

Ideally, champions are not chosen by management. Rather, they emerge from all parts of the company. This notion of champions emerging is critical. If management attempts to pick the winners in terms of pre-identification of those individuals it would like to see become champions or that it believes have the most champion potential, the results are typically disappointing. Thus, the key is to build an internal environment or infrastructure that enables these individuals to step up to the plate. The infrastructure must incorporate properly developed rewards and incentives, effective use of performance appraisals, flexibility in terms of resources, open communication, incentives for interfunctional cooperation, and the elimination of red tape.

The champions program must be well conceptualized. Management must establish the nature and scope of a champion's responsibilities, define a procedure by which champions bring forth their ideas, create a process for approving and empowering champions, and design an appraisal and reward structure tailored to champions while they are involved in a project. The program is augmented by internal communication efforts directed at all employees where elements of the program are explained, and employees are made aware of how to get involved, who is currently active, the status of current projects, and who and what have been successful. The company should also develop a set of characteristics that it looks for in a champion such as self-confidence, calculated risk-taking, demonstrated team and networking skills, and a tendency to be well organized.

TECHNOLOGY-PUSH VERSUS MARKET-PULL

Returning to the innovation process, many companies tend to have an overall orientation that guides or drives this process. Two of the dominant approaches are called *technology-push* and *market-pull*. With technology-push, employees within the firm (usually technically qualified engineers or scientists) see a technical possibility and strive to capitalize on it. They are typically versed in the existing state of the art on the technical side and recognize a means of overcoming an existing technical limitation or obstacle. Alternatively, they see a new way in which a technology might be applied. The tendency with this approach is to be caught up in the technical possibilities, while assuming the marketplace need. Even where a customer need has been clearly identified, many of the substantive issues surrounding whether customers would actually buy the innovation and how competitors are going to react are ignored. Examples of such issues include the level of satisfaction among consumers with whatever they are currently using, their perceived switching costs, the dynamics of their buying process, and the different people that play a role in their buying decisions.

Technology-push approaches also frequently suffer from what is called *perfection syndrome*. Technical people not only see the technological possibilities in an innovation, but they also frequently want to pursue those possibilities as far as they can. They want to perfect the new product or service, adding as many "bells and whistles," or features and functionality, as their research, design, and testing work will allow. In effect, they overengineer the innovation. More often than not, the marketplace wants a new product that is good enough, not the best possible. The additional time and money necessary to make the innovation the best possible drives up prices (and sometimes product complexity) beyond what the customer is willing to pay or results in features the customer is paying for but that he/she does not really want. From the customer's vantage point, a new product or service represents a series of trade-off decisions in terms of what is an acceptable value package.

Conversely, market-pull approaches to innovation start with the customer and are typically driven by marketing people. Market research plays a critical role. Customers are often the source of the new product idea, or at least their input is instrumental in the design and development of the product. While this seems like a safer approach and is consistent with a customer-driven philosophy, it also suffers from limitations. Foremost among these is the assumption that customers know their needs and can describe them in a way that results in new products. Customers generally know what they like and dislike about what is currently available on the market, and the feedback they provide is usually only with this reference point in mind.

We can relate the technology-push and market-pull approaches to the outcomes of the innovation process. Returning to the types of innovation described earlier in this chapter, technology-driven approaches often result in breakthrough products and services, including both discontinuous and dynamically continuous innovations. This is the good news. However, they also produce a lot of failures that can be described as "better mousetraps nobody wanted." These are new products that are technically advanced but for which there is inadequate market demand to justify their introduction. Market-pull approaches frequently result in incremental advances, including both continuous innovation and imitation. While more readily acceptable in the marketplace, such innovations have shorter-term payoffs with less long-run potential. Further, they also produce a common type of failure, the so-called "me-too product hitting a competitive brick wall." In essence, the customer does not see enough uniqueness or difference in the new product and so continues to rely on his or her current solution.

The implication is that neither approach is better. Interfunctional involvement throughout the stages of the new product development process is the key. Innovation management should represent a continuous matching process, where the technical limits and possibilities are explored and matched against an intimate understanding of market segments, the underlying customer needs and buying process, and the competitors' capabilities. Just as important is the ability to envision the customer not simply as he/she is now, but as he or she will be.

INNOVATION STRATEGY AND THE INNOVATION PORTFOLIO

Companies have strategies for increasing sales, cutting costs, financing growth, and managing production or service delivery. They frequently do not have a strategy for innovation. All too often, their innovation activities can be characterized as piecemeal, tactical, and reactive. Resource commitments, priorities, and deadlines for projects are continually being changed. Projects are begun, but most fail to make it to commercialization. Accountability for innovation results is vague or limited. The general approach is cautious, with an emphasis on finding sure-bet winners. The result is a company that is both inefficient and ineffective at innovation.

Strategic innovation represents a different path. Here, the company formulates explicit goals and strategies for innovation, executes those strategies, monitors innovation performance, and then makes adjustments based on deviations between the goals and actual performance. Strategic innovation has the following seven core components:

1. The company makes a strong commitment to an active policy of finding and developing new products, with top management heavily involved in project initiation and support;

2. Innovation is defined as a companywide task, not simply the responsibility of an R&D department or new product development department in isolation;

3. Strategies are formulated for the nature of the new products and services to be developed, including the extent to which innovation projects are concentrated around the firm's current product line or are more diversified, and the desired levels of innovativeness, quality, and customization;

4. Strategies are formulated for the nature of the technologies to be utilized;

5. Strategies are formulated for the types of markets to be served through the firm's innovative efforts, including how new or mature these markets are and the newness of these markets to the firm;

6. There is a clear sense of how aggressive or defensive the innovation efforts of the firm are intended to be and a clear understanding of the planned levels of resource commitment to innovation as a percentage of company revenues;

7. The company has a planned approach for sourcing new product ideas and a policy regarding the relative reliance on external (i.e., outsourced or licensed) versus internal product development.

Just as important is the need for companies to move away from a project mentality and to adopt a portfolio mentality. Earlier it was noted that an effective risk management strategy involves the company's creating and managing a portfolio of innovations. At any point in time, a set of projects is underway. Evidence suggests, for instance, that new-to-the-world products account for about 10 percent of corporate innovation activity, new lines for 20 percent, line extensions for 26 percent, and product revisions for 26 percent. The key is balance across projects. Management attempts to draw a balance of a) high-risk, high-return projects

■ TABLE 7.5

CHARACTERISTICS OF DIFFERENT TYPES OF INNOVATION

Category	Risk	Potential Return	Investment Required	Number of People Involved	Level of Management Approval	Development Cycle
New to the world	High	High	Major	20–35	Director level	3–4 years
New to market	High	High	Major	10–15	Director level	2–4 years
New product line	Moderate	High	Major	10–15	Director level	1–3 years
Extension of existing line	Moderate	Moderate	Moderate	5–6	Business unit level	18 months
Product revision	Low	Moderate	Low	3–5	Product manager	6–12 months
Product support innovation	Low	Low	Low	3–6	Functional manager	1–3 months

against lower-risk, lower-return projects; b) discontinuous or dynamically continuous innovations against continuous innovations and imitations; c) projects with shorter development cycles and payoffs against ones with longer-term outcomes; d) products/services intended for markets the firm currently serves against ones for markets that are new to the firm; and e) projects utilizing new and emerging technologies against those relying on technologies with which the firm is familiar. Table 7.5 illustrates how the characteristics of different types of innovations reflect these trade-offs.

Thinking in terms of a portfolio also implies a different perspective on failure. Given that the portfolio concept is borrowed from finance, consider for a moment a portfolio of financial investments. The wise investor is most concerned with returns achieved on a total set of stocks, bonds, and other investments. He/she does not overreact to the failure of any stock. Rather, the role of failure is recognized and accepted. The same goes for a portfolio of innovations. It is anticipated that some will be major winners, some will be moderate successes, and some will be losers.

Figures 7.4 and 7.5 provide examples of innovation portfolios. While it is up to the individual firm to define the variables on the axes, in Figure 7.4 we have used newness to the market and newness to the company. Figure 7.5 allows for a distinction between product/service innovations and internal process innovations. In both figures, individual projects are positioned within the portfolio based on where they fall on each axis.

Strategic implications can be drawn depending on where a project lies within the portfolio. For instance, products that are not new to the market or to the firm represent a potential source of incremental sales increase but can also cannibalize sales from existing products. Alternatively, products that are very new to the firm but not to the market have proven potential but may not fit well with the firm's distribution network, marketing expertise, information technology, and so on. Similarly, those that are not all that new to the firm but relatively new to the market (e.g., an extension of some earlier innovation of the company) become an issue of fit with the market.

■ FIGURE 7.4

NEW PRODUCT/SERVICE OPPORTUNITIES
AND THE QUESTION OF STRATEGIC FIT

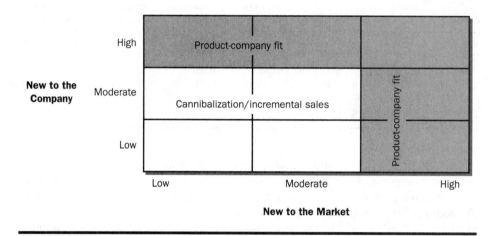

■ FIGURE 7.5

AN ALTERNATIVE INNOVATION PORTFOLIO

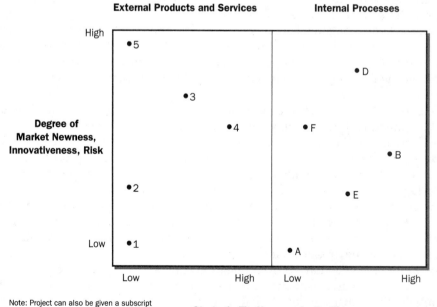

Note: Project can also be given a subscript
reflecting the time until it is implemented

The design of the innovation portfolio also has implications for a firm's structuring of its innovation activities. The products in the portfolio that are newer to the market and not well understood by the firm will tend to require a more centralized new product development team with an emphasis on cross-functional participation and learning. Projects that involve line extensions, product revisions, and product support innovations (not new to the market and with which the company has some experience) require small decentralized teams that emphasize efficiency and speed of delivery.

SETTING INNOVATION GOALS AND MEASURING INNOVATION PERFORMANCE

It is difficult to ensure systematic achievement of management intentions without clearly formulated objectives to guide and motivate activities. Moreover, the manager is unable to assess how the company is doing in a particular area if he/she does not know what the company was trying to accomplish in the first place. As a case in point, assume that management has voiced general criticism regarding a lack of innovation in the company over the past five years. However, because objectives for numbers of products/services, development cycle times, and a host of related performance indicators are absent, judgments are made based simply on perceptions of what competitors did over a similar period or some general notion of what the market required.

Consistent with a portfolio approach to new product development activity, there is a need to establish multiple performance targets. Table 7.6 provides an example of the set of objectives a company or division might specify for the coming three years. Here, objectives have been established in seven areas ranging from types of innovation projects underway to the average development cycle for new products.

A goal that is currently being set in many companies involves the percentage of company revenues that will come from new products and services introduced over the next three to five years. For instance, Page (1993) reported a norm among innovating companies of 38 percent, meaning that five years from now these companies expect 38 percent of their sales will come from products the firm is currently not selling. By setting and widely publicizing this type of goal, management makes clear that innovation is a normal and expected activity.

Closely tied to the establishment of objectives is the need to hold individuals, teams, and departments accountable for innovation performance. The ability to do so is dependent upon the identification of specific performance measures that can be tracked over time. Unfortunately, most companies do not measure their innovation efforts, in part because accounting systems do not deal effectively with innovation. However, where objectives have been quantified, they effectively provide measures that management can track. Thus, each of the objectives specified in Table 7.6 lend themselves to fairly straightforward tracking.

■ **TABLE 7.6**

SETTING INNOVATION OBJECTIVES

A. Projects in development at any one point	11
New products	
■ New to the market	1
■ New to company/new product lines	1
■ New products in existing lines	2
Product revisions	
■ Product improvements/new features	2
■ Products in new markets/market segments	1
■ Product repositionings	1
Product support	
■ New selling approaches	0
■ New distribution approaches	1
■ New marketing approaches	1
■ New administrative approaches	1
B. New product launches	4 per year
C. Average development cycle time*	
■ New products	18 months
■ Product revisions	6 months
D. Average development cost	
■ New products	$2 mil
■ Product revisions	$1.1 mil
■ Product support	$240,000
E. Percentage of total company revenue in three years' time that is to come from products not currently on the market	35%
F. Percentage of each manager's time spent on innovative activity	10%
G. Average ROI on new product development projects	30%

*Defined as period that lapses from allocation of resources to the project until commercial delivery of new product on widespread basis.

An interesting perspective on performance monitoring is provided by Kuczmarski (1996). He proposes a set of ten indices that can be readily calculated on an annual basis (Table 7.7). These include outcome measures that are both financial (e.g., success or hit rate, innovation revenue per employee) and nonfinancial (e.g., innovation portfolio mix), as well as process measures (e.g., process pipeline flow, R&D innovation emphasis ratio). The intent is not to overwhelm the company with too many metrics. In fact, the more typical problem is too few performance measures. Management needs to focus on identifying those measures that best fit the company's competitive situation, its resources, and the amount and type of innovation being emphasized.

■ TABLE 7.7

MEASURES FOR ASSESSING INNOVATION PERFORMANCE

1. Survival Rate
   (3 years)

   Number of commercialized new products still on the market
   +
   Total number of new products commercialized

2. Success/hit rate
   (3 years)

   Number of new products exceeding three-year original revenue forecasts
   +
   Total number of new products commercialized

3. R&D innovation
   effectiveness ratio

   Cumulative three-year gross profits from commercialized new products
   +
   Cumulative three-year R&D expenditures allocated solely to new products

4. R&D innovation
   emphasis ratio

   Cumulative three-year R&D expenditures allocated solely to new products
   +
   Cumulative three-year R&D expenditures

5. Innovation
   sales ratio

   Cumulative third-year annual revenues generated from commercialized new products
   +
   Total annual revenues

6. Newness
   investment ratio

   Cumulative three-year expenditures allocated to new-to-world or country products
   +
   Cumulative three-year new product total expenditures

7. Innovation
   portfolio mix

   Percentage of new products (by number and revenues) commercialized by type
   ■ New to the world or country   ■ Line extension   ■ Repositioning
   ■ New to the company   ■ Product line improvements

8. Process pipeline
   flow

   Number of new product concepts in each stage
   of the development process at year-end

9. Innovation revenues
   per employee

   Total annual revenues from commercialized new products
   +
   Total number of full-time equivalent employees devoted solely to innovation initiatives

10. Return on
    innovation

    Cumulative three-year net profits from commercialized new products
    +
    Cumulative three-year new product total expenditures
    (for all commercialized, failed, or killed new products)

SOURCE: Kuczmarski, T. 1996. *Innovation: Leadership Strategies for the Competitive Edge.* Chicago: NTC Publishing Group: 182.

TECHNLOLOGY AND ENTREPRENEURIAL OPPORTUNITY

Discussions of corporate innovation are incomplete if they do not include the role of technology. We can define technology as the tools, devices, and knowledge that help transform inputs into outputs. Never in history has the pace of technological advance been so fast. Whether it is new polymers, optical data storage, high-tech ceramics, digital electronics, or developments in biochemistry, every facet of business is affected. As a result, just as the contemporary business environment can be characterized as the age of entrepreneurship, so too can it be characterized as the age of technology. In fact, entrepreneurs drive the commercialization of new technologies, and technological developments greatly enhance the level of entrepreneurial activity.

Technology is an important trigger for entrepreneurial activity within corporations, in that it represents both opportunity and threat. For instance, technology is shortening product life cycles, which suggests firms have a smaller window of opportunity, or time period, in which they can act on an innovative opportunity. It also suggests the corporate entrepreneur must have an exit strategy, or harvesting plan, even as the innovation is still in the development stages. Technology is also redefining market segments. Mass markets are disappearing as markets become segmented, fragmented, and niched. This trend creates tremendous new product opportunity in that a single product strategy gives way to customized solutions for different market segments. Markets also become globalized, suggesting distance and size no longer matter, and the playing field between small and large companies is more level. Industry definitions start to become less meaningful as new industries rapidly appear and boundaries blur among existing ones. As a result, the firm finds itself competing in nontraditional markets and facing nontraditional competitors in its existing markets. Under such circumstances, the entrepreneurial firm can redefine the rules of the competitive game like Nucor did with steel and Seatrain did with shipping. Other developments driven by technology include organizational restructuring and changing employee relationships. The communications and information revolutions enabled by technology make possible much flatter organizations, virtual organizations, and organizations where people's offices are wherever the people happen to be at a point in time. The need for the company to own or control assets and people is markedly reduced. All of this facilitates the concept of having a lot of small businesses operating inside one big business.

We have argued above for an innovation strategy in companies, but the innovation strategy should be complemented by a technology strategy. The entrepreneurial firm recognizes the power of technology in achieving sustainable competitive advantage. Achieving such advantage requires that management determine a) how the firm will use technology to position its products/services in the marketplace; and b) how the firm will use technology to enhance its internal processes.

The first of these issues includes the question of how the firm wants to be perceived technologically — as leader, player, or also-ran. An example of such positioning would be the payroll services firm that is the first to manage client payrolls entirely over the Internet. Technology also determines the performance of the company's products on key attributes. If the firm wants its products or services perceived as the safest, fastest, smoothest, smallest, or easiest to use—among other attributes—decisions must be made in terms of how much investment should be devoted to particular technologies.

The other side of competitive advantage involves internal processes. Technologies are a vehicle not only for reducing costs but also for dramatically enhancing internal performance. Order cycle times might be cut in half by adopting a satellite-based vehicle tracking system, while an inventive approach to electronic data interchange might solidify relationships with key clients and distributors. Other technologies allow for the outsourcing of key functions (sometimes to former employees who used to provide the functions internally).

Corporate entrepreneurs are the visionaries who champion efforts in both of these areas. They are frequently not the experts in a given technical area. Rather, they understand what a technology can do. As a result, their mental picture of a product or market or company differs markedly from what everyone else sees.

TECHNOLOGY LIMITS AND PLATFORMS

Firms frequently rely on a number of technologies in providing a product or service to the marketplace, but there are usually one or two core technologies that are the key to the firm's ongoing ability to be competitive with that product or service. These technologies have life cycles. As money and effort is invested in a technology, the initial yield from that investment is often low. At some point, there is a breakthrough development, and the yield of the technology in terms of both new applications and product/service performance takes off. Eventually, the additional potential of the technology begins to slow, even with large investments in continued development. Stated differently, every technology has limits.

As a technology begins to reach its limits, the implications for companies dependent on that technology are immense. Foster (1986, p.32) notes, "Limits determine which technologies, which machines, and which processes are about to become obsolete. . . . Management's ability to recognize limits is crucial to determining whether they succeed or fail, because limits are the best clue they have for recognizing when they will need to develop a new technology." The impending limits of a given technology become especially significant when there is an emerging technology on the horizon. This new technology has yet to be exploited, but it is clearly not subject to the same limits. At some point, users begin to abandon the current technology and jump to the new one (which has its own life cycle). The eventual take off in the new technology's life cycle serves to accelerate the maturation and decline of the old technology.

Further insights can be gained by considering the valuable work of Christensen (1997). He distinguishes between sustaining and disruptive technologies. Sustaining technologies maintain a rate of improvement, giving customers more or better in the attributes they already have. Thus, a currently used technology begins to reach its limits in terms of performance enhancement of the firm's product on one or two key attributes (i.e., quality cannot get much better, speed much faster, or size much smaller). New (sustaining) technologies are employed that allow the firm to continue (or sustain) the trajectory of attribute enhancement.

Disruptive technologies introduce attributes different from those that customers historically value. Consider the microwave oven when it was first introduced or the use of lasers in correcting myopic eyesight. Disruptive technologies might perform poorly on the attributes that are currently important to customers, but they open up entirely new horizons in terms of their capabilities in other areas. Cellular telephones at first did not perform well in terms of reception and reach, but they allowed mobility and communication regardless of time or place. Customers resist using disruptive technologies in applications they know and understand, so these technologies are initially used and valued only in new markets or new applications. Christensen (1997) recounts the resistance on the part of computer manufacturers as the architecture of disk drives eventually shrank from 14 inches to 3.5 inches. Companies failed to see that the reduction in storage capacity enabled other attributes such as lighter weight and lower power consumption that led to the successful introduction of PC's and ultimately led to portable computers.

The threat to mainstream companies is roundabout. The disruptive technology is first employed in new markets (often niche markets ignored by the mainstream firms). Once the disruptive technology has this foothold in the marketplace, sustaining technologies are then applied to improve performance on an array of attributes. In fact, performance improves at a rapid pace, such that the once-ignored (or underserved) needs of customers in established markets are being met as well. Mainstream companies that ignored the disruptive technology suddenly find themselves losing market share to entrepreneurial players who saw the future first. Ironically, by focusing on the existing needs of current customers, the established firm can eventually lose those customers. And when they do finally embrace the disruptive technology, making up the lost ground is almost impossible. Another irony involves the tendency of the mainstream company to continue using technology to improve performance on accepted attributes so that the company overshoots what the marketplace needs and is willing to pay for in terms of those attributes. The firm with the disruptive technology doesn't perform as well on those accepted attributes but eventually performs well enough while also offering a set of new attributes.

The message is that firms cannot afford to ignore either disruptive technologies or the niche markets they initially create. Management must be able to classify technologies as sustaining and disruptive, determine the disruptive technologies that are likely to have a strategic impact on the company's products and markets, and identify the niche markets likely to be created by the new technology. Managers may need to create autonomous structures to facilitate the internal development of disruptive technologies and to ensure the company has a position in emerging markets.

A related concept is that of the technological platform. Here, the firm selects the core technology or technologies around which it defines the future. Platforms are underlying technological capabilities in which a company invests in order to generate a range of different products, applications, and improvements (Kuczmarski et al. 2001). Skills and capabilities with the technologies that define a platform become a core competency of the firm. For its part, a disruptive technology effectively provides a firm with a new platform, redefining not only the limits on the performance possibilities on accepted attributes but also introducing capabilities on new attributes. Thus, mainstream operations in a company might be built around a given platform, but autonomous units might be organized around a new platform.

SUMMARY AND CONCLUSIONS

Innovation in companies represents a classic Catch-22 scenario. Innovation means change, disruption, and accelerated obsolescence of successful products and services. Increased amounts of innovation also means more failure. But not innovating extracts an even higher price. The complacency that comes with a fixed focus on current customer needs and products is an open invitation to disaster . . . but it is a well-disguised threat that hits a company in ways and places and at times that management least expects.

It is not enough for senior executives to simply declare that "entrepreneurship is important in this company and we want a culture of champions and innovation." It is not enough to provide rewards and resources to support innovative efforts. Companies require a strategy for innovation. They need to establish goals for the types and amount of innovative efforts the company will pursue, create and manage a portfolio of innovative projects, have an organized process for managing innovation, and identify appropriate structures for organizing employees around the innovation process. They need to track innovation performance and hold units, departments, and managers accountable for their innovative output.

Technology represents an especially potent tool for the corporate entrepreneur. Its effects both as an opportunity and a threat frequently serve as the triggering event for product and process innovation. In a sense, technology liberates the corporate entrepreneur, freeing him or her from established ways of doing things and from current limitations and structures. The challenge is to properly interpret the technology horizon, which necessitates that the firm "escape the tyranny of the served market" (Hamel and Prahalad 1994). The ability to distinguish sustaining from disruptive technologies and to recognize the corresponding implications for where the marketplace is likely to go becomes the basis for entrepreneurial action and leadership in the corporation.

3M: ADDRESSING CONSUMER NEEDS

Technology and product innovation always have been, and always will be, the lifeblood of Minnesota Mining and Manufacturing Company. 3M started with one product — sandpaper. Today, the $16 billion corporation manufactures 50,000+ products in over sixty countries and continues to apply proprietary technology wherever possible. From light management to health care to fuel cells, 3M innovation is changing the way people live.

At 3M, you won't find managers and employees playing with crayons and staring out windows in an effort to spur their creative juices. Instead, they do what's worked for the company since its inception in 1902; they anticipate customers' needs and devise product solutions. Microreplication was invented in 1964 to make overhead projector lenses lighter. Since then, the technology has been the answer to dozens of consumer problems. For example, laptop computer manufacturers were finally able to introduce smaller, lighter products when 3M used microreplication, which changes the surface structure of materials, to develop a screen that created a brighter image using just one bulb. One bulb doing the job of two allowed for smaller battery size and improved power source capacity. Letting technology work for them, 3M uses microreplication in multiple divisions, including electronics, adhesives, abrasives, reflective materials, and film.

3M's Scotchprint Electronic Imaging System filled the need of screen printing firms with low volume orders. Traditionally, quality advertising displays are expensive and limited in size and shape. The imaging technology made it possible for smaller graphics companies and end users with tight budgets to create and purchase any size and number of ads.

Necessity bred innovation when Scotch™ tape inventor and former CEO William McKnight broke his leg. In an attempt to circumvent the use of heavy plaster casts, 3M acquired a technology for a synthetic material that was lighter and stronger than plaster. Scientists applied their knowledge and improved the application of the technology, creating the first successful fiberglass-reinforced synthetic casting tape.

Certainly the leader in marrying innovation and technology, each of 3M's three major sectors, Industrial and Consumer; Life Sciences; and Information, Imaging, and Electronics, face the 30%/4 goal. That is, thirty percent of all sales must come from products less than four years old. This imperative, initiated by L. D. DeSimone, former CEO, is easily met, however, in a company that seems to hire scientists with lightbulbs as heads.

SOURCE: Kanter, R. M., J. Kao, and F. Wiersema. 1997. *Innovation: Breakthrough Ideas at 3M, DuPont, Pfizer, and Rubbermaid.* New York: HarperCollins Publishers.

REFERENCES

Christensen, C. 1997. *The Innovator's Dilemma.* Cambridge: Harvard Business School.

Foster, R. 1986. *The Attacker's Advantage.* New York: Summit Books.

Hamel, G. 2000. *Leading the Revolution.* Boston: Harvard Business School.

Hamel, G., and C. K. Prahalad. 1994. *Competing for the Future.* Boston: Harvard Business School.

Kanter, R. M., J. Kao, and F. Wiersema. 1997. *Innovation: Breakthrough Ideas at 3M, DuPont, Pfizer, and Rubbermaid.* New York: HarperCollins Publishers.

Kuczmarski, T. 1996. *Innovation: Leadership Strategies for the Competitive Edge.* Chicago: NTC Publishing Group.

Kuczmarski, T., A. Middlebrooks and J. Swaddling. 2001. *Innovating the Corporation.* Chicago: NTC Publishing Group.

Page, A. L. 1993. "Assessing New Product Development Practices and Performance: Establishing Crucial Norms," *Journal of Product Innovation Management* 10: 273–290.

Peters, T. 1997. *The Circle of Innovation.* New York: Alfred A. Knopf.

Synectics. 1993. *Succeeding at Innovation: Report on Creativity and Innovation in U.S. Corporations.* Boston: Synectics.

Thornhill, S., and R. Amit. 2001. "A Dynamic Perspective of Internal Fit in Corporate Venturing," *Journal of Business Venturing* 16 (1): 25–50.

8

CORPORATE STRATEGY AND ENTREPRENEURSHIP

Entrepreneurship is more than a course of action that an individual pursues; it is more than a way of thinking. At the level of the organization, entrepreneurship can provide a theme or direction to a company's entire operations. It can serve as an integral component of a firm's strategy. A strategy, at its essence, attempts to capture where the firm wants to go and how it plans to get there. When entrepreneurship is introduced to strategy, the possibilities regarding where the firm can go, how fast, and how it gets there are greatly enhanced.

Yet, many firms ignore entrepreneurship in their strategies. Their strategic focus emphasizes the achievement of efficiencies in operations, market positions they want to occupy, ways in which they plan to differentiate themselves, or some other competitive variable. While entrepreneurship could potentially be part of any of these strategies, it typically is not included either explicitly or implicitly. In fact, the integration of entrepreneurship with strategy can take many forms. The integration of entrepreneurship implies that innovation and value creation play a significant part in the firm's strategic direction.

In this chapter, we will investigate the relationship between entrepreneurship and company strategy. Forces creating the need for entrepreneurial strategies will be identified within the context of the new competitive landscape. The concept of dominant logic will be introduced, together with the need for entrepreneurship to serve as the dominant logic in a company. Key concepts surrounding strategic management as it relates to entrepreneurship will be explored. The principal elements of an entrepreneurial strategy will be presented. In addition, the chapter will examine critical mistakes made when formulating strategy.

THE CHANGING LANDSCAPE

Companies today find themselves operating in a new competitive landscape. The contemporary business environment can be characterized in terms of increasing risk, decreased ability to forecast, fluid firm and industry boundaries, a managerial mindset that must unlearn traditional management principles, and new structural forms that not only allow for change but also help create it. This new landscape can be described in terms of four powerful forces: change, complexity, chaos, and contradiction (Bettis and Hitt 1995; Hitt and Reed 2000).

No organization is immune to the immense forces of change. The pressures on today's managers and employees are unprecedented. For many managers, the sum of their institutional learning took place in an environment much different from the one they face in the decade ahead. In the past, the playing field was level, if not pitched to their advantage. Many of the rules were obvious. Structure was the manager's friend. Hierarchy provided context and orientation. Time helped, and there was enough of it. Uncertainty was to be avoided. It's not that the rules have been tinkered with. The game itself is different!

Complexity is another critical force in the new landscape. The change alluded to above comes from many different directions, often at the same time. There are new computer technologies, markets, financial systems, demographic patterns, emotional requirements for managing, and communication networks. Competitors come and go. Customer groupings are shifting and becoming more differentiated. Competition involves not only the traditional head-to-head battles but also collaboration with certain firms. Further, change in any one area (e.g., technology) interacts with changes in other areas (e.g., suppliers and customers). The net effect is that there is simply much more to manage than in the past.

Chaos is the third critical force in the new competitive landscape. The common-language meaning of the term *chaos* is *confusion,* and confusion does describe the new business landscape. But the scientific use of the term is perhaps even more descriptive. Chaos theory describes systems with outcomes that are governed by nonlinear differential equations. Random events can cause extreme consequences in the business. The principal managerial implication of chaos theory is that small changes or shocks to the system can have a major impact (hence, things are nonlinear). There is sensitive dependence on initial conditions, which means that causality between one business variable and another business variable is difficult to establish or understand. Further, the scale effects of change are largely unpredictable. Stacey (1996, p.265) described the phenomenon in the following manner: "Under conditions of nonlinearity and randomness, incremental changes that may themselves seem insignificant can precipitate major discontinuous or qualitative change because of the emergent properties triggered by marginal adjustments."

Finally, the business environment is filled with many contradictions, and dealing with paradox becomes a critical aspect of managing in the new competitive landscape. Collins and Porras (1994) explain. "The tyranny of the "or" pushes people to believe that things must be either A *or* B, but not both" (p 43). They argue that such exclusionary thinking is wrong-headed. Rather, managers should

■ **TABLE 8.1**

STRATEGIC INFLECTION POINTS

Example (category)	What Changed	Actions Taken	Results
Wal-Mart (competition)	Superstores enter small communities	Some stores specialize (e.g., become category killers)	Home Depot and Toys 'R' Us thrive; many others perish
PCs (technology)	Price/performance of PCs proved to be far superior	Some companies adapt microcomputers as building blocks; others become systems integrators	Adaptive companies thrive; others face severe difficulties
Demographic time bomb (customers)	Kids have increased computer affinity	Growth of CD-ROM educational and entertainment software aimed at kids	Computers become ubiquitous
Travel agencies (suppliers)	Airlines capped commissions; Internet reservation services appear	Travel agents attempt to charge consumers	Travel agency economics turn tougher; many fail
Telecommunications (de-regulation)	Competition is introduced and intensifies in equipment and long distance service	AT&T divests the Bell operating companies, downsizes, restructures and adapts to a competitive world with consumer marketing	AT&T and the former Bell operating companies' combined valuation is over four times what it was ten years ago

SOURCE: Adapted from Grove, A. S. 1996. *Only the Paranoid Survive.* London: Harper Collins Business.

embrace contradiction by replacing *or* with *and.* For instance, quality can be higher *and* operating costs can be lower. Firms can do more for customers *and* charge them less. Companies can compete with other firms *and* collaborate with them. Products can be standardized *and* customized.

Another way to visualize the changing landscape is from the perspective of what are called *strategic inflection points* (Grove 1996). An inflection point occurs when the old strategic picture dissolves and gives way to the new, allowing the adaptive and proactive business to ascend to new heights. Put another way, a strategic inflection point is when the balance of forces shifts from the old ways of doing business and the old ways of competing to the new. Before the strategic inflection point, the industry simply was more like the old. After this point, the industry is profoundly redefined, often evolving into entirely new structures and value chains. Once the inflection point is reached, there is no going back. The competitive conditions and rules never return to the former state. As a result, firms that do not proactively navigate the inflection point tend to peak and then decline. Some examples of strategic inflection points are illustrated in Table 8.1. The table also summarizes actions taken in response to the inflection point and results achieved.

Since the nature of an inflection point is so unpredictable, how can organizations know when the time is right to make changes? As Grove (1996, p. 35) states, "You don't . . . but you can't wait until you do know . . . timing is everything." If management undertakes a process of adapting to the new while the company is still healthy, and the ongoing business forms a protective bubble in which management can experiment with the new ways of doing things, it becomes possible to capitalize on and retain the company's strengths, keep employees, and maintain the firm's strategic position.

DOES THE DOMINANT LOGIC FIT THE COMPETITIVE LANDSCAPE?

How does a firm achieve sustainable advantage in the new competitive landscape? Addressing this issue requires that we first examine what has been termed the *dominant logic* of the company (Bettis and Prahalad 1995). This very interesting notion refers to the way in which managers conceptualize the business and make critical resource allocation decisions. Every organization has a dominant logic, even if managers do not recognize or formally acknowledge it. The dominant logic at Microsoft would seem to involve a commitment to the Windows standard and the exploitation of a common architecture. At GE Capital, the logic is defined by the company's competence in risk management and deal structuring. Thus, the dominant logic of a company attempts to capture the prevailing mindset, and it drives the overall focus of the systems and routines in the company. Further, it filters and interprets information from the environment; attenuates complexity; and guides the strategies, systems, and behavior of the organization. In fact, managers will often consider only information and intelligence that is believed to be relevant to the firm's prevailing dominant logic.

The dominant logic that is optimal for the firm in today's environment may well be inappropriate for the environment that will exist five years hence. Microsoft may well find that technological developments surrounding the Internet make the Windows standard less relevant — or at least limit its future potential. Stated differently, the dominant logic tends to capture competitive advantage in the present and may be oblivious to future possibilities. The implication is that the dominant logic must be periodically unlearned, and openness to such unlearning should be an integral aspect of the corporate culture. Routines and habits that pertain to the existing dominant logic can inhibit the learning of new processes and operating methods. Thus, a relationship exists between the ability to learn and the need to unlearn. Moreover, the longer that a dominant logic has been in place within an organization, the harder it is to unlearn. Unfortunately, it often takes a crisis before existing assumptions, routines, and systems are questioned. The new competitive landscape can be counted on to produce the kinds of crises and upheavals that illustrate the pitfalls of a well-entrenched dominant logic.

One means of creating a *dynamic* dominant logic is to make entrepreneurship the basis upon which the organization is conceptualized and resources are allocated. As a dominant logic, entrepreneurship promotes strategic agility, flexibility, creativity, and continuous innovation throughout the firm. Further, the overriding focus of the firm is opportunity identification, discovery of new sources of value, and product and process innovation that will lead to greater profitability. And finally, an emphasis on entrepreneurial activity is translated into the objectives, strategies, reward systems, control systems, planning approaches, structure, and so forth of the firm.

THE ROLE OF STRATEGIC MANAGEMENT AND CORPORATE STRATEGY

Achieving sustainable advantage in the new competitive landscape also requires that managers think and act strategically and that they formulate appropriate strategies. In a sense, dominant logic sets the context for the firm's overall direction, while strategy and strategic management more specifically define that direction and determine how well it is accomplished.

Strategic management is a process that deals with the entrepreneurial work of the organization; with organizational renewal and growth; and, more particularly, with developing and utilizing the strategy that is to guide the firm's operations (Schendel and Hofer 1978). In essence, strategic management is the formulation of long-range plans for the effective management of external opportunities and threats in light of a company's internal strengths and weaknesses. This includes defining the company's mission, specifying achievable objectives, developing strategies, and setting policy guidelines. Thus, strategic planning is the primary step in anticipating and managing the firm's external environment and in defining the future of a business.

Importantly, strategic management is more than writing a plan or developing a strategy. It is a way of thinking — one that many managers never really grasp. Strategic thinking requires more of an external than an internal focus. It implies a continuous search for new sources of competitive advantage. It involves looking beyond immediate crises and day-to-day demands and envisioning the market and the firm's position three, five, and ten years from now. It entails an ability to see the big picture, meaning that the manager envisions all of the resources and core capabilities of the firm in terms of how they might be uniquely combined to create new sources of value. Lastly, it implies discipline in identifying a path or position and in ensuring that fellow employees stay focused on the target, while being flexible in the tactical approaches employed. The strategic manager keeps his or her eye on the prize in terms of not being discouraged by serious obstacles, not being distracted by situational opportunities that are inconsistent with the strategic vision, and not giving in to the temptation to take shortcuts.

Coupled with strategic management is the concept of strategy. As noted at the outset of this chapter, a strategy is a statement regarding what the company wants to be and how it plans to get there. Strategy creates a sense of unity, or consistency of action, throughout an organization. In order for people to work toward common objectives, they must know what the objectives are. If employees do not have a strong understanding that innovation is the firm's ultimate aim, then their actions on the job each and every day will not reinforce innovation. As they make choices in their jobs, strategy can provide direction to those choices.

Michael Porter (1996) draws a critical distinction between strategy and operational effectiveness, arguing that managers increasingly are preoccupied with the latter and ignorant of the former. Operational effectiveness is concerned with activities that enable the firm to perform similar activities *better* than competitors perform them. Thus, through the use of total quality management principles, self-directed work teams, downsizing, outsourcing, business process reengineering techniques, or other tools, the company attempts to make current products at lower costs, provide better customer service, offer higher product quality, or otherwise outperform rivals.

Strategy, in Porter's view, is about performing *different* activities than competitors perform or about performing similar activities in *different* ways. Southwest Airlines provides a vivid example. The firm's strategy is built around short-haul routes, frequent flights, travel to midsized cities and secondary airports in larger cities, low-cost fares, and no-frills flights. More fundamentally, the strategy depends on truly empowered employees, a different approach to customers and ticketing, and a unique system for managing ground operations. It is a strategy than enables the firm to turn flights around in record time and to provide a better on-time arrival record than anyone in the business. In the past few years, virtually every other U.S. airline has attempted to mimic some part of the Southwest strategy—an approach that misses the whole point of strategy.

To stay competitive over the short run, the firm must continually improve operational effectiveness. However, there is a point of diminishing returns on this front. And as the firm's managers become more preoccupied with operational effectiveness, they gradually forget about strategy. Meanwhile, the competitive landscape is changing. New players emerge that are capable of competing with established players in spite of small size and limited resources, or firms from seemingly unrelated industries are suddenly competing in the firm's market space. In either instance, these new competitors offer a totally unique value proposition and/or compete in new and different ways. The firm finds it is both unfamiliar with and unprepared for these new circumstances, even though its costs may be lower or its quality higher than either have ever before been.

INTEGRATING ENTREPRENEURSHIP WITH STRATEGY

Not only can entrepreneurship serve as the dominant logic of a company, but it also plays an important role in the firm's strategy. The integration of entrepreneurship with strategy has two aspects, both of which are critical. We will refer to the aspects as *entrepreneurial strategy* and a *strategy for entrepreneurship*.

■ TABLE 8.2

CHARACTERISTICS OF TRADITIONAL STRATEGY
AND ENTREPRENEURIAL STRATEGY

Traditional Strategies	Entrepreneurial Strategies
Security and job preservation	Risk-taking and job creation
Learn one skill	Lifelong learning
Stability, tradition, consistency, robustness	Speed, change, adaptability, agility
Top-down command, hierarchical structure	360-degree integration, flat structure
Capital is equipment	Capital is people's know-how
Regulation	Deregulation
Segregation and compartmentalization	Integration and synergy
Transaction and control	Transformation and empowerment
Status is ascribed	Status is achieved
Scarcity mentality, zero-sum game	Abundance mentality, win-win paradigm

SOURCE: Adapted from: Cooper, A. C., G. D. Markman, and G. Niss. 2000. "The Evolution of the Field of Entrepreneurship." In *Entrepreneurship As Strategy*, edited by G. D. Meyer and K. A. Heppard. (Thousand Oaks, CA: Sage Publishers.)

The first of these is concerned with applying creativity and entrepreneurial thinking to the development of a core strategy for the firm. A great strategy is not an obvious one. Discovering unique positions in the marketplace is difficult, as is breaking away from established ways of doing things. The Dell Direct Method that lies at the core of Dell Computer's strategy is an example of the application of entrepreneurial thinking to strategy. The same can be said about the strategy at Southwest Airlines discussed above. Table 8.2 provides a comparison of some of the underlying traits of traditional strategy versus entrepreneurial strategy.

The second aspect concerns the need to develop a strategy for the entrepreneurial activities of the firm. The strategy for entrepreneurship might cover any number of areas. Six of the most salient decision areas are outlined below.

1. Where does the firm want to be in the entrepreneurial grid? (See Chapter Three.) From an overall standpoint, is the firm's strategy one of high frequency and low degree of entrepreneurship, high degree and low frequency, or some other combination? What is the firm's desired risk profile?

2. To what extent is the entrepreneurial emphasis in the company that of growing new businesses and starting new ventures outside the mainstream of the firm versus transforming the existing enterprise and its internal operations into a more entrepreneurial environment?

3. In what areas does the firm want to be an innovation leader versus an innovation follower vis-à-vis the industry?

4. In what areas of the firm is management looking for higher versus lower levels of entrepreneurial activity? Which business units or product areas

are expected to innovate the most? Which departments are expected to be the real home for entrepreneurship, setting direction and providing leadership for the rest of the firm?

5. What is the relative importance over the next three years of product versus service versus process innovation? What is the relative importance of new versus existing markets?

6. To what extent is innovation expected to come from senior management, middle management, or first-level management? Is there clear direction in terms of the types of innovation expected at each level?

Other issues come into play, some of which were discussed as part of the innovation charter of the firm. (See Chapter Seven.) Examples include the relative emphasis on the outsourcing of innovation and the types of technologies in which the firm is going to invest.

If we compare these two aspects of strategy formulation, both address issues that are external and internal to the firm. However, the application of entrepreneurial thinking to the firm's core strategy is primarily dealing with the following external questions. Where are unfilled spaces in the marketplace? How can the firm differentiate itself on a sustained basis? Where can we lead the customer? Alternatively, the development of a strategy for entrepreneurship is especially concerned with internal questions, including the types of innovative efforts that will receive resources and from where in the company innovations are expected to come. In a sense, it is about stimulating the internal market, or market inside the company, for ideas and innovation. Clearly, the two aspects are related. For instance, internal process innovation in ground operations was critical for Southwest Airlines' being able to differentiate itself as a low-cost, on-time airline.

KEY STRATEGIC CONCEPTS: ENTREPRENEURSHIP AS THE DRIVER

The role of entrepreneurship in strategy and the role of strategy in entrepreneurship can be better appreciated by considering some salient concepts that surround the strategy formulation process. These include strategic advantage, strategic positioning, strategic flexibility, and strategic leverage.

STRATEGIC ADVANTAGE

Markets are dynamic; no one is standing still. Companies leapfrog one another in terms of product improvements, cost reductions, and enhancements to customer service levels. They find themselves in a never-ending battle to preempt, protect against, and surpass competitors. It is all about competitive advantage, which results from "an enduring value differential between the products or services of one organization and those of its competitors in the minds of customers" (Duncan,

Ginter, and Swayne 1998). For its part, strategy is the set of commitments and actions taken by management to first develop and then exploit a competitive advantage in the marketplace.

Yesterday's competitive advantages can be today's disadvantages. Black and Decker's consolidation into a few global-scale facilities in the 1980s proved a disadvantage in the 1990s. Organizational practices, core competencies, and business models confer advantages because of specific factors present under particular conditions over a particular period of time. Not only do the underlying factors subsequently change, but also "the very existence of competitive advantage sets in motion creative innovations that, as competitors strive to level the playing field, cause the advantage to dissipate" (Christensen 2001, p. 109).

Innovation is the key to developing and successfully exploiting competitive advantages. An executive from Enron, for example, states, "Innovation is at the heart of sustaining a company's competitive advantage" (Stein 2000). Innovation coupled with continuous learning provides the edge. The combination brings something new into being: new products, new internal processes, new business models, and new markets. It can enable firms to bring products more rapidly to the market, to customize those products, and to add new functionality to those products.

The challenge is to develop innovation as a core competence of the firm. Moreover, the firm's strategy for entrepreneurship serves to stimulate such innovation. In a global economy, the most successful strategies call for the firm to rely on innovations that offer fundamentally superior value to existing buyers or to create new markets through a quantum leap in buyer value. Companies able to exploit the competitive advantages they own today, while simultaneously using innovation to shape the advantages they intend to own and use tomorrow, increase the probability of long-term survival, growth, and financial success.

STRATEGIC POSITIONING

Strategic positioning is concerned with how the firm wants to be perceived in the marketplace. Positions can be defined on many bases, including attributes or benefits offered, price/quality levels, capabilities relative to competitors, or customers and applications that the firm specializes in. Entrepreneurial strategy is all about positioning. It is a process of perceiving new positions that attract customers from established ones or draw new customers into the market.

Underlying strategic positioning is a distinct set of activities that a company does differently and better than others. These activities represent the linkage both to strategy and to entrepreneurship. Finding and implementing a strategic position that holds meaningful potential for the firm—meaning one that not only represents a unique value proposition but is also meaningfully different from those of competitors—is a fundamentally entrepreneurial challenge. FedEx provides an example. When a package or letter absolutely has to be somewhere and absolutely has to be there quickly, customers rely on this company more than any other. The company's ability to provide fast and highly reliable delivery to virtually anywhere at a reasonable price is tied to the management of its novel hub-and-spoke operating model, an innovative logistics system on the ground, a unique organizational structure, and creative approaches to human resource management activities.

Entrepreneurial thinking can be applied not only to the identification of the strategic position the firm seeks to occupy but also to the way the firm manages each of the underlying activities that make it possible to occupy that position. Further, many trade-offs can come into play among these activities, and entrepreneurial approaches are often needed to ensure activities are combined in ways that do not compromise the value proposition. Activities must fit with and reinforce one another. As Michael Porter (1996, p. 70) notes, "Fit (among key organizational activities) locks out imitators by creating a chain that is as strong as its strongest link." Innovation that enhances value or lowers cost from one activity area can serve to lower costs or increase the value customers receive from a complementary activity area.

Effective strategic positioning is critical for competitive advantage. As with competitive advantage, the appropriateness of the firm's positioning can change both as a function of marketplace developments and of developments affecting the internal value chain of the firm. For example, other firms crowd into similar positions, new customer groups or purchase occasions arise, new needs emerge as societies evolve, new distribution channels appear, new technologies are developed, or new machinery or information systems become available. Firms also become complacent, assuming they "own" a given position, and they stop looking for innovative ways to enhance the position, develop it further, or take it in new but consistent directions. As an exception to the rule, FedEx has extended its effective positioning with creative applications of technology to various internal activities. However, it has also capitalized on and extended the position of Federal Express to a family of related companies, including FedEx Ground, FedEx Freight Custom, FedEx Custom Critical, and FedEx Trade Networking.

STRATEGIC FLEXIBILITY AND ADAPTATION

Firms require appropriate strategic direction to traverse the new competitive landscape successfully, but this direction should be coupled with flexibility. Strategic flexibility involves a willingness to rethink continuously and make adjustments to the firm's strategies, action plans, and resource allocations and to the company structure, culture, and managerial systems. How quickly and adroitly can managers adapt to changes in the competitive set or in competitor strategies, to a shift in the power or change in the structure within the value chain, or to changes in the availability or cost of components and raw materials? These adjustments allow for the fact that management knows where the firm wants to go and how it wants to be positioned but that there are different ways to get there. Flexibility demands keen insights into the organization's resources, capabilities, and competencies.

Michael Hitt and his colleagues have proposed a model for building strategic flexibility into organizations. As illustrated in Figure 8.1, their model starts with

■ FIGURE 8.1

BUILDING STRATEGIC FLEXIBILITY AND COMPETITIVE ADVANTAGE

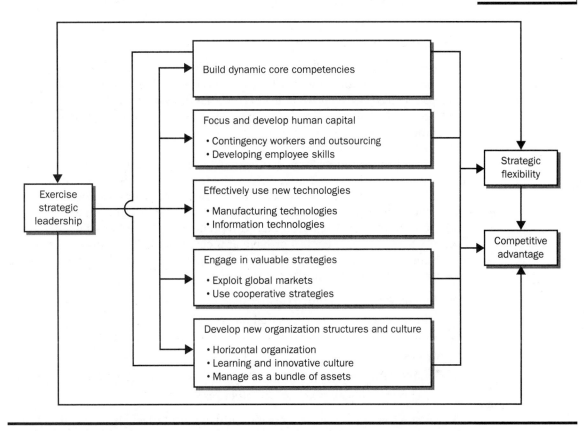

SOURCE: Hitt, M. A., B. W. Keats, and S. M. DeMarie. 1998. "Navigating in the New Competitive Landscape: Building Strategic Flexibility and Competitive Advantage in the 21st Century," *Academy of Management Executive* 12(4): 22–42.

strategic leadership at the top of the organization, which means senior executives who are visionary, entrepreneurial, and transformational (and willing to pay the price of transformation and persevere long enough to see their entrepreneurial visions realized). Assuming this kind of leadership is in place, the following five factors contribute to building strategic leadership: a) a unique set of dynamic core competencies (i.e., competencies that are continually improved and enhanced); b) creative approaches to human capital (e.g., the use of contract labor, outsourcing, and employee sharing in noncore areas of the firm); c) effective incorporation of new and emerging technologies (i.e., technologies that enable the firm to recognize changing market needs or conditions quickly, customize products, and serve different markets in different ways); d) strategic alliances and a global market presence (i.e., a diversified approach to markets and cooperative approach to penetrating those markets); and e) company structures that are flattened and cultures that stress learning and accountability for innovation (i.e., structures and cultures that enable the firm to recognize patterns and trends, make quick adjustments, and continuously experiment in the marketplace).

STRATEGIC LEVERAGE

One vehicle for achieving flexibility is called leveraging. At its most basic level, leveraging refers to doing more with less. Consider the base word *lever.* Acting as a lever, a metal rod or wooden pole enables an individual to dislodge or move an object he or she is unable to move on his or her own. In a similar vein, corporate entrepreneurs and entrepreneurial companies are brilliant leveragers of resources. As Hamel and Prahalad (1994, p. 128) note, "Getting to the future first is more a function of resourcefulness than resources. . . . Resourcefulness stems not from an elegantly structured strategic architecture, but from a deeply felt sense of purpose, a broadly shared dream, a truly seductive view of tomorrow's opportunity." In highly entrepreneurial companies, ambition forever outpaces resources.

The implication is that corporate entrepreneurs are not constrained by the resources they currently control or have at their disposal. They are able to leverage resources in a number of creative ways. Stated differently, the concept of resource leveraging has a number of dimensions:

- Stretching resources much further than others have done in the past;
- Getting uses out of resources that others are unable to realize;
- Using other people's (or firm's) resources to accomplish the entrepreneur's own purpose;
- Complementing one resource with another to create higher combined value;
- Using certain resources to obtain other resources.

Leveraging is not something an individual simply decides to do. It is not a mechanical process — it is a creative process. Firms and managers within firms develop a capacity for resource leveraging. Some are more creative; others are less so. The ability to recognize a resource that is not being used completely, to see how the resource could be used in a nonconventional way, and to convince those that control the resource to let you use it requires insight, experience, and skill. The same can be said for the ability to get team members to work extra hours; convince departments to perform activities they normally do not perform; or put together unique sets of resources that, when blended, are synergistic.

Of all the types of leveraging approaches mentioned above, one of the most powerful concerns the ability to use other people's resources to accomplish the entrepreneur's purpose. Examples of the ways in which this is done include bartering, borrowing, renting, leasing, sharing, recycling, contracting, and outsourcing. These efforts can be directed at other departments and units within the firm or at suppliers, distributors, customers, and other external organizations. They frequently entail both informal initiatives such as the exchange of favors and the use of networks and formal initiatives such as strategic alliances and joint ventures.

Discussions of resource productivity can also be misconstrued, at least in some companies. The leveraging philosophy is not about cutting resources or squeezing them as much as possible in an attempt to increase productivity. Managers seeking to create the lean and mean enterprise often find the end result is more mean than lean. The long-term outcome is frequently less productivity and more inefficiency. Rather, leveraging is about finding and using resources more intelligently, more creatively, and in a more focused manner.

ENTREPRENEURIAL STRATEGY: SOME CONTRIBUTING FACTORS

Strategy does not exist in a vacuum. As suggested earlier, strategy and strategic management go hand in hand. Even the most entrepreneurial of strategies will fail unless it is coupled with management practices that support and reinforce the strategy. Let us consider some of the key ingredients that contribute to a well-conceptualized entrepreneurial strategy.

DEVELOPING AN ENTREPRENEURIAL VISION

Great organizations are driven by clear visions. It is important that senior management conceptualize and communicate a vision of organization-wide entrepreneurship. Vision comes from the top, while entrepreneurial behavior comes from throughout the organization. This shared vision requires identification of a company-specific concept of entrepreneurship, as well as what have been termed *big hairy audacious goals* (or BHAGs for short) that spell out a bold, daunting challenge—one that stretches every member of the company (Collins and Porras 1996).

INCREASING THE PERCEPTION OF OPPORTUNITY

Entrepreneurial behavior is opportunity-seeking behavior. Entrepreneurial strategy represents a quest to find and exploit untapped opportunities—opportunities that arise from areas of uncertainty both inside and outside the organization. If every employee is to be considered a potential entrepreneur, then the ability to recognize opportunity becomes paramount. Employees are unable to see opportunity because they are surrounded by constraints on the one hand and crises on the other hand. Ironically, the very act of pursuing an opportunity tends to subsequently make people more opportunity-aware.

Strategy and objectives must be about people possibilities. These include possibilities in terms of breaking rules, going against the grain, abandoning assumptions, and looking at operations and customers in completely novel ways. It is a continual emphasis on alternative approaches to marketing, human resource management, the use of information technology, and every other facet of business.

OPPORTUNITY ASSESSMENT AND INTERNAL VALUE CREATION

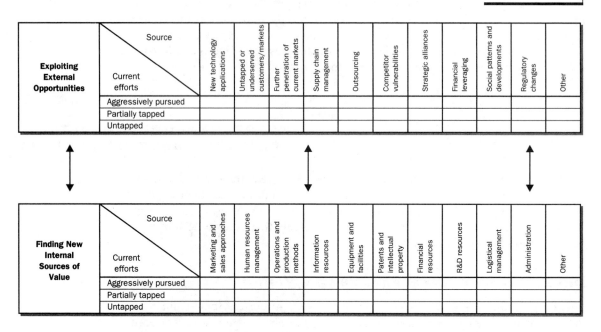

Strategies should be built around the people of the company and should be defined in a manner that is dependent upon and stretches those people.

A useful concept is the opportunity horizon, which represents the outer limit on management's vision regarding the opportunities open to the firm. For many companies, the opportunity horizon is quite constrained. Managers are unable to escape the past, and so future possibilities are little more than extensions of what the company is doing now and where it has been historically. For instance, the needs and demands of current customers so overwhelm management thinking that the firm is unable to imagine unusual ways to create value for new markets or new customer segments. Figure 8.2 represents a framework for use in assessing the firm's (or a given unit's) approach to opportunity.

INSTITUTIONALIZING CHANGE

Change is good. It enriches people, adding to their experiences and deepening their insights. It represents new opportunities for employees. Strategies can sometimes serve to preserve the status quo, in some instances unintentionally. In entrepreneurial companies, strategy should be conceived as a vehicle for change. In fact, in the new competitive landscape, strategy provides focus and direction for change both within the firm and in the marketplace. The opposite of accepting the status quo is to continually challenge every aspect of a business, looking for better ways to do things, processes that can be done differently, and things that can be eliminated.

INSTILLING THE DESIRE TO BE INNOVATIVE

Innovation takes many forms in companies. A strategy that encourages innovation will be effective only if management efforts make clear what types of innovation the company seeks and from where in the company these innovations are expected to come. The concept of an innovation portfolio was introduced in Chapter Seven. The innovation portfolio emphasizes the need to pursue, at the same time, innovations that are higher and lower in risk, discontinuous and continuous, product focused and process focused, and have differing market potentials. The portfolio perspective suggests that innovations can originate from throughout the organization. Not every employee necessarily has to initiate or champion an innovation. But every employee should have some role in one or more innovative initiatives at a given point in time. When 3M created its 15 percent rule, mandating that managers dedicate time to innovation that is not part of their normal job, they were saying that innovation is expected of people who do not necessarily see themselves as innovators. The desire to be innovative stems from a sense of involvement in, ownership of, and responsibility for innovative projects.

INVESTING IN PEOPLE'S IDEAS

Ideas, together with an individual's personal commitment to them, represent the single greatest asset in a company. Unfortunately, companies tend to treat ideas like targets in a shooting gallery, and they come up with the most inventive means of shooting them down. Or their concept of support for ideas begins and ends with a suggestion box. Fostering idea generation requires that management continually plow and fertilize the fields. Investments are needed in intelligence-gathering activities of all types. Infrastructure is needed to support information storage, reporting, and sharing. This must be reinforced by the norms and values of the company. Forums are needed for airing ideas. Pools of capital are required for investing in ideas. Managers at all levels must define their jobs in terms of listening to, productively challenging, endorsing, feeding, sponsoring, and investing in the ideas of employees. The two most precious words in the organization should be "what if?" Approached in this manner, the internal environment of the company becomes a marketplace of ideas; the strategic management becomes a set of activities devoted to making this marketplace work efficiently.

SHARING RISKS AND REWARDS WITH EMPLOYEES

Entrepreneurship is about risk and reward. The relationship is direct but nonlinear. This is a fundamental precept of entrepreneurial behavior and investor behavior. Ignoring the risk-reward relationship when striving to develop entrepreneurial strategies within companies misses the whole point of entrepreneurship. It is not that employees must have the potential to become multimillionaires as a function of entrepreneurial behavior. In fact, the absolute size of rewards is a secondary consideration. However, sustainable entrepreneurship requires that employees experience some of the risk and meaningfully participate in the rewards. The implication is that individuals and teams lose in terms of salary, bonuses, freedom, research support or other resources if projects fail or underperform, and they do quite well when projects are highly successful.

RECOGNIZING THE CRITICAL IMPORTANCE OF FAILURE

Failure is a sign of experience, learning, and progress. Not only can overall projects fail, but the likelihood of project demise is a function of how the champion deals with lots of small failures along the way. Doing something entrepreneurial means experimenting, and experimentation is all about trying something and, when it does not work out, trying something else. Importantly, the experimenter never loses sight of the quest. He or she becomes fairly thickskinned in dealing with rejection and failure but open-minded about ways to adapt or new avenues to attempt. Many attempts are needed before success is achieved.

Learning from failure, as opposed to expecting punishment for it, is promoted in entrepreneurial firms. By encouraging plenty of experimentation and risk-taking, there are more chances for a new product hit. As an example, one of the early founders of 3M, Francis G. Oakie, had an idea to replace razor blades with sandpaper (Von Hipple, Thomke, and Sonnack 1999). He believed that men could rub sandpaper on their face rather than use a sharp razor. He was wrong, and the idea failed in this application. But his idea continued until he developed a waterproof sandpaper for the auto industry — a blockbuster success! In the process, 3M's philosophy of innovation was born. For them, innovation is a numbers game; the more ideas a company has, the better the chances for a successful innovation. Further, one of the underlying principles that guide the strategic management of the company is never to kill an idea, no matter how different or unrealistic the idea appears. This philosophy has paid off for 3M. Antistatic videotape, translucent dental braces, synthetic ligaments for knee surgery, heavy-duty reflective sheeting for construction signs, and, of course, Post-it® Notes are just some of the great innovations developed by the company. Overall, the company has a catalogue of 60,000 products that generate almost $11 billion in sales.

MATCHING STRATEGY WITH STRUCTURE: THE VALUE OF VENTURE TEAMS

We have emphasized the need for companies to develop entrepreneurial strategies as well as strategies for entrepreneurship. The success of both of these is tied to managements' ability to properly structure the company's operations. This is especially true when it comes to strategies for entrepreneurship, for as we shall see in Chapter Ten, different structures will produce different levels and types of innovation. No matter what particular structures emerge, an important building block for structure should be the concept of the venture team.

Quite simply, venture teams represent a means for achieving a major breakthrough in terms of innovation productivity in the firm. This breed of work team is a new direction for many firms. The teams are commonly referred to as self-directed, self-managing, and high performance. Reich (1987) has referred to the term *collective entrepreneurship,* where individual skills are integrated into a group and the team's collective capacity to innovate becomes greater than the sum of its parts. Over time, as group members work through various problems and approaches, they learn about each other's abilities. Specifically, they learn how they can help one another perform better, what each can contribute to a particular project, and how they can best take advantage of one another's experience. Each participant is a role player, and each is constantly on the lookout for small adjustments that will speed and smooth the evolution of the whole. The net result of many such small-scale adaptations, affected throughout the organization, is to propel the enterprise forward.

Venture teams offer corporations the opportunity to capitalize on individual talents together with collective wisdom and energy. An excellent example is Signode, a $750-million-a-year manufacturer of plastic and steel strapping for packaging and materials handling, located in Glenview, Illinois. The company's leaders wanted to chart new directions to become a $1-billion-plus firm. In pursuit of this goal, Signode devised an aggressive strategy for growth by developing new "legs" for the company. It formed a corporate development group to pursue markets outside the company's core business but within the framework of its corporate strengths. It also formed venture teams, but before launching the first of these, top management identified the firm's global business strengths and broad areas with potential for new product lines: warehousing/shipping, packaging, plastics for nonpackaging, fastening and joining systems, and product identification and control systems.

Each new business opportunity was to have the potential to generate $50 million in business within five years. In addition, each opportunity had to build on one of Signode's strengths: industrial customer base and marketing expertise, systems sales and service capabilities, containment and reinforcement technology, steel and plastic process technology, machine and design capabilities, and the production and distribution know-how. The assessment criteria were based on selling to business-to-business markets. The basic technology to be employed in the new business had to already exist, and there had to be a strong likelihood of attaining a major market share within a niche. Finally, the initial investment in the new opportunity had to be $30 million or less.

Based on these criteria, Signode began to build its V-Team (venture team) approach to entrepreneurship. It took three months to select the first team members, and initial teams had three common traits: high risk-taking ability, creativity, and the ability to deal with ambiguity. All participants were multidiscipline volunteers who would work full time on developing new product packaging businesses. The team members came from diverse backgrounds: design engineering, marketing, sales, and product development. They set up shop in rented office space five miles from the firm's headquarters. Not all six teams were able to develop remarkable new ventures. However, the efforts did pay off for Signode because one venture team developed a business plan to manufacture plastic trays for frozen entrees that could be used in either regular or microwave ovens, which did indeed turn out to be a $50-million-a-year business within five years. The V-Team experience rekindled enthusiasm and affected morale throughout the organization. Most importantly, the V-Team approach became Signode's strategy to invent its own future rather than waiting for things to happen.

ANOTHER LOOK AT STRATEGY AND STRUCTURE: THE ACORDIA COMPANIES

The results of an entrepreneurial strategy tied to company structure can be further illustrated by considering the experiences of The Associated Group. Under the vision and direction of L. Ben Lytle, Chairman and CEO, a dramatic restructuring plan was put into effect beginning in 1986 in an attempt to facilitate the entrepreneurial process. In 1983, the company was operating as Blue Cross/Blue Shield of Indiana and was literally bogged down in its own bureaucracy. As a result, The Associated Group (the new name taken by the company rather than Blue Cross/Blue Shield of Indiana) was losing ground in a fast-paced, changing insurance industry. Lytle decided it was time to divide the company legally, emotionally, physically, geographically, and culturally into operating companies named Acordia Companies, ranging in size from 42 to 200 employees. Each separate Acordia company had an individual CEO, vice president, and *outside* board of directors that was delegated full authority to run the business.

By the end of 1991 (1,800 days later and following the implementation of a five-year strategic plan to restructure and infuse entrepreneurial thinking into the organization), much had changed. The opportunities for entrepreneurial individuals within the organization began to expand with the development of these mini-corporations, which were designed to capture market niches and innovatively develop new ones. In 1986, The Associated Group was one large corporation with 2,800 employees serving only the state of Indiana with all revenue generated from health insurance. By the mid-1990s, the company employed over 7,000 people in fifty different companies, serving forty-nine states and generating over 25 percent of its $2 billion in revenue in lines of business outside health insurance. The results, according to Lytle, point to the effectiveness of an entrepreneurial strategy's capturing the imagination of the entire company. The decentralized structure appealed to the builder types in the company who were seeking challenge and accountability for their ideas and innovative abilities.

By 1995, there were thirty-two Acordia companies where corporate clients could obtain all types of insurance-related services including commercial property and casualty coverage, group life and health insurance, third-party claims administration for self-insured benefit plans, and employee benefits consulting. In order to institute self-perpetuating change in the Acordia network, the minicorporation CEOs are encouraged (and rewarded through stock options) to expand their businesses and then spin off certain parts of the business either geographically or by specialty. These spin-offs produce new companies whenever an existing company surpasses 200 employees or there are too many management layers. In addition, the CEOs are evaluated on their ability to identify and nurture additional potential CEOs within their own organization. Thus, the Acordia strategy is to concentrate and divide, which leads to continuous innovation, growth, and entrepreneurial development. It also has placed the company among the elite in *Business Insurance*'s worldwide rankings of brokers.

IMPLEMENTATION ISSUES: FATAL VISIONS

Strategy formulation is half the battle — implementation is the other half. The actual execution of a strategy is almost as important as the strategy itself. Many organizations make unintentional errors while applying a specific strategy to their particular context. Michael Porter (1991) has noted five fatal mistakes to which organizations continually fall prey in their attempts to implement a strategy. These are especially relevant for entrepreneurial strategies:

Flaw 1: Misunderstanding industry attractiveness: There is a tendency to associate attractiveness with those industries that are growing the most rapidly, appear to be glamorous, or use the fanciest technology. Attractiveness has much more to do with high barriers to entry, the ability to differentiate, the existence of few effective substitutes, and the ability to influence suppliers and customers. The more high tech or high glamour a business is, the more likely that many new competitors will enter it and make it less profitable.

Flaw 2: No real competitive advantage: Merely copying, imitating, or slightly improving upon the strategy of competitors is not entrepreneurial. It may seem easier, and it may seem less risky, but it means the venture has no real competitive advantage. To succeed, new ventures must develop unique ways to compete.

Flaw 3: Pursuing an unsustainable competitive position: Firms try to be customer service leaders when customer service innovations are easy to mimic; they attempt to be technology leaders when they do not have the necessary internal capacity to continually produce desirable technical innovations. Alternatively, they pursue strategies that place conflicting demands on different parts of the company.

Flaw 4: Compromising strategy for growth: A careful balance must exist between growth and the competitive strategy that makes a business successful. Pressures exist for companies to maximize sales growth, which often means capitalizing on short-term opportunities that are inconsistent with or distract management from the core strategy. Although fast growth can be tempting in certain industries, it is imperative to maintain and grow strategic advantage as well.

Flaw 5: Failure to explicitly communicate strategy internally: It is essential to communicate the company's strategy clearly to every employee. The assumption that employees know the strategy and understand its implications for how they deal with particular issues or decisions is a dangerous one. Management must be explicit not only regarding the strategy itself but also in what it means for marketing, human resource management, production, and other areas of the firm.

The more that a company's strategy is matched to core competencies and a well-integrated chain of internal activities, the easier implementation will be. However, implementation of strategy is also where flexibility and adaptation are most vital. Implementation involves an iterative process. Action programs are executed, results are assessed, adjustments are made, conditions change, more adjustments are made, certain tactics are abandoned and others added, results are assessed, additional adjustments are made, and so forth. In many instances, one or more of the creative adjustments prove to be the factor that makes a strategy successful over time.

SUMMARY AND CONCLUSIONS

The pervasive dynamism and uncertainty in the new competitive landscape require firms to develop entrepreneurial capacity. Entrepreneurial actions are any newly fashioned behavior through which companies exploit opportunities others have not noticed or exploited. Novelty, in terms of new resources, new customers, new markets, or a new combination of resources, customers, and markets, is the defining characteristic of entrepreneurial actions. When the actions taken in a large firm to form competitive advantages and to exploit them through a strategy are grounded in entrepreneurial actions, the firm is employing an *entrepreneurial strategy.* Further, when establishing direction and priorities for the product, service, and process innovation efforts of the firm, the company is formulating its *strategy for entrepreneurship.*

This chapter has explored the concept of entrepreneurship as the new dominant logic of a firm. In this regard, three factors become evident. First, as a dominant logic, entrepreneurial strategy promotes strategic agility, flexibility, creativity, and continuous innovation throughout the firm. Second, the overriding focus of the firm is opportunity identification, discovery of new sources of value, and product and process innovation that will lead to greater profitability. And third, this strategy is translated into the objectives, reward systems, control systems, planning approaches, structure, and human resource management practices of the

TEXAS INSTRUMENTS

As early as the 1970s, intrapreneurial environments were making millions for corporations. The technological advancements of the time played a major role in companies' abilities to introduce products that would eventually redefine both leisure and commerce activities worldwide.

At Texas Instruments, one employee hit a jackpot when he used the new microchip to invent the Speak 'n' Spell, the first talking toy for children. Amazingly, that person, whose creative idea made millions, wasn't even a member of the company's project development team. TI had supplied funds for the idea to be pursued and developed and received a star performer in return.

At 3M, it's the Genesis program. At TI, it's called the IDEA intrapreneurship program: Identify, Develop, Expand, and Action. TI doesn't hesitate to fund projects with higher-than-average risk.

"Our IDEA program encourages risk-taking because people know this money is throwaway and there is absolutely no aura or taint of failure if projects do not meet their goals," says Nathan Dodge, Director of University Research and supervisor of the program. "We like to use IDEA money for projects that have potentially very high payoff (hundreds of millions of dollars), but our expectation is that they have only a 5 percent or 10 percent chance of success." With IDEA, the third step, Expand, is where any given project comes to a fork in the funding road. If by then the technical and business management aspects of the project/idea do not foreshadow high future value, it isn't converted into the company's R&D system (Action). Like many intrapreneurial companies, TI also requires IDEA projects to fit into the current company philosophy, strategy, and manufacturing competencies.

The ease of project approval indicates how TI can have 150 projects active at one time. A one-page proposal to one of a network of forty volunteer IDEA reps (worldwide) can get any employee $25,000. If Dodge cosigns, employees can be granted up to $50,000. Managers and executives have no say in what projects get funded — something that hinders creativity in many organizations. Annually, TI spends $500,000 to $1 million on the IDEA program. Monies are allowed for labor and expendable materials but not for capital equipment or overhead expenses. The yearly capital investment is pocket change compared to the return on investment Texas Instruments has realized over the past two and a half decades: $500 million in profits and cost savings.

SOURCE: Stevens, T. 1998. "Idea Dollars," *Industry Week* 247 (4): 47.

firm. It is reinforced by the company culture. Moreover, sustainable advantage in the new competitive landscape requires a dominant logic that is dynamic. Entrepreneurship captures such dynamism, with its emphasis on continued innovation of all degrees and types.

REFERENCES

Amit, R. H., K. Brigham, and G. D. Markman. 2000. "Entrepreneurial Management As Strategy." In *Entrepreneurship as Strategy*, edited by G. D. Meyer and K. A. Heppard. Thousands Oaks: Sage Publications.

Bettis, R. A. and M. A. Hitt. 1995. "The New Competitive Landscape," *Strategic Management Journal* 16: 7–19.

Bettis, R. A. and Prahalad, C. K. (1995). "The Dominant Logic: Retrospective and Extension," *Strategic Management Journal* 16: 5–14.

Christensen, C. 2001. "The Past and Future of Competitive Advantage," *Sloan Management Review* 42 (2) 105–110.

Collins, J. C., and J. I. Porras. 1996. "Building Your Company's Vision," *Harvard Business Review* 74 (September–October): 65–77.

Duncan, W. J., P. Ginter, and L. Swayne. 1998. "Competitive Advantage and Internal Organizational Assessment," *Academy of Management Executives* 12 (3): 6–16.

Frohman, M., and P. Pascarella. 1990. "Achieving Purpose-Driven Innovation," *Industry Week* 19 (March): 20–26.

Grove, A.S. 1996. *Only the Paranoid Survive.* London: Harper Collins.

Hamel, G. 2000. *Leading the Revolution.* Boston: Harvard Business School Press.

Hamel, G., and Prahalad, C. K. 1994. *Competing for the Future.* Boston: Harvard Business School Press.

Hitt, M. A., and T. S. Reed. 2000. "Entrepreneurship in the New Competitive Landscape." In *Entrepreneurship As Strategy*, edited by G. D. Meyer and K. A. Heppard. Thousand Oaks: Sage Publications.

Porter, M. E. 1991. "Knowing Your Place—How to Assess the Attractiveness of Your Industry and Your Company's Position in It," *Inc.* 13 (9) (September): 90–94.

Porter, M. E. 1996. "What Is Strategy?" *Harvard Business Review* 74 (6) (November–December): 61-78.

Reich, R. 1987. "Entrepreneurship Reconsidered: The Team As Hero," *Harvard Business Review* 65 (3) (May–June): 77–83.

Schendel, D., and C. Hofer. 1978. *Strategic Management: A New View of Business Policy and Planning.* Boston: Little Brown.

Stacey, R. D. 1996. *Complexity and Creativity in Organizations.* San Francisco: Berrett-Koehler.

Stein, N. 2000. "The World's Most Admired Companies," *Fortune* 142 (7) (October): 182–196.

Von Hipple, E., S. Thomke, and M. Sonnack. 1999. "Creating Breakthroughs at 3M," *Harvard Business Review* 77 (5) (September–October): 47–57.

9

UNDERSTANDING THE OBSTACLES TO CORPORATE ENTREPRENEURSHIP

Company survival depends on constant growth and an ability to defend against the ongoing moves of competitors. Accordingly, many companies have come to recognize the need for entrepreneurship. One survey of executives found that the leading reasons for an emphasis on entrepreneurship inside the corporation are strategic necessity and the maturing of existing businesses (Block and MacMillan 1993). The problem today concerns *how* to make it happen (and, assuming the company can do so, *how much* to let it happen).

The pursuit of entrepreneurship within a company creates new and potentially complex sets of challenges on both theoretical and practical levels. On a theoretical level, companywide entrepreneurship is not included in, or accommodated by, most of the theories, models, or frameworks that have been developed to guide managerial practice. Further, very little progress has been made in developing a theory of corporate entrepreneurship. As a result, little is known about what kind of entrepreneurship is likely under various company structures, control systems, reward approaches, cultures, and other managerial variables. Limited progress in theory building hinders our ability to predict, explain, and shape the environment in which corporate entrepreneurship flourishes.

On a practical level, managers typically find themselves in uncharted territory when it comes to entrepreneurship. They lack guidelines on how to direct or redirect resources towards entrepreneurial strategies. Traditional management practices often don't apply (Table 9.1). Further, most of the infrastructure within a company (systems, structures, policies and procedures, etc.) has been put in place for reasons other than entrepreneurship. Companies develop in ways that enable

■ TABLE 9.1

OBSTACLES AND EFFECTS OF TRADITIONAL PRACTICES

Traditional Management Practices	Adverse Effects
Enforce standard procedures to avoid mistakes	Innovative solutions blocked, funds misspent
Manage resources for efficiency and ROI	Competitive lead lost, low market penetration
Control against plan	Facts ignored that should replace assumptions
Plan long term	Nonviable goals locked in, high failure costs
Manage functionally	Entrepreneur failure and/or venture failure
Avoid moves that risk the base business	Missed opportunities
Protect the base business at all costs	Venturing dumped when base business threatened
Judge new steps from prior experience	Wrong decisions about competition and markets
Compensate uniformly	Low motivation and inefficient operations
Promote compatible individuals	Loss of innovators

SOURCES: Adapted from Sykes, H. B., and Z. Block. 1989. "Corporate Venturing Obstacles: Sources and Solutions," *Journal of Business Venturing* 4(May): 161.

them to efficiently manage the present, which means they are not organized in ways that allow them to create the future. Thus, entrepreneurship typically clashes with the mainstream operations of the firm. More fundamentally, entrepreneurship can be extremely threatening to the people who do the work of the organization because it can be disruptive, uncomfortable, irritating, and distracting. Not surprisingly, there are many in companies who will go out of their way to not only resist an entrepreneurial idea but also to kill it.

In this chapter, we examine the barriers and obstacles within companies that hinder the entrepreneurial process, and a framework for categorizing these obstacles is presented. In addition, a variety of the most consequential constraints are discussed. Insights are provided regarding where to begin efforts to remove the barriers and overcome the obstacles.

A FRAMEWORK FOR UNDERSTANDING THE OBSTACLES

There are, in reality, hundreds of factors within the typical company that constrain entrepreneurship. In fact, there can be so many obstacles that they can make entrepreneurship seem like a hopeless pipe dream. Yet, we find entrepreneurship happening even in the most stifling and bureaucratic of organizations. The key is to first identify the obstacles that represent the greatest threat to new concepts or ideas. The corporate entrepreneur must examine obstacles with an eye towards determining the following:

■ **TABLE 9.2**

CATEGORIES OF ORGANIZATIONAL CONSTRAINTS
ON CORPORATE ENTREPRENEURSHIP

Systems	Structures	Strategic Direction	Policies and Procedures	People	Culture
Misdirected reward and evaluation systems	Too many hierarchical levels	Absence of innovation goals	Long, complex approval cycles	Fear of failure	Ill-defined values
Oppressive control systems	Overly narrow span of control	No formal strategy for entrepreneurship	Extensive documentation requirements	Resistance to change	Lack of consensus over priorities
Inflexible budgeting systems	Responsibility without authority	No vision from the top	Overreliance on established rules of thumb	Parochial bias	Lack of fit
Arbitrary cost allocation systems	Top-down management	Lack of commitment from senior executives	Unrealistic performance criteria	"Turf" protection	Values that conflict with entrepreneurial requirements
Overly rigid, formal planning system	Restricted communication channels	No entrepreneurial role models at the top		Complacency	
	Lack of accountability			Short-term orientation	
				Inappropriate skills/talents	

SOURCE: Morris, M. H. 1998. *Entrepreneurial Intensity*. Westport: Quorum Books, p. 97.

- Which constraints can be ignored?
- Which can be worked around?
- Which can be eliminated?
- Which can be converted into facilitators of entrepreneurship?
- Which must be accepted even if they limit the scope or scale of what the corporate entrepreneur can accomplish?

Given the large number of potential constraints, it is helpful to identify general categories into which they can be grouped. Virtually all the obstacles can be classified into six groups: systems, structure, strategic direction, policies, people, and culture (Morris 1998). These categories are based on an extensive review of the literature on corporate innovation and entrepreneurship, surveys of a number of medium-sized and large industrial organizations, and in-depth assessments of three Fortune 500 companies.

Examples of the specific constraints found within each group are provided in Table 9.2. This set of items is not an exhaustive list but instead includes some of the more pervasive problem areas. Let us examine each of the categories in more detail.

SYSTEMS

Maturing organizations are typically dependent upon a number of formal managerial systems that have evolved over the years. These systems seek to provide stability, order, and coordination to an increasingly complex internal corporate environment. The trade-off, however, is a strong disincentive for entrepreneurship.

For example, employee reward and measurement systems often encourage safe, conservative behaviors and actions that produce short-term payoffs. In some cases, the reward and measurement systems are vague, inconsistent, or perceived as inequitable. Steven Kerr (1975) explains that many managers are guilty of "the folly of rewarding A, while hoping for B." They tend to ask for or expect innovative behavior but actually measure and reward noninnovative behavior. Control systems encourage managers to micromanage the expenditure of every dollar and to establish quantifiable performance benchmarks in as many activity areas as possible. These benchmarks become ends in themselves. They also convey a lack of trust in employee discretion. Budgeting systems provide no flexibility for the funding of bootleg projects or experimentation and tend to reward the politically powerful. Costing systems are frequently based on arbitrary allocation schemes, where any product or project can be made to look untenable simply as a function of the indirect fixed costs that must be recovered.

Planning, although critical for successful entrepreneurship, often serves as an obstacle. The problem occurs when there is an overemphasis on superfluous analysis, on form instead of content, on the document instead of the process, and on professional planners preparing the plan (instead of those charged with actually implementing it). The result is an overly rigid process that is incapable of quickly responding to new opportunities.

STRUCTURE

As a firm designs more hierarchical levels into the organizational structure, the ability to identify market opportunities, achieve management commitment, reallocate resources, take risks, or implement effective marketplace moves becomes problematic. Moreover, hierarchies tend to be accompanied by two other entrepreneurial barriers, top-down management and restrictive channels of communication. The result is frequently intransigence, which leads to a lack of commitment to innovation and change at all levels of the organization.

There is also a tendency to narrow the span of control of managers and to compartmentalize operations as firms mature. The result is oversupervised employees with little room to be creative or improvise. Furthermore, as employees become more segmented and compartmentalized, frames of reference become quite narrow. The ability to integrate perspectives and methods across boundaries is stifled. Meanwhile, accountability for change efforts is sufficiently diffused so that no one has a positive stake in ensuring that change occurs.

Structures that assign responsibility for entrepreneurial activities to managers without delegating adequate amounts of authority represent an additional constraint. Lacking the authority to try new methods or approaches in addressing obstacles or expending required resources, the manager is likely to become frustrated and perhaps cynical.

STRATEGIC DIRECTION

While the desire may be to achieve entrepreneurship throughout the firm, little can be accomplished without meaningful direction from the top. Established firms frequently have sophisticated planning systems that produce comprehensive strategies for marketing, production, and corporate finance but ignore the subject of innovation altogether. In the absence of specific goals for product and process innovation and a strategy for accomplishing such goals, entrepreneurship will only result haphazardly or by chance.

More fundamental, however, is the lack of commitment from senior executives to the principle of institutionalized entrepreneurship. This commitment requires leaders who are visionaries, seeing the firm and its people for what they can be, not what they have been. It requires leaders who are engaged in entrepreneurial processes as they occur throughout the enterprise. Instead, senior management is more typically cautious, suspicious, or completely unaware of efforts to break with tradition and capitalize on opportunity. Middle- and lower-level employees are strongly influenced by the role models found at the top of the organization. What they often find are politicians and technocrats, well versed in the art of corporate survival.

POLICIES AND PROCEDURES

Those involved in entrepreneurial endeavors are, by definition, addressing the unknown. Their efforts are often undermined by organizational policies and procedures that were established to bring order and consistency to the everyday operational requirements of the firm. These requirements tend to be relatively well known. Operating guidelines are established based on the rules of experience, with a premium placed on conservatism. The corporate entrepreneur comes to view these policies and procedures as burdensome red tape, and many find success to be unattainable unless rules are bent or broken.

Two of the most costly side effects of detailed operating policies are complex approval cycles for new ventures and elaborate documentation requirements. These obstacles not only consume an inordinate amount of the entrepreneur's time and energy but also frequently serve as well-designed mechanisms for incrementally dismantling the entrepreneur's innovative concept.

A related problem is the tendency for existing policies and procedures to impose unrealistic timetables and performance benchmarks on entrepreneurial programs. Deadlines and performance standards that reflect everyday operations often create an incentive to compromise on truly novel ideas. The entrepreneur finds it necessary to tailor innovations to performance criteria that reflect the present and the past rather than the competitive requirements of the future.

PEOPLE

The research suggests that people are the greatest obstacle of all. The number one priority in any attempt to increase the entrepreneurial intensity of an organization must be to change people and, specifically, to get them to be accepting of change and tolerant of failure in their work. Entrepreneurship is concerned with change and the management of change efforts. There is, however, a natural tendency for people to resist change. Given the opportunity, employees become comfortable with established ways of doing things. They value predictability and stability and are frequently skeptical of the need for change. Change is viewed as threatening and is met with a defensive, parochial attitude. This is especially the case where employees have no role in the change program.

Furthermore, employees demonstrate a tendency to be preoccupied with the demands of the present, not the future. Correspondingly, it is unrealistic to expect them to adopt a long-term perspective or to recognize the need for continual adaptation. In addition, the entrepreneurial spirit is stifled by a pervading fear of failure that is prevalent in most companies. People come to believe it is better to avoid failure than to risk success. They apparently perceive there is more to lose than to gain. Not that failure must be congratulated; rather, it should be personally detested. But failure is an important medium for learning; it should be embraced as such. The reality is that a majority of new ventures (companies, products, services, processes) fail, suggesting the need for a realistic appraisal of the outcome of any entrepreneurial effort.

Motivating people is also a problem, especially those driven by a need for power and status. Such individuals approach questions of innovation from the standpoint of turf protection. They hoard resources, especially information. They resist open communication and are suspicious of collaborative efforts.

One additional people-related issue concerns a general lack of skills and talents in the entrepreneurial area. While there is ample creative potential in every employee of the firm, many have never learned to develop or channel their creative energies. Some convince themselves that they are incapable of creative thinking. Others refuse to look beyond their current field of reference for ideas and solutions. Still others, on finding a creative solution, lack the skills necessary to bend the rules, build the coalitions, and work through or around the system to achieve successful implementation. Such problems are compounded by the apparent inability of many of those in supervisory positions to motivate and manage creative individuals.

CULTURE

Companies noted as successful innovators tend to foster a strong organizational culture. This culture is built around a central set of values that pervades every aspect of company operations. Employees are continually reinforced to internalize these values, and those who do not internalize them rarely last. These values are the lifeblood of the firm, creating the standards and providing the direction for growth and development.

When companies fail to clearly define what they stand for or do not achieve a consensus over value priorities (e.g., customer needs, quality, efficiency, service, reliability), entrepreneurship will have no focus. Even when priorities exist, values can be inconsistent with current competitive requirements. For instance, the company that stresses reliability or efficiency may find the marketplace puts a much higher premium on flexibility and value for the dollar.

Furthermore, entrepreneurship must itself become part of the organizational value system. This means companywide commitment to innovation, calculated risk-taking, and proactiveness. Such a commitment becomes impossible when the pervading emphasis is on imitation of competitors, conservation, and self-aggrandizement.

MORE ON THE PEOPLE FACTOR

As noted previously, the greatest of all the obstacles is people. Management may be able to fix the structure and remove bureaucratic rules and procedures, but the challenges involved in getting employees to embrace entrepreneurship, change the way they do things, collaborate on projects involving untested (and sometimes crazy) ideas, and give up resources to support entrepreneurial initiatives can be especially vexing. While entrepreneurship represents tremendous opportunity to the firm at large, it threatens the individuals inside the firm. For many employees, entrepreneurship means that current products will be eliminated, budgets will be reallocated, processes will be modified, and someone other than themselves will be a star. As a result, the pathways of most new ideas are blocked by the following:

- Resistance to change
- Making premature and uninformed judgements
- Neophobia: The dread of anything new or novel, fear of the unknown; the sense of embarrassment or humiliation that accompanies the admission that existing products or procedures are inferior to new proposals
- Caution: It's safer to have "the me-too-later" attitude
- Order: Entrepreneurship is a threat to the predictability and continuity on which all businesses are based—a new idea frequently represents a potential or real disruption of this continuity; the unwritten principle in business requires that disruptions be strictly controlled
- Anticipation of the extra trouble in handling and implementing new ideas: "We have enough work as it is"
- Politics: New ideas frequently pose a threat to the organizational stature and vested interests of managers who are anxious to maintain the existing hierarchical structure.

The dilemma of a large institution trying to nurture a people-focused atmosphere while maintaining corporate controls can be managed if disciplined reporting systems are balanced with an environment built around mutual trust and open communication (Sathe 1989). Risk-taking by individuals is strongly related to support, structure, and resources. Management has to act on two fronts simultaneously. One side of the battle involves offering incentives for entrepreneurial efforts and making resources accessible. This can be thought of as the upside. The other side concerns reducing the costs of failure, making employees comfortable with trying things that have a good chance of not working out. It also requires an overt effort to protect entrepreneurial individuals in terms of their career development. We can think of this as management of the downside.

RELATED LIMITATIONS THAT CONSTRAIN THE ENTREPRENEUR

In addition to these general obstacles, entrepreneurial initiatives are held back or derailed because of a number of personal and organizational limitations. In the discussion that follows, thirteen major limitations are identified that affect the success of the corporate entrepreneur.

LACK OF POLITICAL SAVVY: LEARNING TO WORK THE SYSTEM

Unpopular as the term may be, politics is a reality in the work environment. All organizations are inherently political. They are made up of individuals acting in their own interests. To implement corporate entrepreneurship, an innovative intrapreneur must attempt to influence other people, particularly the key stakeholders on whom the concept depends. Failure to identify those stakeholders and to anticipate and manage their behavior can drastically slow the intrapreneur's progress, if not stifle him or her completely.

There are numerous types of political problems that present critical roadblocks to the corporate entrepreneurial process. Many of the obstacles that follow have political undertones or political ramifications associated with them.

LACK OF TIME: CRISIS MANAGEMENT

Employees have jobs to perform. If anything, intensified competition and the information age have resulted in less free time on the job. Many people stay busy simply trying to keep up with the wealth of information that inundates them on the job each day and with the continuous changes in technology that affect how they do their jobs. Further, they continually face crises that require all of their energies. There just isn't a lot of time during the work day to experiment and try new things. A few companies, 3M for example, formally encourage their employees to spend a portion of their time on pet projects.

LACK OF REWARDS FOR INNOVATION: BEYOND TOKENISM

Traditionally, corporations do not necessarily reward (financially or otherwise) employees for being innovative. Many companies have recently implemented reward systems for cost-saving suggestions or ideas presented through structured suggestion programs, but these efforts often represent token gestures. With few exceptions, rewards for innovative thinking and behavior are not systematically built into corporate performance systems.

Corporate entrepreneurs are motivated by all kinds of rewards (e.g., bonuses, free time, profit share, pool of capital to use on future projects, stock options). They should also be ready to share some of the downside risks associated with their concepts or ideas. Like any venture, there should be a risk/reward equation that affects both the venture and the individual or team.

LACK OF GOOD FINANCIAL PROPOSALS: PROJECTING THE NUMBERS

New concepts require financing, and financing requires good financial justification. For this reason, the successful entrepreneur either must be adept at financial projections and calculations or must recruit a member of his or her team who has this knowledge and is willing and able to develop this portion of the venture plan.

The reason for this is quite simple. Boards of directors, presidents and vice presidents, and intracapital (inside money for projects) evaluation committees are not going to invest money in a new venture unless the entrepreneur can demonstrate the potential for a return on the investment that is equal to or greater than the profit margins the company needs to make. Often, corporate entrepreneurs are so in love with their venture idea that they approach these decision makers unprepared, are denied the initial capital to develop an idea, get frustrated, and give up.

In any large organization, funds are limited, and support for new products and services is determined by extensive market research, detailed financial projections, and contingency plans in case the sales projections are overestimated. One entrepreneur at 3M asked for $20 million to continue the research and development of laser disks. In his meeting with the board of directors, his biggest obstacle was criticism of his financial projections and profit margins. Whether the entrepreneur is asking for $20 thousand or $20 million, even from a company as large and innovative as 3M, careful planning and clear projections are a must.

LACK OF PEOPLE DEVELOPMENT SKILLS: AUTOCRACY RULES

Many of today's corporate leaders still adhere to Douglas MacGregor's, top-down "do-as-I-say" style of management. Managers with an autocratic, or Theory X, style are not prone to allowing people to make mistakes. They question the motives and motivation of their employees, assuming they are driven only by financial rewards and security. Consequently, it is difficult for these managers to understand or encourage the excitement a subordinate might have about a new venture idea. It is also difficult for these managers to empower employees or trust the intentions of a potential entrepreneur.

Many managers suffer from what has been termed the "that's-not-my-idea" syndrome. It is hard for them to imagine that one of their subordinates is capable of having and developing a viable innovative product or service. And if the employee does come up with a worthwhile idea, these top-down, controlling type managers often try to take credit for the idea. Frequently, they will want to create a task force or ad hoc committee to look into the idea, effectively taking control away from the corporate entrepreneur.

LACK OF LEGITIMACY: UNTESTED CONCEPT AND UNTESTED ENTREPRENEUR

As discussed briefly in Chapter Four, achieving credibility or legitimacy for an entrepreneurial idea is usually difficult. Since the concept has no real track record (e.g., customers, suppliers, etc.), the corporate entrepreneur encounters internal skepticism. At best, there will be reluctant and lukewarm supporters. At worst, there will be individuals determined to undermine the concept. Building confidence and credibility is a slow, painstaking process; however, it is critical to the survival of the entrepreneurial idea.

Even more important is the legitimacy of the corporate entrepreneur. Companies are apt to invest in an untested concept if the entrepreneur is tested. They may invest in a fairly certain or tested idea even if the entrepreneur is untested. But the likelihood of investing in an untested idea and an untested entrepreneur is slim. Corporate entrepreneurs must find ways to get experience on innovative projects, volunteering to help with the initiatives of others, trying to take leadership roles in teams, and succeeding in their own small initiatives before pushing for big ones.

LACK OF "SEED" CAPITAL: THE PROBLEM OF EARLY RESOURCES

In the initial stages, any new idea requires an adequate supply of resources, including people, materials, and use of the organization's production and service systems. Yet the corporate entrepreneur generally faces severe constraints in the amount of resources available for the new concept. When the idea is new, it is most vulnerable and most in need of refinement and adaptation—and it is least likely to receive financial support at this stage. Further, the intrapreneur, more often than not, is seen as an internal competitor attempting to take resources from someone or something else. This means that even if the intrapreneur could succeed in securing the needed resources, those resources might end up being conceded with reluctance and lingering resentment.

LACK OF OPEN OWNERSHIP: PROTECTING TURF

When Joline Godfrey of Polaroid was trying to create a service business (the development of a photo treasure hunt for vacationers) in a manufacturing company, the marketing department claimed her idea fell into their domain and argued that it was time for them to take over. This is a common occurrence in large organizations. Often, departments are more concerned with protecting their turf than they are with developing new ideas that will benefit the organization. Frequently, the corporate entrepreneur will run into power plays and battles for control over decision making occurring between vice presidents and/or their respective areas. The successful entrepreneur needs to make himself or herself aware of these power plays and, if at all possible, stay out of them. Either that, or he or she must be aligned with the vice president or department that wins the battle.

LACK OF A SPONSOR: SOMEONE TO WATCH OVER YOU

To help assess the political realities, the corporate entrepreneur needs a supporter who oversees the progress of the venture from higher in the organization. Sponsors act as coaches for corporate entrepreneurs. They also act as buffers guarding innovators against unnecessary organizational bureaucratic interference, and allow the corporate entrepreneur to concentrate on his or her venture. Sponsors can help the champion create alliances needed to build venture teams by introducing the entrepreneur to the right people in the organization. They help keep threatening projects undercover for as long as possible. Sponsors are most effective if they have personally championed an idea earlier in their career. When this is the case, they also serve as role models who can offer empathy and optimism through a critical but trusting attitude.

LACK OF ENERGY AND SHARED ENTHUSIASM: THE INERTIA PROBLEM

Inertia represents one of the most serious problems confronting corporate entrepreneurs. It refers to a lack of movement or support, a lack of energy, and the presence of resistance insofar as some new concept or idea is concerned. Block and MacMillan (1993) found five specific types or causes of this dangerous but very real obstacle.

Indifference   The new concept's initial small size renders key parts of the organization indifferent to providing the cooperation required to get the project launched. Although support may be required from engineering, marketing, or the sales force, the concept may receive very little attention simply because the idea is considered insignificant compared to the ongoing business. This can also happen in external relations, with suppliers, customers, and distributors simply ignoring the concept because it is so small.

Distraction   The people responsible for conducting the company's major ongoing business may simply be too distracted by day-to-day pressures. If the concept needs the support of the manufacturing facility for example, this project becomes, at best, a distraction from the principal business and, at worst, a disruptive irritation.

Competition   Competitors can mobilize their clout with distributors and suppliers to deny support to the fledgling venture.

Disaffection   Direct resistance to the corporate entrepreneur's progress and even attempts to subvert him or her can be initiated by people in the organization who either do not believe in corporate entrepreneurship, are envious, or feel that the corporate entrepreneur is disturbing their comfort zones. In particular, staff functions whose mission is to ensure homogeneity in the organization may attempt to stifle the corporate entrepreneur with procedures, rules, and policies. Anything that is new and requires different treatment disrupts and threatens their systems. This attitude can extend beyond the boundaries of the firm to agencies, unions, or any other entity that has a vested interest in preserving the status quo.

Direct threat   Determined opponents of the corporate entrepreneur see him or her as attacking their position or directly threatening their part of the organization. Once again, this type of resistance can extend beyond the organization's boundaries.

LACK OF PERSONAL RENEWAL: THE ISSUE OF REINFORCED DENIAL

Grove (1996) discussed the problems of past success leading individuals to be overconfident in current projects and to exhibit a continued denial of anything new. Senior managers have become successful by having been good at what they do. Over time they learn to lead with their strengths. So it's not surprising that they will keep implementing the same strategic and tactical moves that worked for them during the course of their careers. This can be referred to as *reinforced denial.*

When the environment changes in such a way as to render the old skills and strengths less relevant, many managers almost instinctively cling to their past. They refuse to acknowledge changes around them. They are willing to work harder at the traditional tasks or skills in the hope that their hard work will overcome the change. The new is denied through reinforced belief in past success.

LACK OF URGENCY: FEAR AS GOOD AND BAD

According to Andy Grove of Intel, "The most important role of managers is to create an environment in which people are passionately dedicated to winning in the marketplace. Fear plays a major role in creating and maintaining such passion. Fear of competition, fear of bankruptcy, fear of being wrong, and fear of losing can all be powerful motivators." Thus, fear may be a positive force in the sense that an adrenaline rush catapults people into action, and the constant reminders of these fears can be a sustaining factor.

However, if the fear becomes a negative force such as the fear of punishment or retribution by a superior, then it is a major obstacle to corporate entrepreneurship.

It takes many years of consistent behavior to eliminate fear of punishment as an inhibitor of corporate entrepreneurship. It takes only one incident to introduce it. News of this incident will spread through the organization like wildfire and will discourage everyone from introducing new ideas. Once an environment of fear takes over, it will lead to paralysis throughout the organization and will severely constrain entrepreneurial behavior.

LACK OF APPROPRIATE TIMING: THE RESOURCE-SHIFT DILEMMA

The lack of resources was discussed earlier; however, the actual timing of resource transfer or acquisition is critical as well. Assume the corporate entrepreneur is able to convince senior management to move resources to the new project. The timing of the transfer of resources from the old to the new has to be done with crucial balance in mind. If resources are moved from the old business, the old task, or the old product too early, it can be costly. With a little bit more effort, significant unrealized potential might have been achievable. On the other hand, hanging on to the old business too long could cause opportunities to be missed. The company misses a chance to grab a new business opportunity, add momentum to a new product area, or get aligned with the new order of things. Traditionally, managers act too slowly and too late in their movement of resources, causing the entrepreneurial project to dissipate.

OVERCOMING THE OBSTACLES AND LIMITATIONS

These limitations share a common element—namely, they represent situations in which, to meet the needs of a new project, the corporate entrepreneur must attempt to convince someone or some unit to change current behavior patterns from what the person or unit might prefer to do. Therefore, it is important for the corporate entrepreneur to develop an understanding of methods that can be used to gain influence and shape behavior.

BUILDING SOCIAL CAPITAL

Corporate entrepreneurs must rely on their ingenuity and persistence to build influence. They need to build *social capital,* an inventory of trust, gratitude, and obligations that can be cashed in when the new project is in demand (Blau 1964). Building this capital can be accomplished in a number of ways, including the following:

- Sharing information
- Creating opportunities for people to demonstrate their skills and competence
- Building and using influence networks

GAINING LEGITIMACY

The basic strategy for gaining legitimacy is to use personal influence or influence networks to somehow secure endorsements that will convince the necessary supporters of the corporate entrepreneur's viability and credibility. Entrepreneurs also gain legitimacy through experience on various new initiatives started by others and by first achieving small successes with their own original ideas.

POLITICAL TACTICS

Corporate entrepreneurs find themselves in a wide range of situations in which political skills are critical. The tactics relied upon to achieve legitimacy, garner resources, and overcome inertia and resistance are many and varied. In reality, an unlimited number of political tactics are available to the corporate entrepreneur. One way to organize these possibilities is presented in Table 9.3. Here, another department is blocking the entrepreneur's team by making unreasonable demands. The entrepreneur might employ rule-oriented, rule-evading, personal-political, educational, or organizational-interactional tactics to counteract the demands. These tactics are explained in Table 9.3.

The corporate entrepreneur may apply rule-oriented or rule-evading tactics when he or she is dealing specifically with the unrealistic requests or demands from different departments in the organization. Personal-political tactics can be applied to adverse situations. They relate to the discussion above on building social capital. Educational tactics such as persuasion, explanation, and clarification may be useful in dealing with unreasonable points of view. Finally, the organizational-interactional tactic of gaining greater autonomy or of developing a cross-departmental team may prove valuable in a variety of situations.

Securing endorsements is particularly important for corporate entrepreneurs. If they can rapidly acquire legitimacy, their new project may gain the following significant additional benefits:

■ Earlier customer acceptance
■ Earlier distributor acceptance
■ Earlier revenue streams

RESOURCE ACQUISITION

Block and MacMillan (1993) note, "When it comes to securing resources, accounts of entrepreneurial activity in established corporations are replete with tales of resourceful politicking. Venture managers hijack materials and equipment, appropriate production capacity and personnel time, conceal development activities, and cash in personal favors to secure the resources needed for their new business." The major method of securing the necessary resources is through co-optation or leveraging of the resources currently underutilized by the firm. Starr and MacMillan (1990) identified four distinct strategies for co-optation:

■ TABLE 9.3

EXAMPLES OF POLITICAL TACTICS

Corporate entrepreneurs find themselves in a range of different situations in which political skills are critical. The tactics relied upon to achieve legitimacy, garner resources, and overcome inertia and resistance to change are many and varied. Below are examples of five different categories of tactics available to the entrepreneur. In this case, resources are being withheld by some other department, and the department is making an unreasonable request of the entrepreneur's team in an attempt to undermine the concept or project.

1. **Rule-oriented tactics**

   a. Appeal to some common authority to direct that this request be revised or withdrawn.
   b. Refer to some rule (assuming one exists) that suggests meeting such a request is not necessary.
   c. Require the other department to state in writing why they are making this demand.
   d. Require the other department to consent to having its budget charged with the extra costs involved in meeting their request.

2. **Rule-evading tactics**

   a. Go through the motions of complying with the request but with no expectation of actually completing it.
   b. Exceed formal authority and ignore the request altogether.

3. **Personal-political tactics**

   a. Rely on friendships to induce the other department to modify its request.
   b. Rely on favors, past and future, to accomplish the same result.
   c. Work through political allies in other departments.
   d. Obtain endorsements from senior managers the other department must work with.

4. **Educational tactics**

   a. Use direct persuasion; that is, try to persuade the other department that its request is unreasonable.
   b. Use what might be called indirect persuasion to help the other department see the problem from the entrepreneur's point of view (ask representatives from the other department to sit in on work sessions and observe the difficulty in meeting the request).

5. **Organizational-interactional tactics**

   a. Seek to change the interaction pattern; for example, require the other department to get executive board approval before making such a request.
   b. Have representatives from the other department assigned to the entrepreneur's team.
   c. Seek to have the team take over other responsibilities or be given more autonomy so that the entrepreneur is not dependent on the other department's support.

Based on work on done by G. Straus in his classic work, "Tactics of Lateral Relationships."

SOURCE: Straus, G. 1962. "Tactics of Lateral Relationships," *Administrative Science Quarterly* 7 (September): 166.

Borrowing   Borrowing strategies are employed to secure temporarily or periodically the use of assets or other resources, with the understanding that they will eventually be returned.

Begging   Begging strategies are employed to secure resources by appealing to the owner's goodwill. In this way, venture managers gain the use of the resources without needing to return them, despite the fact that the owner recognizes the value of the assets. In her research, Kanter (1983) identifies many cases of "tin-cupping," in which venture managers begged or scrounged resources from the rest of the firm.

Scavenging   Scavenging strategies extract usage from goods that others do not intend to use or that they might actually welcome an appropriate opportunity to divest themselves of. This approach involves learning about unused or underused resources (e.g., obsolete inventory, idle equipment, or underutilized personnel).

Amplifying   Amplification is the capacity to lever far more value out of an asset than is perceived by the original owner of the asset.

These four strategies allow the entrepreneur to secure resources that would otherwise have to be secured by economic exchange at a much greater cost. There are three critical benefits of relying on these methods of resource acquisition: by appropriating underutilized resources, venture managers reduce the cost of start-up, reduce the risk of start-up by minimizing commitment to various assets, and increase the return on assets of the venture.

FOCUSING ON THE RIGHT OBSTACLES AT THE RIGHT TIME

It is important for corporate entrepreneurs to think in terms of both the immediate and long-term goals for their projects. They can then isolate the key obstacles to accomplishing these goals at differing time periods and prioritize where efforts are to be focused. Once the obstacles are prioritized, the critical opponents as well as supporters can be identified. It is these supporters that should be the focus of an inertia-to-action strategy.

Since the corporate entrepreneur wants to reach agreements that his or her supporters will be enthusiastic about implementing, he or she should attempt to structure "win-win" agreements (agreements that will benefit both parties). Corporate entrepreneurs should seek to reach explicit agreement on the actions that both parties will take to move the project forward. It is especially important to agree on what each party will do to ensure that the next milestone is achieved. The particular issues that the corporate entrepreneur and his or her supporter must address include the following:

- Who will take what specific actions against which opponent?
- What key implementation steps must be taken, and how should those steps be timed?
- How can we tell if things are not going as planned?
- What major contingency plans are needed, and what events will trigger those plans?

When agreement has been reached with these supporters, attention can turn to launching the strategy, focusing the most effort on those activities that will move the project to the next major milestone.

SUMMARY AND CONCLUSIONS

The good news is that companies are discovering the importance of entrepreneurship as a force for positive internal change and for achieving advantage in the marketplace. The bad news is that most companies have developed entrenched mechanisms that discourage entrepreneurial behavior and penalize the corporate entrepreneur. As a result, executives have little guidance in terms of theory or established managerial practice regarding how to make entrepreneurship happen in their companies.

In this chapter, we have attempted to systematically identify the obstacles to entrepreneurship in established companies. A framework was introduced for classifying these obstacles based on whether they were more related to systems, structure, strategic direction, policies and procedures, people, or culture. Virtually any of the potentially hundreds of obstacles found in companies will fall into one of these categories. The categories overlap and are highly interrelated. For instance, control systems include lots of policies and procedures, and they interact with the structure of the company. Reward systems reflect the values that define the culture of the firm. Importantly, the framework of obstacles is actually a blueprint for achieving entrepreneurship. Using this same framework, but turning each of the items on its head, managers can begin to redirect the entire organization.

Related to the obstacles are a number of limitations that affect the success or failure of the corporate entrepreneur. Included here were such things as poor political skills, legitimacy, reinforced denial, inertia, turf protection, and the inability to find a sponsor. A number of strategies were introduced to address or overcome these limitations. Yet, when dealing with barriers and obstacles, there is also a danger in overcomplicating things. Corporate entrepreneurs should exercise appropriate caution in moving forward, without losing sight of the most important objective—ensuring that the project continues to make progress. The essence of overcoming barriers, then, is to keep things simple—identify the few key obstacles, understand them, and plan actions that will solve the most threatening problems.

In the chapters ahead, we will revisit these obstacles. Our objective will be to identify ways in which companies can create environments that eliminate most of them—or at least reduce their negative impact on entrepreneurial behavior.

REFERENCES

Block, Z., and I. MacMillan. 1993. *Corporate Venturing.* Boston: Harvard Business School Press.

Blau, P. 1964. *Exchange and Power in Social Life.* New York: John Wiley & Sons.

Grove, A. S. 1996. *Only the Paranoid Survive.* London: Harper Collins.

Kanter, R. 1983. *The Change Masters.* New York: Simon & Schuster.

Kerr, S. 1975. "On the Folly of Rewarding A, While Hoping for B," *Academy of Management Journal* 18 (December): 769–783.

COMPANY SUPPORT AT LUCENT

For every one corporation that successfully promotes entrepreneurship within the organization, there are dozens of corporations that do not manage their entrepreneurial efforts effectively. After AT&T split into NCR and Lucent in 1996, Lucent's senior vice president, Tom Uhlman, hired consultant Stephen Socolof and developed a strategy to launch the New Ventures initiative.

Excited, but wanting to learn from the mistakes made by other corporations, Uhlman and Socolof spent months picking the brains of Palo Alto's well-known venture capital connoisseurs. What did they learn? For one, that to move quickly and take necessary risks their venture arm had to jettison any conservative corporate structure. Furthermore, they were told that due diligence was important, that providing seed money at certain stages was wise, that they should look outside the firm for business and technical expertise, and of course, that equity compensation was key. Harboring these new characteristics would indeed prove difficult in an organization riddled with seasoned,

traditional managers. But, as the initiative quickly became a full business group and NVG realized that Lucent employed fewer true entrepreneurs with practical business experience than originally thought, NVG made another smart move by hiring "entrepreneurs-in-residence," along with a few technical experts, to help develop ideas and plans and be ready to join a spin-off as president or chief operating officer if necessary.

Since 1997, Lucent's New Ventures Group has helped jumpstart at least twenty-four businesses designed to complement or compete with current revenue streams. Along the way, they have raised $150 million in outside venture capital and contributed $225 million of the company's own funds. Three of the businesses have been assimilated into the parent corporation, one has gone public, and a few irons always remain in the fire. "If you try to nurture that new thing in the same organization, with that same set of people who are today managing fairly substantial businesses using older technology, it

becomes very difficult for this new thing to get much attention," states Bell Labs President Arun Netravali. NVG's success stories are attributable to the fact that the team and the corporation took a new approach to creating a division chartered solely to scout out technology within the corporation that doesn't fit with the current business lines and help researchers develop financial plans, attract venture capital, and get the innovations out the door.

Lucent's NVG blueprint is now being studied and mimicked by other organizations realizing the benefit of entrepreneurial outreach arms. By making entrepreneurial efforts qualitative rather than quantitative, the frequency, implementation, and success of "eureka"-type ideas are changing the face of corporate research and development. Intel, Nortel, and Xerox, for example, have already implemented external entities.

SOURCE: Buderi, R. 2000. "Lucent Ventures into the Future," *Technology Review* 103 (November/December): 1–8.

Morris, M. H. 1998. *Entrepreneurial Intensity.* Westport: Quorum Books.

Raudsepp, E. 1987. *Growth Games for the Creative Manager.* New York: Putnam.

Sathe, V. 1989. "Fostering Entrepreneurship in Large Diversified Firms," *Organizational Dynamics* 18: 20–32.

Starr, J. A., and I. C. MacMillan. 1990. "Resource Co-optation Via Social Contracting: Resource Acquisition Strategies for New Ventures," *Strategic Management Journal* 11 (Summer): 79–92.

DEVELOPING AN ENVIRONMENT TO SUPPORT ENTREPRENEURSHIP

"To be able to *innovate,* the enterprise needs to put—every three years or so—
every single product, process, technology, market, distributive channel,
and internal staff activity on *trial* for life."

—PETER F. DRUCKER

STRUCTURING THE COMPANY FOR ENTREPRENEURSHIP

The design of an organization has many elements, but three overarching ones are the company structure, communication flows, and the control system. This chapter will explore issues surrounding structure and internal communication, while control will be the focus of Chapter Eleven. Structure refers to the formal pattern of how people and jobs are grouped and how the activities of different people or functions are connected. We typically think of structure in terms of some sort of organizational chart filled with boxes, lines, and arrows, suggesting a hierarchical set of relationships regarding who reports to whom. As we shall see, structure is much more than this and has important implications for entrepreneurship.

Structures are created to bring order and logic to company operations. Start-up ventures often begin with very little structure. They operate in a fairly loose and informal manner, and this means they are quite nimble. In fact, the speed and flexibility this provides is one of the major assets of small companies. However, as we saw in Chapter One, companies evolve through life cycles, and the challenges of growth and size make it impossible to operate efficiently or effectively without more formal structures. Once formalized, the structure is not static. It is continually changed as management struggles with the need to balance differentiation of activities and people against integration of activities and people. Unfortunately, structures become increasingly bureaucratic as they evolve, and entrepreneurship suffers.

In this chapter, we will examine the types of structures that develop in companies and the ways in which they discourage entrepreneurial behavior. Alternative approaches to key structural variables will be presented, and examples of companies that have tried radical new approaches to structuring will be highlighted. Let us begin, though, with a look at the key elements that go into the structure of a company.

THE COMPONENTS OF STRUCTURE

At the most basic level, managers attempting to design a company structure are dealing with issues of differentiation and integration. Differentiation is about the ways decision-making authority is distributed, tasks are grouped, and people are assigned to tasks. Integration refers to the ways in which people and functions are coordinated. The actual way in which these issues are addressed entails a whole host of decisions. Stated differently, the design of a structure includes a highly interdependent set of components. Following are some key questions:

- How many levels should there be in the organization?
- What should be the targeted span of control?
- How centralized or decentralized should operations be?
- How formal or informal should structural relations be?
- Should the structure emphasize functional specialization or cross-functional interaction?
- How much of a sense of bigness versus smallness should the structure convey?
- To what extent should the structure emphasize control versus autonomy?
- How rigid versus how flexible should the structure be?
- To what extent should decision making and communication be more top down versus bottom up?

Galbraith (1995) argues that these questions come down to four major policy areas: specialization, shape, distribution of power, and departmentalization. Specialization is concerned with the number and types of specialties to be used in performing the work of the company. More specialization means specific tasks might be performed better, but integration of these tasks into a total outcome is more difficult. If we relate this policy area to innovation, environments that produce discontinuous or dynamically continuous innovation typically require more specialization compared to those producing more continuous innovation or imitation.

Shape has to do with the number of people forming departments or areas at each hierarchical level. If there are more people per department, then fewer levels are required. More people imply a broader span of control, or number of people reporting to a given manager, while fewer levels means the organization is flatter. Flatter structures typically result in better communication and faster decision making and are consistent with delegation of responsibility. Alternatively, structures that are more hierarchical tend to rely on power to settle issues rather than multilevel dialogue and debate.

Distribution of power occurs both vertically and horizontally. Vertically, power can be concentrated in the higher levels of the organization, suggesting a more centralized structure, or it can be pushed down in the organization so that people at lower levels are empowered to make decisions and have discretion over how resources are used. Such decentralized structures are consistent with the encouragement of individual initiative, experimentation, and innovation. The greater the decentralization, the more the challenge becomes one of ensuring these individual efforts are consistent with the strategic direction of the firm, are integrated with other initiatives and activities within the firm, and are representative of more than incremental or marginally profitable advances.

Departmentalization, or the forming of people into departments, groups, or areas, occurs once an organization reaches a certain threshold size in terms of employment. People can be organized in a variety of ways, the most common of which are by functions (e.g., accounting, marketing), product lines (e.g., widgets, gadgets), markets or customer segments (e.g., consumer, industrial, government), geographic regions (e.g., northern Europe, southeastern U.S.), or work flow processes (e.g., new product development processes, customer acquisition and maintenance processes, order processing and fulfillment processes). It is also quite common to use combinations of the above such as processes being organized around products or functional structures existing within geographic regions. The appropriate structure depends on the competitive circumstances (including product and market diversity), strategy, and resources of the firm.

HOW STRUCTURES EVOLVE

If we look at a company when it has first started, and chart the ways in which the structure is changed as the company evolves, no single pattern will exist even between two companies operating under the exact same circumstances. Nonetheless, there are some general directions that we might expect a structure to take as a company grows.

Larry Griener (1972), in his classic work on the organizational life cycle, talks about companies evolving through stages of evolution and revolution. Structure is one of the variables that change over these stages. He suggests the initial structure is highly informal, often without formal titles or any kind of organizational chart. Subsequently, a functional structure is put in place with centralized control. Next comes a decentralized and geographically organized structure built around profit centers. This is followed by a movement towards merged product groups or strategic business units together with centralization of administrative and staff functions at head office. Then the company adopts matrix structures, cross-functional team approaches, the reassignment of head office staff to consultative teams, and process integration. Griener emphasizes a dynamic in which new structures are introduced that enable the company to effectively address emerging conditions at one point but that produce side effects that ultimately require a new structural solution.

A similar picture of structural evolution is painted by Mintzberg (1979). In his schema, most organizations start with entrepreneurial structures, although a minority begin with craft structures. The craft structure is very task focused and is organized around skills, although skills are relatively standardized. There is a very limited administrative component and little supervision required such as with a pottery studio or gasoline station. An entrepreneurial structure involves a vertical division of labor, with the entrepreneur making all the important decisions and providing direct supervision of other employees. Even so, it is a fairly informal and organic structure, with limited administrative infrastructure and no middle management. As they grow in age and size, firms implement an administrative structure (Mintzberg refers to it as bureaucratic). Intermediate levels of supervision are put in place, and the hierarchy of authority is made more elaborate. Meanwhile, a technostructure is developed where efforts to plan and coordinate work are standardized. Thus, a distinction is drawn between designing work and supervising it. So long as the firm concentrates on a few related product lines, they retain the administrative structure. However, as products and markets become more diversified the administrative structure is replaced by a divisional structure. Divisions are created as distinct entities that serve their own markets with a head office that coordinates their activities through an impersonal performance control system. Subsequently, organizations adopt various types of a matrix structure. Here, managers operate with dual or multiple reporting relationships. They may have product responsibility in a geographic region or may work both in marketing and on a major innovative project.

The evolution of structure is not as deterministic as it sounds above, and many variants are possible in a given stage of a company's evolution. The transformations that occur as a company ages, grows, and diversifies include both major redesigns and ongoing adjustments. That is, structural transitions take place that represent changes in kind as well as degree. Levels are added and deleted, control is centralized and decentralized, flexibility is decreased and increased, and so forth.

The company finds that it must continually adjust the structure to reflect both external pressures (e.g., changing competitive conditions, marketplace requirements, technological developments) and internal priorities (e.g., the need to achieve efficiencies, achieve greater coordination, improve responsiveness to the market). A company operates effectively based on a well-coordinated set of relations between structural design, company age and size, the technology of the firm, and the conditions of the industry in which it operates. A move to a new stage of development typically requires that the structure be redesigned and that a new set of relationships among these variables be established. ·

The substantive reorganizations that occur over time affect everyone in the organization. They also have important implications for entrepreneurship. The relative emphasis on entrepreneurship in a company will likely differ depending upon the structure and so will the emphasis on frequency of entrepreneurship (number of events) versus degree of entrepreneurship (level of innovativeness, risk-taking and proactiveness). Unfortunately, entrepreneurship usually is not an overriding consideration in restructuring efforts and so tends to be systematically undermined as the company evolves. Let us explore these relationships in greater detail.

TYPES OF STRUCTURES: LINK TO AN ENTREPRENEURIAL STRATEGY

A lot of attention has been paid by researchers on the fit between the external environment, the strategy of a company, and the company structure. While any number of different structures can be found in companies, some general types of structures have been identified and linked to both strategy and the environment. It is generally argued that the structure of a firm follows from the strategy, although examples exist of structures that, once in place, affect new strategic directions taken by the firm (Chandler 1962; Miller 1996). If entrepreneurship and innovation are integral parts of the firm's strategy, then inconsistencies with certain general types of structure can be problematic.

Miller (1986; 1996) attempts to synthesize contemporary thinking on the strategy-structure linkage. He suggests the structure of a firm can be categorized as one of the following:

- *Simple Structure*—Highly informal with coordination of tasks accomplished by direct supervision and all strategies determined at the top. Little specialization of tasks exists, and there is very limited formalization in terms of programs, rules, or regulations. There is a low degree of bureaucracy, and information systems are unsophisticated. Little need exists for integrating mechanisms, and power is concentrated at the top.

- *Machine Bureaucracy*—A mechanistic and rigid structure in which coordination of tasks is achieved through standardization of work. The structure is hierarchical and very bureaucratic. The need to follow plans and programs is stressed. A large technostructure exists in the firm to design and plan operations. Technology is somewhat automated and integrated into operations. Well-developed information systems exist, but they focus on internal reporting and output tracking rather than on market developments. Power is concentrated among top executives and those who design workflow processes, with little disseminated to middle- or lower-level management.

- *Organic*—Limited hierarchy and highly flexible structure. Groups of trained specialists from different work areas collaborate to design and produce complex and rapidly changing products. Emphasis on extensive personal interaction and face-to-face communication, frequent meetings, use of committees and other liaison devices to ensure collaboration. Power is decentralized and authority is linked to expertise. Few bureaucratic rules or standard procedures exist. Sensitive information-gathering systems are in place for anticipating and monitoring the external environment.

- *Divisional*—Self-contained profit centers exist for producing and marketing different product lines or groups. Divisions can differ significantly from one another in terms of their structures, with some being more organic and others more bureaucratic. There is overall pressure for divisions to conform and for formalization and standardization of procedures and methods.

While divisions tend to become more bureaucratic with time, they operate somewhat independently, with a fair amount of decision-making authority delegated to divisional managers. Control is facilitated by sophisticated management information systems. Coordination across divisions is achieved via interunit committees and a staff infrastructure at head office.

Different types of structures are good for accomplishing particular outcomes under particular circumstances. For instance, simple structures work well in small, rapid-growth ventures operating in fragmented industries where competition is intense. Machine bureaucracies work well in stable, predicable environments and are good for producing high volumes of products and achieving efficiencies in production and distribution. Table 10.1 takes this discussion much further, specifically relating each of these prototypes of structure to the type of environmental conditions under which the structure is most productive and to the types of corporate strategies that tend to be most appropriate. While the table demonstrates logical linkages, it is not intended as an exhaustive summary of the possible sets of relationships that can work effectively.

The configuration of structure, strategy, and environmental conditions should be guided by a theme. Such a theme can capture the vision of senior management, unique organizational competencies, a competitive advantage, or core elements of the company culture. Clearly, entrepreneurship represents a potential theme. Miller (1996, p. 507) notes, "The aspirations of a CEO intent on technological leadership may, for example, produce a strategy of focused R&D, a think-tank culture, and an organic culture."

Let us further explore the role structure plays in accommodating or inhibiting innovative behavior. Innovation requires creative thinking and collaboration. A personal sense of empowerment and room to maneuver are important. Innovation necessitates a level of flexibility in terms of resource utilization and time horizons. Quick decisions are often required during the innovative process, and decision making is both rational and instinctual. Champions and team members must be able to span boundaries within the organization. Innovation is also a communication-intensive activity, including both extensive lateral and vertical communication, much of which is informal and unplanned. Other requirements include ongoing experimentation, continuous failure, and adaptation of the concept or idea.

Not surprisingly, then, major innovation is most likely under structures that most closely mimic the organic structure. Both high degree and frequency of entrepreneurship are consistent with this type of structure. Conversely, the lowest levels of entrepreneurial intensity are likely with machine bureaucracies, or mechanistic structures. Extensive hierarchy and bureaucracy are inconsistent with unstructured problem solving. People are more compartmentalized, which limits communication and encourages resistance to change. Ideas that do not emerge from formal processes and with proper documentation are often ignored. Pursuing multiple and alternative paths to the realization of an entrepreneurial concept is discouraged. Such structures demand fixed rather than flexible goals and well-defined rather than fluid processes.

■ **TABLE 10.1**

FOUR GENERAL TYPES OF STRUCTURES

	Simple Structure	Machine Bureaucracy	Organic	Divisionalized
Characteristics				
Power centralization	All at the top	CEO and designers of worflow	Scientists, techno-crats, and middle managers	Divisional executives
Bureaucratization	Low — informal	Many formal rules, policies, and procedures	Organic	High
Specialization	Low	Extensive	Extensive	Extensive
Differentiation	Minimal	Moderate	Very high	High
Integration and coordination of effort	By CEO via direct supervision	By technocrats via formal procedures	By integrating personnel and task forces via mutual adjustment	By formal committees via plan and budgets
Information systems	Crude, informal	Cost controls and budgets	Informal scanning, open com-munications	Management infor-mation systems and profit centers
Environmental Dimensions				
Technology	Simple, custom	Mass production, large batch/line	Sophisticated product, automated or custom	Varies
Competition	Extreme	High	Moderate	Varies
Dynamism/Uncertainty	Moderate	Very low	Very high	Varies
Growth	Varies	Slow	Rapid	Varies
Concentration Ratio	Very low	High	Varies	Varies
Barriers to entry	None	Scales barriers	Knowledge barriers	Varies

Strategies

	Business Level		Corporate Level	
Favored strategy	Niche differentiation	Cost leadership	Innovative differentiation	Conglomeration
Marketing emphasis	Quality, service, convenience	Low price	New products, high quality	Image
Production emphasis	Economy	Efficiency	Flexibility	Vertical integration
Asset management	Parsimony	Intensity	Parsimony	Varies
Innovation and R&D	Little	Almost none	Very high	Low to moderate
Product-market scope	Very narrow	Average	Average	Very broad

SOURCE: Adapted from Miller, D. 1986. "Configurations of Strategy and Structure: Towards a Synthesis," *Strategic Management Review* 7: 233–249.

Between these two endpoints lie the simple and the divisional structures. The simple structure allows for speed and flexibility. Incremental or continuous innovation is likely if the CEO drives it. At the same time, it is too primitive, undifferentiated, and centralized to support complex innovation. The reliance on simple technologies further limits the likelihood of discontinuous and even dynamically continuous innovation. These characteristics suggest that the degree of entrepreneurship will be low under such structures, and the frequency of entrepreneurship will be low to moderate. Where divisional structures are employed, corporate strategies tend to be the least focused, and the implications for innovative activity are least apparent. As divisions themselves can differ in the extent to which their individual structures are organic or mechanistic, levels of entrepreneurship are likely to vary. For this reason, it is important to track levels of entrepreneurial intensity over time and compare them among divisions (Chapter Fourteen). If the divisional structures tend to become more mechanistic over time, especially where the head office emphasizes measures for standardization and conformity among divisions, degree and frequency of entrepreneurship will suffer. Further, because divisions tend to be built around product lines, markets, and/or geographic regions, they are more likely to produce incremental improvements rather than new-product breakthroughs. They tend to be preoccupied with improving and extending current product lines and with better satisfying the expressed needs and wants of the current customer base. Bold moves that redefine the market and reinvent the industry are generally incompatible with the performance objectives and rewards that guide divisional performance. While the head office may be focused on diversification moves, it is often diversification through acquisition. The implication is that frequency of entrepreneurship will vary considerably among divisions, and degree of entrepreneurship will be low to moderate.

With divisional structures (and possibly machine bureaucracies), significant innovation may require separate structures (separate from mainstream divisions) such as the new ventures division at Procter and Gamble or the Xerox New Enterprises unit. A subsequent problem arises, however, in that innovations that come out of these separate units are often resisted or given lukewarm support by mainstream divisions. The "not-invented-here" mindset prevails, with the mainstream division feeling it is inheriting an unwanted offspring. Success rates are greater if mainstream divisions endorse and take ownership of projects in the separate venture units at inception.

Innovation also affects structure itself, with a number of new and untested structural designs appearing in contemporary organizations (Pettigrew and Fenton 2000). These new company designs are especially conducive to entrepreneurship. Examples include network, cellular, and virtual structures. Let us consider network structures, which are a logical outgrowth of the growing reliance on outsourcing, subcontracting, strategic alliances, and joint ventures (each of which is, parenthetically, a vehicle for achieving innovation). Network structures facilitate new knowledge development and allow firms to leverage their market presence. They can also produce economies in terms of asset utilization. Network approaches entail high degrees of integration across formal boundaries between

■ FIGURE 10.1

THE NETWORK STRUCTURE AT OVE ARUP

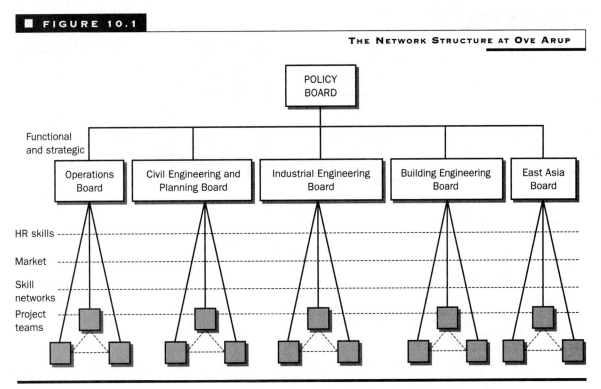

SOURCE: Pettigrew, A., and E. Fenton. 2000. *The Innovating Organization*. London: Sage Publications, p.63.

organizations and units. Pettigrew and Fenton (2000) describe the case of Ove Arup, the large global engineering and consultancy firm. The company was formerly organized around fifty independent units reporting to a main board. As pictured in Figure 10.1, the corporate board has been redefined as a policy board, with five operating boards beneath it and with business operations carried out by groups reporting to one of the operating boards. The groups are organized according to technical, business, or geographic interests and are aligned into networks. In fact, two kinds of networks run horizontally across groups, skill networks and market networks. They link specialists throughout the firm. Strategy and functional committees exist to provide horizontal links at board level. Staff are assigned to particular project teams at a central level by networking through the group leaders. A specific objective in moving to this type of structure was to achieve company-wide innovations.

Another example of experimentation with structure can be found at Saab Training Systems, a unit within Saab that provides computer-aided training equipment for military purposes (Pettigrew and Fenton 2000). Saab has adopted a team-based structure after formerly relying on a hierarchical, functional structure.

■ **FIGURE 10.2**

THE TEAM-BASED STRUCTURE IN SAAB TRAINING SYSTEMS

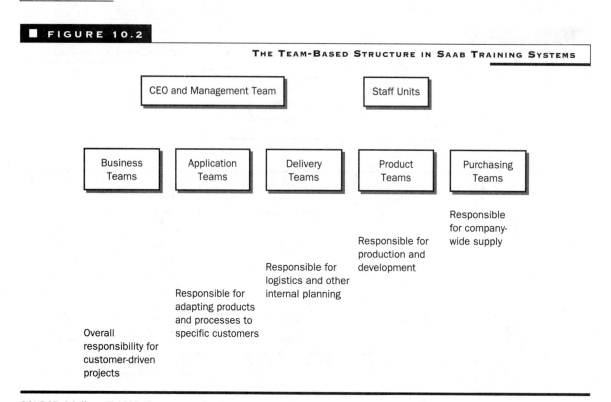

SOURCE: Mullern, T. 2000. "Integrating the Team-Based Structure in the Business Process: The Case of Saab Training Systems." In *The Innovating Organization,* edited by A. Pettigrew and E. Fenton. London: Sage Publications, p.248.

The objective was flexibility. Over forty teams were created, with each reporting to the managing director and management team (a total of two hierarchical levels). When teams exceed a size of eight or so, they split into two teams. The team-based approach is designed around basic business processes, with five different types of teams (Figure 10.2). For instance, business teams are responsible for one or more products and one or more geographic areas. They have overall responsibility for each customer contract. Delivery teams handle logistics for each order, and product teams take care of design and production activities in a project. The mix of teams involved in an order is dissolved once the final project is delivered to the customer. While there is a sequential nature to some of the team activities, the reality is that the teams are highly interdependent. Yet, the desire is to have teams operating almost as individual companies with a high degree of operational freedom and responsibility for innovative product and process development.

■ TABLE 10.2

TOWARD NO BOUNDARIES AT GENERAL ELECTRIC

A lot has been written about the dramatic transformation of General Electric Company over the last twenty years under Chairman Jack Welch.

"One of the keys," says one of Mr. Welch's top lieutenants and his possible successor, "is to assume everybody has a better idea than you."

That kind of attitude, called *boundarylessness* in GE-speak, will be critical for doing business in the 21st century, according to W. James McNerney Jr., president of GE Aircraft Engines in Cincinnati.

"We think we've been successful, but every one of us can become obsolete in a matter of weeks or days, especially in a Web-based world."

Across GE's businesses, ranging from jet engines to finance, Mr. McNerney said, "Our relative advantage is a strong, transportable general management."

He said, "We try hard to make our businesses seem small and nimble to our customers but massive and immovable to our competitors."

Under Mr. Welch in the early 1980s, GE tore apart its old management and businesses and rebuilt them around a management culture that valued ideas from everywhere and valued learning and performance equally.

Mr. McNerney, 49, said, "GE has borrowed ideas such as quick market intelligence from Wal-Mart, lean manufacturing form Toyota Motor Corporation and e-business from everywhere."

Mr. McNerney said GEAE has established an electronic business team within the last couple of months to examine all aspects of how GEAE does business and how it might be improved.

One outgrowth of that has been to establish Websites for each of its airline customers on which they can access information on the status of their engine orders and performance problems on a daily basis.

SOURCE: Boyer, M. 1999. "Boundarylessness Is Big, Big Word at GE," *Cincinnati Enquirer.* November 20.

An increasingly popular approach to structure is called the *boundary-less* organization. General Electric has emphasized this notion, as is summarized in Table 10.2. Eliminating boundaries is actually a component of most of the innovative approaches to structuring discussed earlier. The idea is to take people out of boxes and eliminate artificial barriers that slow things down and create pockets of resistance to change. Boundaries are eliminated within the organization and also between the organization and key outside players. The major external boundary-related changes in companies include the outsourcing of key functions; greater use of strategic alliances with suppliers, distributors, and other firms; and reductions in how diversified companies are (Pettigrew and Fenton 2000). Boundaries are eliminated in many ways, ranging from collaborative R&D efforts to the linking of two organizations via an Internet-based electronic data interchange. Some companies are going much further with such linkages, such as PPG Industries, who has moved from selling paint to General Motors to running the customer's entire painting operation.

■ FIGURE 10.3

ELEMENTS REFLECTED IN NEW ORGANIZATIONAL FORMS

STRUCTURES

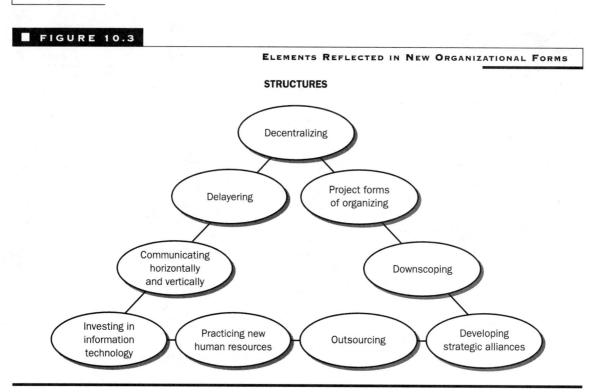

SOURCE: Pettigrew, A., and E. Fenton. 2000. *The Innovating Organization.* London: Sage Publications, p.38.

Experimentation with different organizational designs is increasingly the norm in larger companies. Pettigrew and Fenton (2000) see companies experimenting not only with their structures but also in two closely related areas, processes and the aforementioned boundaries. Figure 10.3 captures many of the principal variables receiving managerial attention. Structural changes such as delayering (removing layers of hierarchy) and decentralization (removing central control) are accompanied by process changes, including the ways horizontal units communicate and interact, the integration of new information technology capabilities, and reliance on new types of human resource management practices in such areas as job design, use of contract labor, and so forth. Changing boundaries occur as the firm relies on outsourcing, strategic alliances, and other methods for linking internal operations to external organizations.

Perhaps the overriding consideration as companies struggle with finding the right structure is the level of turbulence in the external environment. That is, regardless of the type of structure currently in place, as environments become more dynamic, threatening and complex, organizations find that competitive survival forces them to become more entrepreneurial. This, in turn, means they must find ways to move the company towards more organic structures.

AN ENTREPRENEURIAL STRUCTURE AND THE CONCEPT OF CYCLING

So what is a truly entrepreneurial structure? The answer will vary depending on the size, age, products, markets, processes, and technologies of a company. This reality suggests that a firm's structure must be subject to continual experimentation and change. Further, there is an art to designing an entrepreneurial structure, as many of the conventional rules of organizational design must be abandoned. (See Table 10.3 for examples of unconventional approaches.) Galbraith (1995, p. 6) explains, "Organizational designs that facilitate variety, change, and speed are sources of competitive advantage. These designs are difficult to execute and copy because they are intricate blends of many different design policies." However, if we return to the earlier set of questions that must be addressed when designing a structure (i.e., number of levels, span of control, etc.), there are some basic principles to guide the design process.

We believe entrepreneurship flourishes where there are fewer layers or levels in the structure of a company. Further, spans of control are broader. The general orientation is toward a more horizontal and less vertical design. Decentralization and empowerment are the watchwords in terms of operations, while clear vision and strategic direction come from the top. At the same time, the dominant direction in terms of the flow of ideas is bottom up, not top down. The structure also emphasizes simplicity and smallness within a large enterprise by employing such devices as pseudoautonomous units, companies within companies, or empowered teams. Cross-functional interaction and cooperation are priorities, but the clash of ideas from interfunctional interaction is also encouraged. Vehicles are put in place to facilitate extensive and rapid communication among parties at all levels and in all functions. There is less formalization of roles and positions within the structure. Empowerment efforts are not token or random but are designed to be systematic and consistent. Staff functions are kept lean.

Covin and Slevin (1990) propose some additional elements (Table 10.4). They argue that a firm's entrepreneurial behavior correlates positively with the firm's performance when the organizational structure has the following:

1. Managers allowed to freely vary their operating styles;
2. Authority that is assigned based on the expertise of the individual;
3. Free adaptation of the organization to changing circumstances;
4. An emphasis on results rather than processes or procedures;
5. Loose, informal controls with an emphasis on a norm of cooperation;
6. Flexible on-the-job behavior, shaped by requirements of the situation and personality of the employee;
7. Frequent use of group participation and group consensus;
8. Open channels of communication with free flow of information.

■ TABLE 10.3

TWENTY STRUCTURE-RELATED SUGGESTIONS FROM TOM PETERS

1. Insist on a maximum of two levels of management between the bottom and top in any division-sized unit.
2. Most business can be done in independent operating units of 250 or fewer people (with their own boards of directors, including outsiders): Reorganize accordingly within the next 18 months.
3. Within the next nine months, eliminate ALL first-line supervisors.
4. Within the next year, transfer one-third of all staffers at the division level or above to customer-focused operating units (of 250 or fewer people — see No. 2) and then transfer another third the following year.
5. Within four years, reduce corporate staff to a maximum of 10 people per billion dollars in revenue (and no squirreling away "temporary assignees" stolen from divisions).
6. Require remaining members of all "central" (corporate, division) staffs to sell their services to line units at market rates; allow those line units, in turn, to buy any and all services from anybody, anywhere.
7. Destroy all organization charts. Now.
8. All top division/corporate managers: Pledge two days per month to customer visits, two days per month to supplier and distributor visits. And visit, in depth, at least three "neat" companies per year (*outside your industry*).
9. Aim for one-third employee ownership of the corporation within five years.
10. Chief executive officers and division general managers: Within the next 12 months, promote to a position of significant responsibility at least one rabble rouser who doesn't like you or agree with you (on much of anything).
11. Insist that no one serve on a strategic planning staff for more than 24 months. (Twenty-five percent of all strategy staff members should have worked for a customer or competitor.)
12. Make sure all work teams are largely self-contained, encompassing almost all functional skills within their confines.
13. Allow the CEO to sit on a maximum of one outside board.
14. Vacate all facilities more than three stories high.
15. Within 24 months, end all physical segregation of functional departments.
16. At all off-site meetings, make sure that *at least* 25 percent of all attendees are "outsiders" (customers, vendors, etc).
17. In companies with at least $250 million in revenue, create corporate vice president positions for the following: knowledge management, perceived quality and brand-equity management, innovation, industrial design, horizontal systems integration, cycle-time management. (Incumbents will each be supported by a one-person professional staff — max.)
18. Within four years, at last one-third of division-level chiefs should be 32 or younger.
19. Within 24 months, make sure you have at least one non-U.S. board member (firms of $50 million to $1 billion). Companies over $1 billion should have 25 percent non-U.S. board members within four years.
20. Let no senior manager have an office of more than 225 square feet.

SOURCES: Adapted from Peters, T. 1997. *The Circle of Innovation*. New York: Alfred A. Knopf; T. Peters. 1988. *Thriving on Chaos*. New York: Alfred A. Knopf; T. Peters. 1994. *The Pursuit of Wow*. New York: Vintage Books.

The proper blend of decision variables will not guarantee entrepreneurship will occur, nor will an inappropriate blend ensure it does not. However, the appropriate structural design can go a long way toward influencing the types of innovations that are produced and the frequency with which they are produced on a consistent basis over time. Further, and building upon the earlier discussion, the following linkages should be kept in mind:

■ **TABLE 10.4**

OTHER ELEMENTS OF MECHANISTIC VERSUS
ORGANIC ORGANIZATIONAL STRUCTURES

Organic Structure	Mechanistic Structure
Channels of Communications	**Channels of Communications**
Open with free flow of information throughout the organization	Highly structured, restricted information flow
Operating Styles	**Operating Styles**
Allowed to vary freely	Must be uniform and restricted
Authority for Decisions	**Authority for Decisions**
Based on expertise of the individual	Based on formal line management position
Free Adaptation	**Reluctant Adaptation**
By the organization to changing circumstances	With insistence on holding fast to tried-and-true management principles despite changes in business conditions
Emphasis on Getting Things Done	**Emphasis on Formally Laid Down Procedures**
Unconstrained by formally laid out procedures	Reliance on tried-and-true management principles
Loose, Informal Control	**Tight Control**
With emphasis on norm of cooperation	Through sophisticated control systems
Flexible On-Job Behavior	**Constrained On-Job Behavior**
Permitted to be shaped by the requirements of the situation and personality of the individual doing the job	Required to conform to job descriptions
Participation and Group Consensus Used Frequently	**Superiors Make Decisions with Minimum Consultation and Involvement of Subordinates**

SOURCE: Covin, D., and J. Slevin. 1990. "Juggling Entrepreneurial Style and Organizational Structure—How to Get Your Act Together," *Sloan Management Review* 31 (Winter): 44.

More hostile external environment ⟶ Management style must be more entrepreneurial ⟶ Organic structure is needed to facilitate entrepreneurship

More benign or controllable external environment ⟶ Conservative management style is more appropriate ⟶ Mechanistic/ bureaucratic structure is effective

■ FIGURE 10.4

ENTREPRENEURIAL LEADERSHIP, STRUCTURE,
AND THE CONCEPT OF CYCLING

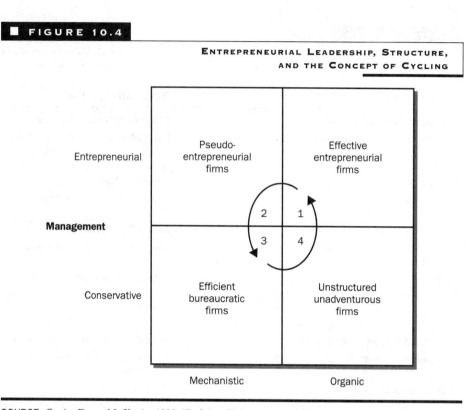

SOURCE: Covin, D., and J. Slevin. 1990. "Judging Entrepreneurial Style and Organizational Structure: How to Get Your Act Together," *Sloan Management Review* 31 (Winter):45.

The work of Covin and Slevin (1990) also helps explain patterns that occur in companies over time. As illustrated in Figure 10.4, there is a need to achieve fit between management style (the relative emphasis on entrepreneurship) and organization structure (more organic versus mechanistic). Thus, a good fit exists with an organic structure and an entrepreneurial emphasis, producing an effective entrepreneurial firm (Cell 1 of Figure 10.4). Similarly, a good fit exists between conservative managerial orientation and a mechanistic structure, resulting in an efficient bureaucratic organization (Cell 3). Organizations are much more problematic when the structure and management style are inconsistent, as in Cells 2 and 4.

An especially intriguing notion is the concept called *cycling*. Here, the successful company is able to move back and forth, or cycle, between Cells 1 and 3 of Figure 10.4. The inference is that firms move through periods of stability and conservatism and periods of innovation and change. Thus, the company may start out as a highly entrepreneurial organization, but growth may create a need for controls, formalization of procedures, and the addition of hierarchy, indicating a move from Cell 1 to Cell 3. At the same time, there is a need not to become stagnant and instead to support ongoing research, new ideas, and innovation, suggesting a need to shift back to Cell 1. And the cycle continues. Obviously, some firms cannot make such transitions without severe disruption. Some get caught in Cells 2 and 4, where external forces create determination among managers to be entrepreneurial but where only token changes are made to the structure, and it remains fundamentally mechanistic. Changes, if they are to be successful, must occur on both dimensions simultaneously.

A different take on cycling might find the company attempting to have parallel structures and management styles. The efficient and conservative manager and a mechanistic style may be appropriate for certain key parts of the business (e.g., processing insurance claims in a large insurance company), while organic structures with entrepreneurial management are applied in units charged with new product and market development.

It should also be remembered that structures are usually designed and modified in reaction to some strategic need in the company. Management sees a need to reduce costs, eliminate duplication of effort, achieve greater coordination, or bring more speed to core aspects of operations. Unless the encouragement of entrepreneurial behavior is an explicit objective when management is redesigning the structure, the probability is great that entrepreneurship will actually suffer under whatever structure is implemented.

CIRCLES INSTEAD OF HIERARCHY

Some companies are taking experimentation and the search for more organic structures further. They are challenging basic precepts and assumptions regarding how a company must be organized. In the process, they reject conventional notions, such as the almost universally accepted idea that companies must be viewed vertically and horizontally. It is intuitively appealing to think in terms of levels in a hierarchy over which authority and responsibility are distributed and to picture departments and functions that specialize in certain activities and that operate laterally or at the same level in the firm. Alternatively, at W.L. Gore and Associates, makers of Goretex, they use the term *unmanagement* to describe an environment with no titles, hierarchy, or conventional structures. The result is more direct lines of communication, no fixed authority, sponsors rather than bosses, and high levels of commitment.

If we refrain from thinking of a hierarchy or an organizational chart with lines and boxes that is narrower at the top and wider at the bottom, then what are some alternative conceptualizations? Certainly, the network and team-based structures discussed earlier represent departures from conventional thinking, but they still have vertical and horizontal dimensions. A very different picture emerges when we think of the organization as a circle.

One of the most intriguing examples of circular structures involves Semco, a Brazilian manufacturer of a diverse mix of industrial products and equipment (Semler 1993). Operating a mature business in a highly turbulent environment, the company decided to slash its bureaucracy from twelve layers of management to three, and it devised a new organizational structure based on circles and triangles. The entire structure consists of three fluid concentric circles. The structure begins with a small innermost circle. It includes six or seven people who are the equivalent of the CEO and senior vice presidents in a conventional structure. These people set and monitor the overall strategic direction of the firm. The second circle includes the seven to ten leaders of the company's business units. The third and very large circle holds everyone else, ranging from machine operators to salespeople to security guards. Within the large circle lie a number of floating triangles. Each triangle consists of a first level manager of a key business function or activity such as marketing, production, engineering, assembly, and so forth. Six to twelve triangles exist for each business unit. The triangles float around in the large circle, suggesting the people in them are moveable. Consistent with the three circles and the triangles, there are only four job categories in the company: counselors (coordinate general policies and strategies), partners (run business units), coordinators (provide first level management of core functions or activities), and associates (everyone else). Coordinators cannot report to coordinators, and associates cannot report to associates, which keeps the structure flat.

There is a fluidity to the Semco structure, in that coordinators can move to other coordinator jobs or move back to associate jobs (without an ill effect on their paycheck). In fact, associates can earn more than coordinators. Further, employees set their own salary and wage rates. Specific limits on the number of coordinators (far fewer of them than the number of foremen, supervisors, and department heads that existed in the company's former structure) force associates to assume more responsibility. Associates make all the decisions on the job that they are comfortable making; after that point, they consult coordinators. The same goes for coordinators, who consult partners at a weekly meeting on those issues with which they feel uncomfortable. When the new structure eliminated managerial positions (what was formerly three distinct levels of management might now be a single coordinator and some associates), it was left to the business units and ultimately the associates to figure out how to redistribute responsibility. In effect, the circle structure not only reduced the number of bosses but also reduced the variety of bosses.

Another approach to structure using circles is proposed by Tropman and Morningstar (1989). As pictured in Figure 10.5, it is a design in which levels are replaced by orbits and in which the orientation toward authority changes with the disappearance of "higher ups." Consistent with the Semco approach, there are three main orbits: the central, or executive, circle; the managerial circle; and the operational, or technical, circle. These authors also suggest the addition of other orbits to capture key external role players such as customers, suppliers, and financiers. Communication among those in different orbits becomes easier and more direct, as is reflected in the lines that connect those in one orbit (say the operational or technical orbit) with those in another (say the executive core) without

■ **FIGURE 10.5**

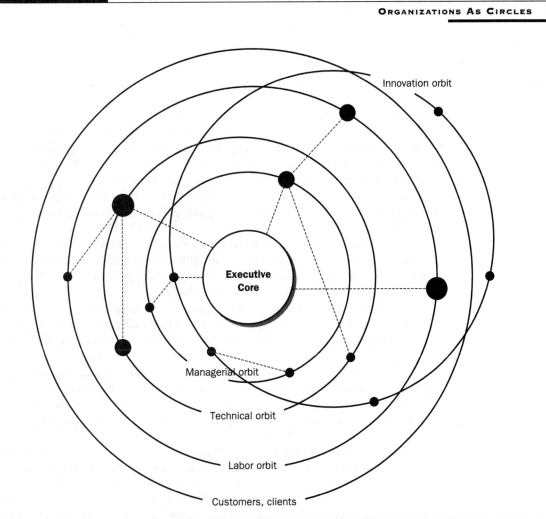

SOURCE: Tropman, J., and G. Morningstar. 1989. *Entrepreneurial Systems for the 1990s.* Westport, CT: Quorum, p. 161.

necessarily going through the people who fall in orbits in between (say the managerial orbit).

A key feature of the structure in Figure 10.5 is that it allows for the creation of new spheres for incubator or experimental programs; hence, innovation spheres can be created and located anywhere in the organization. They can be placed between two spheres, cross various spheres, be placed at the edge or outer periphery of the organization, and so on. Innovative activities thus have a level of independence, but oversight is also applied.

ENTREPRENEURIAL PROJECTS: STRUCTURES WITHIN STRUCTURES

Entrepreneurial projects require structures themselves, and a key issue concerns how project structures fit within the overall organizational structure. In Chapter Seven, we examined some of the popular ways that companies organize units or teams to manage innovation projects. However, there is another consideration. Much happens along the way as an entrepreneurial concept goes from a loose idea to a formal project with an assigned team and budget. The company needs a mechanism that reflects the evolutionary nature of entrepreneurial events inside the organization.

We recommend that companies adopt an approach wherein innovation opportunities are produced through three different internal channels or structural mechanisms. Each of these is described in Table 10.5, in what we have labeled the Entrepreneurial Project Development Framework.

Under this framework, opportunities can be pursued as either "ray of light" projects, "emerging potential" projects, or "mainstream development" projects. Ray of light projects are bootstrapped. An employee (any employee) has an idea and is encouraged to pursue it. He or she begs or borrows resources, pursues the idea in his or her free time, and is concerned with general conceptualization and with demonstrating real market potential. The end product is a short business concept plan that can be sold to management. Management then decides whether to defer, or pass, on the ray of light project, approve it as an emerging potential project, or make it a mainstream development project.

Emerging potential projects (which may have begun as ray of light or emerging potential projects) involve concepts that are brought to some type of review committee, which we shall call the Opportunities Review Board. The makeup of this board might include a mix of levels of management and functional expertise, with members regularly rotating off and on. Special expertise might be added to deal with certain projects. The board members review and approve proposals from employees and are able to allocate seed capital to projects up to some fixed amount. They can also endorse the employee as champion (or assign someone else) and free up 20 percent to 30 percent of the champion's time for his or her pursuit of the project. The seed capital is used to conduct research, for staff assistance, and for related expenses. The end product is a formal business plan that is submitted to the directors. If it is approved, the emerging potential project becomes a mainstream development project.

Mainstream development projects are where the new product, service, and process efforts that have been prioritized by senior management are developed. A formal budget is allocated, and some sort of structure is in place (e.g.,

■ **TABLE 10.5**

THE ENTREPRENEURIAL PROJECT DEVELOPMENT FRAMEWORK

Characteristic	Ray of Light Projects	Emerging Potential Projects	Mainstream Development Projects
Project financing	No budget	Seed capital	Formal budget
Management approval	Not approved	Approved by Opportunity Review Board	Approved by senior management/directors
Supportive research	Exploratory research	Formal market research	Extensive industry, competitive, and customer intelligence
Process followed	Early conceptualizing	Concept refinement/ Prototype testing	Formal NPD process
Initiator/Leader	Driven by initiator/ anyone in company	Champion assigned (20–30% of his/her time)	Driven by new products manager & integrated team
Degree of project risk	Low to medium	Medium	Medium to high
Period of development	Short	Medium	Medium to high
Innovativeness	Low to medium	Medium to high	Medium to high
Outcomes	Produces short (3–5 pages) concept plan	Produces formal business plan	Results in launch or gets canned

a cross-functional new product team is assigned to the project, or a venture team is put together). A systematic process is followed with key performance benchmarks monitored after each major stage. Extensive intelligence is gathered. The end product is typically a major product launch, although it is anticipated that some of these projects may still be terminated or dropped along the way.

The benefits of having three mechanisms for generating innovation are many. First, much more innovation is likely to result. This approach is consistent with the goal of facilitating innovation of all types on an ongoing basis throughout the organization. It encourages a portfolio of innovation projects, helping the firm balance full-scale development activities by having both high-risk, high-return and low-risk, moderate-return projects. Second, innovation is clearly being defined as a corporate-wide task, not R&D in isolation. Third, the likelihood of interfunctional involvement and coordination is much greater. Fourth, employees are more likely to take responsibility for innovation, champions are more likely to emerge, and accountability will not only be for design but also for implementation. Finally, ray of light and emerging potential approaches bring more flexibility and speed to the innovation process and will most likely cost less money than solely relying on a mainstream development for every new product.

SUMMARY AND CONCLUSIONS

We use the term *structure* to describe the formal ways in which a company organizes people and tasks. Entrepreneurship requires structure but is often a victim of the types of structural arrangements created in companies. Companies create structures to manage the existing demands of the business. Entrepreneurship is about creating new things and moving in new directions. As a result, entrepreneurial efforts almost always challenge and often conflict with the structure currently in place.

In this chapter, we have explored the underlying elements that go into the structure of a company as well as some of the more prevalent types of structures that can be found in modern organizations. We have looked at ways in which structures evolve and at how entrepreneurship is systematically constrained as the structure evolves. In general, we have argued that entrepreneurship is facilitated under structures that are more organic in nature. A number of guiding principles were proposed to help make the structure more consistent with continuous entrepreneurship.

It was also emphasized that the structure of a company must be continually re-created. In essence, the structure that works today is likely to demonstrate significant inadequacies eighteen months from now. A complex mix of variables determines the appropriate structure for a company, and those variables are subject to ongoing change. This brings us to an important caveat: structure is a matter of balance (Hamel and Prahalad 1994). Empowerment without direction results in anarchy. Having one hundred independent businesses within one large one can result in lots of wasted resources and missed opportunities unless the linkages among these units are exploited. Similarly, organizations must balance lean and flexible aspects of the organization against the need for administrative controls and some level of bureaucracy in other areas of the firm. They must balance a customer focus against a technological focus.

Structure can be an important facilitator of entrepreneurship because it can give employees a sense that they have room to maneuver and innovate while also allowing their interaction with others in the organization. It can help accommodate a larger volume of entrepreneurial initiatives and also facilitate the speed at which such initiatives move from inception to implementation. Yet, structure does not work in isolation. Its ability to contribute to a more entrepreneurship-friendly environment is a function of interactions between structural elements and other organizational variables. One of the most important of these other variables is the company control system, a subject to which we turn in the next chapter.

REFERENCES

Block, Z., and I. MacMillan. 1993. *Corporate Venturing*. Boston: Harvard Business School.

Chandler, A. 1962. *Strategy and Structure*. Cambridge: MIT.

Cornwall, J., and B. Perlman. 1990. *Organizational Entrepreneurship*. Homewood: Irwin.

CHANGES FOR SURVIVAL

DUPONT

For a company that has been around for nearly two hundred years, DuPont has prided itself on cultivating innovation. Its goal is to upset the natural equilibrium by pushing itself to consider new strategic possibilities that the company's scientists' discoveries make possible. This is made evident, for example, by the entirely new process discovered while making the raw materials for Lycra and by the designing of a new device that measures bacteria in food.

With 1999 sales of $27 billion and operations in sixty-five countries, one of DuPont's most daunting tasks is creating synergies across all of its operating units. Today, the company's focus is toward communication networks. Unless the researchers network and share knowledge, they cannot create a product and bring it to market. At DuPont, networks have become the tools for innovation, which is why DuPont supports over 400 networks that transfer technology throughout the organization.

For example, network members in Detroit, Geneva, and Wilmington produced a structural analysis of an automobile air intake manifold made of DuPont Zytel nylon. The process sensor network transferred sensor technology throughout the company, making it possible for an individual plant to control its emissions and continue to operate. The corporate maintenance leadership team reduced maintenance costs by $200 million in one year. These networks work because all employees are trained to have a lot of mobility within the company. Along the way, people naturally build relationships that lead to networks of allies and mentors.

These strategies have allowed DuPont to achieve and maintain profitability by lowering costs while multiplying research and development dollars. For DuPont, innovation takes the form of small incremental changes in a product or a process with the involvement of many individuals.

ENRON

Quite simply, Enron buys and sells gas and electricity. However, in the last decade, it has gone from a money loser to perhaps the most fundamental agent of change in the industry. The key to Enron's success was its ability to effectively find a way to profit from government regulation. Kenneth Lay, Enron's CEO, is credited with "inventing the natural gas and power trading business."

Trading gas and electric like commodities was thought by many industry experts to be undoable and very risky, yet the concept has been so successful that the company is now exploring ways to trade excess capacity of fiber-optic networks. The process works by taking advantage of all of the natural gas pipelines criss-crossing the forty-eight contiguous states. If a power company in one city needs electricity to cope with a hot spell in August, Enron can find another utility or private generator in another city with a surplus of power, at the right price, and arrange to have it sent to that city. Lay realized that by pushing deregulation, Enron could use all of the natural gas lines to buy gas where it was cheap and ship it to where it was needed.

Lay hired aggressive traders and almost single-handedly created a spot market for gas. In order to accelerate growth, he created several new public companies, all owned by Enron. While others in the gas business felt there was no need for a spot market, Enron found that its new approach could reduce the cost of gas for some utilities by 30 percent to 50 percent. To take it another step further, Enron took advantage of the cheaper free-market gas and began to use it for fuel in electric generation plants—a concept that was forbidden under old federal regulations. Enron went on to build and operate its own gas-fired power plant in Texas, showing that it could compete economically against coal-fired plants—with far less pollution. Today, the company has expanded into Europe and Asia and has launched innovative trading operations in paper, coal, plastics, and Internet bandwidth.

SOURCE: DuPont: Robinson, E. A. 1997. "The Secrets of America's Most Admired Corporations," *Fortune* 135, No. 4 (March): 60–64.

Enron: O'Reilly, B. 2000. "The Power Merchant," *Fortune* 141, No. 8 (April): 148.

Covin, D., and J. Slevin. 1990. "Judging Entrepreneurial Style and Organizational Structures — How to Get Your Act Together," *Sloan Management Review* 31 (Winter): 43–53.

Galbraith, J. 1995. *Designing Organizations.* San Francisco: Jossey-Bass.

Griener, L. 1972. "Revolution and Evolution as Organizations Grow," *Harvard Business Review* 50 (July–August): 37–46.

Hamel, G., and C. K. Prahalad. 1994. *Competing for the Future.* Boston: Harvard Business School.

Miller, D. 1983. "The Correlates of Entrepreneurship in Three Types of Firms," *Management Science* 29, No. 7: 770–791.

Miller, D. 1986. "Configurations of Strategy and Structure: Towards a Synthesis," *Strategic Management Journal* 7: 233–239.

Miller, D. 1996. "Configurations Revisited," *Strategic Management Journal* 17: 505–512.

Mintzberg, H. 1979. *The Structuring of Organizations.* Englewood Cliffs, NJ: Prentice-Hall.

O'Reilly, B. 2000. "The Power Merchant," *Fortune* 141, No. 8 (April): 148.

Pettigrew, A., and E. Fenton. 2000. *The Innovating Organization.* London: Sage Publications.

Semler, R. 1993. *Maverick: The Success Story Behind the World's Most Unusual Workplace.* New York: Warner Books.

Thornhill, S., and R. Amit. 2001. "A Dynamic Perspective of Internal Fit in Corporate Venturing," *Journal of Business Venturing* 16, No. 1: 25–50.

Tropman, J., and G. Morningstar. 1989. *Entrepreneurial Systems for the 1990's.* Westport: Quorum.

11

CONTROL AND ENTREPRENEURIAL ACTIVITY

Control sounds like an oppressive word. It evokes images of restraint, dominance, regulation, rigidity, and conformity. Yet organizations would be reduced to chaos without meaningful control measures. Policies, procedures, and rules are needed to ensure order, achieve coordination, and maintain efficiency. Without them, quality is inconsistent, order schedules are missed, customers are improperly billed, money is spent that should not be spent, and employees take shortcuts. Controls come in many forms, but they ultimately create a sense of accountability and help ensure that company assets are being efficiently employed.

Control systems in companies tend to be simple in the beginning. Over time, they steadily evolve, becoming more sophisticated and complex. Herein lies the problem. As more procedures, systems, and documentation requirements are added, managers are increasingly encouraged to micromanage each and every expenditure and to establish quantifiable performance benchmarks in as many activity areas as possible. These benchmarks can become ends in themselves and can convey a lack of trust in employees. And then there is the issue of efficiency versus effectiveness. Efficiency is concerned with minimizing the amount of expenditures or resources needed to accomplish a task. Effectiveness is concerned with ensuring that the correct tasks are being accomplished. Control systems have historically placed a heavy emphasis on efficiency—sometimes ignoring or even undermining effectiveness issues.

The development of control systems also has implications for the level of entrepreneurship exhibited in a company. It would seem that control systems that attempt to influence the way in which resources are being used (e.g., employee time, facilities and equipment, marketing programs), in addition to monitoring how efficiently they are being used, can at the same time undermine employee motivation and creativity (Morris 1998). Control measures provide structure to tasks and operations within the enterprise, in effect providing criteria on which a given task is evaluated. However, they can become bureaucratic, slowing down the organization, stifling the employee, and encouraging almost mechanical performance to ensure the employee looks good in terms of the control measures (again, becoming an end in themselves rather than a means to an end). Thus, Pinchot (2000) observes, "Many centralized companies with highly sophisticated control systems are, in fact, out of control."

In this chapter, we will examine the relationship between control and entrepreneurship. Types of control measures will be reviewed, together with underlying dimensions of a control system. Approaches to control that encourage entrepreneurial behavior will be explored. Attention will also be devoted to control over a company's financial records and the role of open book accounting in supporting entrepreneurship. Finally, the concept of the profit pool will be introduced as a vehicle for discovering new opportunities within the current operations of a firm.

THE NATURE OF CONTROL IN ORGANIZATIONS

A control system can be defined as those formal and informal mechanisms that help individuals regulate what they do with themselves and other resources on the job. It is about harnessing company resources in a manner consistent with the organization's purpose. Controls are intended to guard against the possibility that people will do something the organization doesn't want them to do or fail to do something they should do. Controls prescribe a set of activities for dealing with situations as they arise.

We should also expand on the question "control over what?" An easy way to address such a question is to conceptualize the application of controls to inputs, processes or behaviors, and outputs. Controls over inputs to the company include such things as hiring practices and purchasing policies. Behavior control focuses on regulating the activities of organizational members through operating procedures and personal evaluations. Output controls involve setting targets for and measuring achievement. The chief concerns are performance goals, performance tracking, and the resolution of performance variances.

The term *control system* implies a carefully constructed and well-integrated set of items. In actuality, the system of controls in an organization is an agglomeration of hundreds and even thousands of documents, policies, procedures, processes, rules, objectives, guidelines, pieces of information, technologies, and equipment. Some of the elements are formal, while others are informal. Thus, control practices arise from conscious managerial efforts and from informal mechanisms that emerge through the spontaneous interactions of workers over time. Further, pieces and parts are continually added, modified, and deleted.

We can conclude that a company does not really design a comprehensive control system and implement it in one fell swoop, nor does it throw out an existing control system and put a new one in place. Rather, the set of control mechanisms evolves, with components subject to change. Changes are typically incremental such as the elimination of a procedure or the addition of a new form. Occasionally,

■ TABLE 11.1

THIRTY SIMPLE ELEMENTS IN AN ORGANIZATION'S CONTROL SYSTEM

Budgets	Travel policies
Production testing and monitoring equipment	Performance reviews
Time clocks	Strategic and operational plans
Objectives	Timetables
Purchasing policies	Rules governing internal communications
Hiring rules	Procedure manuals
Annual employee, department, and division reports	Financial and resource audits
Production schedules	Sales activity reports
Customer satisfaction surveys	Schedules
Job descriptions and job analysis	Financial statements
Sales quotas	Employee tests
Cameras	Spending approval processes
Efficiency measures	Security systems and ID cards
Expense reimbursement procedures	Sexual harassment policies
Hierarchical sign-offs on expense requests	Complaint handling procedures

bolder initiatives are pursued, such as a mandate from senior management to cut paperwork requirements or approval processes by 50 percent.

Table 11.1 provides examples of some of the many elements that might comprise an organization's control system. The list barely scratches the surface but illustrates the diverse set of ways in which behavior in companies is governed, monitored, and evaluated. When they are put together, these elements can have a pervasive impact on employee attitudes, motivation, perceptions, and outlooks. Further, they interact heavily with the structure of the company (see Chapter 10), and they both reflect and influence the culture of the firm (see Chapter 13).

The various control measures and mechanisms can be grouped into four general categories: simple control, technological control, bureaucratic/administrative control, and concertive/cultural control (Cirka 1997). Simple control is the direct personal supervision exercised by the manager over his or her subordinates. Technological control deals with the technology-based techniques used in production and service delivery processes. Bureaucratic and administrative control covers the formal rules, procedures, and policies used in established organizations. Concertive or cultural control is reflected in the shared values, norms, and the conformance to the beliefs of the company.

ORGANIZATIONS OUT OF CONTROL: A STORY OF UNINTENDED CONSEQUENCES

Control is vital in organizations. Without controls, it would be impossible to determine what is going on, distinguish high from low performers, satisfy customers on a consistent basis, be cost competitive, or find ways to continually improve. As companies grow in size and their operations become more diverse, controls become more complex. The problem is that control can feed on itself, continually growing and ultimately strangling an organization. At some point in the evolution of organization, control tends to beget control.

A natural tendency when someone is either not doing something he or she is supposed to do or doing something he or she is not supposed to do is to put a rule or mandated procedure in place. Then management needs paperwork or some other means of monitoring compliance with the rule or procedure. Then, management needs to hire people who will oversee this monitoring process and produce reports. Then, these people start to enhance the monitoring process, adding more procedures and paperwork. Perhaps additional help is needed to handle these new additions to the control system. Eventually, the controllers themselves require control, and a new hierarchy of rules and constraints is put in place so that they can be monitored. And so it goes.

Control initiatives are almost always well intentioned, yet they frequently have unintended consequences. They become problematic for at least four reasons. Let's start with the "trust problem." Most employees desire a certain sense of order in their work lives, and control mechanisms help provide order and accountability. However, as the control measures evolve, they intrude further and further into the way in which an employee performs his or her job. At some point, the employee asks, "What is this company trying to tell me?" when it requires him or her to fill out some superfluous form and/or get approval before he or she can take some ridiculously routine action or when it mandates that he or she follow an unnecessarily detailed procedure. All too often, the conclusion is "They think I'm stupid" or "They think I don't have better things to do with my time" or "They just don't trust me." It is this last conclusion that most undermines the willingness of employees to tap their creative energies, come up with innovative ideas, fight for those ideas, and persevere in getting them implemented.

The next unintended consequence of controls is the "slowness problem." Well-conceptualized controls can eliminate mistakes and wastage, reducing the need to redo some task and ensuring better coordination of resources. The end result can be speed: tasks are accomplished on a timely basis and customers are more quickly satisfied. Again, though, controls evolve to the point that they slow the organization down. If no flexibility exists in how things are done and if there are extremely detailed documentation requirements and elaborate steps that must be followed by the employee, not only will things take much more time, but people are actually being discouraged from working more quickly.

Another unintended result of the control system can be referred to as the "means-end problem." Control systems are meant to be a means towards an end, with the end being the achievement of some desired organizational outcome such as less wastage or fewer mistakes. Consider a rather bizarre example from a major university. Concerned about excessive student drinking and the resultant inappropriate behaviors, the university created an elaborate set of rules and restrictions for parties in fraternity houses. One of the more interesting efforts was something called the "potato chip rule." On the assumption that potato chips were the most popular food item at parties and that consuming more potato chips encouraged party-goers to stay longer and drink more, a rule was put in place limiting the number of potato chips that could be present at a party. Obviously, this meant that the group hosting the party had to take time to count the potato chips, monitor anyone bringing extra chips to the party, and do whatever it took to stay under the mandated limited. They created the position within the fraternity of the "potato chip enforcer." Further, some university employee would have to go around and make sure each and every party was in compliance with the rule. Of course, documents would be needed to track potato chip compliance, and a procedure had to be put in place for dealing with those in violation. Now, all of this seems quite ludicrous, but it captures what happens with overcontrol in companies. Managers get so caught up in trying to create control mechanisms that they lose sight of what the controls were ultimately meant to accomplish. In the example above, one can be sure that the fraternities closely adhered to the potato chip rule (or found inventive ways to get around it). The objective became making sure they *looked good in terms of the control measure.* But the real goal, responsible drinking, was completely lost in the shuffle. From the standpoint of the fraternity members, or the employees in a company, the control system becomes an end in itself, rather than a means to an end.

Then there is the "efficiency-effectiveness problem." It is perhaps the most profoundly disturbing of all the unintended consequences and is directly related to the means-end problem. In simple terms, efficiency is about doing things right, while effectiveness is about doing the right things (Drucker 1985). Again, we can illustrate the problem with an example. A company was concerned about the rapidly growing cost of office supplies. The cost per employee of supplies (an efficiency measure) was up 30 percent from what was thought to be normal. Management was unsure of whether employees were simply being wasteful or taking supplies home for personal use or if there was some other explanation. (Maybe people were just working harder.) Regardless, management put a new rule in place. One of the significant cost increases involved expenditures for legal pads. Up to this point, when an employee needed supplies, he or she simply went to a supply room and took what was needed. Under the new rule, whenever an employee wanted a new legal pad, he or she had to turn in the cardboard backing from the old pad. The rule apparently worked because the result was a reduction in expenditures for legal pads. There was an improvement in the *efficiency* measure, and management was happy. However, the actual effect of the rule was not so simple. Not only did it undermine trust, but also the restriction led people simply to do without pads, especially if they didn't think to hold on to the backing of the ones they had used up. For some, it was just not worth the hassle. Others bought their own pads. Lending pads to one another was certainly being discouraged. Taking pads home was not eliminated because the employee just had to remember to bring the backing in to work. *Effectiveness,* which in this case would be the extent to which employees are better able to do their jobs because they have the necessary office supplies, is either ignored or undermined.

Putting these four problems together, it becomes apparent that the firm with a highly developed and complex control system may actually be controlling the wrong things—or nothing at all. This conclusion is especially likely given the creativity of people and their ability to find ways around things in which they do not believe or see as necessary. In fact, the considerable time that is wasted finding inventive ways around rules and procedures takes away from the time that might have been spent inventing new and better products, services, and processes.

DIMENSIONS OF CONTROL AND ENTREPRENEURSHIP

As management attempts to grapple with the myriad elements of a control system, it is worth stepping back and assessing overall characteristics of the controls that are in place. A control system can be characterized by a variety of attributes: degree of formality and prescriptiveness, desire for conformance and compliance, degree of rigidness, desire for consistency, use of coercive power, distribution of authority and responsibility, desire for individual initiative, level of freedom and discretion, degree of horizontal interaction and communication, and level of detail. Figure 11.1 attempts to summarize these attributes in terms of seven underlying dimensions.

■ FIGURE 11.1

UNDERLYING CHARACTERISTICS OF A FIRM'S CONTROL SYSTEM

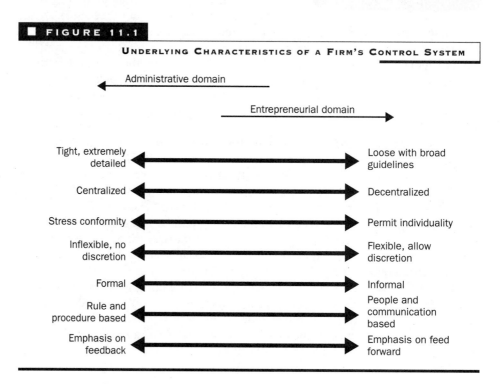

In theory, control systems are designed around attributes such as these in a manner that accomplishes effective outcomes. The principal outcomes sought through control efforts include *risk reduction, elimination of uncertainty, highly efficient operations, goal conformance,* and *specific role definitions.* Unfortunately, outcomes such as these tend to be inconsistent with entrepreneurship. Yet it is our view that control systems can actually facilitate entrepreneurial behavior in firms, as reflected on the right-hand side of Figure 11.1.

Entrepreneurship would appear to be more consistent with *risk tolerance,* rather than risk reduction. Risk tolerance is reflected in a work environment where there is less rigidity in the organizational structure with a greater degree of empowerment and autonomy, areas of responsibility are less clearly delineated, conduct is less prescribed, and administrative consistency is expected. Further, entrepreneurship would seem more likely if the control system allows for *management of uncertainty* rather than seeking to eliminate uncertainty. Uncertainty becomes more manageable when there is less formality and rigidness in the approach to planning for the future, budget mechanisms are more flexible in accommodating new opportunities as they emerge, and organizational goals are focused on achieving ends rather than prescribing means.

In addition, the likelihood of entrepreneurial behavior would seem greater where there is *enlightened efficiency,* and a level of discretion or slack is deliberately designed into cost controls and budgeting, budget deviations are more tolerated, performance measurement is not at fixed intervals, and success measures include both financial and nonfinancial indicators. Also, an internal environment that supports entrepreneurship will most likely focus on *goal congruence.* With the greater degree of freedom and autonomy that might be expected in a more entrepreneurial company, it is expected that self-control and social control would play a larger role than procedural control in aligning the goals of the individual with that of the organization. The control system might be expected to include incentives tied to organizational success factors. Finally, the facilitation of entrepreneurship would appear to be more consistent with *role flexibility,* which can be achieved if employees are empowered to exercise discretion and personal initiative in performing their jobs and the control system focuses more on the outer boundaries for activities and behaviors.

THE ENTREPRENEURIAL PHILOSOPHY OF CONTROL

Managers must periodically ask a simple question: What is our concept of control in this company? If we consider all of the ingredients that go into the complex system of formal and informal controls, is there a guiding philosophy? Stevenson and Jarillo-Mossi (1989) argue that two general philosophies dominate, although clearly many degrees lie between the two. The first is what they term *command and control.* The term has a military connotation, which is appropriate. Control is tight, with orders coming from above and with the expectation that they will be executed

THE CRITICAL ELEMENTS OF AN ENTREPRENEURIAL
PHILOSOPHY OF CONTROL

- Control based on "no suprises"
- Looser but effective control elements
- A mindset of giving up control to gain control
- Empowerment and discretion that is built into the job
- Mutual trust
- Emphasis on self-control
- Organizational slack in terms of resource availability
- Pools of internal venture capital
- Varying levels of control based on the types of entrepreneurial behavior being sought
- Open and shared control information

exactly as they are given. Decisions are made as if superiors are present. Extensive control measures are used to track whether commands are executed and to provide detailed feedback to management.

The second philosophy of control is much more consistent with the creation of an entrepreneurial environment (see also Table 11.2). It is called *no surprises*. The concern is with a control system that generates adequate information on a timely basis for all who really need to know. No one is subject to surprises because of a lack of information. The link is between control and company performance. Management seeks to ensure that overall performance is predictable enough for the company to maintain credibility, achieve coordination among key groups, and properly anticipate resource requirements. Control mechanisms produce indicators or early warning signals of problems before they occur. This approach is very different from one where the purpose is to check up on people or mandate their behaviors on the job.

An entrepreneurial philosophy of control has some related aspects. Consistent with our earlier discussion, it is one in which the control system conveys a sense of trust. If the organization mandates that employees be subjected to electronic time cards to document when they begin and end their work or provide detailed justifications for every expense when they travel, then there is an implicit (and perhaps explicit) statement being made: "We don't trust you to simply do the work you are paid to do without close monitoring, and we don't trust you to spend money wisely when traveling for the company." Now, there are those who will argue that such mechanisms are critical for figuring out where money is being spent and where profits are being made in the business, and that it has nothing to do with trust. Employees are likely to see it differently. More importantly, practices such as these do not reinforce trust or produce an enhanced feeling of empowerment. Trust is an important beginning point in getting employees to move down the path toward trying new things, overcoming obstacles with unconventional approaches, and being willing to experience failure along the way.

Another core principle in the entrepreneurial philosophy of control requires that managers *give up control to gain control*. It is a simple but powerful notion. When a manager gives up control of some activity or area of responsibility and instead allows the employee to handle it, control is being given up. And yet, if the empowered employee responds by being more conscientious, more creative, or harder working, then control is actually being gained. The control is not over the intermediate actions of the employee but over the employee's performance or final output. Control is also gained over the employee's sense of accomplishment and job satisfaction.

Consider the supervisor who lets employees set their own work schedules or determine their own pay rates. By giving up control over these decisions, the manager not only wants to make the employee feel empowered and trusted. More fundamentally, the objective is to get the employee to take ownership, realize the implications of his or her behavior for the company, fellow workers, and herself or himself, and produce an outcome that is better than if the supervisor had simply mandated the decision or performed the activity. Thus, the employee may be more willing to work a less desirable shift, put in extra hours, and agree to a more reasonable wage rate (about which he or she does not complain).

The manager's ability to obtain better results from the employee than would occur if complete control were exercised requires that he or she has a clear strategy that includes answers to the following questions:

- Over what specific activity, responsibility, or requirement is management giving up control?
- Does the employee have or can he or she obtain the proper information to exercise control over the activity or behavior?
- Is it clear that this is a real and permanent relinquishment of control, with no second-guessing?
- What specific impact on behavior is management attempting to have?
- Over what variables is control being gained, and how is it manifested?

If control is, in part, about accountability, then giving up control is about greater accountability. Where there is an elaborate system of control measures, the employee can be secure in the knowledge that, if the control system has been complied with, then his or her accountability is absolved, that his or her responsibility has been fulfilled. He or she need not take any further responsibility for outcomes or the implications of personal behavior for company performance. However, by giving up control to the employee, there is a much deeper sense of responsibility not only for accomplishing a task or behaving in a certain manner but also for the quality of task performance and the impact it has on the organization.

As noted above, to give up control is to empower. Henry Mintzberg (1996, p. 63) explains that "empowerment really means stopping the disempowerment of people—but this just brings us back to hierarchy—for empowerment (typically) reinforces hierarchy." He argues that true empowerment goes beyond tokenism or the delegation of some task or authority as if one were granting a gift to the

■ FIGURE 11.2

RELATING TYPES OF INNOVATION INITIATIVES TO CONTROL

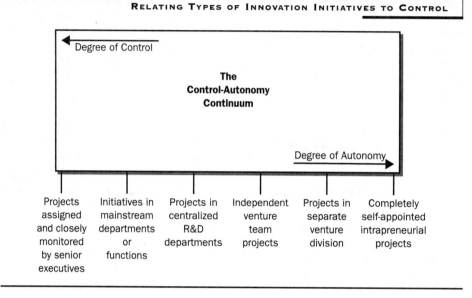

employee from on high. Instead, people get power when it is logically and intrinsically designed into their jobs. This distinction is reflected in the following two scenarios:

Scenario A: The vice president of purchasing invites the purchasing agent to attend a decision meeting from which she is normally excluded, or empowers the purchasing agent to make a particular vendor selection decision when the VP usually makes all such decisions.

Scenario B: The vice president of purchasing sets up a team of purchasing agents to make vendor selection decisions and tells them to come to him only when they are deadlocked on a choice.

It is the latter scenario that not only empowers but also encourages people to apply themselves and to demonstrate initiative. Empowerment means authority is delegated. The employee has a degree of discretion and some level of autonomy. She or he is accountable for a decision or action and the corresponding outcome.

To complete our entrepreneurial philosophy of control, two final points are in order. First, the relationship between entrepreneurship and control is not one of simply getting more entrepreneurship when there is less control. Control is vital for sustained entrepreneurship. The real issue is the nature and intent of the controls and how they are used. However, there does come a point beyond which more control has deleterious effects on entrepreneurial activity.

Secondly, control levels can also be expected to vary with the type of entrepreneurship the company seeks. Incremental innovation can occur in more tightly controlled environments, but discontinuous innovation requires extensive autonomy. One can also link control to the type of structure producing the innovation.

Figure 11.2 illustrates how various innovation structures imply different degrees of control. Levels of control are higher with projects that are sanctioned within a mainstream functional area such as production or marketing. The resultant innovation is apt to be continuous or incremental. Control is replaced by more autonomy with separate new venture divisions. Such separate divisions are more likely to demonstrate much higher levels of entrepreneurial intensity. The implication is that the concept of control in an organization must be flexible in terms of different types of decisions. It should, at the least, distinguish between mainstream operations and innovation activity.

THE CONCEPTS OF SLACK AND INTERNAL VENTURE CAPITAL

A company's control efforts are especially concerned with people and money. Management tries to ensure that employees are earning their pay, the firm is not paying more than it has to for everything from raw materials to travel, items are not purchased that are not really needed, people are not misappropriating funds, and so forth. Moreover, any firm, no matter the size, has limited resources. As a rule, different departments, units, and projects compete for these resources. Recognizing the importance of the above, entrepreneurial firms still find ways to make excess resources available for informal experimentation, unsanctioned trials, and research on formative ideas.

This brings us to an additional feature of entrepreneurial control systems: organizational slack. The concept of slack implies a degree of looseness in resource availability. Employees are able to tap into resources without going through a formal approval process. They can "borrow" expertise, research, money, materials, equipment, and other resources as they develop, test, and refine original concepts. No slack exists when the company is so busy counting everything that can be counted, forcing strict accountability for each penny of a given department's budget and for every minute of an employee's time on the job. Without slack, there is little room to try anything new or different. Experimentation becomes almost impossible.

Managing slack involves a fine balancing act. If money is hanging on trees so that virtually anyone can easily get funding for any new idea, huge amounts will be wasted. Further, there will be little organizational benefit from the subsequent failures that occur. It is important that entrepreneurial champions have to fight for their ideas. Their concepts can only benefit from being challenged and resisted. But if controls are too tight, the incentive to innovate disappears. The time and effort an employee must invest to obtain formal resource support and the high probability that requests will ultimately be rejected lead the employee to conclude that the costs of personal innovation far outweigh any potential benefits. New ideas almost always require initial work to refine, revise, and adapt them into a form that makes sense for the organization. They also require extensive internal selling, and selling is a lot easier if the innovator has data and other evidence to support his or her innovation. But in the absence of slack, it is hard to develop ideas and concepts to the point where they can be sold, and it is difficult to generate supporting evidence. In effect, slack encourages the creation of an underground economy of percolating ideas within the company.

Slack is very much tied to budgeting processes in companies. A tight control system mandates that budgets be prepared for units, departments, functional activities, and projects before money can be spent. It prescribes the format for budgets. Limits are established for the time period covered by the budget. Detailed line item breakdowns are required. Types of expenditures that are and are not permitted in the budget are specified, and *miscellaneous or other* categories are not allowed. Approval of budgets entails meetings at multiple levels in the organization. Alternatively, a budgeting process that allows for slack is more flexible. Time periods covered by different budgets can vary. Expense categories are more broadly defined. In a sense, the budget consists of a number of buckets instead of detailed line items, and the resources in a bucket can be applied creatively to accomplish the basic purpose of that particular bucket.

Although slack applies to operational budgets, it is important that entrepreneurial initiatives not undermine operational needs. Thus, simply having slack is not enough. There is a need to provide financial support for entrepreneurial initiatives in the form of special seed and venture capital funds that are separate from operational budgets. These funds should be available from multiple sources within the firm. Steven Brandt (1986, p. 93) explains, "Creating budget detours is the philosophy and . . . experimentation is the key."

Successful financing schemes are often administered by councils or boards consisting of people at or near the same level in the organization as those applying for the funds (notably, not senior executives). For instance, opportunity review boards might exist in various parts of the company. Each board has permanent members who rotate on and off every two years, and it also has special members who have expertise related to the particular proposal that has been submitted. The membership is principally middle- or lower-level management. Anyone can apply to the fund, and ideas can be fairly rough. A business plan of five pages or less is enough to call a board meeting. The board is empowered to provide staged investments, from fairly-easy-to-get seed money for initial research to increasingly larger amounts that are tied to the achievement of specific development targets. The board might also be given authority to free up an increasing percentage of the employee's time for work on the innovative project.

The key is to try more than one approach. Different funds might be created depending on the scope, scale, and innovativeness of projects. There will usually be limits to the size of a fund and to the amount that can be invested in a project, but both of these might vary considerably depending on the purpose of the fund. Funds might include a deal structure in which the employee gets an equity stake in the concept once it develops past a certain point or an agreement where the employee otherwise shares in the returns. Another option would be to have the employee share in the downside risk, should the concept fail. Pinchot and Pellman

(1999) also suggest the concept of "intracapital," which is a resource bank account awarded to employees who successfully pursue entrepreneurship within the company. The bank account consists of a budget the champion is allowed to spend on his or her next idea without asking anyone for permission. It can be used for research, travel, equipment, self-improvement, or any other expenditure that can reasonably be tied to new project development.

While considering issues surrounding budgetary support for entrepreneurship, it is also worthwhile to question the kinds of initiatives that tend to receive funding in companies. While the evidence is extremely limited, one study examined forty-nine projects (of which twenty-nine received funding) from a convenience sample of large companies (Koen 2000). The most important funding criterion was the strategic fit of the project with the company. Factors differentiating funded from unfunded projects included carefully choosing and developing a good working relationship with an executive champion (sponsor), requesting low initial start-up funding, and the ability to demonstrate marketplace competitiveness. If a project was funded, factors that affected the level of funding included the credibility of the team and market attractiveness.

CONTROL AND COSTS: THE OPEN BOOK REVOLUTION

The entrepreneurial philosophy of control extends to the financial records and books of the company. If there is one thing senior executives seem intent on controlling, it is access to the numbers. The prevalent belief seems to be that employees must never know what the company is spending in various areas, how much salary others are earning, what the salaries of executives are, or what the profits of the business units and the company are. The reasons for such a belief are many, ranging from "it's none of their business" and "it will undermine their motivation" to "they will somehow use it against us" and "competitors will find out." But such thinking is out of step with the current environment and the nature of today's workforce.

An alternative operating model is called *open book management* (Case 1997). It is an approach that attempts to change the link between the employee and the company. Rather than motivating employees to pay attention to quality, efficiency, good customer service, or some other operational concern, open book management gets them to focus on the bottom-line — the success of the business over time. Whereas much managerial time is spent on telling employees *what* the company wants to achieve (goals, performance levels) and *what* employees are expected to do to achieve these goals and levels, with open book management, the emphasis is on *why* things are happening and *why* improved performance is needed in certain areas. Based on a better understanding of these *why*'s, the employee is in a stronger position to discover innovative approaches to *how* goals and performance levels can be achieved. Table 11.3 summarizes the key ingredients constituting the open book approach.

OPEN-BOOK MANAGEMENT AND ENTREPRENEURSHIP:
THE INGREDIENTS

Open-book management is a way of running a company that gets everyone to focus on helping the business make money. It is an approach to business built around the following six principles:

■ Every employee has access to the company's financials and all the other numbers that are critical to tracking the firm's performance.

■ There is an overt and ongoing attempt to get the information in front of the employees.

■ The company teaches the basics of the business (what the numbers mean) to everyone.

■ Employees learn that, whatever else they do, part of their job is to move the numbers in the right direction.

■ People are empowered to make decisions in their jobs based on what they know.

■ Employees have a stake in the company's success, and share in the risk of failure.

SOURCE: Adapted from Case, J. 1995. "The Open Book Revolution," *Inc* 17 (June): 26–43; and Case, J. 1997. "Opening the Books," *Harvard Business Review* 75 (March–April): 118–127.

Open book management strives to get all employees to think and act as owners think and act. The books, financial records, and numbers are shared with everyone so that people see the relationship between what they do and how the company or unit performs. Employees are given training in how to interpret these numbers and how these numbers are influenced by decisions and performance levels in various parts of the company. Courses in business fundamentals are taught to everyone regardless of job description. Scorecards are prepared in which key numbers are regularly communicated to the workforce. Employees see corporate scorecards, business unit scorecards, and department scorecards. If a business unit or department sets a goal in some area, progress is tracked and linked to the numbers on the financial statements. All employees get involved in goal setting, and they see the linkages between the performance goals for their area and overall company performance.

The key to the open book approach is that people take joint responsibility for moving the numbers in the right direction. Employees are encouraged to experiment with creative ways to affect performance. A critical aspect is that employees share directly in rewards when targets are met. In fact, both risks and rewards are tied to the numbers. The rewards are linked to numbers that people regularly see, understand, and can affect. However, when performance comes up short, employees receive less. Compensation plans might vary from gain sharing and stock options to bonuses and salary increases.

For hesitant managers, John Case (1995, p. 29) explains, "Open book management comes with a built-in self-regulator that ought to still the hearts of owners who fear letting go . . . . The most important checks and balances—the numbers—are part of the system. If somebody makes a bad decision, its effects on the bottom line are right up where everybody can see them—and react accordingly."

The open book approach is clearly about trust and enlightened control. It is also consistent with the creation of a more entrepreneurial environment. Not only is this approach built around the concept of taking ownership, but it also encourages employees to look at the relationship between what they do and company performance. This approach facilitates ongoing process innovation as people come to understand how to affect the numbers and as they look for unique ways to accomplish their jobs. Product innovation is also encouraged, since employees can better appreciate the limits to revenue growth from current offerings. As new products and services are added, employees with the open book information get a vivid picture of the ways in which the numbers are affected.

THE CONCEPT OF PROFIT POOLS

Numbers can tell another story about entrepreneurial opportunity, this one on the profit side of the equation. The concept of a profit pool has been proposed by Gadiesh and Gilbert (1998), both of Bain and Company. Simply put, a profit pool is the total profits earned in an industry at all points along the industry's value chain. All the product or service segments in the value chain are identified, and each is assessed in terms of its current and potential profits. Note that the focus is not on revenues because the areas accounting for the most sales are frequently not the most profitable. Figure 11.3 provides an illustration of the profit pool for the U.S. automobile industry. In this example, manufacturing (auto makers) and selling cars (dealers) are responsible for most of the revenues, but auto leasing is the most profitable, followed by insurance.

Profitability can be expected to differ significantly across the segments in the profit pool. Further, each segment can be broken down into individual products (e.g., in the auto example, different auto insurance products), customer groups (e.g., students, fleet buyers), geographic markets (e.g., western Canada, cities in New England with population less than 50,000), and distribution channels (e.g, auto insurance sold through independent agents versus company reps versus the Internet). Profitability measures are generated for each of these subcomponents (or subsegments), and, again, significant differences are likely to appear.

The profit measure itself should be some form of contribution margin. Thus, rather than distort figures by allocating overhead in arbitrary ways, the analyst is concentrating on revenue minus variable costs and direct fixed costs for each segment and subsegment.

By examining where and how money is being made, management can determine where to concentrate entrepreneurial efforts, including the development of new products and markets. A vivid example can be found with U-Haul. The company managed to redefine the entire consumer truck rental business by examining the profit pool and recognizing the potential in accessories (boxes, tape, insurance, carts), even as truck rentals continued to dominate revenues. Once identified, strategies were formulated to maximize control of the profit pool segment.

Profit pool structure can be quite complex. Creative insights are needed to recognize and quantify all of the current and potential components. Signs of

■ **FIGURE 11.3**

THE PROFIT POOL IN THE AUTO INDUSTRY

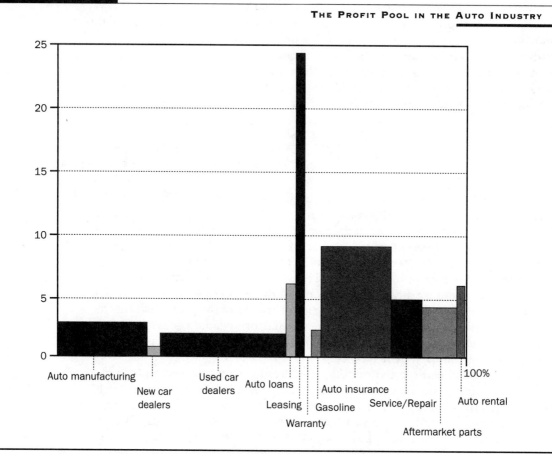

SOURCE: Gadiesh, O., and J. Gilbert. 1998. "Profit Pools: A Fresh Look at Strategy," *Harvard Business Review* 76 (May–June): 142.

untapped profit potential might include the existence of higher barriers to competitive entry in a segment, a product or service that is not well differentiated (but could be), or a subsegment that is being ignored, among others. Gadiesh and Gilbert (1998) suggest some basic questions that can aid in the identification of opportunity through the lens of a profit pool:

- Why have profit pools formed where they have?
- Are the forces that created those pools likely to change?
- How do some profit sources exert influence over others and shape competition?
- Where are the "choke points," or activities that control the flow of profits through the rest of the value chain, and how can they be controlled?
- Will new, more profitable business models emerge?

Interpreting the dynamics of profit pools is difficult. Ongoing changes represent both opportunities and threats to each of the firms in the value chain. Profit levels shift among the segments in the pool over time. New segments emerge, and others cease to exist or are redefined by technological change and other developments in the external environment. What was a deep pool becomes shallow as entry barriers are lowered or differential advantages fade. Power tends to shift over time among the players at different levels in the value chain.

The profit pool concept can also be extended to the value chain within a company. Consider the chain of value creating activities that occur from acquiring resources through production and eventually to satisfying a customer. The myriad activities that constitute the internal value chain are not all profit centers. Some are revenue centers and others cost centers. But each can be linked to the profitability of the unit or company, as was made clear in our discussion of open book management. Each also has subcomponents. When the internal value chain is approached in this manner, an employee can step back from the company and identify untapped or underexploited sources of profit contribution or customer value. Anheuser-Busch was able to do it with creative packaging of beer products, while American Airlines transformed its Sabre reservation service into a profit center called Travelocity. Open book management facilitates this kind of thinking, in that the open and detailed sharing of the numbers helps in the identification of untapped profit pool segments in the company's operations.

The profit pool concept is an important part of the corporate entrepreneur's toolkit. When the profit pool method is approached creatively, new sources of profit within the industry can be identified, priorities can be established for acquisitions and expansion, insights can be produced for targeting new customer groups and distribution channels, and internal operations can be refocused. Ultimately, the business model of the firm can be redefined.

SUMMARY AND CONCLUSIONS

This chapter has looked at control systems in companies and at their implications for entrepreneurship. A control system is a combination of measures, tools, and information that act together to maintain actual performance at a level close to desired performance. The specific measures and tools are intended either to induce desired behavior or to limit dysfunctional behavior.

Control systems can represent a significant obstacle to entrepreneurship, especially when they focus on efficiency to the detriment of effectiveness, encourage micromanagement of resources, and become ends instead of means in terms of their impact on employee behavior. Overreliance on formalization and on procedural control can serve to promote minimally acceptable behavior. Moreover, controls that enforce rigid and conformist behavior are incompatible with innovation and a rapidly changing environment. At the same time, certain characteristics of control can actually serve to facilitate entrepreneurship in companies. The issue is

Is Gateway in Control?

Gateway looked at controls, profits, and costs, just like any successful public company should. Over time, they became an $8 billion industry leader. And from the outside, things looked great. Stock prices rose, as did income. But a closer look revealed a not-so-stable entity.

Good Cow: As if Gateway executives could predict the future, the company has always gone against the grain and geared itself toward consumer rather than commercial sales. Its 60/40 sales ratio is now mirrored by the U.S. consumer and commercial markets for PC sales. This favorable similarity is attributable not only to the plummeting prices, but also to the ease with which its computers can be acquired by the average consumer. With more than 350 stores nationwide, Gateway is proving the critics wrong, catering specifically and successfully to the unacknowledged needs of computer-weary consumers. The cost advantages of Dell's 1984 breakthrough "skip-the-electronics-stores" selling strategy were not destroyed by the retail costs. Gateway still sells computers directly from the factory, but by providing customers with (1) the opportunity to decide hands-on what suits their needs and (2) the ability to learn, free of charge, how to use and benefit from that technology, they are reaching a wider potential customer base. Similar to Intel's growth strategy, Gateway turned the focus to creating a customer for its product rather than creating new products for an already saturated industry. In one month, more than 50 percent of Gateway's income came from the sale of items other than PCs—another bonus to having shelves stocked with accessories and showing customers what computers can do for them. "In a mature industry, the smart players begin to think about how to differentiate around the commodity," says Jeff Weitzen, Gateway CEO, knowing that his cow-painted boxes weren't enough to establish brand recognition and loyalty. Other PC manufacturers are attempting to follow in Gateway's entrepreneurial footsteps, but most are hesitant to cannibalize sales at their retailers.

Bad Cow: Gateway is on the right path to enter the next decade with regard to target markets, inventory control, and brand loyalty, but unless they get control of their financials, they'll have to cut the costs associated with retail operations just to cover manufacturing and distribution costs. The company has lost money, but technically has not suffered in all but one of seven major investments with a combined worth of $425.5 million. In an era of shrinking PC prices and smaller margins, it's no surprise that all PC manufacturers turned elsewhere to make a profit. (Most offer services, value added components, and Internet access.) However, CEO Weitzen decided to enhance revenues by investing in businesses such as AOL, eSoft, OfficeMax.com, ProAct, and Quepasa.com. The strategic investments and purchased shares proved to be costly to Gateway's balance sheet and to its own investors. One financial expert stated that "Gateway's 'other assets' have come to comprise about 130 percent of all the money the company has made in the last $2\frac{3}{4}$ years." Gateway is a perfect example of how things aren't always as they seem outside of the box.

SOURCE: Deborah Claymon, "Strip Malls are Gateway Country" and Cory Johnson, "Gateway Should Stick to Selling Computers," a 3-part Series," *The Industry Standard* (November–January), 2000–2001.

one of balance, in which entrepreneurial firms demonstrate simultaneous "loose-tight" properties.

The question is not one of less control versus more control. The challenge for managers is to redefine the organization's concept of control. A distinction was drawn between a command and control approach versus an early warning approach, and it was argued that the latter is needed in companies striving to be entrepreneurial. Entrepreneurship is facilitated by a less structured, more flexible early warning approach in which mutual trust, discretion, and organizational slack are guiding principles. Other elements of an entrepreneurial philosophy of control were presented, including the concepts of giving up control to gain control and open book management. Flexible control can not only preempt impending problems but can also serve as an active force for effective innovation. Specifically, the control system becomes a vehicle for managing uncertainty, promoting risk tolerance, encouraging focused experimentation, and empowering employees.

Dynamic environments necessitate internal adaptation, and adaptation requires a movement to less formal control and more horizontal communication. Similarly, as organizations move away from hierarchies to flattened structures, the need for managers and management control lessens. Although these may be the general patterns in many companies, the actual levels and types of control should reflect the degree and frequency of entrepreneurship sought by management. If the desire is for infrequent or incremental innovation, controls can be more formal, rigid, and centralized. Breakthrough innovation demands more autonomy and flexibility.

In the final analysis, the impact of control systems transcends the controls themselves. Because of their central role in affecting all members of an organization and all facets of operations, the control system is closely linked to structure, planning systems, goal setting processes, reward systems, and other key components of the organization. Thus, entrepreneurship will be the result of interactive effects among a combination of variables.

REFERENCES

Brandt, S. 1986. *Entrepreneuring in Established Companies.* Homewood: Dow-Jones Irwin.

Case, J. 1995. "The Open Book Revolution," *INC.* 17 (June): 26–43.

Case, J. 1997. "Opening the Books," *Harvard Business Review* 75 (March–April): 118–127.

Cirka, C. 1997. *A Piece of the Puzzle: Employee Responses to Control Practices and Effects on Firm Control Strategy.* Philadelphia: Temple University.

Drucker, P. 1985. *Innovation and Entrepreneurship.* New York: Harper and Row.

Gadiesh, O., and J. Gilbert. 1998. "Profit Pools: A Fresh Look at Strategy," *Harvard Business Review* 76 (May–June): 139–147.

Koen, P. 2000. "Developing Corporate Intrapreneurs," *Engineering Management Journal* 12 No. 2: 3–7.

Mintzberg, H. 1996. "Musings on Management," *Harvard Business Review* 74 (July–August): 61–67.

Morris, M. H. 1998. *Entrepreneurial Intensity.* Westport: Quorum.

Pinchot III, G. 2000. *Intrapreneuring.* San Francisco: Berrett-Koehler.

Pinchot III, G., and R. Pellman. 1999. *Intrapreneuring in Action.* San Francisco: Berrett-Koehler.

Stevenson, H. H., and J. Jarrillo-Mossi. 1989. "Preserving Entrepreneurship as Companies Grow." In *Creativity and Strategy in Mid-Sized Firms,* edited by R. Kuhn. Englewood Cliffs: Prentice-Hall.

12

HUMAN RESOURCE MANAGEMENT AND ENTREPRENEURSHIP

As noted by Schuler (1986, p. 624), "The question to corporations is not whether they should or should not engage in entrepreneurial activity, but rather what can be done to encourage establishment of entrepreneurship." We have emphasized that entrepreneurship, when applied to established companies, takes on unique characteristics and becomes subject to a number of obstacles and constraints not found in most independent start-ups. The magnitude of these constraints suggests that very different approaches to organizational design and management are necessary if entrepreneurship is to be facilitated on an ongoing basis. The challenge is to identify methods for adapting the mainstream operations of large corporations to reflect the cultures and structures that characterize small entrepreneurial firms, while also finding ways to capitalize on the considerable resource base which already exists in established firms. More succinctly, the question becomes, "How do managers create work environments that support the entrepreneurial employee?"

Of all the managerial decision areas that can affect corporate entrepreneurship, human resource management (HRM) would seem one of the more vital. Indeed, the HRM field appears to be experiencing a fundamental transformation from an employee benefits-oriented, bureaucracy-based, tool-driven discipline to one centered around the congruence of the various aspects of the HRM system with business strategies. The argument of Balkin and Logan (1988) that poorly designed compensation and performance appraisal systems may constrain entrepreneurial behavior in established firms is reflective of this transformation. Similarly, a number of observers have suggested that organization-level entrepreneurship can be influenced by a variety of HRM-related policies (Baden-Fuller 1997; Oden 1997; Schuler 1986; Shane 1996).

In this chapter, we will explore the relationship between HRM and corporate entrepreneurship. The underlying nature of HRM is first examined, and core dimensions of a company's HRM system are identified. Based on current classification schemes of HRM-related practices, an assessment is made of practices that facilitate rather than constrain entrepreneurial behavior, including some recent evidence to support these relationships.

CREATING THE WORK ENVIRONMENT

While the entrepreneurial process always involves both individuals and teams, it typically begins with an individual. Concepts are kept alive and teams are nurtured by individuals. The dedicated employee who champions a concept; persists in overcoming internal and external obstacles; accepts responsibility for failure; and, in effect, risks his or her job on the outcome of a venture would seem to be the single most important ingredient in creating entrepreneurship. As De Chambeau and Shays (1984) conclude, "Corporate entrepreneurs cannot be assigned or appointed; they must be volunteers who bring a clear vision of what they want to create."

At the same time, it is our belief that each and every employee within an organization is rich in entrepreneurial potential. Yet, most employees fail to capitalize on that potential. Some of them do not recognize their own potential, while others believe the costs of acting on that potential are greater than the potential benefits. In either case, the challenge to management becomes one of creating a work environment that helps employees understand 1) the kinds of entrepreneurial behaviors sought by the organization; 2) their own innate ability to act in an entrepreneurial fashion; and 3) the incentives for acting in an entrepreneurial fashion and the penalties for failing to do so.

Work environment refers to the context or surroundings in which an employee finds himself or herself when he or she comes to the job each day. It is defined by the set of conditions under which the employee must operate as he or she attempts to accomplish company tasks and personal goals. The employee develops perceptions about the environment based on experiences and interactions over time. Included among these perceptions can be the extent to which the environment expects or permits employees to demonstrate individual initiative, experiment, try new things, persevere in the face of rejection, use resources that have not been formally allocated to them, and related entrepreneurial behaviors.

The work environment is influenced by a host of factors, ranging from current business conditions and how well the business is doing to the management style of the employee's supervisor. While some of these factors are clearly not controllable by senior management, many of them can be controlled or influenced. One of the most potent tools for not only influencing the work environment but also for actually defining it is the company's human resource management (HRM) system.

WHAT IS HUMAN RESOURCE MANAGEMENT?

Human resource management is a broad concept that refers to the set of tasks associated with acquiring, training, developing, motivating, organizing, and maintaining the employees of a company. While some firms still call it *personnel, human resources* is the more prevalent term today, in part because it reflects a more comprehensive and strategic perspective. More specifically, the term reflects the idea that organizational goals and employee needs are mutually compatible if

■ TABLE 12.1

ACTIVITIES OFTEN INCLUDED UNDER HUMAN RESOURCE MANAGEMENT

Interviewing	Pension/retirement plan administration
Vacation/leave processing	Tuition aid/scholarships
Insurance benefits administration	Recreation/social programs
Recruiting (other than college recruiting)	Pre-employment testing (other than drug tests)
Personnel recordkeeping/information systems	Executive compensation
Promotion/transfer/separation processing	Employee assistance plan/counseling
Induction/orientation	Organization development
Wage/salary administration	Productivity/motivation programs
Workers' compensation administration	Thrift/savings plan administration
EEO compliance/affirmative action	Incentive pay plans
Unemployment compensation	Relocation services
Job descriptions	Career planning/development
Payroll administration	Food service/cafeteria
Performance appraisal, management	College recruiting
Disciplinary procedures	Suggestion systems
Job evaluation	Health/wellness program
Performance appraisal, nonmanagement	Attitude surveys
Administrative services	Outplacement services
Maintenance/janitorial services	Drug testing
Exit interviews	Preretirement counseling
Job analysis	In-house medical services
Award/recognition programs	Library
Complaint procedures	Flexible benefits plan administration
Skills training, nonmanagement	Union/labor relations
Supervisory training	Flexible-spending account administration
Security/property protection	Profit-sharing plan administration
Safety training/OSHA compliance	Stock plan administration
Employee communications/publications	International personnel/HR administration
Risk management/business insurance	Child-care center
Human resource forecasting/planning	Community relations/contribution programs
Travel/transportation services	Management development

they are managed properly and that employees represent continued investments on the part of the firm—with continued returns.

A wide array of activities can be included under the general HRM heading, with differences among companies in terms of what they do or do not consider to be part of HR. Table 12.1 provides a summary list of these activities. For simplicity, we can organize most of these into five general categories, which we will explore in further detail. The categories include job planning and design, recruitment and selection, training and development, employee performance evaluation, and compensation and rewards (Figure 12.1). These categories are not all-inclusive, but represent core HRM areas with important strategic implications.

As noted above, a traditional personnel function differs from a human resource management approach in that the latter is more strategic. This means that all of the firm's HR practices are coordinated in a way that reflects a) what is happening in

USING KEY ELEMENTS OF THE HRM SYSTEM TO CREATE
AN ENTREPRENEURIAL ENVIRONMENT

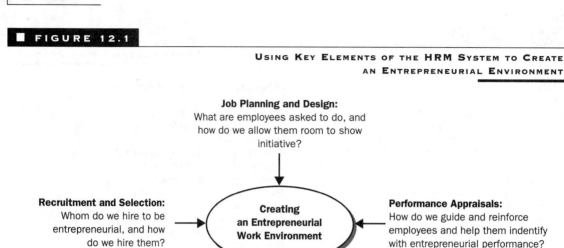

Job Planning and Design:
What are employees asked to do, and
how do we allow them room to show
initiative?

Recruitment and Selection:
Whom do we hire to be
entrepreneurial, and how
do we hire them?

**Creating
an Entrepreneurial
Work Environment**

Performance Appraisals:
How do we guide and reinforce
employees and help them indentify
with entrepreneurial performance?

Compensation and Rewards:
How do we incentivize employees to
be entrepreneurial, take ownership,
and stay with the company?

Training and Development:
How do we help employees
recognize their entrepreneurial
potential and develop the skills to
best capitalize on that potential?

the external competitive environment; b) a longer-term focus; and c) ways in which the skills and behaviors of all employees can be affected in a manner that supports and helps accomplish the overall strategies of the firm. Simply put, *human resource management becomes a means for achieving the company's strategic direction.* For instance, human resource practices associated with recruitment, selection, and training programs are designed to ensure that employees possess the characteristics required for effective organizational performance over time. Performance appraisal, compensation, and discipline programs are designed to provide the appropriate behavioral cues and reinforcements to guide and motivate behaviors associated with key company strategies. It is recognized that different corporate strategies or organizational initiatives require different employee characteristics (knowledge, skills, and abilities) and behaviors. Further, for each human resource practice, there exists design options that are, in fact, options to promote and reinforce different employee characteristics and behaviors. For example, Olian and Rynes (1984) have argued that the appropriate mix of recruitment and selection practices is dependent upon whether organizations were pursuing an entrepreneurial-based strategy or more efficiency-based strategies.

HRM POLICIES AND ENTREPRENEURSHIP

Entrepreneurial activities require employees to act and think in ways not normally associated with nonentrepreneurial or bureaucratic organizations. Thus, one would

expect to find an association between a reliance on particular human resource practices and the levels of entrepreneurship observed in different organizations.

Randall Schuler, a leading scholar in the HRM area, has suggested the following employee characteristics are associated with successful entrepreneurial
efforts: creative and innovative behavior, risk-taking, a long-term orientation, a
focus on results, flexibility to change, cooperation, independent behavior, tolerance of ambiguity, and a preference for assuming responsibility. He also notes that
HRM practices are a reflection of a firm's culture, and others (Cornwall and
Perlman 1990; Hamel 2000; Oden 1999) have suggested corporate entrepreneurship requires a culture built around emotional commitment, autonomy, empowerment, earned respect, and a strong work ethic. Using these desired employee
and cultural characteristics, it becomes possible to identify the HRM policy combinations most conductive to fostering entrepreneurial behavior.

The categories of HRM practices presented above and in Figure 12.1 provide
a useful framework for establishing specific linkages between HRM and entrepreneurship (see also Schuler 1989; Morris and Jones 1995). Beginning with planning choices, innovation and risk-taking behaviors would seem more consistent
with a long-term orientation and an emphasis on formal planning with high
employee involvement. Job-related tasks would need to be broadly defined, with
more decision-making discretion given to employees. Also, greater emphasis
would have to be placed on results over process or procedure. Jobs are likely to be
less structured or constrained by rigid organizational policies. Multiple policies
and procedures, along with centralized decision making, tend to constrain action
alternatives and inhibit the proactive decision making necessary for successful
entrepreneurial events.

Turning to the staffing choices of the firm, entrepreneurial behavior implies less
predictable external environments and internal requirements. The fit between
company direction and available internal resources may be poor. As such, firms
may be forced to rely on a balance of external and internal sources for job candidates. The need to create and maintain an entrepreneurial culture combined with
a reliance on external sources of employees would, in turn, increase the need for
extensive employee orientation and socialization programs. Further, rapid environmental change and continuous product/market innovation can be expected to
produce time pressures as well as variable job demands and requirements. The
result in entrepreneurial organizations is likely to be a reliance on more general,
more implicit, and less formalized selection criteria.

Once a person is selected into the organization, staffing practices are likely to
be designed around broad career paths and multiple career ladders for that
employee. Broad paths and multiple ladders provide exposure to more areas of
the organization and different ways of thinking. This exposure in turn enhances
idea generation and problem solving and encourages cooperative activities.
Staffing procedures in these organizations are apt to be fairly open. Entrepreneurial individuals are goal- and action-oriented. Thus, an employee should not be
selected for, or assigned to, entrepreneurial tasks simply on the basis of past performance on other tasks or because he or she has the basic knowledge and skills
the job requires. Open selection procedures allow for more self-selection into

entrepreneurial positions and hence a better match between the entrepreneurial requirements of the organization and the individual's needs.

Training and development practices can promote entrepreneurial behavior to the extent that training programs are applicable to a broad range of job situations and encourage high employee participation. Changing job demands and the need to keep abreast of the newest technologies suggest a need for continuous, ongoing training as well as for training activities that are less structured or standardized and which focus on individualized knowledge requirements. This type of training approach enables employees to respond in unique ways to new challenges, adapt to dynamic environmental conditions, and feel comfortable with ambiguity. Training programs may also include an attitudinal component, wherein acceptance of change, a willingness to take risks and assume responsibility, and the value of teamwork and shared achievements are central themes. Finally, it may be necessary that political skills be taught to prospective entrepreneurs, including ways to obtain sponsors, build resource networks, and avoid early publicity of new concepts and ventures.

Organizations communicate performance expectations and reinforce desired employee behaviors through their performance appraisal and reward practices, both of which should be designed around specific criteria. Entrepreneurship should be fostered where performance evaluations and discretionary compensation are based on long-term results and on a balance between individual and group performance. Moreover, given that risk implies failure, appraisal and reward systems should reflect a tolerance of failure and offer some employment security. Because entrepreneurial individuals tend to demonstrate a high need for achievement but are also reward conscious, it is important that they be active participants both in setting high performance standards and in designing customized reward systems.

For their part, appraisals will be likely to be conducted at intermittent and irregular time intervals in entrepreneurial organizations, rather than at uniform or fixed intervals. They should be tailored to the life cycle of an entrepreneurial project. This is because entrepreneurial events require time to evolve, with each one encountering unique sets of obstacles and with various projects typically at different stages of development. In addition, entrepreneurial success often depends on the ability of employees to obtain resources from novel sources or in nontraditional ways and occasionally to violate or ignore standard company policies and procedures. Accordingly, performance appraisals will need to emphasize end results or outcomes, rather than the methods employed to achieve those results. The evaluation of employees will need to include explicit measures of innovativeness and risk assumption, which implies some use of qualitative and subjective measures of performance.

With regard to rewards, personal incentives (financial and nonfinancial) are necessary to reinforce the risk-taking and persistence required to implement an entrepreneurial concept. To retain entrepreneurial employees, these incentives must be significant. Individual incentives must be balanced by rewards linked to group performance over longer periods of time, to encourage cooperative, interdependent behavior. Taking responsibility for innovation and achieving a longer-term commitment can be furthered by compensation practices that emphasize external pay equity and incentives such as stock options and profit sharing. The customized nature of these reward systems also suggests that responsibility for their design and implementation should be decentralized or delegated to the divisional or departmental level.

SOME EVIDENCE TO SUPPORT THE RELATIONSHIPS

This discussion has attempted to identify critical HRM practices that are believed to be facilitators of entrepreneurship. However, this list is not intended to be comprehensive; rather, it captures a set of key strategic relationships based on the available evidence, which is quite limited. One of the few studies which attempted to determine if HRM practices actually affect entrepreneurial performance in companies was conducted by Morris and Jones (1995). They conducted a cross-sectional survey of multiple managers in companies representing a wide range of industries. The study focused on human resource management practices as they were being applied to midlevel operational managers (e.g., purchasing, sales, and R&D managers). A total of thirty-six practices in the five categories presented in Table 12.2 (i.e., planning and job design, selection and staffing, training and development, appraisal and compensation) were evaluated. The research attempted to capture the dimensionality reflected in the HRM practices. For instance, respondents were asked to characterize the extent to which selection and staffing practices rely primarily on internal versus external sources for job candidates and are based on implicit versus explicit selection criteria. In addition, levels of entrepreneurship in the companies were measured using a scale similar to the one described later in this book (see Chapter Fourteen).

Using the median scores produced from the survey, firms were split into two groups, those with a stronger entrepreneurial orientation and those with a weaker entrepreneurial orientation. Statistical analysis was then used to determine whether firms that were more entrepreneurial differed from their less entrepreneurial counterparts with regard to their HRM practices. Of the thirty-six items investigated, fourteen demonstrated significant differences (Table 12.3). Those firms demonstrating stronger entrepreneurial orientations were more likely to have selection and staffing procedures designed around multiple career paths and extensive socialization and orientation of new employees. Training and development programs in more entrepreneurial firms were more likely to include high employee participation and active trainee involvement, be group oriented, assume a longer-term or career perspective, be systematic and planned, and be continuous or ongoing. The performance appraisals in these organizations included higher employee involvement and participation in the process, a greater emphasis on individual performance criteria, assessments based more on outcomes or end results, a longer-term performance focus, and explicit encouragement of innovative and risk-taking behaviors. Their compensation practices were more likely to include bonuses and incentives based on long-term performance, an emphasis on job security over high pay, and greater stress on individual rather than group performance.

■ **TABLE 12.2**

HRM POLICIES CONSISTENT WITH ENTREPRENEURIAL BEHAVIOR

General Area	Practices Encouraging Entrepreneurship
Planning/Overall Job Design	Reliance on formal planning
	Long-term orientation in planning and job design
	Implicit job analysis
	Jobs that are broad in scope
	Jobs with significant discretion
	Jobs that are less structured
	Integrative job design
	Results-oriented job design
	High employee involvement
Recruitment and Selection	Reliance on external and internal sources for candidates
	Broad career paths
	Multiple career ladders
	General, implicit, less formalized selection criteria
	Extensive job socialization
	Open recruitment and selection procedures
Training and Development	Long-term career orientation
	Training with broad applications
	Individualized training
	High employee participation
	Unsystematic training
	Emphasis on managerial skills
	Continuous/ongoing training
Performance Appraisal	High employee involvement
	Balanced individual-group orientation
	Emphasis on effectiveness over efficiency
	Result oriented (vs. process)
	Based on subjective criteria
	Emphasis on long-term performance
	Includes innovation and risk criteria
	Reflects tolerance of failure
	Appraisals done based on project life cycle
Compensation/Rewards	Emphasizes long-term performance
	Decentralized/customized at division or department levels
	Tailored to individuals
	Emphasizes individual performance with incentives for group efforts
	Merit and incentive based
	Significant financial reward
	Based on external equity

Further examination of the practices associated with a stronger entrepreneurial orientation suggests that the performance appraisal and training/development areas generated the highest numbers of practices that distinguish more entrepreneurial from less entrepreneurial organizations. Next in order was compensation, followed by selection and staffing and, last, planning and job design.

■ TABLE 12.3

SUMMARY OF SIGNIFICANT DIFFERENCES IN INDIVIDUAL HRM PRACTICES BASED ON THE FIRM'S ENTREPRENEURIAL ORIENTATION

	Nature of the HRM System		Low Entrepreneurial Orientation	High Entrepreneurial Orientation	f	Sig. of f
V11	Multiple/single career path	x = s.d.=	3.29 .86	2.25 1.01	21.80	.000
V12	Extensive/little socialization	x = s.d.=	3.31 .90	2.23 1.16	19.87	.000
V13	High/low employee participation in appraisals	x = s.d.=	3.00 1.26	2.46 1.16	3.72	.050
V16	Long/short-term performance criteria	x = s.d.=	3.57 .88	2.97 1.11	6.43	.013
V17	Encourage/discourage risk-taking	x = s.d.=	3.20 .87	2.79 .92	3.76	.051
V18	Emphasize innovative/ status quo behavior	x = s.d.=	2.97 1.04	2.15 .90	13.05	.001
V21	Active/passive involvement in training	x = s.d.=	2.71 1.18	1.92 .90	10.67	.002
V22	Group/individually oriented training	x = s.d.=	2.94 1.30	2.25 1.25	5.33	.024
V23	Long-/short-term training orientation	x = s.d.=	3.23 1.00	2.33 1.84	17.49	.000
V24	Training designed for all/specific employees	x = s.d.=	2.83 1.10	3.87 1.00	18.22	.000
V26	Ongoing/intermittent training	x = s.d.=	3.54 1.09	2.54 1.21	13.90	.000
V27	Long-/short-term basis for incentives	x = s.d.=	3.66 1.24	3.00 1.30	4.95	.029
V30	Emphasis on job security/high pay	x = s.d.=	2.89 .83	2.41 .94	3.79	.051
V32	Rewards for group/ individual performance	x = s.d.=	3.60 1.12	4.21 .98	6.17	.015

SOURCE: Morris, M. H. and F. Jones. 1995. "Relationships Among Environmental Turbulence, Human Resource Management, and Corporate Entrepreneurship," *Journal of Business and Entrepreneurship* 7: 161–76.

MOTIVATION AND THE CRITICAL ROLE PLAYED BY REWARD SYSTEMS

One of the most visible and influential parts of a company's HRM system is the reward and compensation program. Ultimately, employees come to work each

A MODEL OF MOTIVATION FOR ENTREPRENEURIAL BEHAVIOR

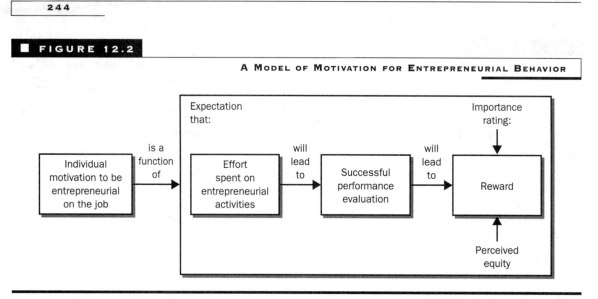

day to achieve rewards. These rewards can take any number of forms. Some people seek financial rewards; others seek power and status; and still others strive for personal and career development, self-actualization, or social rewards (e.g., friendships, camaraderie). Clearly, rewards represent a very potent tool to influence employee behavior on the job, especially the set of rewards over which management has direct control. To better appreciate the role of such rewards, one must start with the question of motivation. The question is not whether an employee is generically motivated or not, but whether he or she is motivated toward specific behaviors. In our case, the concern is with entrepreneurial motivation.

One of the more practical approaches to explaining an employee's motivation to be innovative on the job, take calculated risks, and be proactive is called the expectancy model (Porter and Lawler 1968). Simply stated, this model posits that motivation is determined by 1) how much a person perceives a direct relationship between the effort he or she puts forth and successful performance on the firm's employee appraisal or evaluation system; 2) how much that person perceives a direct relationship between a good performance appraisal and rewards; and 3) whether the company is offering the correct rewards. The expectancy model is illustrated in Figure 12.2.

Let us explore this model in more depth. In a real job situation, some of the specific entrepreneurial tasks toward which the manager desires the employee to expend *effort* could include generating new ideas, doing research or background work to support those ideas, persevering in refining an idea that others have rejected, experimenting with new processes or approaches on the job, and being creative in finding resources to do something new, among others. The *performance evaluation* system refers to management's formal method of evaluating the employee's work output. This might be something as simple as a letter indicating the employee's performance has been excellent, good, average, or poor or as involved as a multiple-item rating survey subjectively filled out by multiple managers and peers and that also incorporates the employee's inputs. *Rewards* refer to the benefit or gain the employee receives in return for his or her work efforts. Rewards can be extrinsic or intrinsic, but again the principal concern is with those rewards that managers control or can affect. Examples include regular pay, bonuses, profit share, equity or shares in the company, expense accounts, job security, promotions, expanded job responsibilities, autonomy, public or private recognition, free time to work on pet projects, money for research or trips to conferences where the employee can learn more about his or her entrepreneurial concept, and much more.

The flow diagram presented in Figure 12.2 can be helpful in identifying some of the reasons an employee might *not* be motivated to act entrepreneurial on the job. Here, we will identify fifteen possible reasons. Keep in mind that the model is all about linkages. The first linkage is between employee effort and management's evaluation of employee performance. Starting with effort, if the employee does not 1) understand what management means by "being entrepreneurial on the job"; or 2) believe it is possible to accomplish entrepreneurial behavior in this company regardless of effort put forth, or 3) perceive that he or she is personally capable of being entrepreneurial, then he or she is likely to be unmotivated. Alternatively, the employee may believe that it is possible to be entrepreneurial, but sees no linkage between doing so and how he or she is evaluated. This can happen because 4) there is no formal appraisal or assessment of the employee; 5) the performance appraisal criteria are unclear; 6) the criteria on which employees are evaluated do not explicitly include innovativeness, risk-taking, and proactive efforts; 7) other nonentrepreneurial criteria receive much more emphasis; 8) the evaluations are done in an arbitrary or unfair fashion; or 9) there are ways to get a good evaluation without actually doing entrepreneurial things (e.g., politicking).

Let's assume that the employee knows that it is possible to be entrepreneurial in this company and if he or she does so, a better performance appraisal will be received. He or she still might not be motivated. The second linkage in Figure 12.2 involves identifying reasons employees might not see a relationship between doing well on the performance evaluation system and receiving a reward. Reasons for this could include 10) managers asking for one behavior, but actually rewarding some quite different behavior; or 11) the employee believes the reward will be earned regardless of the evaluation (e.g., everyone around here gets the same reward); or 12) the employee has found other ways to earn the reward without putting effort toward entrepreneurship (e.g., currying favor with the boss).

Finally, even if the employee sees a link between effort and performance and between performance and reward, he or she may be unmotivated because management is offering the wrong rewards. Examples of problems here could include 13) rewards are being offered that are too small given the effort that is required to push an entrepreneurial initiative through in the face of lots of internal resistance; 14) the type of reward being offered is not the one to which the employee currently attaches the most importance; or 15) the reward is considered inequitable or unfair, possibly because of what the employee knows other people are receiving, especially when he or she thinks these other employees are performing to a lower standard.

These instances are but some of the ways that entrepreneurial motivation becomes a problem. The real job of the manager is to ensure that the employee sees the desired linkages between the types of efforts being requested, the manner in which the employee will be evaluated, and the rewards he or she receives. Just as important is the need to ensure the right rewards are being offered, a task that requires considerable creativity as well as insight into the nature of the company's workers. The new employees entering the corporate environment today bring with them a set of expectations and needs that are not likely to be satisfied by conventional salary packages. Further, the needs of individuals change, so a reward that worked well last year may be unsuccessful this year. Although it may not be feasible to develop distinctive reward and measurement systems for each employee, it is important to include enough flexibility in these systems to at least partially accommodate individual requirements.

The possibilities are actually unlimited when it comes to creative approaches to rewarding entrepreneurial performance. Table 12.4 provides an illustration of what some companies are currently doing. The key here is to use examples from other firms to stimulate ideas, but to then develop programs that fit the personality of the firm, the nature and needs of employees, and the competitive circumstances in which the company finds itself. At the same time, financial rewards do not have to be large, and some of the more glamorous efforts such as stock options and profit-sharing are often less influential than efforts at recognition, compensation time, and rewards that effectively empower a person to pursue his or her ideas within the company.

Just as important as formal rewards is the need for awards. Entrepreneurial firms find novel ways to say "thank you" to their innovative employees. These firms typically have cultures of celebration, where work might be stopped at any time and in any part of the company and a plaque, certificate, pin, bouquet of roses, or one of hundreds of other forms of recognition is given to some employee based on entrepreneurial initiative. The company has ceremonies or rituals that often might seem strange or superficial or even silly to an outside observer but that are rich in meaning to the employees. People in these companies take pride in one another's accomplishments. It is not unusual for the most valued form of recognition to come not from senior management but from the employee's peers.

Effective use of awards requires a clear strategy. Consistent with the expectancy model discussed above, it is vital that management clearly establish (and communicate) the link between the behaviors desired and a given award. Just as important is the need to be consistent in who gets awards, why, and when. Rosabeth Kanter (1994) has identified some additional guidelines for successful employee recognition programs, and these are summarized in Table 12.5.

■ **TABLE 12.4**

EXAMPLES OF CREATIVE APPROACHES TO REWARDING EMPLOYEES

Below are some examples of what some companies are doing with rewards and awards to encourage entrepreneurial behavior among their employees:

- Employees put a percentage of their salary at risk and then can either lose it, double it, or triple it based on team performance;
- Personalized "innovator" jackets, shirts, and leather folders are given to employees who make entrepreneurial contributions;
- When a new idea is accepted by the firm, the CEO awards shares of stock to the employee;
- Employees are given $500 to spend on an innovative idea that relates to their job;
- A firm rents out a major sports stadium, fills the stands with employees, families, and friends, and then has innovation champions run onto the field as their name and achievement appears on the scoreboard;
- A company sets targets, and then 30 percent of incremental earnings above target is placed into a bonus pool that is paid out based on each employee's performance rating;
- Small cash awards are given to employees who try something new and fail—and the best failure of the quarter receives a larger award;
- Some companies have point systems where employees receive differing amounts of points for different categories of innovation contributions. Points are redeemable for computers, merchandise, free daycare, tuition reimbursement, and other types of rewards;
- Small cash amounts are given for innovative suggestions, and then redeemable points (for more significant cash awards) are earned based on how far the suggestion moves through the process of development, approval, implementation, and impact (cost savings or revenue generation);
- A parking spot is reserved for the "innovator of the month";
- Team members working on a major innovation are awarded shares of zero value at project outset, and as milestones are achieved (on time) predetermined values are added to the shares. Milestones not achieved lead to a decline in share value;
- Another firm ties cash awards for employees to a portfolio of innovation activities produced over time, including ideas generated, patents applied for, prototypes developed, and so forth;
- Employees receive recognition for innovation suggestions, and then a drawing is held at the end of the year of all accepted suggestions, with the winner receiving a sizeable financial award;
- One firm has a "frequent innovator" that works like an airline frequent flier program;
- "Hero biographies" are written about an employee, his/her background, and an innovation that he/she has championed. The stories are full of praise and a little humor;
- One firm provides gift certificates within a day of an employee idea being implemented, and another takes employees to a "treasure box" where they can claim from among a number of gifts;
- A company gives employees 15 percent of out-of-pocket savings achieved by their ideas in the first two years of use and, if the idea is for a product, 3 percent of first-year sales;
- The top performing team in terms of innovation is sent to a resort for a week;
- A company gives a savings bond to the employee who raises the most challenging question in management meetings;
- One organization has $500 "on-the-spot" awards for anyone showing special initiative;
- Firms have their own olympics, rodeos, competitions, game shows, hit parades, and murder mysteries in an attempt to recognize initiative and excellence;
- Others have praise and recognition boards, threshold performance clubs, atta-person awards, and some allow innovators to appear in company advertisements.

■ **TABLE 12.5**

PRINCIPLES TO GUIDE THE USE OF AWARDS PROGRAMS TO ENCOURAGE ENTREPRENEURSHIP

Principle 1:	Emphasize success rather than failure. Managers tend to miss the positives if they are busily searching for the negatives.
Principle 2:	Deliver recognition and reward in an open and publicized way. If it is not made public, recognition loses much of its impact and defeats much of the purpose for which it is provided.
Principle 3:	Provide recognition in a personal and honest manner. Avoid providing recognition that is too slick or overproduced, too cheap or superficial.
Principle 4:	Tailor your recognition and reward to the unique needs of the people involved. Having many recognition and reward options will enable management to acknowledge accomplishment in ways appropriate to the particulars of a given situation, selecting from a larger menu of possibilities.
Principle 5:	Timing is crucial. Recognize contributions throughout a project. Reward contributions close to the time an achievement is realized. Be sure people understand why they receive awards and the criteria used to determine rewards.
Principle 6:	Avoid the perception that the awards are being given in a manner that is paternalistic and that seems random and casual.
Principle 7:	Strive for a clear and well-communicated connection between accomplishments and rewards. Be sure people understand why they receive awards and the criteria used to determine awards.
Principle 8:	Follow up on the recognition or award. Reinforce it in meetings, in newsletters, at end-of-the-year meetings, and in employee annual reviews.
Principle 9:	Recognize recognition. That is, recognize people who recognize others for doing what is best for the company.

SOURCE: Adapted from Kanter, R. 1994. *Innovative Reward Systems for the Changing Workplace.* New York: McGraw-Hill Publishers.

SUMMARY AND CONCLUSIONS

The human resource management function can serve a critical role in the formulation and implementation of corporate strategy. This chapter has argued that the overall perspective of HRM as well as the design of particular HRM practices has an impact on the level of entrepreneurship demonstrated within an organization. A number of specific relationships between HRM practices and entrepreneurial behavior in companies were proposed. Further, evidence was reviewed to support a number of these relationships in practice.

At the same time, some of the findings from the survey of companies that was summarized in the chapter were surprising. For instance, levels of entrepreneurship were higher in companies in which training programs were more group than individually oriented and in which compensation/reward practices emphasized job security over high pay. And yet, there may be a logic to these findings as well. For instance, although it appears that training should be customized and career oriented with high levels of employee participation, training also represents an effective venue for giving employees an appreciation of cooperative behaviors and cross-functional perspectives. Such an appreciation is emphasized by many who have studied the phenomenon of entrepreneurship in organizations. It seems that training should include some group characteristics while other HRM variables (e.g., performance assessment) have a more individualistic bent. Alternatively, the finding for compensation/reward practices is more a matter of personal motivation. Some have argued that financial rewards must be appreciable in order to keep the entrepreneurial employee from leaving the firm and going it alone (e.g., Cornwall and Perlman 1990; Peters 1987; Pinchot and Pellman 1999). And yet, the fact that the risks involved with corporate ventures are often more career related than related to an individual's personal financial loss and the fact that a negative connotation is attached to failure in many organizations combine to suggest that entrepreneurship may flourish where employees are given a certain amount of job security.

It is also important that the HRM practices employed by a company demonstrate internal consistency. For instance, encouragement of risk-taking and innovative behaviors would seem consistent with individualized performance assessment and compensation but also with a longer-term orientation, since entrepreneurial events take time to come to fruition. Moreover, individualized appraisal and reward practices would seem consistent with high levels of employee involvement in the training and appraisal areas.

Although this discussion provides direction in terms of where to concentrate efforts when seeking to foster entrepreneurship, the challenge from a managerial standpoint becomes the variable nature of HRM practices and entrepreneurial behavior. Managers must identify desired levels of entrepreneurship and then determine the corresponding levels of particular HRM practices necessary to achieve the entrepreneurship performance goal. There may be very high levels of entrepreneurship that are dysfunctional from an organizational standpoint, in that the overall risk exposure of the firm becomes too great, too many entrepreneurial events are under way to ensure strategic control, and/or resources are being so diverted to entrepreneurial ventures that mainstream businesses are undermined.

Another important task for the HR department within a company is to be the steward for monitoring and assessing entrepreneurial activity in companies. We will discuss methods for doing so in Chapter Fourteen. Not only do organizations need to set goals for entrepreneurial activity, but such goals may also need to be tailored to individual departments and functional areas. Performance then must be tracked for the company as a whole but also for these individual units. Standards will begin to emerge in terms of the levels and the types of entrepreneurship to be expected in a given area. Thus, the emphasis will likely be on product innovation in certain areas, service innovation in other areas, and process innovation in others.

Many questions remain about the ways in which human resources management practices affect entrepreneurship in companies. For example, how important is the relative emphasis on hierarchical vs. egalitarian compensation, on high versus low base salaries, on stock options and perquisites? Further, it would seem relevant to examine various "packages" of HRM practices. A combined package of

INTRINSIC REWARD: SHOWING WHAT YOU KNOW

It's long been said that you learn something new every day. That makes for quite a database of knowledge a person can have, even by the age of 30. And if knowledge really *is* power, imagine the inherent strength of an organization that taps into its employees and enthusiastically supports knowledge sharing. That's the framework of Xerox Corporation's annual Teamwork Day, where teams of empowered employees congregate to "share their successes and best practices with coworkers, customers, suppliers, partners, and other invited guests."

Established in 1983, the concept has grown considerably over the years, going global with technology, and 4,000 people attended Teamwork Day at the 2000 site in Rochester, New York. The excitement and enthusiasm of Teamwork Day results from team exhibits, new product and process presentations, and recognition, but the real benefit is derived from the teams' ability to network and share knowledge. For example,

five teams from five different sites, all working on safety projects, not only were unaware of their competition, but also were unaware of what the other teams were doing. By attending the event, teams met, conversed, and shared to learn from each other's research and avoid duplicated work and wasted labor-hours in the future. "Quality may help a team figure out how to solve a specific problem. But the really big payoff comes when they share that solution with other teams," says Xerox President Anne Mulcahy.

Xerox also uses the event as an opportunity to demonstrate to customers its commitment to quality and customer satisfaction. Xerox's Web site hosts a knowledge database called Eureka, a collection of maintenance tips offered from a multitude of copier repairmen. With 250,000 repair calls per year and 15,000 technical representatives, Xerox expects to save approximately $11 million by the end of their fiscal year because of the valuable information available on the site.

One team participating in Teamwork Day debuted its *Knowledge Miner,* a digital search tool that was created without management sanction or a budget. The team hopes to take its invention to the next level within the company, but Xerox's guidelines for funding new products doesn't come with the event's agenda, and the team doesn't know exactly what the future holds.

For Xerox, Teamwork Day is about recognizing employees and their status as the company's most valuable asset. By providing employees with motivation to think creatively and entrepreneurially and to share their ideas, Xerox will reap the rewards as well—provided that it acts on the ideas. After all, ideas don't make money.

SOURCE: www.xerox.com and Stewart, T. A. 2000. "Water the Grass, Don't Mow, and Wait for the Lightning to Strike," *Fortune* (July): 376–378.

selection, training, and appraisal options might have a different impact on entrepreneurship than the sum of the impacts of the individual practices. In addition, it may be that the HRM practices that facilitate entrepreneurship differ by level in the firm. Not only will the manifestations of entrepreneurship vary at different levels of the firm, but so too might the impact of relying on internal versus external sources of job candidates or of internal versus external equity considerations in fixing compensation levels. Finally, it seems likely that the HRM practices of a company interact with any number of other organizational variables in affecting entrepreneurship. Examples of such variables include company structure, technologies employed, types of budgetary and control systems, and stage of the organizational life cycle.

REFERENCES

Baden-Fuller, C. 1997. "Strategic Renewal: How Large Complex Organizations Prepare for the Future," *International Studies of Management and Organization* 27, No. 2 (Summer): 95–121.

Balkin, D. B., and J. W. Logan. 1988. "Reward Policies that Support Entrepreneurship," *Compensation and Benefits Review* 20: 18–25.

Brandt, S. C. 1986. *Entrepreneuring in Established Companies.* Homewood: Irwin.

Cornwall, J. R., and B. Perlman. 1990. *Organizational Entrepreneurship.* Homewood: Irwin.

Shays, E. M., and F. De Chambeau. 1984. "Harnessing Entrepreneurial Energy Within the Corporation," *Management Review* 73, No. 9: 17–20.

Hamel, G. 2000. *Leading the Revolution.* Boston: Harvard Business School Press.

Kanter, R. M. 1983. *The Change Masters.* New York: Simon and Schuster.

Kanter, R. M. 1994. *Innovative Reward Systems for the Changing Workplace.* New York: McGraw-Hill.

Morris, M. H., and F. F. Jones. 1995. "Human Resource Management Practices and Corporate Entrepreneurship: An Empirical Assessment from the USA," *International Journal of Human Resource Management* 4: 873–896.

Oden, H. 1997. *Managing Corporate Culture, Innovation, and Intrapreneurship.* Westport: Quorum Books.

Olian, J. D., and S. L. Rynes. 1984. "Organizational Staffing: Integrating Practice with Strategy," *Industrial Relations* 23: 170–183.

Peters, T. J. 1987. *Thriving on Chaos.* New York: Alfred A. Knopf.

Pinchot III, G. 1985. *Intrapreneuring.* New York: Harper and Row.

Pinchot III, G., and R. Pellman. 1999. *Intrapreneuring in Action.* San Francisco: Berrett-Koehler.

Porter, L. W., and E. L. Lawler III. 1968. *Managerial Attitudes and Performance.* Homewood, IL: Richard D. Irwin.

Schuler, R. S. 1986. "Fostering and Facilitating Entrepreneurship in Organizations: Implications for Organization and Human Resource Management Practices," *Human Resource Management* 25: 607–629

Schuler, R. S. 1989. "Strategic Human Resource Management and Industrial Relations," *Human Relations* 22, No. 2: 157–184.

Shane, S. 1996. "Renegade and Rational Championing Strategies," *Organization Studies* 17, No. 5: 751–771.

13

DEVELOPING AN ENTREPRENEURIAL CULTURE

INTRODUCTION

How do we get to the fabric of a company, to its essence? What is the stuff the organization is really made of? To answer such questions, we must consider the culture of a company. Like so many other organizational concepts, there is a tendency to think of culture as a metaphor. But culture is very real. It is a word that describes something intangible and imprecise but also something that transcends every aspect of an organization. A simple way to think about culture is that it captures the personality of the company and what it stands for.

Entrepreneurship is not only affected by the culture in a company, but in truly entrepreneurial organizations, it is also a core element of the culture. A culture that is risk averse, or very process driven, is almost by definition discouraging employees from acting in an entrepreneurial manner. At the same time, culture itself is complex and not easily changeable. A noninnovative company could bring in an extremely entrepreneurial CEO, and it could take seven to ten years (or more) for that individual to substantively change the organization's culture.

In this chapter, we will examine the nature of culture and the role it plays in sustaining the entrepreneurial spirit within a company. The values and norms associated with an entrepreneurial culture will be explored, together with the ways in which such a culture is manifested. A number of suggestions will be made for affecting an organization's culture. Attention will also be devoted to the concept of failure, why it is so critical for entrepreneurial success, and new approaches for thinking about and managing failure.

THE NATURE OF CULTURE IN ORGANIZATIONS

Culture can be defined as "an organization's basic beliefs and assumptions about what the company is about, how its members should behave, and how it defines itself in relation to its external environment"(Cornwall and Perlman 1990). Cultures have certain characteristics, regardless of the business (Trice and Beyer 1993). They are collective, meaning that their components are shared by most, if not all, of the people in a firm. They have an emotional aspect, in that employees define and identify with the culture on an emotional level. Although historically based, cultures are dynamic. Thus, a culture reflects the unique history of a group of people interacting over time, but it also is subject to continuous change as people come and go, and is based on developments in the external environment. Cultures are also inherently symbolic. Things such as the way people dress or the types of recognition ceremonies that take place stand for or are expressive of other things, such as individualism or pride of accomplishment. Finally, cultures are fuzzy. They include elements that may seem contradictory or paradoxical. There are often ambiguities in the various symbols, rites, or values found within the firm.

Every company has a culture, but the cultures tend to differ along some key dimensions—for instance, it is possible to talk about positive versus negative cultures. A culture is positive the more that its elements are in line with an organization's vision, mission, and strategies. Further, there is a fit between the culture and the competitive environment in which the firm finds itself. Thus, the more turbulent the environment, the more a positive culture is going to be one built around entrepreneurship. Alternatively, a culture can be described as strong or weak depending on how deeply held and thoroughly permeating are the core values and assumptions of the firm. Service to the customer may be a shared value, but the level of commitment and internalization of that value among employees might be lukewarm. In addition, the culture can be thought of as homogeneous if it is shared generally by all employees, or heterogeneous if there are multiple cultures or subcultures shared by different groups within the organization (e.g., those in R&D compared to those in marketing and sales). Lastly, a culture is more consistent than inconsistent if its elements do not conflict. An example of such conflict might be found when a company does things to reinforce conservatism and avoidance of failure while also pushing symbols of innovation and embracing change.

Understanding characteristics such as these helps to explain why culture is not something that is easily managed. Unlike the decision to develop a new product or change the company structure, the amorphous nature of culture makes it impossible to make precise changes to it at specific points in time. Rather, the leadership of the firm attempts to shape, form, or mold culture with a systematic set of initiatives and forms of reinforcement that are implemented over an extended time period. Stated differently, changing a culture is analogous to trying to turn a large ocean liner around in the ocean. To appreciate how this is done, we must consider the major elements of a culture.

THE PIECES AND PARTS OF CULTURE

The culture of a company touches and influences everything that people do. It is manifested in hundreds of different ways, some planned and many unplanned, some controllable and some that don't readily lend themselves to management control. One way to classify the many components of culture involves distinguishing among the following six elements:

1. Values: The things that employees think are worth having or doing or are intrinsically desirable; values express preferences for certain behaviors and outcomes; entrepreneurial values might include creativity, integrity, perseverance, individualism, achievement, accountability, ownership and change, among others;

2. Rules of conduct: Accepted norms and rules in the company; the behaviors that represent accepted ways to attain outcomes; the general understanding regarding everything from ethical behavior to how an employee dresses, to whom an employee speaks, and appropriate behavior styles in a meeting;

3. Vocabulary: The language, acronyms, jargon, slang, signs, slogans, metaphors, gestures, gossip, and even songs that are commonly used in the company—could include proverbs such as 3M's "never kill a product idea";

4. Methodology: The perception of how things actually get accomplished in the company, such as the reliance on rational processes, politicking, or rule-bending—for instance, having a sponsor and preparing a business plan with certain key ingredients might be part of the methodology for innovating in a company;

5. Rituals: Rites, ceremonies, and taboos, including random recognition ceremonies, annual off-site conferences, Christmas parties, as well as how employees are welcomed, let go, retire; the awarding of a pink Cadillac at Mary Kay Cosmetics is a ritual;

6. Myths and Stories: The histories, sagas, mythologies, and legends of an organization; includes a sense of "who are the heroes in this company"; entrepreneurial companies not only have legends and ways to continually retell stories of how past heroes did unusual things but they also create new heroes and role models all the time;

If we consider these elements in more basic terms, cultures consist of *substance and forms* (Trice and Beyer 1993). Substance refers to shared systems of values, beliefs, and norms. Forms are the concrete ways in which the substance is manifested in the organization. They are observable, and include everything from vocabulary, myths, rituals, and ceremonies, to ways of dressing and office décor. The forms are the means by which the substance of the culture is expressed, affirmed, and communicated.

In Figure 13.1, this distinction is taken a step further. Culture is pictured as existing at three different levels: assumptions, values, and artifacts. Tying this to the discussion above, the first two levels are more about substance, and the third is concerned more with forms. The first level includes invisible aspects of which people are not necessarily conscious or that they simply take for granted. At this level one finds basic assumptions about people, what it takes to be successful in the marketplace, and a host of other aspects of work and the environment. Employees are likely to make assumptions about the importance of entrepreneurship for company success, the motivations and innate entrepreneurial potential of

■FIGURE 13.1

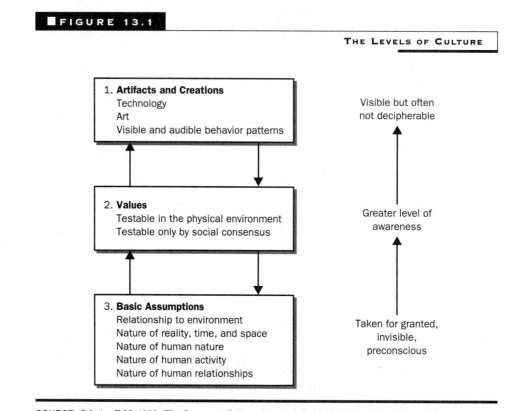

1. **Artifacts and Creations**
   Technology
   Art
   Visible and audible behavior patterns

Visible but often
not decipherable

2. **Values**
   Testable in the physical environment
   Testable only by social consensus

Greater level of
awareness

3. **Basic Assumptions**
   Relationship to environment
   Nature of reality, time, and space
   Nature of human nature
   Nature of human activity
   Nature of human relationships

Taken for granted,
invisible,
preconscious

SOURCE: Schein, E.H. 1999. *The Corporate Culture Survival Guide.* San Francisco: Jossey-Bass.

the people in the company, what it takes to accomplish entrepreneurship within the organization, and so forth. It can be quite difficult to determine the assumptions held by employees of a company, but they play a critical role in determining behavior.

The second level is one at which people are more conscious or generally aware. Here we find the commonly-held values within the organization. Although not really visible or tangible, values have clear meaning to employees. Examples of important values in an entrepreneurial context are cited above and will be explored in more detail later in this chapter.

At the third level are the artifacts and creations that symbolize company culture. Artifacts are highly visible or observable manifestations of the culture. They include rituals, rules of conduct, methodology, myths, and vocabulary. Although artifacts are visible, their meaning or interpretation is not always clear. For example, management could design the physical layout of offices to encourage openness, quick communication, information sharing, and innovation partnerships among employees. For their part, employees might interpret the artifact differently. They could conclude that it conveys a desire to encourage collectivism over individualism, reflects distrust and an attempt to check up on them, or is a reflection of tight spending and efficiency. The ultimate meaning of the artifact or creation is arrived at over time, based on how it is managed, messages that are reinforced, and the interplay of the artifact with other components of the culture.

The inference is that, if the goal is to create work environments that support entrepreneurship, culture underlies all the other components of the workplace (i.e., reward systems, company structures, control systems, the strategic direction of the firm, etc.). In fact, these other components can themselves capture elements of the culture. The entrepreneurial potential of a positive, strong, and consistent culture is significant, leading one team of researchers to conclude: "Organizational cultures can enhance and inspirit us. They can remove us from the boxes and traps in which we exist, making our lives richer and giving meaning to our daily tasks. [This] is the goal of cultural management" (Tropman and Morningstar 1989).

CORE IDEOLOGY AND THE ENVISIONED FUTURE

Entrepreneurial companies have a vision. They have a sense of what they are and what they want to become. They also understand the things about their organizations that are subject to change and those that should never change. Collins and Porras (1994) argue that a great vision starts with a "core ideology." By using the term *core* they capture elements of an organization that should not change as products mature, markets evolve, technologies emerge, or the leadership of the company comes and goes. Thus, the core ideology includes *core values*, or what the company stands for, as well as *core purpose*, or the reason the company exists.

Core values are the essential and enduring principles and tenets of an organization. Meaningful levels of entrepreneurship cannot be sustained over time unless entrepreneurship is reflected in the core values of the firm. For instance, Sony Corporation's core values include being a pioneer, doing the impossible, and encouraging individual ability and creativity. At the Walt Disney Company, creativity, dreams, and imagination form some of the core values. Complementing these values is the core purpose, which is a source of guidance and inspiration to the organization. Again, entrepreneurship should be implicit in the firm's core purpose. The reason for being at 3M is to solve unsolved problems innovatively, while the purpose at Mary Kay Cosmetics is to give unlimited opportunity to women. Cintas Corporation, the leader in professional uniforms, exists to exceed its customers' expectations. Each of these purposes go well beyond suggesting that entrepreneurship might be important—they allow for bold initiatives in accomplishing a purpose that transcends the current products and processes of the company.

The other part of a vision concerns what the organization aspires to become, which Collins and Porras (1994) refer to as the "envisioned future." While the core purpose can be a never-ending quest, the envisioned future is about setting clear and compelling goals that the company commits to achieve over the next ten or twenty years. It is coupled with a vivid description of what it will take to get there. General Electric set the goal of being Number 1 or Number 2 in every market it served, Nike sought to crush Adidas, and Sam Walton set revenue goals that seemed completely unrealistic to people outside Wal-Mart. These are ambitious goals that take on a life of their own and stimulate ongoing progress in an organization. They require extraordinary effort, and there is a real chance of failure. Goals motivate people and evoke passion and conviction. Once they are achieved, the company sets new ones.

GENERIC CULTURE TYPES

Among those who study culture, one of the great debates concerns whether there are general properties of cultures that can be found in many different organizations or, alternatively, if each culture is unique unto itself. With the former view, researchers have proposed a number of typologies or classifications of culture types. The idea is that most companies will tend to fit one of the categories contained within a given typology. Table 13.1 outlines some examples of these typologies. They differ considerably, reflecting different underlying variables. Some are based on levels of control, others on the extent to which the company is more people oriented or task oriented, and still others on psychological traits.

Prominent among the perspectives presented in Table 13.1 is the work of Deal and Kennedy (2000). They argue that distinct types of cultures evolve within companies and that these types have a direct and measurable impact on strategy and performance. Companies are social environments, with tribal habits, well-defined cultural roles for individuals, and various strategies for determining inclusion, reinforcing identity, and adapting to change. Moreover, their cultures will generally be related to one of the following four prototypes:

1. The Process Culture: A world of little to no feedback where employees find it hard to measure what they do. Instead, they concentrate on how it is done. The hierarchy is tight and employees tend to be cautious fence sitters. Avoidance of failure is important. Processes themselves can develop to the point where they stifle the company and operations become quite bureaucratic.

2. The Tough-Guy/Macho Culture: A world of competitive individualists who regularly take high personal risks and get quick feedback on whether their actions were right or wrong. The structure fluctuates. Financial stakes of not succeeding can be high, as can rewards from succeeding. The orientation is more short term, and employee turnover can be high.

3. The Work Hard/Play Hard Culture: Fun and action are the rules here, and employees take few risks, all with quick feedback. To succeed, the culture encourages employees to maintain a high level of relatively low-risk activity. Much gets done in this culture, as it is very action oriented. The

■ **TABLE 13.1**

Culture Type	Dominant Ideologies	Authors
Type A	Hierarchical control, high specialization, short-term employment, individual responsibility, individual decision making	Ouchi, 1981
Type J	Clan control, low specialization, lifetime employment, collective responsibility, collective decision making	
Type Z	Clan control, moderate specialization, long-term employment, individual responsiblilty, consensual decision making	
Process	Low risk, "cover your tail" mentality, tight hierarchy	Deal and Kennedy, 2000
Tough-guy/macho	High risk, quick feedback, fluctuating structure	
Work hard/play hard	Moderately low risk, race to the quick, flexible structure	
Bet the company	Very high risk, slow feedback, clear-cut hierarchy	
Sensation–thinking	Impersonal, abstract, certainty, specificity, authoritarian	Mitroff and Kilmann, 1975
Intuition–thinking	Flexible, adaptive, global notions, goal driven	
Intuition–feeling	Caring, decentralized, flexible, no explicit rules or regulations	
Sensation–feeling	Personal, homelike, relationship-driven, nonbureaucratic	
Apathetic	Demoralizing and cynical orientation	Sethia and Von Glinow, 1985
Caring	High concern for employees, no high performance expectations	
Exacting	Performance and success really count	
Integrative	High concern for employees with high concern for performance	
Paranoid	Fear, distrust, suspicion	Kets DeVries and Miller, 1984
Avoidant	Lack of self-confidence, powerlessness, inaction	
Charismatic	Drama, power, success, abject followership	
Bureaucratic	Compulsive, detailed, depersonalized, rigid	
Schizoid	Politicized, social isolation	

SOURCE: Trice, H.M., and J. Beyer. 1993. *The Cultures of Work Organizations.* Englewood Cliffs, NJ: Prentice Hall.

orientation here is also fairly short term. Often there is strong customer focus and sales orientation.

4. The Bet-the-Company Culture: An environment of big-stakes decisions in which considerable time passes before employees know whether decisions have paid off. It is a high-risk, slow-feedback environment with a clear-cut hierarchy. Decisions are deliberate because of the risk. Pressure is ongoing. These firms often produce major technological breakthroughs and high-quality inventions.

While a number of variables are considered in this taxonomy, especially prominent are risk and the speed with which the company receives feedback on the appropriateness of its decisions. Both of these factors are associated with entrepreneurship. The degree of risk associated with the company's activities (risk avoidance or low risk, calculated or managed risk, high risk) says something about the amount and types of entrepreneurial initiatives that will be pursued. Cultures that have a stronger process orientation are likely to discourage entrepreneurial behavior; whereas a bet-the-company culture will likely pursue entrepreneurship that is high on degree but low on frequency (see Chapter 3). Similarly, limited market feedback or accountability, such as when a firm enjoys captive demand or monopoly market conditions, does not foster entrepreneurial behavior, and rapid feedback encourages a higher frequency but lower degree of entrepreneurial activity.

Even if the elements of a firm's culture are consistent with entrepreneurship, and even if that culture is relatively strong, companies striving to maintain an entrepreneurial cuture in today's environment face an additional challenge. In recent years, firms have actively pursued a number of strategic initiatives that can unintentionally serve to undermine the basic culture of the organization. Specifically, as managers aggressively pursue such strategies as outsourcing, downsizing, reengineering, mergers, and leveraged buyouts, they often fail to consider the (potentially significant) implications of these initiatives for the firm's culture, and, by extension, for entrepreneurship.

ELEMENTS OF AN ENTREPRENEURIAL CULTURE

Above we have discussed how types of culture might affect levels of entrepreneurship in a company. We now turn to a more fundamental question: What is an entrepreneurial culture? As we have seen, a culture has many elements. The challenge lies in determining the ones that are most conducive to entrepreneurship. A look at the perspectives presented in Table 13.2 may shed some light. The table presents a synopsis of work done by different writers on how culture relates to innovation and entrepreneurship. While it may appear that a variety of elements comes into play, there is a certain commonality to the things being emphasized. If we synthesize these perspectives, the entrepreneurial culture would seem to have the following elements:

- People and empowerment focused;
- Value creation through innovation and change;
- Attention to the basics;
- Hands-on management;
- Doing the right thing;
- Freedom to grow and to fail;
- Commitment and personal responsibility;
- Emphasis on the future and a sense of urgency.

It must also be kept in mind that most large organizations are quite complex. Their internal environments are filled with competing demands, a multiplicity of tasks and commitments, and people operating under differing time horizons. As a

■ **TABLE 13.2**

COMPONENTS OF AN ENTREPRENEURIAL CULTURE: THREE PERSPECTIVES

Timmons (1999)	Cornwall and Perlman (1990)
Clarity, being well organized	Risk
High standards, pressure for excellence	Earned respect
Commitment	Ethics of integrity, trust, credibility
Responsibility	People
Recognition	Emotional commitment
Esprit de corps	Work is fun
	Empowered leadership throughout firm
Peters (1997)	Value wins
	Relentless attention to detail, people, structure, and process
Listening	Effectiveness and efficiency
Embracing change	
Customer focus	
Total integrity	
Excellence	
Involve everyone in everything	
Experimentation	
Fast-paced innovation	
Small starts and fast failure	
Visible management	
Measurement/accountability	

result, organizations are confronted with a number of conflicting value choices. The creation of an entrepreneurial culture is not simply a matter of identifying a value to be emphasized; it is also choosing between values that conflict with one another and coexist in an organization—that is, management must strike a balance among certain values.

Tropman and Morningstar (1989) examine what they term *primary values* and draw implications for entrepreneurship. As illustrated in Figure 13.2, value choices must be made in ten areas. Each set of values is pictured as a continuum, and the points that have been placed along each continuum indicate the type of balance an entrepreneurial firm might try to strike. For instance, most companies have multiple purposes (often pursued by various subcultures in the firm), but the entrepreneurial firm has strong focus on one overriding purpose. The point becomes to achieve a balance while having a dominant emphasis. The same goes for the relative emphasis on excellence versus satisfactory performance and comfort. Entrepreneurial firms set priorities in terms of the areas in which they are truly superlative and driven in terms of performance, while in other areas they may simply be "good enough." Organizations can also contain considerable diversity, and conflicts arise among different interest groups (e.g., men versus women, minorities versus majorities, union members versus management, and so forth). The balance here involves respecting differences while finding areas of commonality or similarity between class or group interests and overall organizational interests. It is just as important

FIGURE 13.2

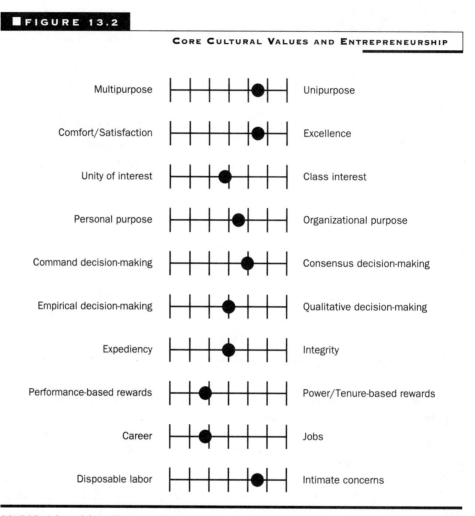

CORE CULTURAL VALUES AND ENTREPRENEURSHIP

Multipurpose		Unipurpose
Comfort/Satisfaction		Excellence
Unity of interest		Class interest
Personal purpose		Organizational purpose
Command decision-making		Consensus decision-making
Empirical decision-making		Qualitative decision-making
Expediency		Integrity
Performance-based rewards		Power/Tenure-based rewards
Career		Jobs
Disposable labor		Intimate concerns

SOURCE: Adapted from Tropman, J.E. and G. Morningstar. 1989. *Entrepreneurial Systems for the 1990s.* Westport, CT: Quorum.

to capitalize in a positive way on the friction between various interests, as we saw in our discussion of creative abrasion in Chapter Six. Similar conclusions apply to personal goals of individuals in the firm and to organizational goals.

The need for entrepreneurial firms to empower employees would seem to indicate a consensus form of decision making. However, companies must move quickly, and building consensus on every issue is not realistic. A major issue is the relative reliance on quantitative or fact-based and numbers-driven decision making versus a more qualitative approach. Consider the earlier discussion of calculated risk-taking, which implies a careful attempt to identify and quantify key risk factors. Yet, innovating and venturing into the unknown do not always lend themselves to hard numbers. Judgment, instinct, and subjective assessments play a vital role in entrepreneurship. With regard to integrity versus expediency, the placement along the continuum is not meant to suggest a firm should not demonstrate the highest integrity at all times. Rather, it must do so while also stressing the need to get things done. Too often, the entrepreneurial firm becomes overzealous in terms of its action orientation, and integrity suffers. The high pressure and strong work ethic of the entrepreneurial manager are not always shared by other employees and team members. There is a need for sensitivity toward those who view it as a job. They may put in an honest day's work but are not willing to give the daily fifteen-hour efforts an entrepreneur gives. Entrepreneurial behavior clearly must be motivated and is most consistent with performance-based rewards. Yet, entrepreneurship attempts to exist in corporations where power and tenure-based rewards are the expected norm, so again some balance is required. Finally, entrepreneurship is very people based, and so the balance on that continuum is much closer to the "intimate concerns" side. One can go too far here, though, moving beyond people's professional needs and intruding into their personal lives.

There is one more element to consider when thinking about the architecture of the company culture. We use the term *healthy discontent* to describe an emphasis on constant improvement. Employees in entrepreneurial firms are not complacent, even after a major achievement. They always want to go one better. They look at daily processes and think, "We can do this in a better way." They are always critiquing, raising positive criticisms, and challenging the way things have been or are. Managers at all levels get their hands dirty, spend time out in the field, visit customers, ride along on delivery routes, and so forth. Healthy discontent also requires a balancing act, since it can easily become negative and give rise to defensiveness and political gamesmanship.

ENTREPRENEURIAL LEADERSHIP THROUGH CULTURE: THE CINTAS CORPORATION

Culture is rich in entrepreneurial companies. An excellent case in point can be found by considering the Cintas Corporation. Cintas is the world's leading provider of corporate identity uniforms, with annual sales exceeding $1.9 billion. The company has grown for thirty-one consecutive years, with sales increasing at a compound rate of 25 percent and profits at a rate of 33 percent. An investment of $1,000 in Cintas stock when it went public in 1983 would be worth over $50,000 today.

Cintas proactively manages its company culture. For instance, it is ownership driven. Most of the executives have the majority of their net worth invested in Cintas stock. Employees are referred to as partners. At its core, the company culture is defined around the following four distinguishing characteristics:

I. We are professional:
- We are thorough in everything we do.
- We have a spartan attitude about our business.
- We do what is right, not what is expedient. We practice "tough-minded management."
- We believe in people.
- A professional looks professional.
- We are courteous.
- We are enthusiastic.

II. We live by the rules and have high ethical and moral standards:
- We separate business and personal affairs.
- We comply with all laws and regulations.
- We never compromise the personal and ethical standards of each other.

III. We act with a sense of urgency in everything we do:
- Exceeding customer and fellow partners' needs is the simple, overriding business necessity.
- We attend to every detail of our business with a sense of urgent enthusiasm, professionalism, and thoroughness.
- We view every detail as critical to our future success.

IV. We have a sense of positive discontent:
- We are never satisfied with the status quo.
- We constantly strive to improve the process, the systems, the product and the service.
- We are not grumblers and complainers; we are constantly looking for opportunities.

This culture drives a very entrepreneurial enterprise. Cintas prides itself on an infrastructure unmatched in the industry, innovative in-plant engineering and equipment design, ongoing product development, outstanding employee training programs, and award-winning marketing. In a recent year, the company completed the integration of a major acquisition (Unitog), expanded uniform rental presence into nine new cities, opened 11 new uniform rental plants, added 200 full-service uniform routes, expanded the customer base by 50,000 new business customers, and expanded distribution of its line of corporate first aid kits into three new cities while adding 45 first aid service routes.

As we have noted elsewhere, entrepreneurship pays off. The company is ranked in the top one-third of *Information Week*'s 500 Leading Information Technology Innovators and has been recognized as one of the world's most valuable companies in *Business Week*'s Global 1000.

EXPLORING A KEY VALUE: INDIVIDUALISM

Entrepreneurship does not happen without individuals. Someone must champion a concept, persevere in the face of resistance and rejection, make adaptations, and keep the idea alive. But it also does not happen without teams. A motivated, coordinated group of individuals, each having his or her own skills and contributions to make, is critical for moving an entrepreneurial event through what can be

■ TABLE 13.3

MERITS OF INDIVIDUALISM VERSUS COLLECTIVISM

Positive Aspects

Individualism	Collectivism
■ Employee develops stronger self-concept, more self-confidence	■ Greater synergies from combined efforts of people with differing skills
■ Consistent with achievement motivation	■ Ability to incorporate diverse perspectives and achieve comprehensive view
■ Competition among individuals encourages greater number of novel concepts and ideas; breakthrough innovations	■ Individuals treated as equals
■ Stronger sense of personal responsibility for performance outcomes	■ Relationships more personalized, synchronized, harmonious, while interpersonal conflicts are discouraged
■ Linkage between personal effort and rewards creates greater sense of equity	■ Greater concern for welfare of others, network of social support available
	■ More consensus regarding direction and priorities
	■ Credit for failures and successes equally shared
	■ Teamwork produces steady, incremental progress on projects

Negative Aspects

Individualism	Collectivism
■ Emphasis on personal gain at expense of others, selfishness, materialism	■ Loss of personal and professional self to group/collective
■ Individuals have less commitment/loyalty, are more "up for sale"	■ Greater emotional dependence of individuals on the group or organization
■ Differences among individuals are emphasized	■ Less personal responsibility for outcomes
■ Interpersonal conflicts are encouraged	■ Individuals "free ride" on efforts of others, rewards not commensurate with effort
■ Greater levels of personal stress, pressure from individual performance	■ Tendency toward "group think"
■ Insecurity can result from overdependence on self	■ Outcomes can present compromises among diverse interests, reflecting need to get along more than need for performance
■ Greater feelings of loneliness, alienation, and anomie	■ Collectives can take more time to reach consensus, may miss opportunities
■ Stronger incentive for unethical behavior, expediency	
■ Onus of failure falls on the individual	

■FIGURE 13.3

THE RELATIONSHIP BETWEEN ENTREPRENEURSHIP AND AN EMPHASIS ON THE
INDIVIDUAL VERSUS THE GROUP OR COLLECTIVE

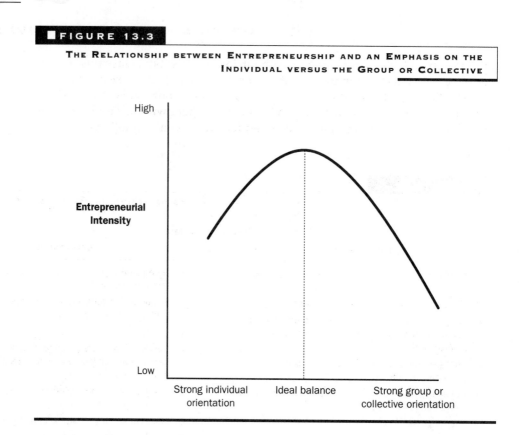

a lengthy process filled with obstacles. This brings us to a value that exists in most companies, even if management is unaware of it: individualism versus collectivism.

Individualism refers to a self-orientation, an emphasis on self-sufficiency and control, the pursuit of individual goals that may or may not be consistent with those of the employee's colleagues, and a value system where people derive pride from their own accomplishments. A group or collective orientation involves the subordination of personal interests to the goals of the larger work group, an emphasis on sharing, a concern with group welfare, and antipathy towards those outside the group.

In a work context, there are positive and negative aspects to both individualism and a group or collective orientation. Table 13.3 provides a summary of these pros and cons. In essence, an individualistic ethic may foster development of an individual's self-confidence; lead to a greater sense of personal responsibility; create more of a competitive spirit; and produce higher-risk, breakthrough innovations. It can also produce selfishness, higher levels of stress, and interpersonal conflict. A group orientation offers the advantages of more harmonious relationships between individuals, greater synergies, more social support, and can result in a steady stream of incremental improvements and moderate innovations. On the downside, the team or group focus can entail the loss of individual identity; greater emotional dependency; a tendency to "free ride" on the efforts of others; compromises rather than optimizing behavior; and "group think," in which individuals get locked into a singular shared way of viewing or approaching a problem.

The ability to achieve sustained entrepreneurship in a company is dependent upon a balance between the need for individual initiative and the spirit of cooperation and group ownership of innovation. This balance is pictured in Figure 13.3. As the entrepreneurial process unfolds, the individual champion requires not just specialist expertise but also teams of people, some of whom can fill multiple roles. Members of these teams are able to collaborate in meeting tight timelines, identifying and overcoming unanticipated obstacles, and finding angles and opportunities that often redefine the original concept, putting it on a more successful path. Sometimes it is the entrepreneur who keeps the team on track, and other times it is the team that is the voice of reason and consistency.

A DIFFERENT VIEW OF FAILURE

The culture in the entrepreneurial firm embraces failure. Managers recognize that failure goes hand in hand with innovating. In fact, if an employee is not failing now and again, he or she is probably not trying anything new. Yet, in most companies, failure is something employees often avoid at all costs, instead opting for the safer middle route. Fear of failure is a certain recipe for mediocrity.

Failure is *perceived*, and this reality explains much of the problem in organizations. Employees attach certain costs to it. They do not want to have the onus of failure attached to their names. It is these perceived costs that should be the focus of management. Consider a very different situation, bankruptcy, which is clearly a type of failure. Bankruptcy laws in the United States are extremely liberal. While we can debate the pluses and minuses of such liberal laws, there is one major benefit. Liberal bankruptcy laws serve to reduce the perceived cost of failure associated with entrepreneurial start-ups. They are an incentive for innovation.

Now consider a large corporation. The manager should ask himself or herself a simple question: How can I reduce the perceived cost of failure that employees associate with innovation or entrepreneurial behavior in this firm? Answering this question implies the manager has a clear sense regarding the specific costs associated with failure. Is it job loss, a smaller pay raise, a missed promotion, a blemished record, loss of autonomy, personal embarrassment, loss of stature, or something else? An interesting exercise is to ask people in organizations to cite people they know who have attempted something entrepreneurial, then failed, and then paid a clear price in terms of job loss or some of these other significant costs. They are often hard-pressed to come up with specific examples. This reality further reinforces the perceptual nature of failure. It may be that much of the perceived cost of failure is psychological. But these costs can be reduced by openly recognizing failures in a very positive way, while continually reinforcing the valuable learning that

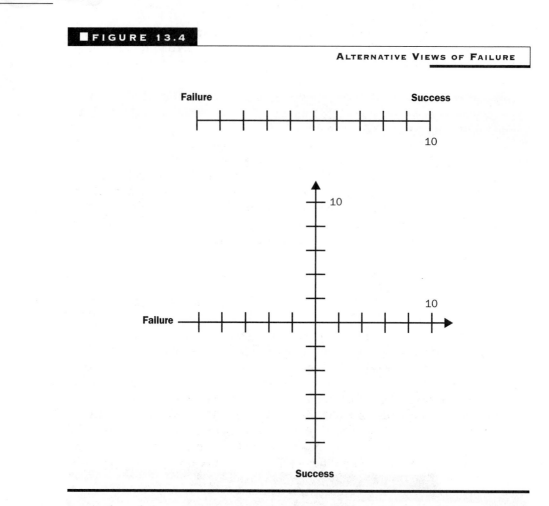

■ FIGURE 13.4

ALTERNATIVE VIEWS OF FAILURE

results from failure. At Enron, for example, managers pride themselves on the fact that even failures that might end up on the front page of a major newspaper do not destroy careers, while at Johnson and Johnson a favorite maxim is "Failure is our most important product."

Companies also should distinguish among the different types of failure. *Moral* failure, which occurs when there is a breach of ethics or an employee acts in an immoral fashion, should be addressed aggressively with a zero tolerance policy. *Personal* failure is related to inadequacies in skills, understanding of an assignment or task, motivation levels, and so forth. It is dealt with through personal counseling, coaching, and training. *Uncontrollable* failures are those that occur in part because of events or forces beyond the control of the individual employee. This is where much of the failure associated with entrepreneurship comes into play. The employee had an interesting idea or concept, approached it with skill and passion, but things did not work out as expected. These failures should be celebrated and should be the subject of systematic documentation and learning efforts.

The real problem, however, has to do with how we conceptualize failure. As pictured at the top of Figure 13.4, people tend to view failure and success as opposites. Success is a line along which an employee moves. Movement in one direction produces increments of success, and movement in the other direction results in increments of failure. The problem here is that, if an employee is succeeding more, then he or she assumes that he or she is failing less. Or, if the employee is failing, they must not be succeeding. Entrepreneurial companies take an alternative view, as pictured at the bottom of Figure 13.4. Both success and failure can be occurring at the same time, in that a firm can have any number of successful initiatives and any number of failures. Something that is not all that successful is not viewed as being somewhat of a failure. Importantly, avoiding failure in no way ensures success. Experiencing failures can enhance the likelihood of success, but only if learning is taking place.

SUMMARY AND CONCLUSIONS

In this chapter, we have examined the need to embed entrepreneurship into the culture of an organization. The nature of culture has been explored and, although it is a complex and time-consuming undertaking, it was argued that culture can be managed. Culture exists at different levels, and manifests itself through a variety of symbols. There also may be types of cultures, each of which has implications for the frequency and degree of entrepreneurship in the organization. In addition, key elements of an entrepreneurial culture were presented.

A difference exists between entrepreneurial leadership and an entrepreneurial culture. An organization can have one or more people at the top who drive innovative performance. But if those people leave, innovative performance will go as well, unless it has been embedded in the culture. Kotter (1996, p. 156) notes, "Culture changes only after you have successfully altered people's actions, after the new behavior produces some group benefit for a period of time, and after people see the connection between the new actions and the performance improvement." So, management does not change the culture and then entrepreneurship happens. Rather, a company moves to an entrepreneurial culture through a process of transformation that includes ongoing innovation, continuous reinforcement, results, extensive internal communication, and working through coalitions. It is a slow process involving focused changes to artifacts, steady redefinition and prioritization of values, and the eventual permeation of the underlying assumptions that define why the company exists and how things get done.

The movement toward an entrepreneurial culture is well summarized in Timmon's (1999) "Chain of Greatness," which is illustrated in Figure 13.5. Vision coupled with learning produce an entrepreneurial mindset throughout the organization. Accountability and responsibility for innovative initiatives are assigned and assumed, as employees take ownership of these initiatives and of the organization

■FIGURE 13.5

THE CHAIN OF GREATNESS

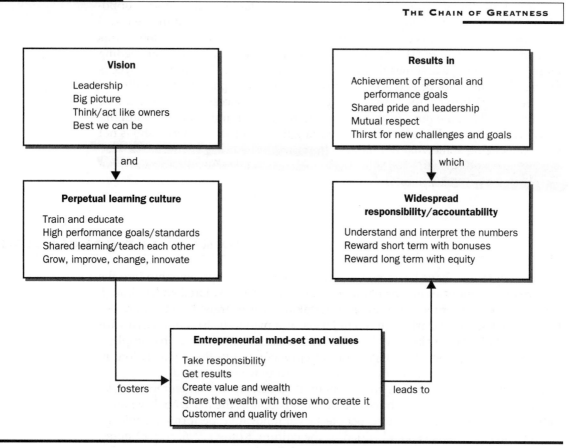

SOURCE: Timmons, J. 1999. *New Venture Creation.* Burr Ridge, IL: Irwin McGraw-Hill.

itself. The end result is a strong, positive, and consistent culture that is achievement driven, pride inducing, and personally fulfilling for employees. The chain of greatness becomes both reinforcing and perpetuating.

The chapter also explored the role of individualism versus collectivism in companies. While significant emphasis is placed these days on teams and groups, managers must not forget the vital role played by individuals in affecting entrepreneurship. The design of jobs, company structures, and performance appraisals and rewards should balance incentives for individual initiative and risk-taking against reinforcements for teamwork and group outputs.

Last, we took a look at the value of failure. Entrepreneurial companies accept the reality that failure goes with the territory. It is a sign of progress, and its

WHEN CHANGE ISN'T TEMPORARY

Reengineer, redesign, alter, transform, restructure . . . every management trend comes prepackaged with synonyms, acronyms, and adages perfect for creating a buzz in the workplace. Trends are temporary, however, and are not followed by everyone all of the time. Over the past decade, companies have been on a continuous trend, cutting costs, streamlining, and flattening, much to the chagrin of the hard-working employee. For every action, there is an equal and opposite reaction. As organizations attempt to restructure their hierarchies and missions, it is only natural that their actions be met with fear, rigidness, and inflexibility.

Take Jaguar of North America, for example, where the pressure of mounting nationwide changes finally frustrated dealership managers beyond tolerance. The tension started when Ford purchased the company in 1990 and began reengineering its manufacturing process and eventually restructuring the organization. One third of the staff was let go, operations was split into three divisions, and titles and perks were stripped away. As a result of falling sales and profits, the energy focus quickly turned to improving customer service. Vice President of Customer Care, Dale Gambill, thought he understood how dealers were feeling and reacting to the recent changes— with distrust and lack of enthusiasm. When Gambill confronted a group of manager-dealers about improving customer service, his speech was abruptly stopped. "Hey, let's forget the customer for a minute here. You aren't taking care of us," stated one dealer in reference to the recent changes. Gambill reported that the group spent two days vocalizing their frustrations, which included lack of vision, competing values among departments, and not receiving feedback about mistakes. Manager-dealers were annoyed with the fact that they were constantly putting out fires rather than training others how to prevent them. Gambill and Jaguar president Mike Dale quickly formulated a strategy to appease the dealers and mitigate future changes. Those who were emphatic enough to speak for the masses were enlisted and empowered to identify and solve problems. Employee Involvement Groups were formed and morale and service quickly turned around. Compliance to a new way of doing things is easier said than done, but when the rules and goals are common and known to everyone on the playing field, the game becomes much easier.

Change wasn't easily instilled at GTE Mobilnet when the company set out to establish itself as the leader in cellular phone customer service. What started out as a project task force became a full-time group of change agents employed to address the needs and complaints of the operating units as new policies swarmed over the organization. Even with personnel geared toward minimizing the adverse effects of change, resistence was still met: "When we went back and explained how things were going to change, they stared at us like, 'What have you done?' We sure didn't get any standing ovations." Specifically, one customer service initiative involved distributing new phones with batteries already installed and charged. The salespeople loved the idea, but the service employees were not thrilled. "We've had to overcome their objections one by one, piece by piece, bit by bit," stated one change agent. Employees simply didn't uderstand why they needed to bother with some of the initiatives presented.

Organizational change, whether among functional processes or human resource systems, must be accompanied with a logical explanation. If employees can relate to and fully understand the benefit of change, no matter how long-term, they will be much more likely to acclimate themselves to new way of doing what they've done for so long. Reengineering efforts aren't always successful, and experts say that part of the fault lies among management ranks. When management is unable to stay focused on one company goal for an extended period of time, employees generally exhibit similar behavior. Resistance to passing management fads is commonplace in organizations of all sizes and shapes. Effective, permanent change requires diligence and the ability to appeal to employees' values and emotions. Just like customers, they need to "be sold" before they'll ever "buy in."

SOURCE: Fisher, A. B. 1995. "Making Change Stick," *Fortune* (April): 121–130.

absence is an indicator that nothing new is being attempted. Of course, employees tend to be skeptical when the boss says it is okay to make mistakes. The need is for systematic management of failure, in which a philosophy of failure is widely communicated, rewards and awards are given for entrepreneurial initiatives that do not work out, and efforts are formally organized to document and derive learning lessons from failed efforts.

REFERENCES

Cornwall, J., and B. Perlman. 1990. *Organizational Entrepreneurship.* Homewood: Irwin.

Collins, J. C., and J. I. Porras. 1994. *Built to Last.* New York: Harper Business.

Deal, T., and A. Kennedy. 2000. *Corporate Cultures.* Reading: Perseus Publishing.

Hamel, G. 2000. *Leading the Revolution.* Boston: Harvard Business School Press.

Kets de Vries, M., and D. Miller. 1984. *The Neurotic Organization.* San Francisco: Jossey Bass.

Kotter, J. 1996. *Leading Change.* Boston: Harvard Business School Press.

Mitroff, I., and J. Kilmann. 1975. "Stories Managers Tell: A New Tool for Organizational Problem-Solving," *Management Review* 64, No. 7: 18–28.

Ouchi, W. 1981. *Theory Z: How American Business Can Meet the Japanese Challenge.* Reading: Addison-Wesley.

Peters, T. 1997. *The Circle of Innovation.* New York: Alfred A. Knopf.

Sethia, N., and M. A. Von Glinow. 1985. "Arriving at Four Cultures by Managing the Reward System." In *Gaining Control of the Corporate Culture,* edited by R. Kilmann et al. San Francisco: Jossey-Bass.

Timmons, J. 1999. *New Venture Creation.* Burr Ridge: Irwin McGraw-Hill.

Trice, H., and J. Beyer. 1993. *The Cultures of Work Organizations.* Englewood Cliffs: Prentice-Hall.

Tropman, J., and G. Morningstar. 1989. *Entrepreneurial Systems for the 1990s.* Westport: Quorum.

IV

ENTREPRENEURIAL ORIENTATION AND THE FUTURE

---■---

"It is time for a new generation of leadership to cope with new problems and opportunities.
For there is a new world to be won."

—JOHN F. KENNEDY

---■---

14

Planning And Measuring The Organization's Entrepreneurial Activity

INTRODUCTION

Planning is essential to the success of any undertaking. Carefully prepared entrepreneurial plans are simply the formulation of goals, objectives, and directions for the future of an innovation. The absence of a plan could mean failure before even starting the entrepreneurial project.

As the organization aggressively pursues the future, there needs to be a continual assessment or measurement of the actual levels of entrepreneurial activity and the results produced. If corporate entrepreneurship is to succeed as a viable strategy for today's organizations, then there must be an emphasis on the measurement process to validate the methods employed for entrepreneurial activity. Rather than becoming merely a *program* for a company to institute, corporate entrepreneurship needs to be a *process* that infiltrates and permeates the entire organization, very much like the quality movement which addressed the measurement and assessment factors of systems and procedures in order to develop better processes (Hodgetts 1998). In this same manner, the corporate entrepreneurship activities must be measured and assessed for their effectiveness. In this chapter, we examine a framework of planning for corporate entrepreneurship, the methods currently available for assessment and measurement, and the importance of continued process improvement in every phase of an entrepreneurial strategy.

DEVELOPING THE ENTREPRENEURIAL PLAN

Planning is the management key to reducing uncertainty and the risks associated with change. Although we can never predict the future, planning is a process that allows ventures to stay on track through the preparation, development, and execution stages of the entrepreneurial process.

Pitfalls in planning are abundant—no one says it's easy! Table 14.1 outlines planning pitfalls, problem indicators, and solutions. These should be carefully considered before embarking on any entrepreneurial pursuit. The comprehensive

■ **TABLE 14.1**

PITFALLS IN ENTREPRENEURIAL PLANNING

(Read carefully before assessing your venture plan)

Pitfalls	Indicators	Possible Solutions
1. No realistic goals	■ Lack of time frame for accomplishing things ■ Lack of priorities ■ Lack of action steps	*Set up a timetable with specific steps to be accomplished at each elapsed time period.*
2. Failure to anticipate road blocks	■ No admission of possible road blocks ■ No contingency or alternative plans	*List the possible obstacles you face along with any flaws or weaknesses in your plan, with alternatives written out that state what you "might have to do."*
3. No commitment or dedication	■ Too much procrastination ■ Missed appointments ■ No desire to put up money of your own ■ Project appears to be a hobby or whim for you ■ Appearance of making a fast buck	*Act quickly and be sure to follow up on all professional appointments. Be ready and willing to demonstrate a financial commitment: "Put your money where your mouth is!"*
4. Lack of demonstrated experience (business/technical)	■ No experience in the specific area of your venture ■ Lack of understanding of the industry into which your venture fits ■ Failure to convey to others a clear picture of what, how, why your venture works, and who will buy it	*Always explain your experience and background for this venture. If you lack specific knowledge or skills, attempt to get help from those who possess the skills. (Demonstrate that you and those helping you are a team.)*
5. No market niche (segment)	■ Uncertainty regarding who will buy your idea ■ No proof of need or desire for your idea ■ Assuming there will be customers or clients just because you think there will be	*Have an established market segment at which you are specifically aiming your venture. Be able to demonstrate why you chose that market and the steps you are taking to prove that there is a need or desire for your idea.*

venture plan, which should be the result of research meetings and reflections upon the entire direction of the new venture, is the major tool used today in conveying the essential components of a new concept, market feasibility, financial capability, and contingent directions that sponsors, interested resource providers, and other key parties need to see. In today's turbulent environment, the entrepreneurial plan (business plan) has become the minimum that is expected for any entrepreneurial venture.

■ **TABLE 14.2**

HELPFUL HINTS FOR DEVELOPING THE CORPORATE VENTURE PLAN

I. Executive Summary
- No more than three pages. This is the most crucial part of your plan because you must capture the reader's interest.
- What, How, Why, Where, etc., must be summarized.
- Complete this part after you have finished the plan.

II. Venture Description Segment
- The name of the venture or concept.
- A background of the industry with history of your company (if any) should be covered here.
- The potential of the new venture should be described clearly.
- Any uniqueness or distinctive features of this venture should be clearly described.

III. Marketing Segment
- Convince executives that sales projections and competition can be met.
- Use and disclose market studies.
- Identify target market, market position, and market share.
- Evaluate all competition and specifically cover why and how you will be better than them.
- Identify customer communication requirements and approaches for key target audiences.
- Demonstrate pricing strategy since your price must penetrate and maintain a market share to produce profits. Thus the lowest price is not necessarily the best price.

IV. Operations and Development Segment
- Describe the advantages of your location (zoning, tax laws, wage rates). List the production needs in terms of facilities (plant, storage, office space) and equipment (machinery, furnishings, supplies).
- Describe the access to transportation.
- Indicate proximity to your suppliers.
- Mention the availability of labor in your location.
- Provide estimates of manufacturing costs — be careful; too many entrepreneurs underestimate their costs.
- Identify key technical obstacles to be overcome, and the costs and timetable for addressing them.

V. Management Segment
- Supply resumes of all key people in the management of your venture.
- Carefully describe the legal structure of your venture (sole proprietorship, partnership, or corporation).
- Cover the added assistance (if any) of advisers, consultants, and directors.
- Give information on how and how much everyone is to be compensated.

VI. Financial Segment
- Give actual estimated statements.
- Describe the needed sources for your funds and the uses you intend for the money.
- Develop and present a budget.
- Create stages of financing for purposes of allowing evaluation by investors at various points.

VII. Critical Risks Segment
- Discuss potential risks before executives point them out, such as:
- Price cutting by competitors
- Any potentially unfavorable industry-wide trend.
- Design or manufacturing costs in excess of estimate.
- Sales projections not achieved
- Product development schedule not met
- Difficulties or long lead times encountered in the procurement of parts or raw materials
- Greater than expected innovation and development costs to stay competitive
- Provide some alternative courses of action

VIII. Harvest Strategy Segment
- Outline a plan for the orderly transfer of company assets (ownership).
- Describe the plan for transition of leadership.
- Mention the preparations needed for continuity of the business.

IX. Milestone Schedule Segment
- Develop a timetable or chart to demonstrate when each phase of the venture is to be completed. This shows the relationship of events and provides a deadline for accomplishment.

SOURCE: Kuratko D.F., J.S. Hornsby, and F.J. Sabatine. 1999. *The Breakthrough Experience*. Muncie, IN: Midwest Entrepreneurial Education Center.

We begin with a few reminders about what a corporate venture plan should accomplish. An effective plan will do the following:

1. Describe every aspect of a particular innovative concept, including the underlying economic model;

2. Specify the nature of the opportunity the concept is intended to capitalize upon;

3. Include a marketing plan;

4. Clarify and outline financial needs;

5. Identify potential obstacles and alternative solutions;

6. Establish milestones for continuous and timely evaluations; and

7. Serve as a communication tool for assessment purposes.

It is also important to recognize the key elements in the plan. Table 14.2 provides some helpful hints regarding the construction of each segment of a plan.

The corporate venture plan is a major tool used in guiding the direction of a proposed venture or new concept, as well as the primary document in managing it. But the plan is more than a written document—it is an ongoing process that starts when corporate entrepreneurs begin to gather information and then continues as projections are made, implemented, measured, and updated. It is a way of thinking and operating. The clearer the plan, the more powerful it becomes as a tool for continuous evaluation. Table 14.3 provides a comprehensive assessment tool for each component of the venture plan.

ASSESSING THE CORPORATE ENTREPRENEURIAL PROJECT

A critical task in assessing a corporate venture project is to determine the likelihood of the new concept getting off the ground by undertaking solid analysis and evaluation. Corporate entrepreneurs must put their ideas through this analysis to discover if they contain any fatal flaws.

ASK THE RIGHT QUESTIONS

Many important evaluation-related questions should be asked. Ten sets of preliminary questions that can be used to screen an idea are presented here:

I. Is it a new product or service idea? Is it proprietary? Can it be patented or copyrighted? Is it unique enough to get a significant head start on the competition? Or can it be easily copied?

II. Has a prototype been tested by independent evaluators who try to systematically attack the system or product? What are its weak points? Will it stand up? What level of research and development should it receive over the next five years? If a service, has it been tested on customers? Will customers pay their hard-earned money for it?

Text continues on page 286.

■ TABLE 14.3

There are ten components of a business plan. As you develop your plan, you should assess each component. Be honest in your assessment since the main purpose is to improve your business plan and increase your chances of success. For instance, if your goal is to obtain external financing, you will be asked to submit a complete business plan for your venture. The business plan will help a funding source to evaluate your business idea more adequately.

Assessment

Directions: The brief description of each component will help you write that section of your plan. After completing your plan, use the scale provided to assess each component.

5	4	3	2	1
Outstanding	Very Good	Good	Fair	Poor
Thorough and complete in all areas	*Most areas covered but could use improvement in detail*	*Some areas covered in detail but other areas missing*	*A few areas covered but very little detail*	*No written parts*

The Ten Components of a Business Plan

1. Executive Summary: This is the most important section because it has to convince the reader that the business will succeed. In no more than three pages, you should summarize the highlights of the rest of the plan. This means that the key elements of the following components should be mentioned.

The executive summary must be able to stand on its own. It is not simply an introduction to the rest of the business plan. This section should discuss who purchases your product or service, what makes your business unique, and how you plan to grow in the future. Because this section summarizes the plan, it is often best to write this section last.

Rate this component:

5	4	3	2	1
Outstanding	Very good	Good	Fair	Poor

2. Description of the Business: This section should provide background information about your industry, a history of your company, a general description of your product or service, and the specific mission that you are trying to achieve. Your product or service should be described in terms of its unique qualities and value to the customer. Specific short-term and long-term objectives must be defined. You should state clearly what sales, market share, and profitability objectives you want your business to achieve.

Key Elements	Have you covered this in the plan?	Is the answer clear? (yes or no)	Is the answer complete? (yes or no)
a. What type of venture will you have?			
b. What products or services will you sell?			
c. Why does it promise to be successful?			

continued

■ **TABLE 14.3**

CONTINUED

d. What is the growth potential?			
e. How is it unique?			

Rate this component:

5	4	3	2	1
Outstanding	Very good	Good	Fair	Poor

3. Marketing: There are two major parts to the marketing section. The first is research and analysis. Here, you should explain who buys the product or service—in other words, identify your target market. Measure your market size and trends, and estimate the market share you expect. Be sure to include support for your sales projections. For example, if your figures are based on published marketing research data, be sure to cite the source. Do your best to make realistic and credible projections. Describe your competition in considerable detail, identifying their strengths and weaknesses. Finally, explain how you will be better than your competitors.

The second part is your marketing plan. This critical section should include your market strategy, sales and distribution, pricing, advertising, promotion, and public awareness. Demonstrate how your pricing strategy will result in a profit. Identify your advertising plans, and include cost estimates to validate your proposed strategy.

Key Elements	Have you covered this in the plan?	Is the answer clear? (yes or no)	Is the answer complete? (yes or no)
a. Who will be your customers? (target market)			
b. How big is the market? (number of customers)			
c. Who will be your competitors?			
d. How are their businesses prospering?			
e. How will you promote sales?			

f. What market share will you want?			
g. Do you have a pricing strategy?			

Rate this...

5		3	2	1
Outsta...	...ry...	Good	Fair	Poor

4. Ope... ...to describe the issues surrounding production or service deliver...

		...overed ...plan?	Is the answer clear? (yes or no)	Is the answer complete? (yes or no)
b.				
c.				
d.				
e.				

Rate this...

5			2	1
Outstand...		...ood	Fair	Poor

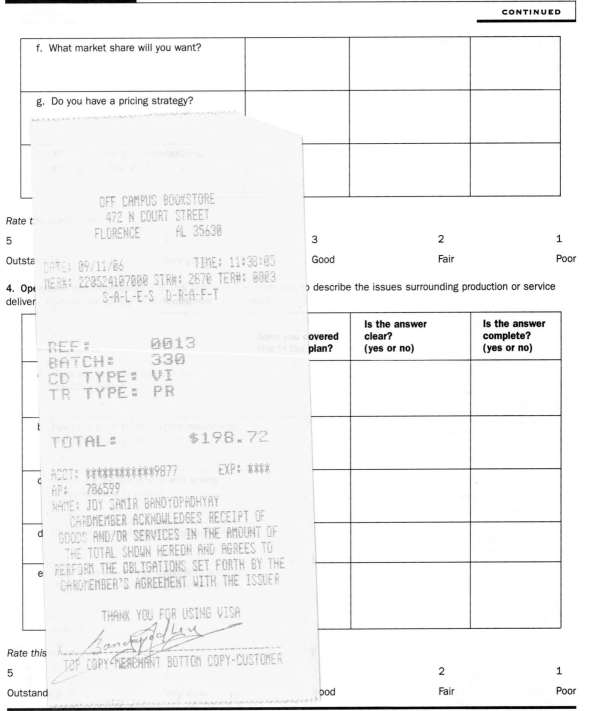

OFF CAMPUS BOOKSTORE
472 N COURT STREET
FLORENCE   AL 35630

DATE: 09/11/06   TIME: 11:38:05
MER#: 220524107000 STR#: 2870 TERM: 0003
S-A-L-E-S D-R-A-F-T

REF: 0013
BATCH: 330
CD TYPE: VI
TR TYPE: PR

TOTAL= $198.72

ACCT: ***********9877   EXP: ****
AP: 706599
NAME: JOY SAMIR BANDYOPADHYAY
     CARDMEMBER ACKNOWLEDGES RECEIPT OF
GOODS AND/OR SERVICES IN THE AMOUNT OF
THE TOTAL SHOWN HEREON AND AGREES TO
PERFORM THE OBLIGATIONS SET FORTH BY THE
CARDMEMBER'S AGREEMENT WITH THE ISSUER

     THANK YOU FOR USING VISA

TOP COPY-MERCHANT BOTTOM COPY-CUSTOMER

continued

CONTINUED

■ **TABLE 14.3**

5. Management: Start by describing the management team, their unique qualifications, and how you compensate them (including salaries, employment agreements, stock purchase plans, levels of ownership, and other considerations). Discuss how your organization is structured and consider including a diagram illustrating who reports to whom. Also include a discussion of the potential contribution of the board of directors, advisers, or consultants. Finally, carefully describe the legal structure of your venture (i.e., sole proprietorship, partnership, or corporation).

Key Elements	Have you covered this in the plan?	Is the answer clear? (yes or no)	Is the answer complete? (yes or no)
a. Who will manage the business?			
b. What qualifications do you have?			
c. How many employees will you have?			
d. What will they do?			
e. How much will you pay your employees and what type of benefits will you offer them?			
f. What consultants or specialists will you use?			
g. Where will the venture or project fall within the organizational structure?			
h. What regulations will affect your business?			

Rate this component:

5	4	3	2	1
Outstanding	Very good	Good	Fair	Poor

6. Financial: Three key financial statements must be presented: a balance sheet, an income statement, and a cash flow statement. These statements typically cover a one-year period. Be sure you state any assumptions and projections you made when calculating the figures.

Determine the stages in which your business will require financing and identify the expected financing sources. Also, clearly show what return on investment these sources will achieve by investing in your business. The final item to include is a break-even analysis. This analysis should show what level of sales will be required to cover all costs. If the work is done well, the financial statements should represent the actual financial achievements expected from your business plan. They also provide a standard by which to measure the actual results of operating your business. They are a very valuable tool to help you manage and control your business.

Key Elements	Have you covered this in the plan?	Is the answer clear? (yes or no)	Is the answer complete? (yes or no)
a. What is your total expected business income for the first year? Quarterly for the next two years? (Forecast)			
b. What is your expected monthly cash flow during the first year?			
c. What rates of return will accrue?			
d. What sales volume will you need in order to make a profit during the first three years?			
e. What will be the break-even point?			
f. What are your projected assets, liabilities, and net worth?			
g. What are your total financial needs?			
h. What are your funding sources?			

Rate this component:

5	4	3	2	1
Outstanding	Very good	Good	Fair	Poor

7. Critical Risks: Discuss potential risks before they happen. Here are some examples: price-cutting by competitors, potentially unfavorable industry-wide trends, design or manufacturing, costs that could exceed estimates, sales projections

continued

CONTINUED

■ TABLE 14.3

that are not achieved. The idea is to recognize risks and identify alternative courses of action. Your main objective is to show that you can anticipate and control (to a reasonable degree) your risks.

Key Elements	Have you covered this in the plan?	Is the answer clear? (yes or no)	Is the answer complete? (yes or no)
a. What potential problems have you identified?			
b. Have you calculated the risks?			
c. What alternative courses of action are there?			

Rate this component:

5	4	3	2	1
Outstanding	Very good	Good	Fair	Poor

8. Harvest Strategy: Ensuring the survival of an internal venture is hard work. A founder's protective feelings for an idea built from scratch make it tough to grapple with such issues as management succession, corporate rivalries, and harvest strategies. With foresight, however, entrepreneurs can keep their dreams alive, ensure the security of their ventures, and usually strengthen their businesses in the process. Thus a written plan for succession in your business is essential.

Key Elements	Have you covered this in the plan?	Is the answer clear? (yes or no)	Is the answer complete? (yes or no)
a. Have you planned for the orderly transfer of the venture assets if ownership of the business is passed to this corporation?			
b. Is there a continuity of business strategy for an orderly transition?			

Rate this component:

5	4	3	2	1
Outstanding	Very good	Good	Fair	Poor

9. Milestone Schedule: This is an important segment of the business plan because it requires you to determine what tasks you need to accomplish in order to achieve your objectives. Milestones and deadlines should be established and monitored on an ongoing basis. Each milestone is related to all the others and together they comprise a timely representation of how your objective is to be accomplished.

Key Elements	Have you covered this in the plan?	Is the answer clear? (yes or no)	Is the answer complete? (yes or no)
a. How have you set your objectives?			
b. Have you set deadlines for each stage of your growth?			

Rate this component:

5	4	3	2	1
Outstanding	Very good	Good	Fair	Poor

10. Appendix: This section includes important background information that was not included in the other sections. This is where you would put such items as resumes of the management team, names of references and advisers, drawings, documents, licenses, agreements, and any materials that support the plan. You may also wish to add a bibliography of the sources from which you drew information.

Key Elements	Have you covered this in the plan?	Is the answer clear? (yes or no)	Is the answer complete? (yes or no)
a. Have you included any documents, drawings, agreements, or other materials?			
b. Are there any names of references, advisers, or technical sources you should include?			
c. Are there any other supporting documents?			

Rate this component:

5	4	3	2	1
Outstanding	Very good	Good	Fair	Poor

continued

■ **TABLE 14.3**

CONTINUED

Summary: Your Plan

Directions: For each of the business plan sections that you have assessed in the Components section, circle the assigned points on this review sheet and then total the circled points.

Components	Points				
1. Executive Summary	5	4	3	2	1
2. Description of the Business	5	4	3	2	1
3. Marketing	5	4	3	2	1
4. Operations and Development	5	4	3	2	1
5. Management	5	4	3	2	1
6. Financial	5	4	3	2	1
7. Critical Risks	5	4	3	2	1
8. Harvest Strategy	5	4	3	2	1
9. Milestone Schedule	5	4	3	2	1
10. Appendix	5	4	3	2	1

Total Points: _____

Scoring:

50 points: Outstanding! The ideal business plan. Solid.

45–49: Very Good.

40–44: Good. The plan is sound with a few areas that need to be polished.

35–39: Above average. The plan has some good areas but needs improvement before presentation.

30–34: Average. Some areas are covered in detail and others need improvement.

20–29: Below Average. Most areas need greater detail and improvement.

Below 20: Poor. Plan needs to be researched and documented much better.

SOURCE: Kuratko, D.F. and R.M. Hodgetts. 2001. *Entrepreneurship: A Contemporary Approach*, 5th ed. Fort Worth, TX: Harcourt College Publishers.

III. Has it been taken to trade shows? If so, what reactions did it receive? Were any sales made? Has it been taken to distributors? Have they placed any orders?

IV. Is the product or service easily understood by customers, bankers, venture capitalists, accountants, lawyers, and insurance agents?

V. What is the overall market? What are the market segments? Can the product penetrate these segments? Are there special niches that can be exploited?

VI. Has market research been conducted? Who else is considered part of the market? How big is the market? How fast is it growing? What are the trends? What is the projected life cycle of the product or service? What degree of penetration can be achieved? Are there any testimonials from customers and purchasing agents? What type of advertising and promotion plans will be used?

VII. What distribution and sales methods will be used—jobbers, independent sales representatives, company sales force, direct mail, door-to-door sales, supermarkets, service stations, company-owned stores? How will the product be transported: company-owned trucks, common carriers, postal service, or air freight?

VIII. How will the product or service be produced or delivered? How much will it cost? For example, will it be produced in-house or by others? Will production be by job shop or continuous process? What is the present capacity of company facilities? What is the break-even point?

IX. Will the business concept be developed and licensed to others or developed and sold off?

X. Can the company get, or has it already lined up, the necessary skills to operate the business venture? Who are the workers? Are they dependable and competent? How much capital will be needed now? How much more in the future? Have major stages in financing been developed?

A single strategic variable seldom determines the ultimate success or failure of a new corporate venture. Instead, in most situations, a combination of variables influences the outcome. Thus it is important to identify and investigate these variables before the new idea is put into practice. The results of a feasibility criteria approach enable the corporate entrepreneur to judge the idea's business potential. The feasibility criteria approach, developed as a criteria selection list, allows insights into the viability of a venture and is based on the following questions:

1. *Is it proprietary?* The product does not have to be patented, but it should be sufficiently proprietary to permit a long head start against competitors and a period of extraordinary profits early in the venture to offset start-up costs.

2. *Are the initial production costs realistic?* Most estimates are too low. A careful, detailed analysis should be made so that no large unexpected expenses crop up.

3. *Are the initial marketing costs realistic?* Answering this question requires the entrepreneur to identify target markets, market channels, and promotion strategy.

4. *Does the product have potential for very high margins?* This potential is almost a necessity for a fledgling company. The financial community understands gross margins and, without the promise of high margins, obtaining funding can be difficult.

5. *Is the time required to get to market and to reach the break-even point realistic?* In most cases, faster is better. In all cases, the venture plan is tied to this answer, and an error here can spell trouble later on.

6. *Is the potential market large?* In determining the potential market, the entrepreneur must look three to five years into the future because some markets take that long to emerge.

7. *Is the product the first of a growing family?* If it is, the venture will be more attractive to investors. After all, if a large return is not made on the first product, it might be realized on the second, third, or fourth product.

8. *Is there an initial customer?* Sponsors and backers are impressed when a venture can list its first ten customers by name. This pent-up demand also means that the first quarter's results are likely to be good and the focus of attention can be directed to later quarters.

9. *Are development costs and calendar times realistic?* Preferably, development costs should be minimal. A ready-to-go product gives the venture a major advantage over competitors. If there are costs, they should be complete and detailed and tied to a month-by-month schedule.

10. *Is this a growing industry?* Industry growth is not absolutely essential if profits and company growth are evident, but with no industry growth, there is less room for mistakes. In a growing industry, good companies do even better.

11. *Are the product and the need for it understood by the financial community?* If financiers can grasp the concept and its value, chances for funding will increase. For example, a portable heart-monitoring system for post-coronary patient monitoring is a product that many will understand. Undoubtedly, some of those hearing the presentation for the product will have already had coronaries or heart problems of some sort.

The comprehensive corporate venture plan discussed earlier in the chapter provides the most accurate assessment instrument (Table 14.3). First developed as a planning document, the venture plan becomes the critical assessment and measurement tool for the entrepreneurial project.

THE IMPORTANCE OF ORGANIZATIONAL-LEVEL MEASUREMENT AND ASSESSMENT

Sustainable entrepreneurship requires that managers are involved in ongoing efforts at assessment. The entire concept of assessment revolves around the measurement of processes and outcomes. Thus, attention is given to outcomes but also and equally to the experiences that lead to those outcomes. Effective assessment strategies pay attention to the processes that help explain the attainment or non-attainment of a particular outcome. Banta et al. (1996) found that the power of assessment is that of a cumulative, ongoing effort in the spirit of continuous improvement. Assessment is most likely to lead to improvement when it is part of a larger set of conditions that promote change. In many respects, this notion of assessment as a process of continuous change and improvement echoes the Japanese outlook on improvement known as *kaizen*—a philosophy of continuous improvement with a two-hundred-year view of the future. Although it is probably not necessary — or possible — to view assessment within a two-hundred-year framework, it is possible and important to take at least a perspective that incorporates the possibility of assessment changes and improvements over the next twenty or thirty years.

Unfortunately, assessment and organizational improvement are often perceived as exercises to be implemented in response to an urgent need—shareholder pressure, stakeholders' opinions, market pressure, image, and so forth. Effective assessment programs become embedded in the organizational culture. They are acknowledged, discussed, deliberated, reviewed, and refined. Effective assessment is perceived as an integral part of the overall mission, and it focuses, very simply, on learning. In this context, assessment becomes one of the driving forces in creating what Peter Senge (1990) calls *learning organizations,* organizations in which people continually expand their capacity to create the results they truly desire, in which new and expansive patterns of thinking are nurtured, in which collective aspiration is set free, and in which people are continually learning how to learn together" (p. 3). Assessment at its best is all of these things—and more.

Some attempt has been made to model behavior within entrepreneurial firms, and these efforts have implications for measurement efforts. As an example, Jelinek and Litterer (1995) looked at entrepreneurial companies and found difficulties in analyzing them using traditional organization theory. They proposed that a new model be used that focuses on shared cognitions among those in the firm. They posited that this new model could account for the constant innovation resulting from entrepreneurial activity and approach it as systemic flexibility. The authors pointed to shared management and measurement as a structural element for facilitating an organizational culture and strategy that achieves entrepreneurial activity. At the operational level, measurement systems are the key for recognizing anomalies (signals for mindful alertness) that can be information for coordinated decision making that produces results (exploiting opportunities).

So at the surface, the purpose of measurement in highly entrepreneurial firms appears to be radically different from what it is in less entrepreneurial firms. Shared management and measurement systems in more entrepreneurial companies have much to do with the firm's propensity for "ambiguity absorption." The managerial system of the entrepreneurial firm is adept at dealing with high levels of ambiguity in the environment, contributing to organizational flexibility. The ambiguity absorption factor seems to be supported not only in models that focus on cognitions, but also in those that emphasize behaviors. In their entrepreneurial posture model, Covin and Slevin (1991) focus on the frequency and nature of product innovations as one of the defining behaviors. The authors make it clear that systems must be designed for flexibility to take advantage of opportunities that arise as entrepreneurial managers are mindfully tracking product/market life cycles and opportunities.

The importance of assessment can also be seen when considering the relationship between corporate entrepreneurship and firm performance in large organizations. This relationship has been assessed differently across time. During the 1980s, for example, some argued that it was difficult if not almost impossible for people to act entrepreneurially in what often had become bureaucratic organizational structures (Morse 1986). At the same time, however, others were suggesting that for companies of any size (in terms of sales volume and number of employees, among other dimensions), entrepreneurial actions were possible, should be encouraged, and could be expected to enhance firm performance (Burgelman 1984; Kanter 1986).

Witnessed throughout the 1990s was a virtual revolution with respect to the perceived value of entrepreneurial actions as contributors to organizational success. This significant change paralleled the rapid emergence of profound adjustments in how companies defined their business, utilized their human resources, and competed in the global economy. Speaking to this matter, Zahra, Kuratko, and Jennings (1999) point out that "some of the world's best-known companies had to endure painful transformation to become more entrepreneurial. These companies had to endure years of reorganization, downsizing, and restructuring. These changes altered the identity or culture of firms, infusing a new entrepreneurial spirit throughout their operations. Change, innovation, and entrepreneurship became highly regarded words that describe what successful companies must do to survive." Extending this position to the current day, it can be noted that the beginning of the 21st century is a time period during which entrepreneurial actions are recognized widely as the path to competitive advantage and success in firms and agencies of all types and sizes (Covin, Slevin, and Heeley 2000). Moreover, some argue rather convincingly that a lack of entrepreneurial actions in the fast-paced and complex global economy may be a recipe for failure (Zahra 1999).

The discussion up to this point has implied that entrepreneurial actions can be measured. While reliable and valid measures have yet to be developed at the level of the individual, progress has been made at the organizational level. Building on the work of Miller and Friesen (1982), a number of researchers have reported success both in measuring a company's entrepreneurial orientation and in linking that orientation to various strategic and performance variables.

Researchers have demonstrated statistically significant relationships between entrepreneurial actions and a number of indicators of company performance (Kuratko, Ireland, and Hornsby 2001). Examples of such indicators include profits, the income-to-sales ratio, the rate of growth in revenue, the rate of growth in assets, the rate of growth in employment, and a composite measure of twelve financial and nonfinancial criteria (Covin and Slevin 1990; 1991; Davis, Morris, and Allen 1991; Miller and Friesen 1982; Morris and Sexton 1996; Peters and Waterman 1982; Zahra 1986). This linkage between entrepreneurial actions and performance appears to be especially strong for companies that operate in increasingly turbulent environments.

METHODS OF MEASURING ENTREPRENEURIAL ACTIVITY

A central thesis of this chapter is that entrepreneurial actions should be monitored and measured on an ongoing basis. Measurement at the level of the individual can be useful in helping managers and others to examine and refine their own leadership styles and in characterizing employee behavior over time. At the organizational level, measures can be used to benchmark and track entrepreneurial performance, establish norms and draw industry comparisons, establish entrepreneurship goals, develop strategies, and assess relationships between entrepreneurial actions and company performance variables over time.

As mentioned earlier, there is no one agreed-upon method for measuring entrepreneurial activity. However, we present two instruments that assess a number of critical factors in the corporate entrepreneurial process. One instrument developed by Michael H. Morris is the Entrepreneurial Performance Index (EPI) presented in Table 14.4. The items in this questionnaire capture both the degree and frequency of entrepreneurship, as well as the underlying dimensions of innovativeness, risk-taking, and proactiveness. In addition, product, service and process innovation are covered. Various studies in which these measures have been employed have reported more than satisfactory statistics for their reliability and validity (Morris and Sexton 1996).

Measurement through the EPI also provides numerous opportunities for further questions by the organization. For example, the relative importance of degree and frequency when measuring entrepreneurial actions may actually vary depending on certain strategic factors, such as the pace of technological change in an industry, the levels of competitive intensity, or the heterogeneity of market demand. Also, the conditions under which degree or frequency is the strongest contributor to performance need to be assessed. It is also necessary to determine if frequency contributes more to short-term results, whereas degree is better able to impact long-term outcomes. Although hypothetical, such a possibility is implicit in the work of Hamel and Prahalad (1991). Using a baseball analogy of hitting many singles versus attempting to hit a home run, they emphasize the value of companies pursuing multiple smaller projects at a time as opposed to their pursuing one potentially breakthrough project. A risk-reward trade-off is involved in which the former are thought to generate short- and intermediate-term profits, whereas the latter significantly impacts long-term profitability. In any event, the EPI is a powerful assessment tool that captures the degree and frequency of entrepreneurship at the organizational level.

Another instrument developed by Donald F. Kuratko, Jeffrey S. Hornsby, and Ray V. Montagno is the Corporate Entrepreneurship Assessment Instrument (CEAI) illustrated in Table 14.5. It is a diagnostic tool for evaluating how supportive the corporate environment is.

Let us examine some of the elements that compose the CEAI. While the literature illustrates a wide variety of corporate entrepreneurial factors, there are a few elements that are consistent throughout the writings in this field. One is the appropriate use of rewards. Theorists stress that any reward system, to be effective, must consider goals, feedback, emphasis on individual responsibility, and rewards based on results. A second element is management support, which relates to willingness of managers to facilitate entrepreneurial projects. Resources (including time) and their availability is a third element recognized in many of the writings. Employees must perceive the availability of resources for entrepreneurial activities. A fourth consistent element is organizational structure, which is identified in various ways yet always appears as an essential factor. Finally, risk-taking appears as a consistent element in that employees and management must have a willingness to take a risk and must have a tolerance for failure should it occur. Table 14.6 identifies these common factors and the literature that supports them.

Text continues on page 299.

■ **TABLE 14.4**

<u>THE ENTREPRENEURIAL PERFORMANCE INDEX</u>

Company Orientation

For the following statements, please circle the number that best corresponds to your level of agreement with each statement:

Our company is characterized by:

	Strongly Agree			**Strongly Disagree**	
1. A high rate of new product/service introductions compared to our competitors (including new features and improvements);	1	2	3	4	5
2. An emphasis on continuous improvement in methods of production and/or service delivery;	1	2	3	4	5
3. Risk-taking by key executives in seizing and exploring chancy growth opportunities;	1	2	3	4	5
4. A "live and let live" philosophy in dealing with competitors;	1	2	3	4	5
5. Seeking of unusual, novel solutions by senior executives to problems via the use of "idea people," brainstorming, etc;	1	2	3	4	5
6. A top management philosophy that emphasizes proven products and services, and the avoidance of heavy new product development costs;	1	2	3	4	5
7. A charismatic leader at the top.	1	2	3	4	5

In our company, top-level decision making is characterized by:

	Strongly Agree			**Strongly Disagree**	
8. Cautious, pragmatic, step-at-a-time adjustments to problems;	1	2	3	4	5
9. Active search for big opportunities;	1	2	3	4	5
10. Rapid growth as the dominant goal;	1	2	3	4	5
11. Large, bold decisions despite uncertainties of the outcomes;	1	2	3	4	5
12. Compromises among the conflicting demands of owners, government, management, customers, employees, suppliers, etc;	1	2	3	4	5
13. Steady growth and stability as primary concerns.	1	2	3	4	5

■ **TABLE 14.4**

CONTINUED

New Product Introduction

		Significantly Less	Same		Significantly More
1. What is the number of new products your company introduced during the past two years?					
2. How many product improvements or revisions did you introduce during the past two years?	1	2	3	4	5
3. How does the number of new product introductions at your organization compare with those of your major competitors?	1	2	3	4	5
		Not at all			To a great extent
4. To what degree did these new product introductions include products that did not previously exist in your markets ("new to the market")?	1	2	3	4	5

New Service Introduction (for those who sell services)

		Significantly Less	Same		Significantly More
1. What is the number of new services your company introduced during the past two years?	1	2	3	4	5
2. How many existing services did you significantly revise or improve during the past two years?	1	2	3	4	5
3. How does the number of new service introductions your company made compare with those of the competitors?	1	2	3	4	5
		Not at all			To a great extent
4. To what degree did these new service introductions include services that did not previously exist in your markets ("new to the South African market")?	1	2	3	4	5

New Process Introduction

		Significantly Less	Same		Significantly More
1. Please estimate the number of significant new methods or operational processes your organization implemented during the past two years. Examples of process innovations include: new systems for managing customer service or inventories, an improved process for collecting receivables, a major new sales or distribution approach, etc.	1	2	3	4	5

continued

■ TABLE 14.4

CONTINUED

Key Business Behavioral Dimensions.

The following questions relate to the approaches that underlie the way your organization conducts business. Please circle the number that best represents the relative emphasis your organization places on the two criteria given. The number 1 indicates that more emphasis is placed on the left and 5 more emphasis on the right.

1. Our organization's current strategic orientation is:

Influenced primarily by the resources we currently control.	1	2	3	4	5	Influenced primarily by the perception of untapped opportunity.

2. With regard to new opportunities, our organization tends to:

Commit fairly quickly, capitalize, and move to the next opportunity.	1	2	3	4	5	Approach with an evolutionary commitment that tends to be of long duration.

3. Our organization's approach to investing resources in new opportunities tends to involve:

Multiple stages with minimal commitment at each stage.	1	2	3	4	5	A single stage with complete commitment upon decision.

4. When managing or controlling resources, we tend to:

Episodic use, renting, leasing, contracting, and outsourcing of resources.	1	2	3	4	5	Ownership, purchase, control, and employment of the resources we use.

5. Our organization's management structure can be characterized as:

A flat structure with multiple informal networks.	1	2	3	4	5	A hierarchical structure with clearly defined authority and responsibility.

6. Our organization's compensation and reward system is:

Value based and team based with unlimited earnings potential for employees.	1	2	3	4	5	Resource based, driven by short-term performance data, with limited earning potential for employees.

CEAI: CORPORATE ENTREPRENEURSHIP ASSESSMENT INSTRUMENT

We are interested in learning about how you perceive your workplace and organization. Please read the following items. Using the scale below please indicate how much you agree or disagree with each of the statements. If you strongly agree, write "5." If you strongly disagree, write "1." There are no right or wrong answers to these questions so please be as honest and thoughtful as possible in your responses. All responses will be kept strictly confidential. Thank you for your cooperation!

Strongly disagree	Disagree	Not sure	Agree	Strongly agree
1	2	3	4	5

Section 1: Management Support for Corporate Entrepreneurship

1. My organization is quick to use improved work methods.
2. My organization is quick to use improved work methods that are developed by workers.
3. In my organization, developing ideas for the improvement of the corporation is encouraged.
4. Upper management is aware of and very receptive to my ideas and suggestions.
5. A promotion usually follows from the development of new and innovative ideas.
6. Those employees who come up with innovative ideas on their own often receive management encouragement for their activities.
7. The "doers" on projects are allowed to make decisions without going through elaborate justification and approval procedures.
8. Senior managers encourage innovators to bend rules and rigid procedures in order to keep promising ideas on track.
9. Many top managers are known for their experience with the innovation process.
10. Money is often available to get new project ideas off the ground.
11. Individuals with successful innovative projects receive additional rewards and compensation for their ideas and efforts beyond the standard reward system.
12. There are several options within the organization for individuals to get financial support for their innovative projects and ideas.
13. People are often encouraged to take calculated risks with ideas around here.
14. Individual risk takers are often recognized for their willingness to champion new projects, whether eventually successful or not.
15. The term "risk taker" is considered a positive attribute for people in my work area.
16. This organization supports many small and experimental projects realizing that some will undoubtedly fail.
17. An employee with a good idea is often given free time to develop that idea.
18. There is considerable desire among people in the organization for generating new ideas without regard for crossing departmental or functional boundaries.
19. People are encouraged to talk to employees in other departments of this organization about ideas for new projects.

Section 2: Work Discretion

20. I feel that I am my own boss and do not have to double-check all of my decisions with someone else.
21. Harsh criticism and punishment result from mistakes made on the job.
22. This organization provides the chance to be creative and try my own methods of doing the job.
23. This organization provides the freedom to use my own judgment.
24. This organization provides the chance to do something that makes use of my abilities.
25. I have the freedom to decide what I do on my job.
26. It is basically my own responsibility to decide how my job gets done.
27. I almost always get to decide what I do on my job.
28. I have much autonomy on my job and am left on my own to do my own work.
29. I seldom have to follow the same work methods or steps for doing my major tasks from day to day.

continued

■ **TABLE 14.5**

CONTINUED

Section 3: Rewards/Reinforcement

30. My manager helps me get my work done by removing obstacles and roadblocks.
31. The rewards I receive are dependent upon my work on the job.
32. My supervisor will increase my job responsibilities if I am performing well in my job.
33. My supervisor will give me special recognition if my work performance is especially good.
34. My manager would tell his/her boss if my work was outstanding.
35. There is a lot of challenge in my job.

Section 4: Time Availability

36. During the past three months, my work load kept me from spending time on developing new ideas.
37. I always seem to have plenty of time to get everything done.
38. I have just the right amount of time and work load to do everything well.
39. My job is structured so that I have very little time to think about wider organizational problems.
40. I feel that I am always working with time constraints on my job.
41. My co-workers and I always find time for long-term problem solving.

Section 5: Organizational Boundaries

42. In the past three months, I have always followed standard operating procedures or practices to do my major tasks.
43. There are many written rules and procedures that exist for doing my major tasks.
44. On my job I have no doubt of what is expected of me.
45. There is little uncertainty in my job.
46. During the past year, my immediate supervisor discussed my work performance with me frequently.
47. My job description clearly specifies the standards of performance on which my job is evaluated.
48. I clearly know what level of work performance is expected from me in terms of amount, quality, and time lines of output.

Scoring Scales

Scale 1: Management support for corporate entrepreneurship

Statement

1	1	2	3	4	5
2	1	2	3	4	5
3	1	2	3	4	5
4	1	2	3	4	5
5	1	2	3	4	5
6	1	2	3	4	5
7	1	2	3	4	5
8	1	2	3	4	5
9	1	2	3	4	5
10	1	2	3	4	5
11	1	2	3	4	5
12	1	2	3	4	5
13	1	2	3	4	5
14	1	2	3	4	5
15	1	2	3	4	5
16	1	2	3	4	5
17	1	2	3	4	5
18	1	2	3	4	5
19	1	2	3	4	5

Subtotals: _____ + _____ + _____ + _____ + _____ = _____

Scale Score = Total Score (19): _____

■ **TABLE 14.5**

Scale 2: Work Discretion

Statement

Statement					
20	1	2	3	4	5
*21	5 = 1	4 = 2	3	2 = 4	1 = 5
22	1	2	3	4	5
23	1	2	3	4	5
24	1	2	3	4	5
25	1	2	3	4	5
26	1	2	3	4	5
27	1	2	3	4	5
28	1	2	3	4	5
29	1	2	3	4	5

Subtotals: _____ + _____ + _____ + _____ + _____ = _____

Scale Score = Total Score (10): _____

*Item 21 is reverse-scored

Scale 3: Rewards/Reinforcement

Statement

Statement					
30	1	2	3	4	5
31	1	2	3	4	5
32	1	2	3	4	5
33	1	2	3	4	5
34	1	2	3	4	5
35	1	2	3	4	5

Subtotals: _____ + _____ + _____ + _____ + _____ = _____

Scale Score-Total Score (6): _____

Scale 4: Time Availability

Statement

Statement					
*36	5 = 1	4 = 2	3	2 = 4	1 = 5
37	1	2	3	4	5
38	1	2	3	4	5
*39	5 = 1	4 = 2	3	2 = 4	1 = 5
*40	5 = 1	4 = 2	3	2 = 4	1 = 5
41	1	2	3	4	5

Subtotals: _____ + _____ + _____ + _____ + _____ = _____

Scale Score = Total Score (6): _____

*Items 36, 39, and 40 are reverse-scored

continued

■ **TABLE 14.5**

CONTINUED

Scale 5: Organizational Boundaries

Statement

*42	5 = 1	4 = 2	3	2 = 4	1 = 5
*43	5 = 1	4 = 2	3	2 = 4	1 = 5
*44	5 = 1	4 = 2	3	2 = 4	1 = 5
*45	5 = 1	4 = 2	3	2 = 4	1 = 5
46	1	2	3	4	5
*47	5 = 1	4 = 2	3	2 = 4	1 = 5
*48	5 = 1	4 = 2	3	2 = 4	1 = 5

Subtotals: _____ + _____ + _____ + _____ + _____ = _____

Scale Score-Total Score (6): _____

*Items 42, 43, 44, 45, 47, and 48 are reverse-scored

■ **TABLE 14.6**

COMMON DIMENSIONS THAT ENHANCE ENTREPRENEURIAL ACTIVITY WITHIN ORGANIZATIONS

Factor	Research Citations
Appropriate Use of Rewards	Scanlon, 1981; Souder, 1981; Kanter, 1985; Sathe, 1985; Fry, 1987; Block & Ornati, 1987; Sykes, 1992; Barringer & Milkovich, 1998.
Management Support	Souder, 1981; Quinn, 1985; Hisrich & Peters, 1986; Sykes, 1986; MacMillan, Block, & Narasimha, 1986; Sykes & Block, 1989; Stevenson & Jarillo, 1990; Damanpour, 1991; Kuratko et al., 1993; Pearce, Kramer, & Robbins, 1997.
Resource Availability	Von Hippel, 1977; Souder, 1981; Sathe, 1985; Kanter, 1985; Sykes, 1986; Hisrich & Peters, 1986; Katz & Gartner, 1988; Sykes & Block, 1989; Damanpour, 1991; Stopford & Baden-Fuller, 1994; Das & Teng, 1997; Slevin & Covin, 1997; Burgelman & Sayles, 1986.
Organizational Structure	Souder, 1981; Burgelman, 1983; Sathe, 1985; Hisrich & Peters, 1986; Sykes, 1986; Schuler, 1986; Burgelman & Sayles, 1986; Bird, 1988; Sykes & Block, 1989; Guth & Ginsberg, 1990; Damanpour, 1991; Covin & Slevin, 1991; Zahra, 1991; Zahra, 1993; Brazeal, 1993; Hornsby et al., 1993; Naman & Slevin, 1993.
Risk Taking	Burgelman, 1983; Burgelman, 1984; Sathe, 1985; Kanter, 1985; Quinn, 1985; MacMillan, Block, & Narasimha, 1986; Sykes, 1986; Ellis & Taylor, 1988; Bird, 1988; Sykes & Block, 1989; Sathe, 1989; Stopford & Baden-Fuller, 1994.

SOURCE: Adapted from Hornsby, J. F., D. F. Kuratko, and R. V. Montagno. 1999. "Perceptions of Internal Factors for Corporate Entrepreneurship: A Comparison of Canadian and U.S. Managers," *Entrepreneurship Theory & Practice* 24, No. 2: 11.

Based on an analysis of these consistent elements in the available research, Kuratko, Montagno, and Hornsby (1990) developed a multidimensional scale consisting of five factors to summarize the major subdimensions of the concept of entrepreneurship in organizations. These dimensions include: management support for corporate entrepreneurship, reward and resource availability, organizational structure and boundaries, risk-taking, and time availability. Subsumed under each of these factors were various procedures and policies that may exist in an organizational setting.

This scale provides an organization the opportunity to measure five distinct internal factors that should be recognized in promoting entrepreneurial activities within an organization. These factors represent a parsimonious description of the internal organizational characteristics that influence middle managers to foster entrepreneurial activity.

The instrument also has practical implications for managers. As just one example, the CEAI can be used as an assessment tool for evaluating corporate training needs in the areas of entrepreneurship and innovation. Companies have initiated such programs over the years to identify areas that require attention if the firm is to encourage entrepreneurial and risk-taking activities (Kuratko and Montagno 1989; McWilliams 1993). The results of one empirical analysis indicated that a training program designed to enhance corporate entrepreneurship significantly affected perceptions of the environment by managers (Kuratko, Montagno, and Hornsby 1990). Therefore, the instrument can be used as a diagnostic tool for determining areas where training may be needed if a company is considering initiating corporate entrepreneurship activities. Determining these training needs can set the stage for improving middle managers' skills and increasing their sensitivity to the challenges of building and supporting a corporate entrepreneurship program.

DEVELOPING A CONTINUOUS ENTREPRENEURIAL PROCESS

When developing a continuous entrepreneurial process in organizations, today's managers need to follow the examples of the quality movement mentioned earlier in this chapter. Some of the key ingredients of this quality movement have clear applications in developing an entrepreneurial process (Juran 1989). Three of those ingredients are recognize managers, conquer fear, and accept the process as a continuous challenge.

RECOGNIZE MANAGERS

Recognition takes a number of different forms, including financial rewards, days off, vacation trips, choice parking spots (typically for a week or a month), pictures placed on the "Manager of the Month" wall, and names added to a plaque of distinguished managers. The latter are often displayed prominently in one area of the

building and are typically referred to as walls (or halls) of fame. Although companies will develop their own recognition system, there are a handful of characteristics that apply to all efforts: 1) recognition should always be positive and should be
given to those actions that have resulted in success; 2) recognition should be given
openly and should be publicized throughout the company or division; 3) recognition should be carefully tailored to the needs of the people so that everyone is motivated to pursue the reward; 4) rewards should be given soon after they have been
earned; and 5) the relationship between the achievement and the reward should be
clearly understood by the personnel.

At Marlow Industries (located in Dallas, Texas), in addition to the company's
Hall of Fame, other awards include service awards, perfect attendance awards,
good housekeeping awards, team recognition awards, individual team bonuses,
and profit sharing. Marlow Industries is a $12-million-per-year company with 160
employees. At San Jose, California based Solectron, there are a series of awards
including the chairman/CEO award, which is given for performance, innovation,
and invention. This company employs 22,000 worldwide with sales reaching
$89 billion.

CONQUERING FEAR

Conquering fear is a principal element for successful entrepreneurial programs.
People fear change, expression of opinions (especially negative ones), taking the
initiative on projects, making decisions, and failing. Mostly this fear arises out of
the perceived outcomes that face the employee.

The Wallace Company of Houston, Texas is a prime example of this characteristic. The company filed for Chapter 11 bankruptcy after winning the Malcolm
Baldrige Award for Quality (the U.S. Chamber of Commerce National Award).
The demands of winning caused everyone in the company to fear changing anything. Financial difficulties were encountered and even though cutbacks and lay-
offs were necessary, management failed to make the tough decisions. Ironically, it
was the quality improvement process that originally brought the Wallace Company through difficult times. Because people had been involved in meetings, discussions, and quality efforts, there had been a willingness to speak out, admit
mistakes, and reorganize.

CONTINUOUS IMPROVEMENT

The continuous improvement process is typically viewed as incremental and addi-
tive, rather than explosive and revolutionary. It is usually characterized more by
"rapid inching" than by dramatic, totally disruptive progress. This concept means
organizations would rather move a foot each day than remain where they are for an
indefinite period of time while waiting to make a giant leap forward. A close look at
the nature of the continuous improvement process helps explain the logic behind it.

Continuous improvement actually relies on two developments: consistent,
incremental gains and radical innovation. This is similar to the difference between

■ **TABLE 14.7**

A COMPARISON OF CONSTANT IMPROVEMENT AND INNOVATION

	Constant Incremental Improvement	Radical Innovation
1. Effect	Long term and long lasting but undramatic	Short term but dramatic
2. Pace	Small steps	Big steps
3. Time frame	Continuous and incremental	Intermittent and non-incremental
4. Change	Gradual and constant	Abrupt and volatile
5. Involvement	Everybody	A select few "champions"
6. Approach	Collectivism, group efforts, systems approach	Rugged individualism, individual ideas and efforts
7. Mode	Maintenance and improvement	Scrap and rebuild
8. Spark	Conventional know-how and state of the art	Technological breakthroughs, new inventions, new theories
9. Practical requirements	Little investigation, great effort to maintain improvement	Large investigation, little effort to maintain improvement
10. Effort orientation	People	Technology
11. Evaluation criteria	Process and efforts for better results	Results for profit
12. Advantage	Works well in slow-growth economy	Better suited to fast-growth economy

SOURCE: Adapted from Hodgetts, R. M., D. F. Kuratko, and J. S. Hornsby. 1999. "Quality Implementation in Small Business: Perspectives from the Baldridge Award Winners," *SAM Advanced Management Journal* 64, No. 1 (Winter): 37–47.

incremental and radical innovation discussed in Chapter 7. While the latter is certainly desired, companies give it less emphasis because it is unpredictable and non-incremental. Organizations seem to understand the distinction between continuous incremental improvements and radical innovation but to concentrate exclusively on the former. An exception is Zytec Corporation, of Redwood Falls, Minnesota. The company trains employees to appreciate the fact that radical innovation can move a company from one level to another but that constant improvement helps the firm improve further while waiting for an innovative leap forward. Thus, while radical innovation is critical at Zytec, constant improvement is viewed as a more critical factor in the overall picture. Table 14.7 provides a comparison of these two processes and helps illustrate why both are needed and the challenge is to strike the right balance.

SUMMARY AND CONCLUSIONS

In this chapter, we examined the framework of planning for corporate entrepreneurship, the methods currently available for assessment and measurement, and the importance of continued process improvement in every phase of the entrepreneurial strategy.

Planning is essential to the success of any undertaking. Carefully prepared entrepreneurial plans are simply the formulation of goals, objectives, and directions

"WHIRLPOOL HOUSE GRADUATES"

Real World + Whirlpool Sales Trainers = Real Whirled. But instead of 24/7 dramatic video coverage, these residents are pitching sales techniques at each other, turning themselves into product experts, and entertaining executives at all hours of the day. Real Whirled participants are those that will be training the sales associates in stores like Home Depot and Sears and telling them why Whirlpool products are better than the competition. Now, when a customer says "So what?" to a salesperson about an appliance feature, that customer will get a valid answer.

We are led to wonder what could possibly cause the number one major appliance manufacturer in the world to put eight market-training representatives in one house for two months. The live-in concept arose from Whirlpool's realization that it wasn't focusing enough on the consumer — taboo in the new economy. In the last decade, Whirlpool has been unable to find a growth avenue worth pursuing in the domestic market. Even with nine impressive brand names, 60,000 employees, and 1999 net sales of $10.5 billion, Whirlpool wants more than to be happy with the way things are. "It seems like such a no-brainer, but we tend to get away from spending time with the consumer," states Jackie Seib, the national manager of training for sales and operations.

The whole experience has taught the "house graduates" a few new things. First, *those who do, teach.* One graduate believes what he says when he tells managers and customers that a particular washing machine is the quietest he's ever used. Second, graduates have learned to empathize with the customer because *real life has real problems.* Third, learning the importance of *selling solutions instead of specifications* means that customers will get what they really need, not something that's beyond their budget. Last, to *create a compelling buying experience* is to create a customer for life. These four phrases can and should fit into any organization if it plans to cultivate and keep its customers.

With 40 million sold annually, the home appliance industry has long been in a stage of maturity in the United States. This fact has driven Whirlpool not only to focus on providing the best available customer service but also to match its established U.S. leadership in the global market. Whirlpool is way ahead of the competition as number one in both North America and Latin America. Worldwide, it has plenty of room to build on its strengths. It is only number three in Europe and remains as a growing force in Asia. The company seeks to set the standards against which the global major domestic appliance industry is measured. Based on strategies like Real Whirled and the networked home solutions initiative (partnership with Cisco and Sun Microsystems) and with record sales throughout the company in 1999, Whirlpool is on the right path in the pursuit of excellence.

SOURCE: Balu, R. 1999. "Whirlpool Gets Real with Customers," *Fast Company* 30 (December): 74–75; 2000. www.whirlpool.com."

for the future of an innovative concept. The absence of a plan could mean failure before efforts have even really begun.

As the organization aggressively pursues the future, there needs to be a continual assessment or measurement of the actual levels of entrepreneurial activity and the results produced. If corporate entrepreneurship is to succeed as a viable strategy for today's organizations, then there must be a recognition of the measurement process to validate the methods employed for entrepreneurial activity. Rather than becoming merely a *program* for a company to institute, corporate entrepreneurship needs to be a *process* that infiltrates and permeates the entire organization, very much like the quality movement which addressed the measurement and assessment factors of systems and procedures to develop the processes better. In this same manner, the corporate entrepreneurship activities must be measured and assessed for their effectiveness.

Organizations that commit to the planning of the corporate entrepreneurial process and carefully measure and assess its progress will realize a number of benefits. Kuratko, Ireland, and Hornsby (2001) examined the gains experienced by one corporation through the power of entrepreneurial actions. They found a number of significant results including the following: 1) increased quality of output; 2) greater competitiveness; 3) higher profitability; 4) the opportunity to use a participative management approach that allows employees to play a role in decision making; and 5) a way of learning from past experiences and using this information to achieve realistic, attainable entrepreneurial goals.

To achieve these objectives, companies have two routes: they can lead from strength by doing what they do best, and/or they can work to correct mistakes and deficiencies. Entrepreneurial firms rely on both of these approaches, although they place strongest emphasis on the first, identifying those processes or systems at which they are most successful and working to improve these still further. In a manner of speaking, they follow the "attack yourself" rule by analyzing their faults and aiming to get better and better. In the process, they become entrepreneurial leaders.

REFERENCES

Banta, T. W., J. P. Lund, K. E. Black, and F. W. Oblander. 1996. *Assessment in Practice.* San Francisco: Jossey-Bass.

Burgelman, R. A. 1984. "Designs for Corporate Entrepreneurship," *California Management Review* 26: 154–166.

Covin, J. G. and D. P. Slevin. 1990. "New Venture Strategic Posture, Structure, and Performance: An Industry Life Cycle Analysis," *Journal of Business Venturing* 5, No. 2 (March): 123–125.

Covin, J. G., and D. P. Slevin. 1991. "A Conceptual Model of Entrepreneurship as Firm Behavior," *Entrepreneurship Theory and Practice* 16, No. 1 (Fall): 7–25.

Covin, J. G., D. P. Slevin, and M. B. Heeley. 2000. "Pioneers and Followers: Competitive Tactics, Environment, and Firm Growth," *Journal of Business Venturing* 15: 175–210.

Davis, D., M. Morris, and J. Allen. 1991. "Perceived Environmental Turbulence and Its Effect on Selected Entrepreneurship, Marketing, and Organizational Characteristics in Industrial Firms," *Journal of Academy of Marketing Science* 19 (Spring): 43–51.

Hamel, G., and C. E. Prahalad. 1991. "Corporate Imagination and Expeditionary Marketing," *Harvard Business Review* 69 No. 4: 31–93.

Hodgetts, R. M. 1998. *Measures of High Quality Performance.* New York: Amacom.

Hodgetts, R. M., D. F. Kuratko, and J. S. Hornsby. 1999. "Quality Implementation in Small Business: Perspectives from the Baldrige Award Winners," *SAM Advanced Management Journal* 64, No. 1 (Winter): 37–47.

Hornsby, J. S., D. F. Kuratko, and S. A. Zahra. "Middle Managers' Perception of the Internal Environment for Corporate Entrepreneurship: Assessing a Measurement Scale," *Journal of Business Venturing* (Forthcoming 2002).

Jelinek, M. and J. A. Litterer. 1995. "Toward Entrepreneurial Organizations: Meeting Ambiguity with Engagement," *Entrepreneurship: Theory and Practice* 19, No. 3: 137–168.

Juran, J. M. 1989. *Juran on Leadership for Quality.* New York: Free Press.

Kanter, R. M. 1986. "Supporting Innovation and Venture Development in Established Companies," *Journal of Business Venturing* 1: 47–60.

Kuratko, D. F., and R. V. Montagno. 1989. "The Intrapreneurial Spirit," *Training & Development Journal* 43, No. 10 (October): 83–87.

Kuratko, D. F., R. V. Montagno, and J. S. Hornsby. 1990. "Developing an Intrapreneurial Assessment Instrument for an Effective Corporate Entrepreneurial Environment," *Strategic Management Journal* 11: 49–58.

Kuratko, D. F., R. D. Ireland, and J. S. Hornsby. 2001. "The Power of Entrepreneurial Actions: Insights from Acordia, Inc.," *Academy of Management Executive* (in press).

McWilliams, B. 1993. "Strengths from Within—How Today's Companies Nurture Entrepreneurs," *Enterprise* 6, No. 4 (April): 43–44.

Miller, D., and P. H. Friesen. 1982. "Innovation in Conservative and Entrepreneurial Firms: Two Models of Strategic Momentum," *Strategic Management Journal* 3, No. 1: 1–25.

Morris, M. H., and D. L. Sexton. 1996. "The Concept of Entrepreneurial Intensity," *Journal of Business Research* 36 No. 1: 5–14.

Morse, C. W. 1986. "The Delusion of Intrapreneurship," *Long Range Planning* 19: 92–95.

Peters, T. J., and R. Waterman. 1982. *In Search of Excellence: Lessons from America's Best Run Companies.* New York: Harper & Row.

Schmidt, W. H., and J. P. Finnigan. 1993. *The Race without a Finish Line.* New York: John Wiley & Sons.

Senge, P. M. 1990. *The Fifth Discipline: The Art & Practice of the Learning Organization.* New York: Doubleday.

Zahra, S. A. 1986. "A Canonical Analysis of Corporate Entrepreneurship Antecedents and Impact on Performance," In *Best Paper Proceedings,* edited by J. Pearce and R. Robinson, 46th Annual Meeting, Academy of Management, 71–75.

Zahra, S. A. 1993. "Environment, Corporate Entrepreneurship, and Financial Performance: A Taxonomic Approach," *Journal of Business Venturing* 8, No. 4: 319–340.

Zahra, S. A. 1999. "The Changing Rules of Global Competitiveness in the 21st Century," *Academy of Management Executive* 13, No. 1: 36–42.

Zahra, S. A., D. F. Kuratko, and D. F. Jennings. 1999. "Entrepreneurship and the Acquisition of Dynamic Organizational Capabilities," *Entrepreneurship: Theory & Practice* 23, No. 3: 5–10.

15

ENTREPRENEURSHIP IN GOVERNMENT ORGANIZATIONS

People tend to think of public sector organizations as monopolistic entities facing captive demand, enjoying guaranteed sources and levels of financing, and being relatively immune from the influences of voters, stakeholders, and political institutions such as legislatures and courts. Not only are most of the elements of this stereotype inaccurate, but the contemporary public sector organization also faces unprecedented demands from a society that grows more complex and interdependent by the day.

The external environment of today's public sector organizations can be characterized as highly turbulent, which implies an increasingly dynamic, hostile, and complex set of environmental conditions. One has only to consider the typical public medical facility. There are more beds than patients, competition is arising from entirely new sources, technological change is continuous, medical liability pressures are intense, costs are rising faster than the general rate of inflation, those who cannot pay must be served, and skilled labor is in short supply.

Organizational theory has long held that external change leads to internal adjustments in structure, strategy, and operational methods (Lawrence and Lorsch 1967). Thus, contingency theorists posit that the relatively stable and predictable business environments of the 1950s and 1960s led to the development in the private sector of many large, mechanistic organizations. Alternatively, they suggest that small, more organic structures appear to be more appropriate when organizations are faced with high levels of environmental change (Burgelman 1983; Burns and Stalker 1961; Miller 1983).

A related school of thought suggests that entrepreneurship represents an effective strategic response to environmental turbulence. Discontinuities in the environment threaten existing modes of operation, and they also create numerous opportunities for innovative behavior. When they are conceptualized at the organizational level, there is a growing body of evidence to suggest that, under conditions of turbulence, a company's entrepreneurial orientation is positively associated with numerous measures of corporate performance (Davis, Morris, and Allen 1991; Morris and Sexton 1996; Zahra 1986).

More recently, considerable attention has been devoted to the need for alternative frameworks to guide the management of public sector organizations. Various observers have emphasized a need to reinvent and streamline government and to introduce to the public sector such market-related mechanisms as competition, market segmentation, user fees, and a customer focus (Moody's 1999; Osborne and Gaebler, 1992; Peters 1987). Others have argued for the development of creative, risk-taking cultures inside of public organizations, and, in this context, the term *public sector entrepreneurship* has been introduced (Bellone and Goerle 1992; Doig and Hargrove 1987; Lewis 1980; Ramamurti 1986).

Does entrepreneurship really apply in a public sector context? In this chapter, we will explore this question. A key objective of the chapter is to better integrate principles and concepts from the entrepreneurship literature with perspectives from the public administration literature, a linkage that has largely been ignored. Based on this foundation, priorities are established for the creation of entrepreneurial government organizations.

PERSPECTIVES FROM PUBLIC ADMINISTRATION

Although almost exclusively associated with private sector activity, the term *entrepreneurship* has appeared in the public administration literature with increasing frequency over the past decade. It is a term that is often used loosely and applied in a number of diverse ways. For instance, one stream of research seeks to identify pioneers who have affected dramatic change in public sector organizations (e.g., Cooper and Wright 1992; Doig and Hargrove 1987; Lewis 1980; Ramamurti 1986). The work of Mitchell and Scott (1987) is consistent with this approach. They suggest that entrepreneurship is one of three criteria upon which the legitimacy of real administrative authority rests. These research efforts are grounded in a type of "great man" model, which presupposes that only a select few have the vision and skill necessary to provide substantive leadership in public sector organizations. Thus, Lewis (1980, p. 233) notes, "The outstanding fact that differentiates public entrepreneurs from ordinary managers and politicians is their ability to alter the existing allocation of scarce public resources in fundamental ways."

Entrepreneurship has alternatively been conceptualized in terms of the initiation of political movements or the creation of new public organizations that serve to produce meaningful social, political, or economic change (Adam and Moodley 1986; Drucker 1995; Wilson 1973). Two related contemporary examples might be the impact of the Afrikaner movement through the National Party to introduce statutory "innovations" that served to facilitate apartheid in South Africa over a forty-year period, and the more recent efforts of the African National Congress in facilitating the peaceful move to democracy, majority rule, and a significant reallocation of societal resources. Such movements, rather than being a function of any one person, are more linked to the efforts of groups of dedicated individuals.

A third relevant research stream suggests that entrepreneurship may be a by-product of the application of strategic management and leadership principles to public enterprises (e.g., Nutt and Backoff 1993; Mokwa and Permut 1981). To the extent that strategic management and leadership produce a directed, longer-term, external focus coupled with open communication and participative decision making, public sector organizations are thought to be more likely to identify new opportunities and generate new process and service innovations, thereby affecting organizational transformation (Behn 1991; Davies and Griffiths 1995; Nutt and Backoff 1993).

A fourth approach can be found in the "reinventing government" literature. Popularized by Osborne and Gaebler (1992), the notion of reinventing has generated considerable discussion (Carroll 1996; Fox 1996; Kamesnsky 1996; Khademian 1995; Moe 1994; Sweeney and Hyde 1995). Although criticized for having no theoretical foundation and consisting of disjointed sets of conflicting concepts, principles, and approaches, reinventing government centers around three major initiatives (Fox 1996; Kettle 1995; Reynolds 1994). These include *downsizing,* or reducing the size of government; *reengineering,* or significantly redesigning the processes by which the work of government gets accomplished; and *continuous improvement,* or raising quality standards for service through participative management, bottom-up reform, and intrinsic motivation. Reinvention implies empowered employees who are able to effect innovative solutions to "customer" problems and needs, and the ability to be innovative is believed by advocates to be facilitated by each of these initiatives. Accordingly, employees at the lowest levels are encouraged to act entrepreneurially.

Yet another pertinent research stream concerns privatization (Moore 1992; Savas 1987; Savas 1992). Privatization entails reducing public sector involvement in service provision by effectively outsourcing certain responsibilities to the private sector. Thus, the public sector is leveraging resources by encouraging entrepreneurship in private firms.

These differing approaches suggest an acknowledgment of the potential applicability of entrepreneurship to public sector management, but there is little consensus as to what this means. The fact that concepts and theories from the corporate entrepreneurship literature have not been applied to a public sector context raises important questions. Is this because the work on corporate entrepreneurship is context specific and therefore limited in its perceived usefulness? Are public sector organizations so different that they require an entirely different theoretical approach? Let us explore these issues in more detail.

REVISITING CORE CONCEPTS OF ENTREPRENEURSHIP

As noted in other parts of this book, the term *entrepreneurship* has historically referred to the efforts of an individual who takes on the odds in translating a vision into a successful business enterprise. In this book, we have approached entrepreneurship as a *process* that can occur in organizations of all sizes and types. Thus, we talk of "creating value by bringing together a unique combination of resources to exploit an opportunity" (Stevenson, Roberts, and Grousbeck 1989).

As we have seen in earlier chapters, this process requires both an entrepreneurial event and an entrepreneurial agent. The event refers to the creation of a new product, service, process, or entity. The agent is an individual or group who assumes personal responsibility for bringing the event to fruition. Further, the entrepreneurial process has attitudinal and behavioral components. Attitudinally, it refers to the willingness of an individual or organization to embrace new opportunities and take responsibility for effecting creative change. Behaviorally, the process includes the set of activities required to (a) identify and evaluate an opportunity; (b) define a business concept; (c) identify the needed resources; (d) acquire the necessary resources; and (e) implement, operate, and harvest the venture.

In Chapter 3, it was noted that entrepreneurial attitudes and behaviors have three key underlying dimensions of innovativeness, risk-taking, and proactiveness. To the extent that an undertaking demonstrates some amount of innovativeness, risk-taking, and proactiveness, it can be considered an entrepreneurial event and the person behind it can be considered an entrepreneur. Further, any number of entrepreneurial events can be produced in a given time period. Accordingly, entrepreneurship is a question of degree and frequency. Organizations can be characterized, then, in terms of their entrepreneurial orientation or intensity, which is a reflection both of how many entrepreneurial things they are doing and how innovative, risky, and proactive those things tend to be.

APPLICATION OF THESE CORE CONCEPTS TO THE PUBLIC SECTOR

In spite of the growing attention devoted to the phenomenon, a generally accepted definition of public sector entrepreneurship has yet to emerge. Examples of proposed definitions include the following:

- An active approach to administrative responsibility that includes generating new sources of revenue, providing enhanced services, and helping to facilitate increased education and involvement of citizens (Bellone and Goerle 1992);

- A continuous attempt to apply resources in new ways so as to heighten the efficiency and effectiveness of public institutions (Osborne and Gaebler 1992);

- The purposeful and organized search for innovative changes in public sector organizations and operations (Linden 1990).

Themes that emerge from these definitions include the notion that a process is involved, that entrepreneurship is ongoing, and that the end result is innovative, proactive behavior. Each of these notions is consistent with the mainstream entrepreneurship literature as discussed above. Building on that literature and these themes, we can make minor modifications to the efforts of Stevenson and his colleagues at Harvard to produce the following working definition: *Public sector entrepreneurship is the process of creating value for citizens by bringing together unique combinations of public and/or private resources to exploit social opportunities.*

The basic steps in this process that were identified earlier should be no different in a public sector context. Figure 15.1 provides an example of the application of these steps to a public university. Some of the tools and concepts from the private sector that are useful when trying to understand or facilitate developments in each stage of the process are equally applicable in the public sector (e.g., window of opportunity, leveraging of resources), while others must be adapted (e.g., criteria for evaluating an opportunity, sources of entrepreneurial concepts, harvesting strategies), and still others are not really applicable (e.g., competitive entry wedge, criteria for selecting financing sources).

Entrepreneurship also has the same underlying dimensions when applied in a public context. However, innovativeness will tend to be more concerned with novel process improvements, new services, and new organizational forms. Examples might include voter registration from our automobiles, day-care service for a welfare mother in a job training program, or a public/private joint venture to address AIDS awareness. Risk-taking involves pursuing initiatives that have a calculated likelihood of resulting in loss or failure. While public sector organizations cannot incur bankruptcy, failure can result through nondelivered services; cutbacks in service levels, programs, or organizational units; staff reassignments; and budget cuts. While high visibility typically means risk-taking is moderate to low, the public sector does undertake highly risky ventures such as the controversial luggage-handling system at the Denver, Colorado, airport some years ago. There is also career-related risk in the public sector, for although it is difficult to fire people, advancement can be hampered by visible failures. Proactiveness entails an action orientation and an emphasis on anticipating and preventing public sector problems before they occur. This action orientation includes creative interpretation of rules, skills at networking and leveraging of resources, and a high level of persistence and patience in affecting change.

As noted above, an organization's overall entrepreneurial orientation, or intensity, is the result of combining the number of entrepreneurial events that are taking place (frequency) with the extent to which these events are innovative, risky, and proactive (degree). Figure 15.2 represents a graphical representation of entrepreneurial intensity hypothetically applied to six different public organizations. The Social Security department is characterized in terms of few events and events that are not very innovative, risky, and proactive. Alternatively, the public transit authority may be pursuing many events (e.g., new route structures, partnerships with downtown retailers, buses that are vividly painted), each of which is a fairly modest innovation. A very different approach might find the Division of Motor Vehicles not pursuing that many events, but the ones it does implement are fairly entrepreneurial (e.g., driving examinations in simulators, automobile registration using the Internet). The implication is that different levels of entrepreneurial intensity are appropriate for different public sector organizations and that organizations might pursue different strategies depending on their relative emphasis on frequency versus degree.

■FIGURE 15.1

THE ENTREPRENEURIAL PROCESS APPLIED TO A PUBLIC UNIVERSITY

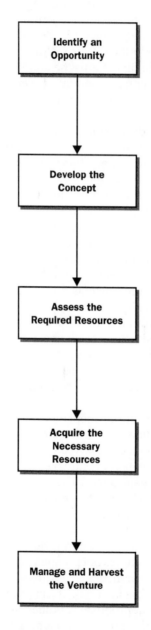

Identify an Opportunity

Changing demographics
Emergence of new market segments
Process needs
New technologies
Funding and regulatory changes
New promotional channels
New sources of funding

Develop the Concept

New organizational structures/forms
New curricula/programs
New satellite campuses/sites
New fund-raising methodologies
New recruitment programs
New tuition financing schemes
New tuition structures

Assess the Required Resources

Needs for skilled employees
Needs for capable students
Needs for funding
Needs for community support
Support from accrediting bodies
Support from professional societies
Support from government agencies

Acquire the Necessary Resources

Early tuition payments
Reliance on faculty expertise
Lobbying efforts with legislatures
Leveraging schemes/outsourcing
Partnerships with NPO's
Joint ventures with companies
Licensing of inventions and new knowledge
Barter
Debt
Gifts
Profits from university-run businesses

Manage and Harvest the Venture

Implementation of business concept
Monitoring of performance
Payback to resource providers
Achievement of performance goals
Absorption of new business concept into mainstream
Operations
Shutdown of venture

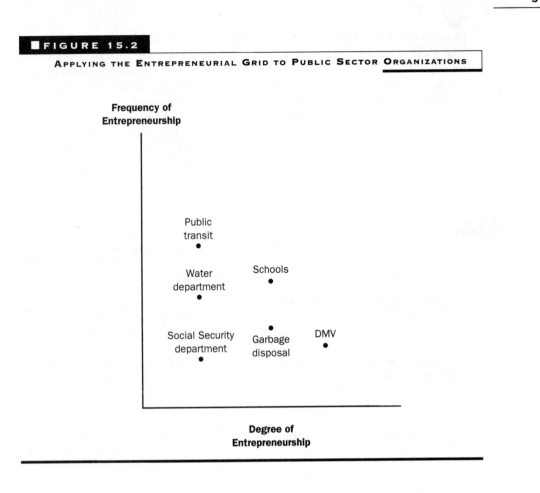

■FIGURE 15.2

APPLYING THE ENTREPRENEURIAL GRID TO PUBLIC SECTOR ORGANIZATIONS

UNIQUE CHARACTERISTICS OF PUBLIC SECTOR ORGANIZATIONS

When applied to existing firms, entrepreneurship takes on distinct characteristics and becomes subject to a number of obstacles and constraints not found in most independent start-ups. The magnitude of these constraints has led many to conclude that unique approaches to organizational design and management are necessary if entrepreneurship is to be facilitated on an ongoing basis (Cornwall and Perlman 1990; Harvard Business Review 1995; Jennings & Seaman 1990; Tropman and Morningstar 1989). At the same time, the literature on corporate entrepreneurship is relatively limited and focuses almost exclusively on large private sector organizations. As such, little guidance has been provided regarding its application in other contexts, most notably the public sector.

On the surface, public sector entrepreneurship would seem to have much in common with entrepreneurship in a large corporation. Both types of organizations typically have formalized hierarchies; established stakeholder groups with competing demands; deeply entrenched cultures; detailed rules and procedures to guide operations; a desire on the part of managers for power and security; and fairly rigid systems governing financial controls, cost allocations, budgeting, and employee rewards. Managers in both types of organizations are often more concerned with internal than external developments, and tend to focus more on considerations of process than on outcomes. Further, they are not independent, do not "own" the innovations they develop, and confront very finite limits on the rewards that they can receive. They have more job security, are not personally

■ TABLE 15.1

MANAGEMENT IN BUSINESS AND GOVERNMENT

Management Variables	Private Sector	Public Sector
Goals	Focused, opportunity driven, externally linked, hierarchical	Complex, problem driven, internally linked, subject to ongoing adjustments as government responds to interest group pressures
Governability	Shareholder control exercised through directors and key managers	Consensus and diversity driven, governments operate within a comfort zone and adjust implementation priorities to achieve this
Planning and control	Plans are a general mandate for both action and evaluation Control focuses on profits and business results	Plans focus on long-term government objectives Short-term control is through detailed control of staffing, budgetary, and purchasing inputs; long-term control seldom looks beyond electoral success or failure
Budgets	A vehicle for implementation and control	A vehicle for the negotiation of comfort zones and for demonstrating respect for diverse needs A vehicle for managing complex allocative tensions
Communication	Development of common values, communicating change, evaluation of results	Defusing problems, developing support for solutions Maintenance of comfort zones
Core management values	Strategic, performance, and results oriented Key success criterion is business success	Delivery of services within the constraints generated by budgets and comfort zones Equality of treatment Key success criteria—complex, nonmarket driven Avoiding failure, maintaining support for government

SOURCE: Cullen, R. B., and D. P. Cushman. 2000. *Transitions to Competitive Government.* Albany, N.Y.: State University of New York, 46.

assuming the financial risks associated with the project, and have access to an established pool of resources.

Alternatively, characteristics that distinguish public sector organizations from private firms have been explored by various authors (Bower 1977; Cullen and Cushman 2000; Rainey, Backoff, and Levine 1976). With such comparisons, one must keep in mind the considerable diversity that exists among organizations in both sectors and particularly among those in the public sector. Some key differences are summarized in Table 15.1. Briefly, public sector organizations:

- Do not have a profit motive, and instead are guided by social and political objectives; typically seek to achieve a multiplicity and diversity of objectives; these objectives and performance toward them are harder to measure;
- Have less exposure to the market and its incentives for cost reductions, operating economies, and efficient resource allocation; resources tend to be allocated based on equity or fairness considerations and political pressures;
- Receive funds indirectly from an involuntary taxpayer rather than directly from a satisfied and voluntary customer;
- Have difficulties in identifying the organization's "customer," because there are typically a number of different publics being served by a given agency, department, or unit;
- Produce services that have consequences for others beyond those immediately involved; have greater accountability for the indirect consequences of their actions;
- Are subject to public scrutiny, such that major decisions have to be made with transparency; decisions must involve consensus among and consultation with a variety of interest groups and constituencies;
- Face risk/reward trade-offs that strongly favor avoiding mistakes.

These differences raise fundamental questions regarding not simply whether entrepreneurship *can* be applied in public enterprises but also whether it *should* be applied.

IS PUBLIC SECTOR ENTREPRENEURSHIP REALLY VIABLE?

Public employees are not in a position to put taxpayer monies at significant risk, and this, combined with the difficulties in measuring risk/return trade-offs in the public sector, usually makes high-risk pursuits inappropriate. In addition, high visibility and a need for consensus in decision making suggest that incremental change is more realistic than bold innovation. Also, the lengthy periods of time required for an entrepreneurial event to unfold are inconsistent with public sector budgeting and reelection cycles. Moreover, bureaucracy and the civil service system serve to protect the status quo, ostensibly from the arbitrary or politically influenced behavior of political leaders and public executives. Because entrepreneurship often involves disrupting the status quo and effecting organizational change, again there would seem to be a potential inconsistency.

At a more fundamental level, some might argue that entrepreneurship can result in innovative devices (e.g., user fees, redevelopment agencies, off-budget enterprises, investment revenues, tax-increment financing, and development fees) for circumventing voter approval and increasing the autonomy of public officials and public administrators, thereby undermining democracy. Further, entrepreneurship entails the pursuit of opportunity regardless of resources currently controlled, while public sector managers are limited often by legislative or regulatory statute to using only those resources formally assigned to their organizations. Finally, the mission, structure, and major initiatives of the public organization are dictated from outside sources (legislative bodies, councils, authorities). Public managers are expected to implement these dictates in a reasonably effective and efficient manner. Entrepreneurship, alternatively, represents an internal dynamic that can serve to redirect the strategic course of an organization, potentially putting it in conflict with its stated mission or mandate. Similarly, entrepreneurial efforts can lead public enterprises to generate new services or fund-raising schemes that effectively put them in competition with private sector enterprises, which the private sector might argue is a form of unfair competition.

The counterargument is that there have always been elements of innovation and entrepreneurship in public sector organizations (e.g., Jordan 1990; Moore 1983) and that the issue is more one of formally defining the entrepreneurial role and then determining appropriate degrees and frequencies of entrepreneurship for a given organization or unit. Returning to our definition, creating value for customers, putting resources together in unique ways, and being opportunity driven are not inherently in conflict with the purpose of public agencies. There is, we could further suggest, a growing need for entrepreneurial approaches in public administration. The contemporary environment confronting public sector managers is far more complex, threatening, and dynamic than in years past. The ability of organizations to recognize and adequately respond to their changing circumstances is severely limited not only by resources but also by the management philosophies and structures that characterize public enterprises.

Bureaucracy has many advantages and can be quite effective when an organization is operating in a relatively stable and predictable environment. However, when the organization is faced with circumstances in which funding is not dependable, client demographics and needs are in flux, technology is rapidly changing, social and environmental pressures are increasing, skilled labor shortages are the norm, citizens are calling for privatization, litigation is rampant, and a host of other discontinuities continue to present themselves, the bureaucratic framework fails to provide the flexibility, adaptability, speed, or incentives for innovation that are critical for effectively carrying out the mission of the public enterprise. There are, of course, different degrees of bureaucratization, and the higher the degree, the greater the potential conflict with entrepreneurship.

Bellone and Goerle (1992) agree that potential conflicts do exist between public entrepreneurship and democracy but suggest that these can be bridged with what

■ **TABLE 15.2**

COMPARING INDEPENDENT, CORPORATE, AND PUBLIC SECTOR ENTREPRENEURS

	Independent Entrepreneur	Corporate Entrepreneur	Public Sector Entrepreneur
Primary motive	Wants freedom; goal orientated and self-reliant; achievement motivated	Wants freedom and access to corporate resources; goal orientated and self-motivated, but also responds to corporate rewards and recognition	Power motivated and achievement motivated; may think in grandiose terms; not constrained by profit motive
Time orientation	End goals of 5–10 year growth of the business	End goals of 3–15 years, depending on type of venture	End goals of 10–15 years; begins with impressive short-term success and then implements long-term plan as series of short-term programs
Skills	Knows business intimately; more business acumen than managerial or political skills	Strong technical skills or product knowledge; good managerial skills; weak political skills	Strong political skills; able to develop power sources beyond those formally assigned; adept at using public relations and the media to advantage
Attitude toward system	Frustrated by system, so rejects it and starts his or her own	Dislikes system but learns to work within it and manipulate it	Tends to redesign or restructure the system to accomplish his or her own ends
Focus	External; markets and technology	Internal and external; builds internal networks and finds mentors or sponsors	Learns to co-opt or use external forces to accomplish internal change; builds constituencies of support among politicians, unions, the private sector, the media, and the community
Risks and failure	Assumes considerable financial and personal risk; clearly identifies key risk factors and tries to minimize them; sees failure as learning experience	Likes moderate risks; principal risks are career related; sensitive to need to appear orderly within corporation; hides risky projects so can learn from mistakes without political cost of public failure	Calculated risk-taker; takes big organizational risks without taking big personal risks by managing the process by which risky decisions are made; tends to deviate from rules only slightly at first, then progressively more; since failure is harder to define, will manage events to promote positive outcomes
Courage and destiny	Self-confident, optimistic, bold	Self-confident, optimistic, bold; cynical about the system but believes he or she can manipulate it	Self-confident, optimistic, bold; high tolerance for ambiguity; uses ambiguity as a source of managerial discretion

they refer to as a *civic-regarding entrepreneurship.* This concept emphasizes accountability in that the principles of democratic theory are incorporated into the design of any entrepreneurial initiatives. In noting that "a strong theory of public entrepreneurship requires a strong theory of citizenship" (p.133), they argue that such initiatives should be developed in ways that facilitate citizen education and participation.

They cite as examples of ways to accomplish such participation citizen budget committees, advisory boards, vehicles for elevating citizen choice (e.g., vouchers), and volunteerism.

In practice, the public sector entrepreneur confronts unique obstacles. Ramamurti (1986) discusses multiplicity and ambiguity of goals, limited managerial autonomy and high political interference, high visibility, skewed reward systems, a short-term orientation (reinforced by budget and election cycles), and restrictive personnel policies. To these we would add lack of competitive incentives for improved performance, difficulties in segmenting or discriminating among users, and lack of accountability among managers for innovation and change. Approached differently, however, obstacles such as these can be used to facilitate entrepreneurial behavior. For instance, goal ambiguity is a potential source of discretion to the entrepreneurial manager, the media can be used as a source of power, and outsiders can be co-opted to enable public sector managers to take organizational risks without taking personal risks (Ramamurti, 1986).

This brings us to a final question: "Who is the public entrepreneur?" Perhaps the most researched issue in the entrepreneurship literature has involved identifying the psychological and sociological traits associated with the entrepreneurial personality. Pinchot (1985) has taken this work further in attempting to characterize the corporate entrepreneur and contrast him/her with the start-up entrepreneur. In Table 15.2, we have attempted to extend Pinchot's efforts (see Chapter Five) to incorporate findings on the public sector entrepreneur. The key characteristics being proposed include the following: a mix of power and achievement motivation; an ability to work strategically, beginning with small steps; strong political and external networking skills; calculated risk-taking; self-confidence; and an ability to tolerate and use ambiguity as a source of discretion. Further, and in spite of the inherent obstacles, the public sector work environment may represent a level of ambiguity, flex, and contradiction in values such that there is room for the entrepreneur to develop and act on such characteristics.

Although an integration of concepts from the entrepreneurship literature with those from public administration provides a conceptual foundation from which to approach public sector entrepreneurship, it is also helpful to consider the perspectives of those who actually work in the public sector.

PERSPECTIVES FROM PUBLIC SECTOR MANAGERS

In a recent study (Morris and Jones 1999), a large cross-section of public sector managers was surveyed for the purpose of gaining insights into their attitudes and opinions on the nature and role of entrepreneurship in their organizations. These managers were asked to identify individual and organizational characteristics they most associated with entrepreneurship in the public sector. Findings are summarized in Table 15.3. At the level of the individual, entrepreneurship was most associated with the following: self-confidence, strong drive, strong leadership abilities,

■ **TABLE 15.3**

PUBLIC SECTOR MANAGER—PERCEPTIONS OF PERSONAL AND ORGANIZATIONAL CHARACTERISTICS ASSOCIATED WITH ENTREPRENEURSHIP

	Mean	Standard Deviation
The Entrepreneurial Person*		
Self-confident	1.62	.77
Strong drive	1.70	.76
Strong leadership abilities	1.74	.79
Good organizer	1.79	.77
Self-disciplined	1.81	.78
Vision	1.81	.93
Action-oriented	1.84	.92
Persistent	1.87	.80
Good analytical skills	1.95	.84
Independent	1.99	.92
Resourceful	2.04	.93
Bold	2.05	.92
Concerned for public good	2.25	1.08
Strong moral values	2.29	1.02
Risk-taker	2.42	1.09
Good political skills	3.22	1.20
Good political connections	3.38	1.13
Lucky	3.62	1.12
The Entrepreneurial Organization*		
Strong leader at the top	1.86	.96
Good planning system	1.95	.95
Customer-driven	2.00	.93
Efficient operations	2.01	.87
Hands-on management	2.02	.97
Leader in the development of new program/services	2.05	.99
Better informed about regulatory policies	2.10	.91
Few layers of management	2.12	1.03
Long-term orientation	2.20	.89
Competitive orientation	2.20	1.03
Willing to pursue risks	2.41	1.03
Long-term funding stability	2.47	1.08
Recruit outside experts	2.61	1.14
Creative system for rewarding employees	2.63	1.32
Tolerant of failure	2.66	1.07
Face pressure to privatize	2.68	1.19
Small in size	2.68	1.28
Protected from political influence	2.93	1.38

*4-point scale: 1 = definitely applies; 4 = does not apply

good organizational skills, vision, and self-discipline. Least associated with the entrepreneurial individual were luck and good political connections. When managers were asked if people with entrepreneurial characteristics are born that way, less than 40 percent expressed agreement.

Alternatively, when it comes to the entrepreneurial organization, a strong leader at the top, good planning systems, a customer-driven orientation, efficient operations, and hands-on management were the leading characteristics. Nearly half (48.6 percent) of respondents associated the term *entrepreneurship* more with a type of person, 8 percent saw it predominantly as an organizational characteristic, and 43.5 percent indicated that it applies equally to both.

In general, the public sector managers saw a role for entrepreneurship in their organizations. When they were asked to respond to the statement "entrepreneurship does not really apply to organizations such as mine," 58.6 percent either disagreed or strongly disagreed. This does, however, suggest that a sizable minority questions the role of entrepreneurship. In a similar vein, ratings of the applicability of entrepreneurship on a 5-point scale from very relevant (equals 1) to not at all relevant (equals 5) produced a mean response of 2.32 (s.d. equals 1.04). At the same time, 86.4 percent perceived that fostering entrepreneurship would have a somewhat positive or significantly positive impact on organizational performance. The leading payoffs from higher levels of entrepreneurship were increased efficiency, productivity (mentioned by 39.9 percent of respondents), improved service delivery (mentioned by 28.2 percent), cost reductions (mentioned by 21.3 percent), improved employee morale (mentioned by 19.1 percent), and reduced dependency on tax revenue (mentioned by 9 percent).

Respondents also supported the notion that the environment in public sector organizations can be designed in ways that help employees develop their entrepreneurial tendencies (88.5 percent agreed or strongly agreed). When responding to the statement, "No matter how entrepreneurial an individual employee might be, it is virtually impossible for an organization to act entrepreneurial," 62.2 percent of the managers disagreed or strongly disagreed.

As summarized in Table 15.4, respondents generally perceived that the most entrepreneurial individuals could be found in middle management (23.2 percent) and in mainstream functional areas (16.8 percent), both of which overlap with one another, as well as at an executive or senior management level (19.4 percent). The greatest opportunities for entrepreneurship were perceived to exist at the top management level (41.5 percent of responses), in a variety of functional areas throughout the organization (29.2 percent), at a middle management level (12.3 percent), and in service delivery/direct customer contact areas (8.5 percent). The areas in which entrepreneurship is seen as most critical were planning/ organizing/budgeting (33.1 percent), service delivery (28.7 percent), operations (21.9 percent), and human resources (9.5 percent).

In spite of the above, the public sector environment was not seen as being supportive of entrepreneurship. A large majority of respondents either strongly agreed (23 percent) or agreed (54 percent) with the statement, "The civil service environment discourages the entrepreneurial individual," with 7.2 percent disagreeing or

■ **TABLE 15.4**

THE IMPORTANCE OF ENTREPRENEURSHIP WITHIN
SPECIFIC FUNCTIONAL AREAS OF THE FIRM

The Most Entrepreneurial People	%
Middle management	23.2
Top management	11.4
In a variety of functional areas	16.8
Lower management	10.1
All management levels	9.2
Among professionals	7.6
Nonmanagerial levels	5.9
Other	7.8
The Greatest Opportunities for Entrepreneurship	
At top management level	41.5
In a variety of major functional areas/throughout the organization	29.2
At middle management level	12.3
In areas of direct contact with customers	8.5
In small autonomous departments	6.2
Nowhere in the organization	1.5
Other	0.8
Where Entrepreneurship Is Most Critical	
Planning/organizing/budgeting	33.1
Service delivery	28.7
Operations	21.9
Human resources	9.5
Marketing and communications	3.2
Everywhere in organization	2.4
Nowhere in organization	2.4
Other	0.8

strongly disagreeing. Most of the managers (74.1 percent) also indicated agreement with the notion that public sector organizations naturally become less entrepreneurial as they get larger.

The leading obstacles to entrepreneurship, as rated by these managers, are summarized in Table 15.5. Extensive policies/procedures/red tape was identified as the leading obstacle, followed by personnel restrictions (hiring, firing), limitations to amounts of rewards, and limited managerial autonomy. These are quite similar to obstacles identified in the corporate entrepreneurship literature. In fact, distinct public sector characteristics such as multiplicity of goals, high visibility, and difficulties in defining the customer were not rated all that highly as obstacles. In a separate, open-ended question, respondents suggested that the leading obstacles were inadequate rewards and incentives (27.3 percent), bureaucracy and red tape (19.5 percent), and autocratic management (13.6 percent).

■ TABLE 15.5

OBSTACLES TO ACHIEVING ENTREPRENEURSHIP WITHIN
PUBLIC SECTOR ORGANIZATIONS

Obstacle	Rank
Policies/procedures/red tape	1
Restrictions on personnel policies (hiring and firing)	2
Limited size of rewards/competition	3
Limited managerial autonomy	4
Lack of a profile motive	5
Interference from politicians	6
Pressure to emphasize equity over efficiency	7
Ambiguity of goals	8
Lack of competition among organizations	9
Public sector unions	10
Short-term orientation	11
Multiplicity of goals	12
Reward system that penalizes failure	13
High public visibility	14
Difficulty in defining our customers	15

Public sector managers tended to rate their organizations as being only modestly entrepreneurial. Their ratings averaged 2.63 on a 5-point scale, where higher scores indicate more entrepreneurial. Assessments of employee receptivity to change found approximately the same proportions rating employees as receptive as rating them resistant to change. An examination of particular management activities found respondents reporting that the greatest levels of entrepreneurship could be found in training efforts, servicing clients, and delegation of tasks, while the least entrepreneurial activities were compensation of employees and morale-boosting/motivating. Close to two-thirds (63.5 percent) of respondents indicated that their agencies had developed new services or service delivery systems over the past two years, and the median number of such innovations was three.

Finally, respondents made suggestions for the single most important thing that their organizations could do to encourage more entrepreneurship. The leading answers were improved rewards and recognition for innovation and risk-taking (29.1 percent of the responses); active promotion of employee participation, empowerment, and accountability (27.4 percent); and elimination of red tape (7.7 percent).

HOW TO GET THERE

A number of suggestions can be made regarding how government organizations must be transformed. A beginning point is the introduction of market mechanisms, which is much of the theme of Osborne and Gaebler (1992) in *Reinventing Government*. They discuss the need to focus on the following ten themes:

■ *Competition:* finding creative ways to introduce competition and the corresponding incentives for greater efficiency, more resource productivity, greater responsiveness to customers, encouragement of innovation, and enhanced employee morale. Competition can be public versus private, private versus private (e.g., outsourcing to private bidders), or public versus public (e.g, school vouchers).

■ *Citizen empowerment:* involving citizens in ownership and control of services, so that people feel they own the streets, schools, and other public assets.

■ *Focus on outcomes:* measuring results or outcomes of programs, not inputs, such as through the creation of revenue centers.

■ *Mission over rules and regulations:* focusing decisions and resource allocations not on rules, but on the fundamental purpose of the public agency and defining this fundamental purpose in terms of needs of citizens instead of particular services or programs.

■ *Customer orientation:* developing an obsession with customer service and satisfaction, in which the focus is on value creation, customization to diverse groups, management of points of customer contact or interface, service quality, and continuous customer feedback.

■ *Proactiveness:* instilling a focus on the future combined with an emphasis on anticipation and prevention of problems before they occur.

■ *Earning over spending:* searching for nontax revenues, developing creative user-fee structures, charging impact fees, renting out unused or underutilized resources, selling or generating revenue from assets.

■ *Decentralization:* focusing on participatory management, flattened organizational structures, decision making that is pushed down in the organization, empowerment and rewards for champions, more broadly defined jobs and more autonomy, and an expectation of innovation from the bottom up.

■ *Partnerships over adversarial relationships:* working with private sector employers and nonprofit organizations to develop creative solutions to problems and share resources.

■ *Other market mechanisms:* finding creative ways to manage both supply and demand for services such as with impact fees, emissions trading, tax credits, vouchers, incentives to private sector suppliers, and shared risk-taking with private sector and nonprofit organizations.

At the root of Osborne and Gaebler's suggestions is the need to move away from arguments regarding whether there should be less government or more government and instead concentrate on the kind of governance that society wants.

Entrepreneurial governance brings a flexible, dynamic, and innovative approach to the process by which problems are collectively solved and society's needs are met. Government defines itself less in terms of rowing and more in terms of steering. The challenge is not to create bureaucracies that "do," but instead to design nimble units that "lead," that capitalize on opportunity by putting together unique resource combinations.

Useful direction is also provided by Cullen and Cashman (2000), who discuss the transition to competitive government. Table 15.6 summarizes this concept as it relates to government effectiveness, business/government roles, approach to resources, cycle time management, and communication. These authors argue for a strategic approach to affecting this transition. Although their focus is on national government, the approach is applicable to government bodies at all levels. In essence, critical strategic questions are first raised about the three core missions of government: enhanced competitiveness, creation of social value, and governability. Based on the responses to these questions, objectives are established, and elements of a transition strategy are proposed, together with performance benchmarks and verifiable outcomes. Support objectives and strategies are then established for government functions and services and then for five key elements of general management reform: strategic leadership, cycle time management, performance management, comfort zone management, and results-based financial management.

Finally, a more operational perspective is provided by Linden (1990), who proposes an action agenda for public sector managers. His agenda begins with *strategic thinking and acting*. Here, public managers move away from planning for planning's sake and a preoccupation with the plan document itself. Instead, the focus is on a vision of what can be, on thinking strategically, and on determining the elements that need to be in place to have a maximum chance for success with minimal resistance. Next comes *holding on and letting go,* in which the manager lets others interpret and implement the vision; gives some autonomy; and, in a sense, gives up control to gain control. This step is followed by *creating a felt need for change,* in which the manager sells the importance of change, defines change in terms of opportunities for employees, empathizes with fear and resistance to change, and presents disconfirming data regarding assumptions. It is important to *start with small steps,* in which the priority is action, not pronouncements, task forces, or the "paralysis of analysis." The manager attempts to move quickly on an innovation agenda, but one step at a time. Experimentation is stressed, and the manager reinforces those who pick up the banner. The manager also strives to *use structural changes* to reinforce and validate new approaches on the assumption that attitudinal change will follow structural change. Examples include the use of boards of advisers, rotation of department heads, flattening of the structure, and formal roles for citizen participation. Along the way, the manager has mechanisms to *deal with risk,* including efforts to minimize exposure. Risk can be managed by starting new initiatives with volunteers, through the use of pilot projects, and by keeping initial expectations low. The manager does not focus on failures, but instead highlights and rewards accomplishments, while stressing what is being

■ **TABLE 15.6**

TRANSITION FROM TRADITIONAL GOVERNMENT TO COMPETITIVE GOVERNMENT MANAGEMENT

Traditional (Function Driven) Government Management	Competitive (Performance Driven) Government Management
Effective Government	
The government role is to supply services and infrastructure, fund these operations from users and taxpayers, and provide an environment where persons are treated equitably and business can develop.	Effective government is government that adds value by delivering improvements in competitiveness, social value, and governability.
Unless government is failing, it is presumed to be working.	Performance focuses on desired products.
Evaluation cycle dominated by government budget and election cycles.	Evaluation focuses on short-term impacts and relative performance.
Business/Government Roles	
Government sets the business environment. The business role is to generate national competitiveness.	Government and business need to work together to improve societal competitiveness.
Resources	
Government budgets and legislative mandates are used to control allocations and drive priorities.	Resources are a management variable.
Performance is seen as a function of spending allocated resources.	Performance is a function of delivering results on time and within budget.
Cycle Time Management	
The management task is to fit management needs into preset cycles. The emphasis is on queuing customers to fit these preset cycles, reducing risks, and increasing efficiency.	Cycle time management is a key variable to managing the impacts of change and reducing the comfort zone tensions created by change.
Communication	
The key communication task is to take the credit for national progress and to respond to failure by either denying or obscuring it. Where problems must be recognized, the communications task shifts to simple dramatic solutions which defer evaluation.	Cycle-based and proactive communication.
	Impacts are managed as part of a delivery and communication strategy. Expectations and benefits are managed throughout the government planning and implementation cycle.

SOURCE: Cullen, R.B., and D.P. Cushman. 2000. *Transitions to Competitive Government*. Albany: State University of New York, 49.

learned. Lastly, the manager's ability to *use political skills* is especially important. The manager respects the culture of the organization even while attempting to change it. He/she builds coalitions, understands and uses informal networks, seeks common areas of consensus, and develops talents for persuasion.

SUMMARY AND CONCLUSIONS

This chapter has argued that entrepreneurship is a universal construct and can be applied in public sector organizations. The definition, nature of the process, and underlying dimensions of entrepreneurship are fundamentally the same regardless of the context. There are, however, fundamental differences in organizational realities, suggesting that the goals, constraints, approaches, and outcomes related to successful entrepreneurial efforts are unique in public sector organizations.

It would appear that public sector managers increasingly recognize entrepreneurship as a salient concept for their operations. They are coming to perceive entrepreneurship as a key factor in promoting efficiency, improving productivity, and delivering better service to the public. Further, it is applicable at both the individual and organizational levels, but more so at the individual level. At both levels, the traits they associate with entrepreneurship tend to reflect proactiveness and innovativeness more than risk-taking. There is also more emphasis placed on process innovation relative to product or service innovation.

It is noteworthy that some of the most distinctive characteristics of the public enterprise (visibility, multiplicity of goals and constituencies) are not viewed by public sector managers as especially serious obstacles to entrepreneurship. Instead, factors that managers in private companies struggle with, such as red tape and limits on rewards, are the ones also emphasized by public sector managers. There is also a tendency to view middle management and functional area management as being the most entrepreneurial, while perceiving the greatest opportunities for entrepreneurship to lie at a senior management level. And yet, excessive control by top management is viewed as a major obstacle to entrepreneurship. One might conclude that there is a tendency to look "up the organization" for entrepreneurship.

Strong leadership is clearly necessary to overcome an environment that severely constrains entrepreneurial behavior. Senior management must first establish goals and strategies for entrepreneurship. An important component here is the need to determine where within their organizations to place the entrepreneurial priorities. Different degrees and amounts of entrepreneurial behavior would seem appropriate depending on the agency, department, functional area, or other organizational unit of analysis, and managerial expectations should reflect such differences.

It is also imperative that senior management perform the symbolic behaviors that reinforce the priority given to innovative thinking. Employee values and attitudes must be the focal point—especially the tendencies to resist change and to avoid failure at all costs. The facilitation of entrepreneurship comes down to people, individuals who will champion innovation and change. Mintzberg (1996, p.82), in suggesting that public sector professionals need to be freed both from the direct controls of bureaucracy and the narrow pressures of market competition, notes that "government desperately needs a life force . . . there is no substitute for human dedication."

Reward and measurement systems would appear to represent especially useful tools for accomplishing some of this required attitudinal change, yet in practice they appear to serve as a leading obstacle. Training is also important. While it is debatable as to whether someone can be taught to be an entrepreneur, public sector employees would benefit from a better appreciation for the process nature of entrepreneurship, including such issues as opportunity identification and assessment, formulation of plans for new concepts, capitalizing on goal conflict and ambiguity, risk-management strategies, and networking to obtain resources, among others.

There is no formal blueprint or model regarding how entrepreneurship can be accomplished in the public sector. The key appears to be experimentation. While public sector managers do not have the luxury of being able to experiment freely with structures, control systems, rewards, communication systems, or budgeting methods, there is typically more room for flex than acknowledged by so-called "bureaucracy bashers."

Perhaps more significant for interpreting the suggestions made in this chapter is the fact that public sector organizations everywhere confront an erosion of the tax base, significant expansion of the audiences they serve, heightened public visibility and accountability, and strong pressures to reflect diversity and affirmative action requirements. As such, we believe that the discussion here holds important implications for public sector organizations in any democratic political environment but especially those organizations experiencing higher levels of environmental turbulence.

There remain a lot of unanswered questions concerning entrepreneurship in the public sector. Although sound measures exist for assessing entrepreneurial intensity in private sector organizations, more work is needed to facilitate measurement efforts in the public sector. Measures of innovation, risk-taking, and proactiveness most likely must be tailored to reflect the distinct types of opportunities that exist in the public organizations. Further clarification is needed regarding how an entrepreneurial event can be designated and quantified in these organizations. In a related vein, it will prove useful to develop a categorization of types of public sector innovations and to relate these to appropriate time frames, structures, incentives, and resource requirements. Developments in the quantification of entrepreneurship will also make it possible to establish linkages between levels of entrepreneurship and the various obstacles that characterize the public sector environment, on the one hand, and measures of organizational performance, on the other. This also assumes further progress in refining output, as opposed to input, measures of performance in these organizations. Research is needed as well to establish norms for entrepreneurial performance in different types of public organizations. Such norms will prove invaluable in goal setting and performance benchmarking.

In the final analysis, we are not proposing entrepreneurship as a comprehensive framework intended to replace various models of public sector management, including models rooted in bureaucracy. However, the emergence of alternative models (e.g., the reinvention movement) suggests that conventional bureaucracy

CHANGE IN THE OLDEST BUREAUCRATIC SYSTEM

It isn't so uncommon anymore for humans to trade in their salaries and health plans for independence and a piece of the profit pie. Thus, employers are forced to offer stock options, day care, and flextime just to recruit and retain full-time employees, let alone *motivated* employees. Some organizations, however, such as the U.S. Government, are not for profit and cannot afford to reward favorable employee behavior extrinsically. Mr. Frank Sabatine was well aware of this when, in 1997, he was appointed as Chairman of the Indiana State Board of Tax Commissioners. With this new title came new responsibilities outlined in the governor's "Smaller and Smarter Government" initiative, which included analyzing the agency and making changes that would improve performance while making the Indiana property tax system simpler, fairer, and conducive to economic development. There would be no profit sharing to work toward, no IPO. How was Sabatine to instill new methods and attitudes in such a bureaucratic system?

In addition to an education in political science, Sabatine had extensive vocational experience in management, leadership, and entrepreneurship. Sabatine quickly set out to reorganize the agency, thereby changing the cultural attitude. Managers and employees alike had to give presentations and interview for the positions they really wanted. This hurt some and excited others. The key to the success of Sabatine's reorganization was finding five division managers to help maintain and promote an energetic, efficient agency. After conducting several structured interviews, looking for characteristics such as a high energy level, the courage to do the hard things, an entrepreneurial perspective, and an overall knowledge of the job, Sabatine and the two other commissioners found the following five division managers that lived up to their expectations in just ten months:

APPEALS DIVISION MANAGER

Hired/trained eighteen employees, created a new system to process appeals, established new procedures and rules of evidence for the appeals hearing process, trained appeals hearing officers to write more comprehensive final determinations for cases on appeal, and processed more than half of the 5,000 outstanding appeals in less than two years.

ASSESSMENT DIVISION MANAGER

Eliminated the auditing program, downsized the number of field officers and increased their responsibilities to include real estate assessing functions, established a reporting system to measure activities and travel, increased accountability, and developed a local Assessors Operations Manual.

BUDGET DIVISION MANAGER

Developed detailed training manuals and hands-on training workshops for all budgeting personnel and redesigned the public hearing process to give local taxpayers the opportunity to raise objections concerning local budgets.

OPERATIONS DIVISION MANAGER

Developed an employee handbook, conducted "train the trainer" programs for all division leaders, implemented electronic information sessions for local officials, and developed a Web page to make communications with off-site officials and taxpayers more convenient.

DIVISION OF TAX REVIEW

Developed an assessment study methodology and conducted an assessment quality study of a large Indiana county, created a research request tracking system and a customer satisfaction survey instrument, established more user-friendly databases and developed and conducted several training workshops used to educate local officials on the methods used to evaluate the quality of assessing.

These "champions" were motivated intrinsically by having the freedom within their divisions to implement whatever strategy they felt would get the job done. The trickle-down effect Sabatine had hoped for worked since the attitudes and desire for change from the division managers were contagious to their subordinates. All involved shared a vision, enjoyed taking initiative, and thrived on chaos—very similar to the rewards of being an entrepreneur, without the risk. The public sector had successfully introduced major organizational change — and made it stick.

SOURCE: Sabatine, Frank J. 1999. "Creating a New Government Culture: The Search for Champions," *The Journal of Leadership Studies* 6, No. 4 (Summer/Fall): 34–49.

is an increasingly inadequate solution. Our conclusion is that entrepreneurship must be an integral component in whatever models or frameworks are adopted. Entrepreneurship implies an innovative, proactive role for government in steering society toward an improved quality of life. This includes generating alternative revenues, improving internal processes, and developing novel solutions to inadequately satisfied social and economic needs.

REFERENCES

Adam, H., and K. Moodley. 1986. *South Africa without Apartheid: Dismantling Racial Domination.* Berkeley: University of California Press.

Behn, R. D. 1991. *Leadership Counts. Lessons for Public Managers From the Massachusetts Welfare Training and Employment Program.* Cambridge: Harvard University.

Bellone, C. J., and G. F. Goerle. 1992. "Reconciling Public Entrepreneurship and Democracy," *Public Administration Review* 52, No. 2: 130–134.

Bower, J. L. 1977. "Effective Public Management," *Harvard Business Review* 55, No. 2 (March/April): 135.

Burgelman, R. A. 1983. "A Model of the Interaction of Strategic Behavior, Corporate Context, and the Concept of Strategy," *Academy of Management Review* 8 (January): 32–47.

Burns, T., and G. Stalker. 1961. *The Management of Innovation.* London: Tavistock.

Carroll, J. D. 1996. "Reinventing Public Administration," *Public Administration Review* 56, No. 3: 245–246.

Cooper, T. L., and N. D. Wright, eds. 1992. *Exemplary Public Administrators: Character and Leadership in Government.* Baltimore: Johns Hopkins University.

Cornwall, J. R., and B. Perlman. 1990. *Organizational Entrepreneurship.* Homewood: Irwin.

Cullen, R. B., and D. P. Cushman. 2000. *Transitions to Competitive Government: Speed, Consensus and Performance.* Albany: State University of New York.

Davies, S., and D. Griffiths. 1995. "Kirklees Metropolitan Council: Corporate Strategy in a Local Authority." In *Cases in Strategic Management,* 2nd edition, edited by C. Clarke-Hill and K. Glaistar. London: Pitman.

Davis, D., M. Morris, and J. Allen. 1991. "Perceived Environmental Turbulence and Its Effect on Selected Entrepreneurship, Marketing and Organizational Characteristics in Industrial Firms," *Journal of the Academy of Marketing Science* 19 (Spring): 43–51.

Doig, J. W., and E. C. Hargrove, eds. 1987. *Leadership and Innovation: Entrepreneurs in Government.* Baltimore: Johns Hopkins University.

Drucker, P. F. 1995. "Really Reinventing Government," *The Atlantic Monthly* 275 (February): 49–61.

Fox, C .J. 1996. "Reinventing Government As Postmodern Symbolic Politics," *Public Administration Review* 56, No. 3: 256–262.

Harvard Business Review. 1995. "How Can Big Companies Keep the Entrepreneurial Spirit Alive?" 73 (November–December): 183–189.

Jennings, D. F., and S. L. Seaman. 1990. "Aggressiveness of Response to New Business Opportunities Following Deregulation: An Empirical Study of Established Financial Firms," *Journal of Business Venturing* 5 (October): 177–89.

Jordan, F. 1990. *Innovating American.* New York: The Ford Foundation.

Kamensky, J. M. 1996. "Role of the Reinventing Government: Movement in Federal Management Reform," *Public Administration Review* 56, No. 3: 247–255.

Kettle, D. F. 1995. "Building Lasting Reform: Enduring Questions, Missing Reforms." In *Inside the Machine: Appraising Governmental Reform,* edited by D. F. Kettle and J .J. Diluilo, Jr.. Washington: Brookings Institute.

Khademian, A. M. 1995. "Reinventing a Government Corporation: Professional Priorities and a Clear Bottom Line," *Public Administration Review* 55, No. 1: 17–28.

Lawrence, P., and J. Lorsch. 1967. *Organization and Environment.* Boston: Harvard University, Division of Research.

Lewis, E. 1980. *Public Entrepreneurship: Toward a Theory of Bureaucratic Power.* Bloomington: Indiana University.

Linden, R. 1990. *From Vision to Reality: Strategies of Successful Innovators in Government.* Charlottesville: LEL Enterprises.

Miller, D. 1983. "The Correlates of Entrepreneurship in Three Types of Firms," *Management Science* 29 (July): 770–791.

Mintzberg, H. 1996. "Managing Government, Governing Management," *Harvard Business Review* 74 (May–June): 75–83.

Mitchell, T., and W. G. Scott. 1987. "Leadership Failures, the Distrusting Public, and Prospects of the Administrative State," *Public Administrative Review* 47, No. 2: 445–452.

Moe, R. C. 1994. *Thickening Government: Federal Hierarchy and the Diffusion of Accountability.* Washington: Brookings Institute.

Mokwa, M., and S. Permut. 1981. *Government Marketing.* New York: Praeger.

Moody's Public Finance. 1999. *Perspectives on Municipal Issues.* New York, NY: Moody's Investors Service.

Moore, B. H., ed. 1983. *The Entrepreneur in Local Government.* Washington: International City Management.

Moore, J. 1992. "British Privatization — Taking Capitalism to the People," *Harvard Business Review* 70, No. 1 (January–February): 115–124.

Morris, M. H., and D. Sexton. 1996. "The Concept of Entrepreneurial Intensity: Implications for Company Performance," *Journal of Business Research* 36, No. 1: 5–14.

Morris, M. H., and F. Jones. 1999. "Entrepreneurship in Established Organizations: The Case of the Public Sector," *Entrepreneurship Theory and Practice* 24, No. 1: 71–91.

Murray, M. A. 1975. "Comparing Public and Private Management: An Exploratory Essay," *Public Administration Review* 35, No. 4 (July/August): 366–367.

Nutt, P. C., and R. W. Backoff. 1993. "Transforming Public Organizations with Strategic Management and Strategic Leadership," *Journal of Management* 19, No. 2: 299–349.

Osborne, D., and T. A. Gaebler. 1992. *Reinventing Government: How the Entrepreneurial Spirit Is Transforming the Public Sector.* Reading: Addison-Wesley.

Peters, T. J. 1987. *Thriving on Chaos.* New York: Alfred A. Knopf.

Pinchot, G. 1985. *Intrapreneuring.* New York: Harper and Row.

Rainey, H. G., R. W. Backoff, and C. H. Levine. 1976. "Is Management Really Generic," *Public Administration Review* 36, No. 2 (March/April): 233–244.

Ramamurti, R. 1986. "Public Entrepreneurs: Who They Are and How They Operate," *California Management Review* 28, No. 3: 142–158.

Reynolds, L. 1994. "Can Government Be Reinvented?" *Management Review* 83, No. 1 (January): 14–21.

Savas, E. S. 1987. *Privatization : The Key to Better Government.* Chatham: Chatham House Publishers.

Savas, E. S. 1992. "Privatization in Post-Socialist Countries," *Public Administration Review* 52, No. 6 (November–December): 573–581.

Skoldberg, K. 1994. "Tales of Change: Public Administration Reform and Narrative Mode," *Organization Science* 5, No. 2: 219–238.

Stevenson, H. H., M. J. Roberts, and H. I. Grousbeck. 1989. *Business Ventures and the Entrepreneur.* Homewood: Irwin.

Sweeney, J. C., and A. C. Hyde. 1995. "The Public Manager 1995 Annual Survey," *The Public Manager* 24, No. 2 (Summer): 56–64.

Tropman, J. E., and G. Morningstar. 1989. *Entrepreneurial Systems for the 1990s.* Westport: Quorum Books.

Wilson, J. Q. 1973. *Political Organizations.* New York: Basic Books.

Zahra, S. A. 1986. "A Canonical Analysis of Corporate Entrepreneurship Antecedents and Impact on Performance." In *Best Paper Proceedings,* edited by J. Pearce and R. Robinson. 46th Annual Meetings: Academy of Management.

16

SUSTAINING ENTREPRENEURSHIP TODAY AND TOMORROW

Entrepreneurship is a phenomenon that has become quite captivating both to those in the classroom and in the boardroom. Unfortunately, too many people are caught up in the excitement of the entrepreneurial event itself or with inspiring stories of individual entrepreneurs. Although it is easy to become enamored with the idea of entrepreneurship, such infatuation misses the real point. The true value of entrepreneurship as a managerial concept lies in the extent to which it helps us to *better understand how organizations operate and succeed.*

Such understanding has been the focus of the preceding chapters of this book. We have seen that entrepreneurship is a thread that can be woven through many facets of a company. It can serve as the dominant logic, as a measurable objective, as part of corporate strategy, as an element in the company culture, as a performance criterion for use in employee appraisals and compensation programs, and more. There are entrepreneurial approaches to managerial tasks (i.e., entrepreneurial strategies, entrepreneurial methods of resource acquisition, entrepreneurial structures), and there are entrepreneurial outcomes from managerial efforts (i.e., new ventures, products, processes, technologies and markets). Companies, units within companies, and employees within units can all be characterized in terms of their levels of entrepreneurial intensity.

Levels of entrepreneurship within organizations are not constant. They not only vary across departments and units, but they also vary considerably over time. Even the most entrepreneurial of companies goes through cycles, with ebbs and flows in terms of the frequency and degree of entrepreneurial activity. While some companies struggle to muster even a minimal amount of entrepreneurial activity, *all* companies battle mightily to sustain entrepreneurship over time.

In this final chapter, we examine the issue of sustainability. We begin with the need for individuals to develop a personal model or approach to entrepreneurial endeavors—one they can use on a sustainable basis. Following this, the concept of triggers is introduced, together with an identification of the leading types of events that trigger entrepreneurial behavior in companies. The need to manage triggers, while creating an ongoing sense of urgency in the organization is discussed. Other vehicles for sustaining entrepreneurship such as enlightened experimentation and organizational learning are explored. Finally, we take a look at the entrepreneurial organization of tomorrow and the paradoxes that will define that organization.

DEVELOPING A PERSONAL APPROACH
TO THE ENTREPRENEURIAL PROCESS

There are innumerable models of how a given entrepreneurial project might be successfully initiated and completed in a company. The effectiveness of any one model depends on the scope and scale of the project, the team members involved, the nature of the organization, and conditions in the external environment. And yet, there are certain principles to which the individual entrepreneur or champion may always want to adhere. Stated differently, corporate entrepreneurs should develop a personal approach to any entrepreneurial opportunity and, although the approach should be tailored to the individual's skills and talents, it should reflect a few basic considerations. The following eight principles represent a foundation around which the corporate entrepreneur can design his or her personal model:

- Solidify a relationship with a sponsor;
- Build a flexible team structure;
- Insulate the project and keep it quiet as long as possible;
- Become a guerrilla;
- Promise less but deliver more;
- Experiment and produce early wins;
- Manage project momentum;
- Attempt to set the parameters.

The champion begins with a strategy for getting a sponsor, an activity that is much more involved than simply obtaining the endorsement for a project from someone at a higher level in the organization. (See Chapter Five.) Sponsor selection must be approached systematically, since the entrepreneur is looking for someone with relevant credibility, someone who will be around, and someone with whom he or she has a personal fit. A relationship must be established and then carefully nurtured. It is a two-way relationship predicated on trust and mutual investments. The willingness of a sponsor to protect the champion and the project, to provide advice and contacts, and to be associated with a project requires a significant investment. Defending a champion when he or she steps out of line or steps on someone's toes is a lot to expect from a sponsor. Motivating the champion when he or she wants to give up is another, often unexpected, role of the sponsor. The corporate entrepreneur must have a well-planned approach for reciprocating this investment. Communication styles, as well as the medium and frequency of communication are important. Honesty, especially regarding setbacks, budgetary problems, and an inability to meet targets is vital. So, too, is the need to stick to an agreed-upon path, produce evidence of progress, and provide the sponsor with research and other ammunition for dealing with critics. Knowing when to use the sponsor and when not to and ensuring that the champion does not "embarass" the sponsor are also part of the approach.

The social skills necessary for managing the sponsor relationship are also needed for building a team. The entrepreneur is looking for two things when he or she is constructing a team: skill sets that complement his or her own skills and people who believe in the concept or vision. Teams will have formal and informal members, and relationships with both must be cultivated. Champions develop a sense of the type of team structure that works best for them. They ensure that individual roles are well communicated and agreed to and that a consistent and mutually acceptable decision-making style is employed. The entrepreneur's approach includes techniques for motivating the team, reinforcing members, sharing achievements, and accepting responsibility for all that goes wrong.

Entrepreneurial projects are most vulnerable in their infancy. Flaws exist, elements have not been completely thought through, and aspects of the project look extremely threatening to one or more stakeholders in the organization. The corporate entrepreneur must develop a strategy to protect a project from early mortality. The goal is to insulate projects from detailed scrutiny by senior managers, departments not involved in the project, or other potential critics. Such insulation can be achieved in various ways. Endorsement by the sponsor and other senior managers, creation of an unofficial advisory group, and involving key departments in some tangible way can be sources of insulation. However, these activities create visibility and must be balanced against a strategy of working underground and keeping publicity to a minimum. Many entrepreneurial successes come about because the team "bootlegged" their time (after hours, lunches, dinners, etc.), kept the project under cover in the formative period, and built credibility for the project before unveiling it. Also, the less entrepreneurs can appear to be openly competing for someone else's resources, the better. Insulation can also be achieved by placing a project outside the mainstream of the company structure and by "buying" a window of time for project development before there will be any formal review.

The heart and soul of the entrepreneur's approach concerns how he or she deals with a lack of resources, with bureaucratic obstacles, and with rejection of critical requests. Champions must be guerrillas, with a personal style for gaining access to resources they do not control, circumventing obstacles, and keeping ideas alive that have been killed (Table 16.1). Individuals differ in terms of their salesmanship abilities, political skills, tenacity, and skills at the creative employment or manipulation of resources. These differences suggest the style an entrepreneur employs will be, by definition, highly individualistic. It is a style that must reflect the champion's strengths and compensate for his or her weaknesses.

■ **TABLE 16.1**

THE DECISION-MAKING STYLES OF CORPORATE ENTREPRENEURS

Research on characteristics of entrepreneurs has generally focused on personality traits and demographics. Less attention has been devoted to behavioral characteristics of entrepreneurs. Corporate entrepreneurs need to develop a personal style or approach to the entrepreneurial process, and their styles are likely to include a number of behavioral characteristics. In a study in which start-up entrepreneurs were compared to corporate managers, Busenitz and Barney (1997) demonstrate that entrepreneurs are more likely than corporate managers to employ certain biases and heuristics when making decisions. Two specific biases and heuristics emphasized by entrepreneurs follow:

Overconfidence

The tendency for a decision-maker to be overly optimistic in their initial assessment of a situation, and to be slow to subsequently incorporate additional information about a situation into their assessment because of their initial overconfidence.

Representativeness

A willingness to generalize about a person or phenomenon based on only a few attributes of that person or only a few observations of a specified phenomenon. In effect, small, non-random samples of data are being relied upon. The unreliability inherent in such limited data is ignored or underestimated by the decision-maker.

These short cuts allow the entrepreneur to decipher lots of inputs efficiently and make quick decisions under conditions of uncertainty. As corporate entrepreneurs deal with much of the same uncertainty, they might be expected to rely on some of the same biases and heuristics. At the same time, reliance on them makes the corporate entrepreneur vulnerable to attack from within, as the corporate environment typically places a premium on systematic data collection and conservative interpretation of information.

SOURCE: For the complete study, see Businitz, L. and J. Barney. 1997. "Differences Between Entrepreneurs and Managers in Large Organizations: Biases and Heuristics in Strategic Decision-Making," *Journal of Business Venturing* 12, No. 1: 9–30.

Another aspect of the entrepreneur's model or approach to projects concerns the management of expectations. The rule here is simple: underpromise and overdeliver. If the project's potential is overemphasized from the outset (or is exaggerated by those not involved in the project), expectations can be so high that there will never be satisfaction with whatever the team produces. Again, a balance is involved, since the entrepreneur wants to get key people excited about a project and its possibilities. He or she conveys a vision of what can be but is conservative in terms of specific performance levels that will be achieved at specific points in time. Subsequently, he or she never fails to exceed these performance levels, initially by small amounts and eventually by significant amounts. Conservatism is especially critical with regard to the expectations of those who are not involved as sponsors, endorsers, contributors, or participants in the project.

The earlier the champion can show progress, the better. This can be difficult, since some projects demand a significant level of preliminary research and development activity before anything tangible can be produced. The champion requires a strategy for producing deliverables, or some kind of evidence that a project is moving forward, things are being accomplished, and benchmarks are being met. These deliverables might include favorable market research findings (e.g., surveys, focus groups, test markets), technical test results, simulations, drawings, prototypes, feedback from beta test sites, endorsements from key accounts, or any number of other signs of progress. This kind of action orientation should be coupled with a sense that a consistent stream of small victories are occurring, because the champion has established a series of targets that reflect the logical evolution of a project.

The preceding two principles can be taken a step further. The champion should have in mind an overall time horizon over which a project will unfold. Expectations are managed across this time horizon and are steadily raised. Similarly, small wins evolve into more significant accomplishments. The point becomes that a project has momentum, and the momentum builds over time. As momentum builds, the champion is able to achieve buy-in with key individuals and departments on a logical and sequential basis. Momentum that peaks too early can find attention subsequently shifting to other projects and priorities. At the same time, the lack of a sense that things are building in the early and middle stages of a project will often result in defections by key people and loss of key resources.

Finally, the entrepreneur must have an approach for influencing the rules of the game. The more a champion must make a project work within the context of someone else's rules, the harder it is to succeed. Further, those rules are subject to change in midstream. Champions should look for ways to set or negotiate the parameters under which the venture team operates. Examples of areas over which the entrepreneur should seek agreement at the outset of a project include the establishment of performance benchmarks that make sense given the type of project being pursued, acceptable processes for obtaining approvals for expenditures, decisions over which the champion has discretion, an overall project time frame and time frames for individual project stages, reporting responsibilities, and the amount of control the champion has over various resources (including people).

As the corporate entrepreneur develops a personal model or process for managing entrepreneurial initiatives, he or she may find it helpful to refer regularly to the so-called Ten Commandments of the Intrapreneur (Table 16.2). These were coined some years ago by Gifford Pinchot and remain highly relevant today. Moreover, the principles cited earlier capture the essence of many of these commandments.

We can see these principles and commandments in action by considering the case of 3M's now famous Post-it Notes. An adhesives engineer at 3-M was able to secure a sponsor in his manager, gather a few excited engineers to help on the project, and certainly keep this "unsticky" adhesive underground until they could find some practical use for it. Breaking some of the traditional rules and realizing they would ask for forgiveness later, the team left samples of the adhesive pads on the desks of all the clerical personnel at the Minneapolis headquarters. They used a similar approach (and some CEO letterhead) to get the product (which was not yet in production) on the desks of executive secretaries of Fortune 500 CEOs. The subsequent applications of this new idea allowed the project to rise up from

■ **TABLE 16.2**

THE TEN COMMANDMENTS OF AN INTRAPRENEUR

1. Come to work each day willing to be fired.
2. Circumvent any orders aimed at stopping your dream.
3. Do any job needed to make your project work, regardless of your job description.
4. Build a network of good people to assist you.
5. Develop a spirited team; choose and work with only the best.
6. Work underground as long as you can—publicity triggers the corporate immune mechanism.
7. Be loyal and truthful to your sponsor.
8. Remember that it is easier to ask for forgiveness than for permission.
9. Be true to your goals, but be realistic about the ways to achieve them.
10. Be thoroughly engaged, take ownership, and persevere.

SOURCE: Adapted Pinchot, III, G. 1985. *Intrapreneuring.* New York: Harper and Row. Adapted by permission of Harper Collins Publishers.

having been underpromised to the point where it could be overdelivered. Today, Post-it Notes account for a sizable portion of 3-M's total company revenues.

COMPANIES NEED TO MANAGE THE TRIGGERING EVENTS

What are the factors that lead individuals within an established company to develop and implement something new? It would seem that the decision to act entrepreneurially occurs as a result of interactions among organizational characteristics, individual characteristics, and some kind of precipitating event. We will call this precipitating event a *trigger.* The trigger provides the impetus to behave entrepreneurially when other conditions are conducive to such behavior. Although it is generally recognized that entrepreneurship involves a process, the ability to manage and facilitate that process on an ongoing basis requires that managers understand what gets things going in the first place.

Based on the research that has been conducted, we might be tempted to conclude that entrepreneurship in established companies is primarily externally driven. For example, it appears that the positive relationship between the entrepreneurial orientation of a company and its bottom-line performance is especially strong when it must cope with a dynamic, threatening, and complex external environment (Covin and Slevin 1989; Davis, Morris, and Allen 1991; Miller and Friesen 1982; Zahra 1993). Stevenson et al. (1999) indicate a stronger need for entrepreneurial management when firms face diminishing opportunity streams, rapid changes in the external environment, and shortened decision windows (The implications would appear to be that the principal triggers for corporate entrepreneurship are aggressive competitor moves, changes in industry or market structure, regulatory threats, and other external factors.) Others point out that the factors in the external environment and the organization interact, challenging managers to respond creatively and act in innovative ways (Zahra and O'Neil 1998).

"TRIGGERING" EVENTS FOR CORPORATE ENTREPRENEURSHIP

Specific customer request	Senior management initiative
Competitor threat or action	Personal initiative on the part of one or more employees
Changes in people's lifestyles/expectations	Ongoing innovation program in the firm
New sales targets	Strategic growth target
Public relations/image	New marketing initiative
Substitute product or service	Diversification
Declining market share	Availability of new equipment
Declining profits	Availability of new resources
Declining sales	Availability of new distribution channel or method
Improved quality control	New management
Poor quality of an existing product or service	Perception of increasing risk
Rising costs	Vertical integration
Problem with existing logistical performance	Geographical expansion
Specific customer complaint	Internal opportunities
Supplier request	Inventory problems
Availability of new IT or on-line systems	Staff training
Regulatory requirement	Horizontal integration
Decreasing size of the market	New investment by a supplier
New investment by a buyer	Change in accounting practices
Supplier complaint	

SOURCE: Schindehutte, M., M. H. Morris, and D. F. Kuratko. 2000. "Triggering Events, Corporate Entrepreneurship and the Marketing Function," *Journal of Marketing Theory and Practice* 8, No. 2 (Spring): 18–30.

Yet, people in established companies pursue ideas that come to them simply because the ideas intrigue them, they believe in them, or they take exception to the fact that others have rejected their ideas. Also, some companies have planned programs for innovation regardless of what is happening in the external environment at a given point in time, or they have cultures in which initiation of innovation is simply expected. Examples include Proctor & Gamble, 3-M, Compaq, Intel, and Merck. Thus, various internal triggers would seem to be relevant, such as senior management directives, targeted employee rewards, resource availability, and problems in controlling costs.

Table 16.3 summarizes the more prevalent triggers for entrepreneurial activity in corporations. Some of these are more specific than others (e.g., a particular customer complaint), and some can be broken down in more detail (e.g., employee initiative, inventory problems). In addition, there is potential overlap among some of the items (e.g., declining profits and rising costs). Nonetheless, they do tend to capture the range of triggering events that commonly influence innovative behavior in established organizations.

Just as important is the need to identify relevant ways in which triggers can be grouped or categorized. Following are five key ways for grouping triggering events:

■ internal/external source;

■ opportunity-driven/threat-driven;

- technology-push/market-pull;
- top-down/bottom-up;
- systematic or deliberate search/chance or opportunism.

Although there are other ways in which these initiating factors could be classified, each of the ones identified has potential strategic relevance. For instance, it may be that resource requirements differ markedly for entrepreneurial projects triggered by internal developments as opposed to those initiated principally by external developments and for technology-driven projects versus market-driven projects. Triggers from outside the company such as technological change may tend to produce entrepreneurial projects that are more innovative or that represent bigger departures from the status quo than do triggers from inside the company. Triggers related to the actions of competitors might lead to more imitation, and those related to a threat from a substitute product might produce more innovative solutions. Managerial support may be more easily obtainable for entrepreneurial projects triggered by threats (e.g., an impending government regulation) as opposed to opportunities (e.g., an untapped market niche). The same may be true for those where the source of the trigger is more top down as opposed to bottom up. Further, in terms of outcomes, if the trigger is some successful action by a competitor, then the entrepreneurial project may represent a reactive response that comes too late to have any marketplace impact. Similarly, it may be that entrepreneurial events that are in response to a particular supplier or customer request are associated with higher levels of success.

In one exploratory survey directed at a sample of twenty large companies, Morris et al. (2000) attempted to discern the relative reliance on the triggers identified in Table 16.3. Senior executives were asked to identify up to five entrepreneurial initiatives that had been pursued within their companies in the past three years. A total of eighty-two entrepreneurial initiatives were identified. Internal factors were surprisingly prevalent among the most frequently mentioned triggers, including employee initiative, a strategic program, a new growth target, a new marketing initiative, and public relations/image. The principal external triggers were a specific customer request, a competitor threat, and a change in people's lifestyles or expectations.

The study also drew a distinction between planned and unplanned triggers, those that were internal versus external to the company, and those that were more controllable versus uncontrollable by management. The largest proportion of the triggers tended to be planned, internal, and controllable. The entrepreneurial initiatives were more likely to be driven by perception of opportunity as opposed to threat. Further, a large majority of respondents indicated the effort to discover the idea or concept was planned/deliberate/conscious as opposed to random/accidental/coincidence. In about a quarter of the cases, the idea or concept was a fairly unexpected development. Over two-thirds of the initiatives were driven by an awareness of demand in the marketplace (market-pull) as opposed to being novel innovations for which the firm is trying to create a market. Projects to attract new customers tended to be pursued more so than did projects for retaining existing customers.

It is also noteworthy that all of the projects had an internal champion and this person tended to initiate the project. The champion's primary motivation tended to be growth of revenues or profits, personal satisfaction, and job requirements. The single biggest overall factor motivating entrepreneurial behavior included profit opportunity, managerial leadership, and the passion and drive of individual employees.

A number of implications can be drawn from this discussion for the concept of sustainable entrepreneurship. The ability to encourage entrepreneurship on an ongoing basis requires that managers first identify the types of triggers that are prevalent in the company and determine if any key triggers are not occurring for particular reasons. There is a need to systematically review triggering events for both successful and unsuccessful products, services, and processes that have been pursued by the firm over the past five years. Further, managers should apply the groupings or categories above and then look for associations between types of triggers and types of entrepreneurial projects and between types of triggers and the outcomes of entrepreneurial endeavors.

Companies must also develop an understanding of the needs and motives of potential champions, since certain types of individuals may respond more to particular triggers. In addition, firms may find that the composition of venture teams is associated with the type of trigger that drives a particular project. For instance, teams dominated by R&D or technical personnel may be driven more by internal and planned triggers, and those teams that have a strong marketing emphasis may be driven more by external and unplanned triggers. Finally, it is likely that certain types of triggers will be more salient under particular industry and market conditions.

By studying the triggering process in their organizations, managers can gain insights regarding the triggers to be emphasized under a given set of circumstances, how resources and incentives should be allocated to facilitate certain triggers, and ways in which the organization should be structured so as to take maximal advantage of particular types of triggers. In the final analysis, planning and the strategic management of the triggering process become vital for sustainable entrepreneurship.

CREATING A SENSE OF URGENCY

What are the top managerial concerns in large, established organizations? For most companies, making innovation happen has become either the Number 1 priority or is very high on the priority list (Leifer et al. 2000). Corporate leaders have come to appreciate the critical need for innovation in response to the new competitive landscape, but they also are coming to recognize that their organizations are not inherently good at innovating. Even companies that spend tens of millions of dollars on research and development often demonstrate relatively low innovation productivity. The problem is not whether firms can focus attention and resources in a manner that makes a new product or service happen at a particular point in time (although many do struggle with this, and making an innovation happen inside the firm is not the same thing as making it successful in the marketplace). The problem is sustainable innovation—making innovation happen on an ongoing basis and throughout the company.

In the preceding section, triggers for corporate entrepreneurship were discussed. Many of these triggers involve threatening conditions such as a competitor's preemptive moves, loss of key accounts, or costs that undermine company profitability. The message seems to be that companies seek entrepreneurial behaviors from their employees when they are in trouble, and the sense of crisis motivates employees to make innovation happen. The reality is that employees are always capable of entrepreneurial behavior, but most of the time they and their bosses do not perceive the need for innovation and change. Such complacency has a number of causes, ranging from strong financial performance of the firm (at least for the moment) and a preoccupation with the demands and crises of day-to-day operations to a tendency to underestimate the extent to which things are changing in the external environment. Further, innovation is disruptive. And, managers have a natural tendency to exalt in the past accomplishments and reputation of the firm, even when those accomplishments have little to do with current marketplace conditions and that reputation may no longer be deserved.

The great challenge for any company wishing to achieve sustainable entrepreneurship is creating an ongoing sense of urgency throughout the organization. When there is a crisis, employees feel the urgency, but when the crisis is surmounted, complacency eventually sets in. Management must create an environment where urgency is felt all the time. Urgency in this context refers to a compelling sense that organizational survival depends on change. It is an imperative that suggests that the company either innovates or falls behind—there is no middle ground. It is a permanent mandate for making the company's products and processes obsolete. Urgency is a call for immediate action, a pressing need to do things differently, a belief that time is running out.

Entrepreneurial companies instill in their employees a burning desire to make things better. People demonstrate a combination of paranoia (someone is out there right now figuring a superior way to do this), competitiveness (we can out-innovate anyone), pride (with our people and passion, magic is possible), and obsession (we are focused and will not quit before we reach the top of the mountain).

A beginning point in creating urgency is to rethink the fundamental assumptions that underlie the business. Following are six key assumptions management may wish to adopt:

- Our best employees, and even our good employees, have professional options that do not involve our company;
- Customer loyalties are fleeting; creating a "wow" experience for customers is impossible if we are not continually finding new and better approaches;

■ **TABLE 16.4**

DOES THE COMPANY HAVE A SENSE OF URGENCY?

Urgency is something that pervades the entrepreneurial company and is reflected in many facets of daily operations. Below are ten questions that can be used to gauge the extent to which management has created a sense of urgency within an organization.

1. How big is the comfort zone surrounding managers at each level in the organization? Are managers regularly expected to challenge one another's comfort zones?

2. Does the company measure itself against the best, but even more so against itself?

3. If a customer complains or is not satisfied, does the company measure how quickly the situation is rectified, and has that time been reduced by at least 10 percent in the past year?

4. Do managers in the company want to change the world?

5. Which of the following is most emphasized in the company: (a) thorough and well-formulated analysis; (b) properly managed consensus-building; (c) sensitivity to process and procedure; or (d) a willingness to take action and make something happen?

6. If timetables are not met, are the perceived costs or penalties significant?

7. How much of this year's sales must come from products that did not exist three years ago?

8. To what extent can decision-making be characterized as a promise of compromise to satisfy multiple constituencies?

9. When managers talk about "the future," are they referring to a time that is twenty, ten, five, or two years from now?

10. How much of a sense of regret do managers feel for missed opportunities and missed targets?

- The gap between us and the competition is smaller than we think in those situations where we are ahead and is larger than we think in those situations where we are behind;

- The latest, greatest technology has problems, but we cannot afford to ignore it;

- Our business model is working, and yet it needs to be fixed;

- The firm could be out of business in 24 months.

Coupled with the need for different assumptions are some caveats. Creating a sense of urgency is different from creating a sense of crisis. Urgency is a call to action, but it is not about short-sightedness, expediency, or change for the sake of change. The imperative for innovation and change does not preclude the need for strategy and planning. Further, a sense of urgency does not lessen the need to build operations around sound business fundamentals. In fact, such fundamentals as a customer focus, a quality emphasis, value for money, and investing in employees should be the focal point of the concern for urgency. There becomes an urgent need to find new ways of delighting customers, to achieve even higher levels of quality, and so forth.

One means for taking stock of the relative level of urgency versus complacency in organization is for managers to periodically assess their operations using the ten questions presented in Table 16.4. Indicators of a strong sense of urgency include managers having relatively small comfort zones, the existence of some standard that a certain percentage of sales must come from new products, a sense that the future is now, a primacy placed on action over analysis or compromise, and a greater concern with missing the boat rather than sinking the boat (see Chapter 3) when it comes to the pursuit of new opportunities. Moreover, the pressure for improvement is not simply because of what someone else is doing — the company benchmarks itself against itself. There is an expectation that no matter how well the company performs in a given area, it must raise the bar for itself and everyone else.

DIFFERENT APPROACHES TO RESEARCH AND EXPERIMENTATION

Urgency is ultimately driven by an appreciation for how things are changing outside the company. The new competitive landscape requires that managers be thoroughly immersed in various components of the external environment. It is difficult to lead through innovation if management is insulated from the patterns and trends in markets, the supply chain, technology, regulation, and so forth.

Yet, traditional approaches to monitoring and measuring what is happening in the external environment tell very little of the story. For example, conventional methods of market research usually fail to uncover breakthrough opportunities. Instead, they confirm things that management already knows, or they produce insights that are relatively superficial (e.g., interest is uncovered in a new feature, or some negative aspect of the product is identified). Mainstream customers have difficulty describing needs for products that have yet to be invented. Further, respondents to market research projects typically answer questions based on the products they are using at present, and this frame of reference limits their ability to imagine alternative solutions to their needs. Most tools for assessing external developments focus on the present and the past, not on what is to come.

Companies must break out of these constraints by adopting new and different ways for looking at the external environment. A simple example can be found in what Andreasen (1988) calls *backward marketing research*. Arguing that most research on customers provides management with little that is actionable, the approach turns the conventional marketing research process on its head. Projects are conducted backwards, and the company first determines how the research results will be implemented (i.e., specific managerial actions), then what the report must look like in order to implement the results, then what analysis is needed to fill in the tables in the report, then what sort of data is needed to carry out those analyses, and so forth. Because the approach involves action-oriented managerial involvement from the outset, the research is likely to be more focused, with much deeper and more relevant perspectives regarding untapped market segments and customer needs.

An even more provocative example of looking at the marketplace through a different lens can be found in the work of von Hippel and his colleagues (1999). Working with 3-M and other companies, they have developed a technique called *lead user research*. The technique is predicated on the fact that many commercial innovations are initially thought of and prototypes are made by users or customers (companies, organizations, or individuals) instead of manufacturers, and that there are users who are well ahead of market trends and whose needs go well beyond those of the average user. These lead users are innovators, not only trying new approaches before early adopters or the majority of the market but also often inventing new approaches because no one is addressing their needs.

Lead user research requires that the firm go through a process of exploring markets, determining current trends, identifying innovative users who are ahead of the trend, and then bringing these lead users together to help the company develop breakthrough innovations. The company seeks lead users from its own markets but also from other fields facing similar problems in different and often more extreme forms. Thus, a research team involved with medical imaging found radiologists who were lead users, but these radiologists led them to specialists in pattern recognition and people working on images that show the fine detail in semiconductor chips. The entire process lasts at least six months on average and is summarized in Table 16.5.

In addition to the need for alternative approaches to research, companies can stay immersed in the marketplace through a process of continuous experimentation. To experiment is to test, run trials, or try alternative approaches. Artists, athletic teams, and medical professionals understand that experimentation is not only a natural part of what they do but that it is also vital for their survival. The most natural place of all for experimentation is a business. Unfortunately, managers all too often seek the sure bet, not wanting to implement something new until they have eliminated as much uncertainty as possible (which often means following other firms) and are relatively certain of marketplace success. When facing a dynamic, threatening, and complex external environment, this approach becomes problematic — market conditions continue to change, and market windows are too short.

To become an innovation factory, companies must first become experimentation factories. This means experimenting *in the marketplace* with new products, product variants, new product applications, new marketing and distribution approaches, new payment schemes, and so forth. Firms can no longer afford to gamble on one major breakthrough idea that systematically moves through an extended new product development process and is introduced only after it has been perfected. Rather, the mindset becomes one of lots of trials. As noted by two keen observers of corporate innovation processes:

> Staking out uncharted territory is a process of successive approximations. Think about an archer shooting arrows into the mist. The arrow flies at a distant and indistinct target, and a shout comes back, "right of the target" or "a bit to the left." More arrows

A LOOK AT LEAD USER RESEARCH

Eric von Hippel and his colleagues have demonstrated the value of lead user research in identifying opportunities for breakthrough innovation. They outline a process that begins with the formation of a cross-disciplinary team of four to six people, each of whom spends twelve to fifteen hours a week on the project. Projects last six months on average. The project then moves through the following four phases:

Phase 1: Laying the Foundation

During this initial period, the team identifies markets it wants to target and the type and level of innovations desired by key stakeholders within the company. If the team's ultimate recommendations are to be credibly received, these stakeholders must be on board early.

Phase 2: Determining the Trends

It's an axiom of the process that lead users are ahead of the trend. But what is the trend? To find out, the team must talk to experts in the field they are exploring—people who have a broad view of emerging technologies and leading-edge applications in the area being studied.

Phase 3: Identifying Lead Users

The team now begins a networking process to identify and learn from users at the leading edge of the target market and related markets. The group's members gather information that will help them identify especially promising innovations and ideas that might contribute to the development of breakthrough products. Based on what they learn, teams also begin to shape preliminary product ideas and to assess the business potential of these concepts and how they fit with company interests.

Phase 4: Developing the Breakthroughs

The goal is to move the preliminary concepts toward completion. The team begins this phase by hosting a workshop with several lead users, a half dozen in-house marketing and technical people, and the lead user team itself. Such workshops may last two to three days. During that time, the participants first work in small groups and then as a whole to design final concepts that precisely fits the company's needs. After the workshop, the project team further hones the concepts, determines whether they fit the needs of the target market users, and presents recommendations to senior management.

SOURCE: von Hippel, E., S. Thomke, and M. Sonnack. 1999. "Creating Breakthroughs at 3M," *Harvard Business Review* 77, No. 5 (September–October): 47–57.

are loosed, and more advice comes back until the cry is "bull's-eye!" What counts most is not being right the first time but the pace at which the arrows fly. How fast can a company gather insights into the particular configuration of features, price, and performance that will unlock the market, and how quickly can it recalibrate its product offering. (Hamel and Prahalad 1991, p. 87)

Experimentation allows the firm to alter the risk/return equation. Although conventional thinking has it that risk goes up if a company innovates more, experimenting with more innovations actually reduces risk. It is a risk-management strategy. By increasing the number of market opportunities a firm is exploring at any one time, management increases the rate at which market knowledge is accumulated. The key is that experimentation becomes a process of learning and adaptation. In a sense, innovation becomes experimentation becomes innovation.

■ **TABLE 16.6**

ESSENTIALS FOR ENLIGHTENED EXPERIMENTATION

Experimentation must be tied to organizational learning. Innovation requires the right managerial systems for performing experiments that will generate the information needed to develop and refine products quickly. Stefan Thomke provides the following guidelines for a new approach to experimentation:

Organize for Rapid Experimentation

■ Examine and, if necessary, revamp entrenched routines, organizational boundaries, and incentives to encourage rapid experimentation.

■ Consider using small development groups that contain key people (designers, test engineers, manufacturing engineers) with all the knowledge required to iterate rapidly.

■ Determine what experiments can be performed in parallel instead of in sequence. Parallel experiments are most effective when time matters most, cost is not an overriding factor, and developers expect to learn little that would guide them in planning the next round of experiments.

Fail Early and Often, but Avoid Mistakes

■ Embrace failures that occur early in the development process and advance knowledge significantly.

■ Don't forget the basics of experimentation. Well-designed tests have clear objectives (what do you anticipate learning?) and hypotheses (what do you expect to happen?). Also, mistakes often occur when you don't control variables that could diminish your ability to learn from the experiments. When variability can't be controlled, allow for multiple, repeated trials.

Anticipate and Exploit Early Information

■ Recognize the full value of front-loading, identifying problems upstream, where they are easier and cheaper to solve.

■ Acknowledge the trade-off between cost and fidelity. Experiments of lower fidelity (generally costing less) are best suited in the early exploratory stages of developing a product. High-fidelity experiments (typically more expensive) are most effectively used later, to verify the product.

Combine New and Traditional Technologies

■ Do not assume that a new technology will necessarily replace an established one. Usually, new and traditional technologies are best used in concert.

■ Remember that new technologies emerge and evolve continually. Today's new technology might eventually replace its traditional counterpart, but it could then be challenged by tomorrow's new technology.

SOURCE: Thomke, S. 2001. "Enlightened Experimentation: The New Imperative for Innovation," *Harvard Business Review*, 79, No. 2 (February): 67–75.

Further, the beauty of continued experimentation is that it puts failure right where it belongs — front and center. A chemist expects to fail many times before coming up with the right formulation. Thomas Edison's light bulb was the result of over one thousand complex experiments. Each failed attempt provides learning and results in adaptation. Companies that become experimentation factories must also accept failure as the natural indicator of progress. It starts to become clear that innovation is not a dichotomy in which a new product is either a failure or success. Rather, a major success is the result of a series of failures and minor successes.

A company's capacity for rapid experimentation has been enhanced by new information-based technologies. Advance in such areas as simulation, the rapid making of prototypes, and combinatorial chemistry permit faster learning at lower cost. Building on these technologies, Thomke (2001) uses the term *enlightened experimentation* to capture the emerging ability of companies to dramatically increase the amount, speed, and quality of their experiments with new products and processes. Doing so requires that firms organize their experimentation efforts differently, with early and open sharing among departments, removal of boundaries between departments or units, use of small development groups, and experiments conducted in parallel rather than in sequence. It requires that they develop a healthy attitude toward failure, as noted above, and distinguish failures from mistakes, the latter of which produces little new or useful information. Another element involves experimenting so as to generate as much information as possible in the early stages of project development, even if early experiments are markedly rougher and more incomplete than they would be once much more is known. Last, rather than choosing between a new and old technology, companies must learn ways to combine or jointly use the new and traditional technologies in their development efforts. Table 16.6 further describes the four essential elements of enlightened experimentation.

LEARNING THAT NEVER STOPS

When a company is confronted with dynamic, threatening, and complex change in the external environment, it is forced to adapt. Adaptation typically involves various forms of innovation. For their part, adaptation and innovation are dependent on the ability to learn, and learning requires timely and relevant information. Accordingly, much emphasis is placed today on the *learning organization* and the *learning manager*.

Senge (1990) refers to a learning organization as one that continually improves through its capacity to learn from its experiences. Learning in this context refers to the acquisition of new knowledge by employees who are able and willing to apply the knowledge in making decisions or influencing others in the organization. It also includes the unlearning of old routines as a parallel activity to the learning of new routines. Unlearning is especially important in an entrepreneurial context, since long-held assumptions and past experiences that hold little relevance for the contemporary environment frequently act as blocks to an entrepreneurial project.

Underlying the learning process is the organization's ability to find or generate information, organize or code it, process it, store it, generate reports from it, interpret it, share it, and act on it. Our concern is with the company's ability to learn in ways that facilitate entrepreneurship, and this is a notable area of weakness in companies. Most companies do not have systematic methods to ensure learning. In one study, Block and MacMillan (1993) found that, among firms that tend to engage in more entrepreneurial activity, few conducted any systematic study or review of projects. They reported a number of reasons including the following:

a) key people involved with the project may have left the firm;

b) the champion responsible for the project may have been reassigned to a distant location;

c) a number of individuals may have participated, with each having been involved with a different aspect of the experience at a different time;

d) few records may have been kept;

e) accounting figures are not always consolidated and readily accessible.

Furthermore, many entrepreneurship-related experiences may not have been positive, and there may be a certain reluctance to unearth the skeletons of such negative experiences. For these reasons and more, each effort at corporate entrepreneurship starts off as a new process and evolves in its own way.

As Block and MacMillan (1993, p. 312) aptly conclude, "Managers are often very curious about what *other* companies have done and how their ventures have performed but overlook the most relevant learning of all—the learning that can be extracted from their own venturing experience. Such experience has been achieved at great expense to the organization, and to ignore or discard it is to squander an irreplaceable asset."

Organizations must be prepared to track each entrepreneurial project or effort to identify underlying reasons for success or failure. By constructing project histories, management can extract maximal "learning" from the entrepreneurial experience. If organizations are to learn and use what is learned to improve future performance, they must make a systematic effort to get the facts, examine them carefully, and draw conclusions about what to do and what to avoid in the future. The objective should always be to discover what errors occurred at any stage of the entrepreneurial project; why those errors occurred; and, most significantly, how would they be avoided in future projects. Following are ten critical areas that should be the focus of learning efforts within a given company:

- Champion styles that work and do not work;

- Venture team structures that are most effective for certain types of innovation projects;

- Models of successful projects in terms of key steps or stages, and the identification of the models that best fit different types of projects;

- Approaches to goal setting and monitoring that keep projects on track;

- Methods of opportunity identification that are especially productive given the nature of the company, industry, and market;

- Ways of achieving the appropriate balance between autonomy and control on innovation projects;

- Venture funding approaches that encourage successful projects;

- Human resource management policies that encourage individual initiative and group collaboration around innovation projects;

■ **TABLE 16.7**

MAXIMIZING LEARNING FROM CORPORATE ENTREPRENEURIAL PROJECTS

There are three levels of learning effort that organizations can implement to gain the most benefit from each entrepreneurial project that develops.

Level 1

The project champion writes a report about the experience, including a statement of the most important things learned and recommendations for the future, designed to help the firm's overall entrepreneurial effort. A useful question for the champion to address is "If you could do this project over again, what would you do differently?" This first level of learning effort represents the simplest and easiest approach. It will yield information that is useful but far from complete.

Level 2

Key project and senior management people hold one or more meetings to discuss the progress of the project. Reports should be written that present conclusions and recommendations for future actions. The company should hold separate meetings dedicated to assessing the project experience, or it can perform this assessment as part of the agenda of other meetings held in connection with the entrepreneurial activity. If it decides to hold separate meetings, they can be conducted either periodically or at the time a project changes its status in some way (e.g., by being terminated, combined with an existing unit, or established as an ongoing business unit).

Level 3

The company conducts a full-fledged, in-depth study of the entrepreneurial experience, which will probably require the participation of people from outside the firm to obtain objectivity as well as expertise. The third level involves a really significant research project—one that is time-consuming and may be quite difficult to accomplish. An undertaking of this magnitude should probably be reserved for very major projects involving amounts of money that are highly significant to the firm.

SOURCE: Adapted from Block, Z. and I. MacMillan. 1993. *Corporate Venturing.* Boston: Harvard Business School.

■ Techniques for optimally managing the timing and allocation of resources (funds, functional specialists, staff people, facilities, and equipment) across the stages of a project;

■ Effective means of getting mainstream units in the company to adopt or assume ownership of projects developed by venture teams.

Each entrepreneurial effort represents an experiment. Learning is critical not only to enable management to redirect the individual employee more effectively but also to enable management to gather cumulative information on the entrepreneurial experiences that will help encourage and nurture activity more effectively in the future. Table 16.7 identifies some ways in which companies can maximize learning.

Learning occurs not only at an organizational level across different entrepreneurial projects but also within the projects themselves. That is, for a project to evolve from point A to point B to point C, learning must take place. The more innovative the project, and the more it breaks truly new ground, the more learning is required in order to move the project forward. Existing knowledge in the company proves inadequate, and much more exploration is necessary. McGrath (2001) has provided evidence that, with highly innovative projects requiring high levels of exploration, learning effectiveness is greater when teams are given more autonomy both in setting goals and in conducting operations. Alternatively, when teams are working on less innovative projects or ones in which the existing knowledge base of the company is more adequate, learning effectiveness is enhanced when goals are clearly specified and there is less operational autonomy.

ORGANIZATIONS DESIGNED AROUND PARADOXES

Not all corporate entrepreneurs produce dramatic breakthroughs. Ironically, those that attempt to overthrow the establishment frequently find that the returns they achieve can be less than those received by less ambitious entrepreneurs. This is an example of the fundamental paradoxes confronting corporate entrepreneurship. The entrepreneurial organization of tomorrow will be one filled with paradoxes and will require managers who are adept at managing them. Below are some of the more vexing paradoxes that surround the entrepreneurial efforts of companies in the 21st century.

THE PARADOX OF BIGNESS AND SMALLNESS

Smallness matters, but so does bigness. Small firms are quick and flexible. They can innovate on the fly. The technological revolution has empowered them to operate globally, while creative leveraging strategies enable them to compete on the same playing field with much bigger firms. As a result, many large companies are transforming themselves into confederations of small, fairly independent companies. And yet, being larger offers the important benefits of scale and scope. The ability of bigger companies to achieve economies, leverage the value chain, capitalize on strategic partnerships, and exploit opportunities in distribution is unsurpassed. As a case in point, Netscape will continue to be an important player as the Internet evolves principally because it is part of AOL Time Warner.

THE PARADOX OF RISK AND RETURN

The relationship between what the corporate entrepreneur does and the outcomes or returns achieved is not a simple one. It is often assumed that major breakthroughs or higher risk ventures generate higher returns. But this is not always the case, since returns are influenced by timing, managerial competence, market conditions, and a host of environmental factors. Even if all of these factors are controlled, doing something that is highly entrepreneurial only raises the *possible ceiling* on returns if the venture is successful. Actual returns are unique to the venture.

The general level of risk facing any corporate entrepreneur will increase in the coming years simply because more entrepreneurial activity will be occurring.

Within this broader context, the probability of failure will be higher for those individuals and organizations that pursue both very low and very high levels of entrepreneurial activity. The highest returns will come to those who can sustain a balance of degree and frequency of entrepreneurial activity over time.

THE PARADOX OF THE INDIVIDUAL AND THE TEAM

Corporate entrepreneurship requires a visionary champion with drive and commitment. However, a dedicated team of specialists and generalists is also needed. The problem becomes one of emphasizing both individualism and collective teamwork at the same time. Unfortunately, a policy or procedure that offers incentives for an individual's action can serve as a disincentive for collective action. Similarly, a preoccupation with teams will come at the expense of entrepreneurial leadership.

Nonetheless, in an age of multiple careers and lessened organizational loyalty, the corporate entrepreneur will have to be less of a team dictator and more of a team member. He or she will have to share ownership and control with team members. The objective will be to build a project based on core competencies and to focus on the continued development of knowledge assets that can deliver these competencies. Thus, the internal team itself becomes fluid or subject to change.

THE PARADOX OF FLEXIBILITY AND CONTROL

Large corporations have downsized, restructured, and reengineered in a quest to become faster and more flexible. The question becomes one of maintaining flexibility while also being able to exert sufficient control over resources and operations. In the years ahead, entrepreneurial companies will focus less on accumulating assets and achieving control through ownership and more on building a fluid adaptable organization that is highly leveraged. That is, they will be able to achieve market penetration through external alliances and networks, not through an increase in their physical asset base. They will effectively gain control by giving up control.

THE PARADOX OF CONSTRUCTIVE AND DESTRUCTIVE BEHAVIOR

Corporate entrepreneurship requires both stability and turbulence. Where there is an established infrastructure, corporate entrepreneurship is facilitated. Yet, turbulence creates opportunities for proactive entrepreneurs. There is a related paradox in that entrepreneurship is both constructive and destructive. Entrepreneurial individuals create the new, and in doing so, they preemptorily make existing products, services, and processes obsolete. Within companies, entrepreneurs make what have heretofore been well-functioning operations unnecessary. In the future, this creative destruction will accelerate, as corporate entrepreneurs find they must continually make their own products obsolete. Along the way, whole new entrepreneurial opportunities will be created for recycling, retrofitting, and identifying alternative distribution channels (reaching new markets) for the products being displaced.

THE PARADOX OF SUCCESS AND FAILURE

Although it is normal to think in terms of winners and losers in business, sustained entrepreneurship is not that simple. Entrepreneurs are often competitive, with a need to win. They are replacing conventional managers who have a need to avoid failure. Yet, many entrepreneurs fail multiple times. They can frequently describe an entire portfolio of successes and failures, where one solid hit is followed by a strikeout and two ground outs and then a home run.

Within failure are the seeds for success. Corporate entrepreneurs must increasingly believe in the "successful failure," in which lessons from unsuccessful efforts are used to adapt concepts and ideas into something that will work. This is important on two levels. By definition, a general increase in new product and service introductions means a higher failure rate. Similarly, as individuals find themselves involved in more entrepreneurial activity, they will also begin to fail more often. Success will increasingly be a function of the entrepreneur's ability to overcome the psychological fear of and avoidance of failure that is ingrained in virtually all of us.

DOMAINS, PORTFOLIOS, AND A CYCLE OF REVOLUTION

In addition to managing paradox, the dynamic organizations of tomorrow will be ones that are capable of merging strategic action with entrepreneurial action on an ongoing basis. Strategic management focuses on achieving competitive advantage within a particular industry and market context. Entrepreneurship seeks to exploit opportunities others have missed or ones that have not been completely exploited. Thus, strategic actions provide the context within which entrepreneurial actions are pursued (Ireland et al. 2001). Figure 16.1 illustrates the interface between the strategic actions (advantage-seeking behavior) and the entrepreneurial actions (opportunity-seeking behavior) of a firm.

To create wealth, firms will need to establish linkages between entrepreneurial actions and strategic actions within six dominant domains (Ireland et al. 2001). First, the competitive mindset of managers must be based on *innovation,* and innovation efforts of the firm must be managed strategically. The objective is innovations that are well timed, consistent with marketplace realities, difficult to imitate, and that fit well with the firm's core competencies. Further, entrepreneurial and strategic actions are used to create and exploit *networks* of relationships between the organization and other organizations and individuals. Such networks provide the firm with access to competitively valuable information, enable faster market penetration, allow for risk sharing, and enhance the firm's innovation capabilities.

■ FIGURE 16.1

CREATING WEALTH THROUGH ENTREPRENEURIAL AND STRATEGIC ACTIONS

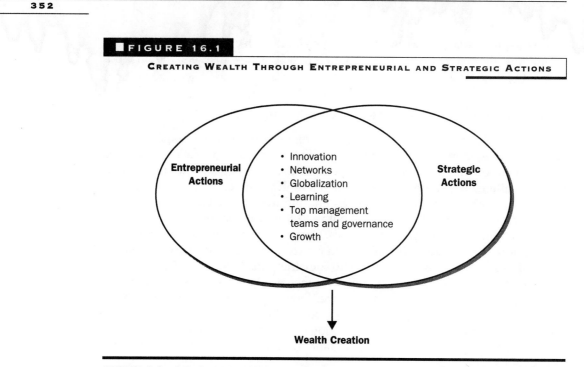

Wealth Creation

SOURCE: Ireland, R. D., M. Hitt, S. M. Camp, and D. L. Sexton. 2001. "Integrating Entrepreneurship and Strategic Management Actions to Create Firm Wealth," *Academy of Management Executive* 15, No. 1 (February): 1.

In addition, entrepreneurial and strategic actions must combine to facilitate *internationalization,* or the exploitation of global opportunities. Tapping global markets requires product innovations, innovations in management systems and structures, and innovative use of networks and alliances, all of which must be managed strategically. Another key domain is *organizational learning.* Companies must make a strategic commitment to learning and to rapid transfer of knowledge throughout the organization. As we saw earlier in this chapter, learning is intimately tied to successful entrepreneurship. A key task of company leadership is to enhance the firm's abilities to use intellectual assets both strategically and entrepreneurially. The next domain is concerned with the *top management team and governance structures* in the firm. Top management teams must have a shared entrepreneurial vision that they translate into goals and strategies. Their role is not that of passive observer. Instead, they are intimately involved in innovation and serve as key players in networks to support entrepreneurial and strategic actions. Boards of directors must also be accountable for entrepreneurial direction and performance. Last, entrepreneurial actions and strategic actions are linked to the types of *growth opportunities* sought by the firm. Growth can come from changes in the external environment or from inefficiencies in existing markets. No matter the rate of growth, the objective is managed growth and properly designed and executed strategies.

One purpose of strategic leadership in companies is to ensure innovation does not occur in a vacuum — that the spirit and enthusiasm that go with entrepreneurship do not lead managers to forget the fundamentals. Consider the findings of a recent study. Researchers examined 1,435 companies that had been listed among the 500 largest any time since 1965 (Collins 2000). They sought to identify companies that were able to make a shift from good to great performance (defined as having generated cumulative shareholder returns greater than three times the market average over fifteen years). Only 11 of the 1,435 companies showed a sustained and verifiable shift from good to great. This stunning finding led to the following conclusion:

> The truth is, there's nothing new about being in a New Economy. Yes, the Internet is a big deal, but electricity was bigger. And in each evolution of the economy over the past 150 years, the best executives have adhered to the same basic principles, with rigor and discipline. I can't tell you exactly what a corporation will look like 50 or 100 years from now. But I can promise this: If you toss out all the time-proven fundamentals, you'll have no chance whatsoever of building an enduring, great company. (Collins 2000, p. 208)

Two other perspectives are useful as we try to draw a picture of the entrepreneurial organization of tomorrow. The first of these concerns portfolios — and specifically, conceptualizing the company as a collection of portfolios. Portfolio thinking is about a strategic balance in which the firm balances a mix of objectives such as risk versus return, income versus growth, and short-term versus long-term performance. Organizations will be built around four major portfolios:

- The portfolio of competencies–the set of skills and capabilities that capture what the organization does best. The strategic direction of the firm will be designed around these competencies, and outside providers will be relied upon for most of the activities not reflected in these competencies. In the leading entrepreneurial firms, core competencies will include the ability to innovate, adapt, and manage change. Management will recognize the need to invest in both exploitative (of current resources and markets) competencies and exploration (of new frontiers) competencies.

- The portfolio of resources–the set of financial, physical, human, organizational, relational, and intellectual resources that are innovation enabling. Although organizations are repositories of all kinds of resources, the leaders recognize that certain resources are instrumental for innovation and define the limits on the innovation capacity of the firm. The portfolio is managed in a way that these resources complement one another. Within the resource portfolio might also be found a portfolio of different kinds of entrepreneurs within the company and a portfolio of partners and alliances.

- The portfolio of innovations–a balanced mix of new product, service, and process projects. The leaders will be those companies that pursue multiple innovations at a given time, including new-to-the-world or new-to-the-market innovations, new lines, lines extensions, and incremental improvements. Projects will routinely benefit one another through systematic experimentation and learning.

■ The portfolio of ventures and small businesses–the devolution of the company into a confederation of small businesses that have autonomy but whose contributions can be seamlessly coordinated and integrated. Individual ventures will vary in terms of their levels of entrepreneurial intensity and position in the organizational life cycle.

From a portfolio perspective, the company becomes a large incubator. Ideas, concepts, products, and ventures are regularly spawned in this incubator. The company creates environments that support the growth and development of ideas into concepts, then into products or processes, then into ventures (or into additions to existing ventures). Further, products and ventures mature and are harvested.

Finally, the organization of tomorrow will be one that continuously cycles through periods of rapid evolution and periodic revolution. Change will be the norm. The company will alternate between exploiting a given innovation or technology platform (while experimenting with others) and ultimately moving to new platforms. Ongoing changes in structure, strategy, elements of culture, approaches to rewards, and so forth will be interrupted by major strategic inflection points, in which more dramatic change is required. Moreover, the company will cycle through the entrepreneurial grid, alternating between periods of high entrepreneurial intensity and lower entrepreneurial intensity. (See Chapter Three.) Thus, the dominant positioning of the firm might be continuous/incremental entrepreneurship over a given period of years and then periodic/discontinuous for a number of years. There will also be cycles within cycles, since individual units within the company vary in terms of their own entrepreneurial intensity and the nature of their own operating environments.

SUMMARY AND CONCLUSIONS

Times have certainly changed in terms of how entrepreneurship is perceived in a corporate setting. In the 1970s, the word *entrepreneurship* was simply not associated with large corporate environments. During the 1980s, many argued that it was difficult, if not almost impossible, for people to act entrepreneurially in bureaucratic organizational structures (Morse 1986). At the same time, a few observers began to suggest that entrepreneurial actions were possible for companies of any size, should be encouraged, and might be expected to enhance firm performance (Burgelman 1984; Kanter 1985). During the latter part of the 1980s and throughout the 1990s, there was a veritable revolution with respect to the perceived value of entrepreneurial actions. This significant change paralleled the profound adjustments companies were making in terms of how they defined their business, utilized their human resources, and competed in the global economy. Zahra, Kuratko, and Jennings (1999) note:

Some of the world's best-known companies had to endure a painful transformation to become more entrepreneurial. They had to endure years of reorganization, downsizing, and restructuring. These changes altered the identity or culture of these firms, infusing a new entrepreneurial spirit throughout their operations . . . *change, innovation,* and *entrepreneurship* became highly regarded words. (p. 5)

Extending this position to the current day, the beginning of the 21st century is a time when entrepreneurial actions are recognized widely as the path to competitive advantage and success in organizations of all types and sizes (Covin, Slevin, and Heeley 2000). Moreover, a lack of entrepreneurial actions in today's global economy is a recipe for failure.

In the new competitive landscape, the opportunities and threats are revolutionary in nature — that is, they happen swiftly and are relentless in their frequency, affecting virtually all parts of an organization simultaneously. The business environment is filled with ambiguity and discontinuity, and the rules of the game are subject to constant revision. The job of management effectively becomes one of continual experimentation — experimenting with new structures, new reward systems, new technologies, new methods, new products, new markets, and much more. The quest remains the same: sustainable competitive advantage. The fundamentals remain the same: great products, creating real value for customers, highly motivated employees, providing products when and where the customer chooses. But the path is less clear. It is our belief that entrepreneurship represents the guiding light, the road map, and the motivating force for companies as they attempt to find their way down this path.

Achieving an entrepreneurial orientation is not something that management can simply decide to do. Corporate entrepreneurship is not a fad, and it does not produce instant success. It requires considerable time and investment, and there must be continual reinforcement. By their nature, organizations impose constraints on entrepreneurial behavior. To be sustainable, the entrepreneurial spirit must be integrated into the mission, goals, strategies, structure, processes, and values of the organization. Flexibility, speed, innovation, and entrepreneurial leadership are the cornerstones. The managerial mindset must become an opportunity-driven mindset, where actions are never constrained by resources currently controlled.

A sustainable entrepreneurial orientation will drive organizations to new heights in the 21st century. This new millennium has been characterized as an age of instant information, with an ever-increasing development and application of technology, experimental change, revolutionary processes, and global competition. It has also been called an age of turbulence and paradox, but we prefer to call it simply *the entrepreneurial age.* It is an age where excellence is achievable only if those who manage companies are willing to do the following:

- Expect more than others think is practical;
- Dare more than others think is wise;
- Risk more than others think is safe; and
- Dream more than others think is possible.

The future belongs to the dreamers and doers.

Samsung's "Cycle of Change"

Corporate innovation and intrapreneurship can take place via numerous methods. At Samsung Electronics, methods utilized include deprecating past accomplishments, instilling new values, and simply making chaos. Jong Yong Yun came to Samsung in 1969 and earned his way through the ranks until he took over as CEO in 1997.

In 2000, Yun earned Asia's Businessman of the Year award from *Fortune* magazine for his part in making the company culture less bureaucratic and more entrepreneurial. To be eligible, an executive must not only run a company with at least $750 million in annual sales but must also have "a penchant for risk, a clear vision for the future, a feel for new technology, and skill in leading people."

After a streak of losing money on low-priced television sets and microwaves in the mid-90s, Yun's change at Samsung involved placing the company in the forefront of digital convergence and on a path to triple revenues over the next six years. Yun restructured the balance sheet, sold $1.9 billion

in assets, and focused on the company's environment. Earnings for Samsung rose more than tenfold to $2.7 billion in 1999, while stock rose 214 percent.

Reinventing the company, however, took more than just slashing debt and stirring up the talent pool. Yun put much effort into eliminating the corporation's bureaucratic trends and hierarchical structure. He energized and empowered complacent members of the management team, a complacency he attributed to a recent economical crisis in the East, which had forced his and other companies to sacrifice profits for market share. Now, 17 global product managers have responsibility for the entire value chain, and managers are performing appropriately since their salaries and bonuses are based significantly on their entrepreneurial contributions to the bottom line. He cut costs by reducing inventory 75 percent, from a four-month to a one-month supply, and capitalizing on the company's core strengths, rolled out thirty new digital products in one year.

Samsung Electronics has made collaborations with Dell and Apple Computer and will supply the mobile phones for the 2001 Olympics. Such partnerships will enable Samsung to stay ahead of the rapidly changing technological market with leading edge products.

Less than 10,000 of the 23 million businesses in America qualify as large firms, but regardless of how high tech the nation becomes, they are going to be around for a long time to come. To maintain their competitive edge, most will be forced to restructure the corporate vision and mission, encouraging innovative thinking and funding entrepreneurial projects. Samsung already leads the market in digital phones, computer monitors, and other electronic components, but Yun wants more: "You have to break the old ways of thinking and doing business by creating chaos."

SOURCE: 2000. "Samsung's Tech Wizard." *Fortune* Magazine On-Line.

References

Andreasen, A. 1988. *Cheap but Good Marketing Research*. Homewood: Dow Jones-Irwin.

Block, Z., and I. MacMillan. 1993. *Corporate Venturing*. Boston: Harvard Business School.

Burgelman, R. 1984. "Managing the Corporate Venturing Process," *Sloan Management Review* 25, No. 2: 33–48.

Collins, J. 2000. "Don't Rewrite the Rules of the Road," *Business Week* (August): 206–208.

Covin, J. G., and D. P. Slevin. 1989. "Strategic Management of Small Firms in Hostile and Benign Environments," *Strategic Management Journal* 1, No. 10: 75–87.

Covin, J. G., and M. P. Miles. 1999. "Corporate Entrepreneurship and the Pursuit of Competitive Advantage," *Entrepreneurship Theory and Practice* 23, No. 3: 47–64.

Covin, J. G., D. P. Slevin, and M. B. Heeley. 2000. "Pioneers and Followers: Competitive Tactics, Environment, and Firm Growth," *Journal of Business Venturing* 15, No. 2 (March): 175–210.

Davis, D., M. Morris, and J. Allen. 1991. "Perceived Environmental Turbulence and Its Effect on Selected Entrepreneurship, Marketing, and Organizational Characteristics in Industrial Firms," *Journal of Marketing Science* 19 (Spring): 43–51.

Hamel, G., and C. K. Prahalad. 1991. "Corporate Imagination and Expeditionary Marketing," *Harvard Business Review* 69, No. 4: 81–92.

Ireland, R. D., and M. A. Hitt. 1999. "Achieving and Maintaining Strategic Competitiveness in the 21st Century: The Role of Strategic Leadership," *Academy of Management Executive* 13, No. 1: 43–57.

Ireland, R. D., M. Hitt, S. M. Camp, and D. L. Sexton. 2001. "Integrating Entrepreneurship and Strategic Management Actions to Create Firm Wealth," *Academy of Management Executive* 15, No. 1 (February): 1.

Kanter, R. 1985. "Supporting Innovation and Venture Development in Established Companies," *Journal of Business Venturing* 1, No. 1: 47–60.

Leifer, R., C. McDermott, G. O'Connor, L. Peters, M. Rice, and R. Veryzer. 2000. *Radical Innovation*. Boston: Harvard Business School.

McGrath, R. 2001. "Exploratory Learning, Innovative Capacity, and Managerial Oversight," *Academy of Management Journal* 44, No. 1: 118–133.

Miller, D., and P. Friesen. 1982. "Innovation in Conservative and Entrepreneurial Firms: Two Models of Strategic Management," *Strategic Management Journal* 3, No. 1: 1–25.

Morris, M. H. 1998. *Entrepreneurial Intensity*. Westport: Quorum.

Morris, M., Z. Zahra, and M. Schindehutte. 2000. "Understanding Factors That Trigger Entrepreneurial Behavior in Established Companies." In *Entrepreneurship and Economic Growth in the American Economy*, edited by G. Libecap. Amsterdam: JAI Press.

Morse, C. W. 1986. "The Delusion of Intrapreneurship," *Long Range Planning* 19, No. 2: 92–95.

Senge, Peter. 1990. *The Fifth Discipline*. New York: Doubleday Currency.

Stevenson, H. H., and J. C. Jarillo-Mossi. 1986. "Preserving Entrepreneurship As Companies Grow," *Journal of Business Strategy* 7, No. 1(Summer): 10.

Stevenson, H. H., M. J. Roberts, and D. E. Grousbeck. 1999. *New Business Ventures and the Entrepreneur*. Homewood: Richard D. Irwin.

Thomke, S. 2001. "Enlightened Experimentation: The New Imperative for Innovation," *Harvard Business Review* 79, No. 2: 67–75.

von Hippel, E., S. Thomke, and M. Sonnack. 1999. "Creating Breakthroughs at 3M," *Harvard Business Review* 77, No. 5: 47–57.

Zahra, S. A. 1993. "Environment, Corporate Entrepreneurship, and Financial Performance: A Taxonomic Approach," *Journal of Business Venturing* 8, No. 4: 319–340.

Zahra, S. A., and H. M. O'Neil. 1998. "Charting the Landscape of Global Competition: Reflections on Emerging Organizational Challenges and Their Implications for Senior Executives," *The Academy of Management Executive* 12, No. 4: 13–21.

Zahra, S.A., D. F. Kuratko, and D. F. Jennings. 1999. "Corporate Entrepreneurship and the Acquisition of Dynamic Organizational Capabilities," *Entrepreneurship Theory and Practice* 23, No. 3: 5–10.

INDEX